Thinking Through the Past

Thinking Through the Past

A Critical Thinking Approach to U.S. History

Volume II: Since 1865

John Hollitz

COMMUNITY COLLEGE OF SOUTHERN NEVADA

HOUGHTON MIFFLIN COMPANY   Boston   New York

Sponsoring Editor: Patricia A. Coryell
Senior Associate Editor: Jeffrey Greene
Senior Project Editor: Carol Newman
Production/Design Coordinator: Deborah Frydman
Senior Manufacturing Coordinator: Marie Barnes

Cover design: Len Massiglia.
Cover image: *Ohio Magic,* 1945 by Ben Shahn, Fine Arts Museum of San Francisco, Mildred Anna Williams Collection, 1948.14.

Printed in the U.S.A.
Library of Congress Catalog Card Number: 96-79467
ISBN: 0-669-33488-x

2 3 4 5 6 7 8 9-DH-00 99 98 97

Contents

3

6

Ideology and History: Closing the "Golden Door"

7

The Problem of Historical Causation: The Election of 1928

8

History "From the Top Down": Eleanor Roosevelt, Reformer 176

11

12

13

Why Historical Interpretation Matters: Assessing the "Reagan Revolution"   **313**

Preface

This book was inspired by the idea that interpretation is at the heart of history. That is why learning about the past involves more than mastering facts and dates, and why historians often disagree. As teachers, we know the limitations of the deadly dates-and-facts approach to the past. We also know that encouraging students to think critically about historical sources and historians' arguments is a good way to create excitement about history and to impart understanding of what historians do. The purpose of *Thinking Through the Past,* therefore, is to introduce students to the examination and analysis of historical sources.

FORMAT

To encourage students to think critically about American history, *Thinking Through the Past* brings together primary and secondary sources. It gives students the opportunity to analyze primary sources *and* historians' arguments, and to use one to understand and evaluate the other. By evaluating and drawing conclusions from the sources, students will use the methods and develop some of the skills of critical thinking as they apply to history. Students will also learn about a variety of historical topics that parallel those in U.S. history courses. Unlike most anthologies or collections of primary sources, this book advances not only chronologically, but pedagogically through different skill levels. It provides students the opportunity to work with primary sources in the early chapters before they evaluate secondary sources in later chapters or compare historians' arguments in the final chapters. Students are also able to build on the skills acquired in previous chapters by considering such questions as motivation, causation, and the role of ideas and economic interests in history.

At the same time, this book introduces a variety of approaches to the past. Topics in *Thinking Through the Past* include social, political, cultural, intellectual, economic, diplomatic, and military history. The chapters look at history "from the top down" and "from the bottom up." Thus students have the opportunity to evaluate history drawn from slave quarters as well as from state houses. In the process, they are exposed to the enormous range of sources that historians use to construct arguments. The primary sources in these volumes include portraits, photographs, maps, letters, fiction, music lyrics, laws, oral histories, speeches, movie posters, magazine and newspaper articles, cartoons, and architectural plans.

The chapters present the primary and secondary sources so students can pursue their own investigations of the material. Each chapter is divided into five parts: A brief introduction, which sets forth the problem in the chapter; the Setting, which provides background information pertaining to the topic; the Investigation, which asks students to answer a short set of questions revolving around the problem discussed in the introduction; the Sources, which in most chapters provides a secondary source and a set of primary sources related to the chapter's main problem, and, finally, a brief Conclusion, which offers a reminder of the chapter's main pedagogical goal and looks forward to the next chapter's problem.

INSTRUCTOR'S RESOURCE MANUAL

The format of *Thinking Through the Past* is designed to be effective in various classroom situations. Students in large classes can work through this book with minimal instructor assistance. Yet the format also provides students in seminars, small classes, and discussion sections the opportunity to share with one another the excitement of thinking about the past. The Instructor's Resource Manual is designed to enhance the effectiveness of *Thinking Through the Past* in all these classroom settings. The manual contains discussion of the sources in each chapter and explanations of how they relate to the chapter's main problem and pedagogical goals. It also contains questions to stimulate classroom discussion and suggestions for evaluating students' learning.

ACKNOWLEDGMENTS

Many people contributed to this book. I want to thank my students, without whom it never would have been created. I owe thanks to many others as well. Richard Cooper and Brad Nystrom at California State University, Sacramento listened patiently to unformed ideas and offered helpful suggestions at the initial stages of this project. Alan Balboni, DeAnna Beachley, Gary Elliott, Michael Green, and Charles Okeke, colleagues at the Community College of Southern Nevada, offered sources, ideas, and encouragement. Marion Martin, Inter-Library Loan librarian at CCSN, provided unfailingly cheerful and efficient assistance. D. C. Heath editors James Miller and Pat Wakeley made many helpful suggestions. Susan Zorn of Houghton Mifflin copyedited the manuscript with extraordinary skill, while Jeffrey Greene and Carol Newman performed their editorial tasks with professionalism and good humor. Numerous colleagues around the country reviewed chapter drafts and offered insightful suggestions.

They were very generous with their time, and their ideas were invaluable. The reviewers were:

Karen Blair, *Central Washington University*
Joan Chandler, *University of Texas—Dallas*
Myles Clowers, *San Diego City College*
Julian Del Gaudio, *Long Beach City College*
Ronald Faircloth, *Abraham Baldwin Agricultural College*
Gerald Ghelfi, *Rancho Santiago College*
David Godschalk, *Shippensburg University*
Robert Goldman, *Virginia Union University*
Nancy Isenberg, *University of Northern Iowa*
John Jameson, *Kent State University*
Benjamin Newcomb, *Texas Technological University*
Vince Nobile, *Chaffey Community College*
Mario Perez, *University of California—Riverside*
Edward Pluth, *St. Cloud State University*
John Rector, *Western Oregon State University*
David Schmitz, *Whitman College*
Luther Spoehr, *Lincoln School*
Emily Teipe, *Fullerton College*
Stephen Weisner, *Springfield Technical Community College*
Marianne Wokeck, *Indiana University—Purdue University at Indianapolis*
Walter Weare, *University of Wisconsin—Milwaukee*
Marli Weiner, *University of Maine*

My biggest debt, however, is to Patricia. For patience, support, and much more, this book is dedicated to her.

J.H.

Thinking Through the Past

Introduction

"History," said Henry Ford, "is more or less bunk." That view is still shared by many people. Protests about the subject are familiar. Studying history won't help you land a job. And besides, what matters is not the past but the present.

Such protests are not necessarily wrong. Learning about ancient Greece, the French Revolution, or the Vietnam War will hardly guarantee employment. In spite of the desire of many employers for "well-rounded" job candidates, a history course or two probably won't get most students any closer to a good job. Likewise, who can deny the importance of the present compared to the past? In many ways the present and future are more important than the past. Pericles, Robespierre, and Lyndon Johnson are dead; presumably, anyone reading this is not.

Still, the logic behind the history-as-bunk view is flawed because all of us rely upon the past to understand the present, as did even Henry Ford. Besides building the Model T, he also built Greenfield Village outside Detroit because he wanted to recreate a nineteenth-century town. It was the kind of place the automotive genius grew up in and the kind of place he believed represented the ideal American society: small-town, white, native-born, and Protestant. Greenfield Village was Ford's answer to changes in the early twentieth century that were profoundly disturbing to him and to many other Americans of his generation: growing cities, the influx of non-Protestant immigrants, changing sexual morality, new roles and new fashions for women, and greater freedom for young people.

Ford's interest in the past, symbolized by Greenfield Village, reflects a double irony. It was the automobile that helped to make possible many of the changes, like those in sexual morality, that Ford detested. The other irony is that Ford used history—what he himself called "bunk"—to try to better the world. Without realizing it, he became a historian by turning to the past to explain to himself and others what he disliked about the present. Never mind that Ford blamed immigrants, especially Jews, for the changes he decried in crude, hate-filled tirades. The point is that Ford's view of America was rooted in a vision of the past, and his explanation for America's ills was based on historical analysis, however unprofessional and unsophisticated.

All of us use historical analysis all the time, even if, like Ford, we think we don't. In fact, we all share a fundamental assumption about learning from the past: One of the best ways to learn about something, to learn how it came to be, is to study its past. That assumption is so much a part of us that we are rarely conscious of it.

Think about the most recent time you met someone for the first time. As a way to get to know this new acquaintance you began to ask questions about his or her past. When you asked, "Where did you grow up?" or "How long have you lived in Chicago?" you were relying on information about the past to learn about the present. You were, in other words, thinking as a historian. You assumed that a cause-and-effect relationship existed between this person's past and his or her present personality, interests, and beliefs. Like a historian, you began to frame questions and to look for answers that would help to establish causal links.

Because we all use history to make sense of our world, it follows that we should become more skilled in the art of making sense of the past. Ford did it crudely, and ended up promoting the very things he despised. But how exactly do you begin to think more like a historian? For too many students, this challenge summons up images of studying for history exams: cramming names, dates, and facts and hoping to retain some portion of this information long enough to get a passing grade. History seems like a confusing grab bag of facts and events. The historian's job, in this view, is to memorize as much "stuff" as possible. In this "flash-card" approach, history is reduced to an exercise in the pursuit of trivia, and thinking like a historian is nothing but an exercise in mnemonics—a system of improving the memory.

There is no question that the dates, events, and facts of history are important. Without basic factual knowledge historians could no more practice their craft than biologists, chemists, or astrophysicists could practice theirs. But history is not a static recollection of facts. Events in the past happened only once, but the historians who study those events are always changing their minds about them. Like all humans, historians have prejudices, biases, and beliefs. They are also influenced by events in their own times. In other words, they look at the past through lenses that filter and even distort. Events in the past may have happened only once, but what historians think about them, the meaning they give to those events, is constantly changing. Moreover, because their lenses perceive events differently, historians often disagree about the past. The supposedly "static" discipline of history is actually dynamic and charged with tension.

That brings us to the question of what historians really do. Briefly, historians ask questions about past events or developments and try to explain them. Just as much as biology, chemistry, or astrophysics, therefore, history is a problem-solving discipline. Historians, like scientists, sift evidence to answer questions. Like scientists, whose explanations for things often conflict, historians can ask the same questions, look at the same facts, and come up with different explanations because they look at the past in different ways. Or they may have entirely different questions in mind and so come away with very different "pasts." Thus history is a process of constant revision. As historians like to put it, every generation writes its own history.

But why bother to study and interpret the past in our own way if someone else will only revise it again in the future? The answer is sobering: If we don't write our own history, someone else will write it for us. Who today would accept as historical truth the notion that the Indians were cruel savages whose extermination was necessary to fulfill an Anglo-Saxon destiny to conquer the continent for democracy and civilization? Who today would accept the "truth" that slaves were racially inferior and happy with their lot on southern plantations? If we accept these views of Indians and black slaves, we are allowing nineteenth-century historians to determine our view of the past.

Instead, by reconstructing the past as best we can, we can better understand our own times. Like the amnesia victim, without memory we face a bewildering world. As we recapture our collective past, the present becomes more intelligible. Subject to new experiences, a later generation will view the past differently. Realizing that future generations will revise history does not give us a license to play fast and loose with the facts of history. Rather each generation faces the choice of giving meaning to those facts or experiencing the confusion of historical amnesia.

Finding meaning in the facts of the past, then, is the central challenge of history. It requires us to ask questions and construct explanations—mental activities far different and far more exciting than merely memorizing names, dates, and facts. More important, it enables us to approach history as critical thinkers. The more skilled we become at historical reasoning, the better we will understand our world and ourselves. Helping you to develop skill in historical analysis is the purpose of this volume.

The method of this book reflects its purpose. The first chapter discusses textbooks. History texts have a very practical purpose. By bringing order to the past, they give many students a useful and reassuring "handle" on history. But they are not the Ten Commandments, because, like all works of history, they also contain interpretations. To most readers these interpretations are hard to spot. Chapter 1 examines what a number of college textbooks in American history say and don't say about the role of African-Americans during Reconstruction, the period immediately after the Civil War. By examining selections from several texts and asking how and why they differ, we can see that texts are not as objective as readers often believe.

If textbooks are not carved in stone, how can historians know anything? To answer this question, we turn next to the raw material of history. Chapter 2, on the living and working conditions of wage earners in industrializing America, examines the primary sources historians use to reconstruct and interpret the past. What are these sources? What do historians do with them? What can historians determine from them?

With a basic understanding of the nature and usefulness of primary sources, we proceed in Chapter 3 for a closer evaluation. This chapter on the images of the Populists and their political opponents shows how careful historians must be in using primary sources. Does a source speak with one voice or with many? How can historians disagree about the meaning of the same historical facts? By carefully evaluating primary sources in this chapter, you can draw your own conclusions about the nature of the agrarian revolt in the late nineteenth century.

You can also better understand how historians often derive different conclusions from the same body of material.

Chapter 3 is good preparation for the evaluation in Chapter 4 of one historian's argument about the role of the yellow press in the Spanish-American War. In this chapter you can begin to use primary sources to reach a conclusion about a historian's argument. Inasmuch as historians still disagree about the reasons for the war with Spain, the essay and the primary sources in this chapter provide another opportunity to see how subjective historical interpretation can be.

One of the most important sources of disagreement among historians is the question of motivation. What drove people to do what they did in the past? The good historian, like the detective in a murder mystery, eventually asks that question. Chapter 5 illustrates the importance of motivation by examining what was behind the promotion of a new housing style in the early twentieth century known as the bungalow. That topic also demonstrates that historians often look in some unlikely places to understand the past.

Motives in history are, of course, related to ideas, the subject of Chapter 6. What power do ideas exert in history? What is their relationship, for example, to the motives examined in the previous chapter? In Chapter 6 we try to answer these questions by examining the role of ideology in closing the doors to large-scale immigration in the early twentieth century.

The problem of motivation is also closely linked to the study of historical causation. Differences in historians' interpretations usually involve different views about the causes of things. In considering the questions of motivation and ideology, Chapters 5 and 6 moved beyond the question of what happened to the question of why. Chapter 7, on the bitter presidential election of 1928, moves even deeper into the realm of why. It considers how numerous factors may interact to produce historical change. It also demonstrates the relationship between the ability of historians to discriminate among historical causes and their power to explain the past.

Chapter 8 turns from causation to the influence of a single individual in the past. In this chapter we examine the activities of Eleanor Roosevelt as First Lady. Few First Ladies were more admired, or hated. What can historians learn about an era by focusing on one prominent individual like Eleanor Roosevelt? In the past, many historians believed that history was nothing more than the biography of great people. How much can students of history learn about the past by looking at it this way, that is, "from the top down"? How much do they miss by doing so? Such questions are, of course, related to the topics of previous chapters: historical evidence, motivation, and causation.

The next chapter examines history from the opposite perspective—"from the bottom up." What can historians learn by looking at the people at the bottom of a society? What challenges face historians who try? During World War II, a good place for looking at history this way is in the slums of Detroit, one of America's greatest war-production centers. Chapter 9 examines the race riot that occurred there in 1943. We will see who the rioters were and why their lives are important to historians.

Having considered the questions of motivation and causation in history and examined the past from different perspectives, in Chapter 10 we examine how historians synthesize, or combine small pieces into a large picture. The topic of this chapter is the impact of anticommunist hysteria on postwar popular culture. Aside from the question of causation, this chapter considers the problems historians face when they try to trace the influence of one large force in history.

Many of the preceding chapters have used a single historical essay and an accompanying set of primary sources to examine problems of evidence, motivation, ideology, causation, grand forces, and writing of history from both the "top down" and the "bottom up." The next chapter offers an opportunity to pull together the lessons of previous chapters. Chapter 11 compares what two historians have written about a single topic, the war in Vietnam. We will consider the way the United States fought this war, historians' explanations for the way it turned out, and the lessons they draw from the experience. This requires that we examine the actions of a small but influential set of individuals as well as the attitudes of many ordinary Americans. Thus explaining America's biggest military loss enables us to consider, in a single topic, such questions as motivation, the role of grand historical forces, and the role of the individual in history.

The goal of Chapter 12 is similar to that of Chapter 11: a synthesis, or pulling together, of lessons learned in preceding chapters. Here, however, the emphasis is on the problems of historical evidence, causation, and the role of ideology. Chapter 12 contains two essays on the rise of the women's movement in the 1960s and 1970s and a small collection of primary sources. It asks you to compare and analyze conflicting arguments, using not only primary sources but also insights drawn from previous chapters.

All of the chapters in this volume have a common purpose: to encourage you to think more like a historian and to sharpen your critical thinking skills. Chapter 13 returns to a point emphasized throughout this volume: The pursuit of the past cannot occur apart from a consideration of historical interpretation, and differences in historical interpretation matter not just to historians but to everyone. This final chapter examines various interpretations of the "Reagan Revolution." It contains two accounts of the Reagan administration's legacy and primary documents that illuminate both interpretations. In addition, it underscores the way our view of the past can be used to justify policies and practices in a later time.

By the end of this volume, you will have sharpened your ability to think about the past. You will think more critically about the use of historical evidence and about such historical problems as motivation, causation, and interpretation. Moreover, by exploring several styles of historical writing and various avenues to the past—from approaches that emphasize politics or economics to those that highlight social developments or military strategy—you will come to understand better, not only the historian's craft, but also the importance of the past. In short, you will think more like a historian.

Chapter 1

Historians and Textbooks:
The "Story" of Reconstruction

The textbook selections in this chapter illustrate different assumptions about the meaning of post–Civil War Reconstruction history.

Sources

1. Reconstruction (1906), THOMAS W. WILSON
2. The Negro in Reconstruction (1922), CARTER WOODSON
3. The Ordeal of Reconstruction (1966), THOMAS A. BAILEY
4. Radical Reconstruction in the South (1991), DAVID M. KENNEDY and THOMAS A. BAILEY

*I*n one of the most memorable scenes in movie history, Rhett Butler tells Scarlett that he's leaving her. When Scarlett asks what she will do, Rhett answers, "Frankly, my dear, I don't give a damn." It was the climax of *Gone with the Wind,* starring Clark Gable as Rhett and Vivian Leigh as Scarlett O'Hara. The David O. Selznick film, based on a best-selling novel, was the biggest picture of 1939.

The film's success should have surprised no one. It had all the right elements: strong-willed characters, tempestuous romance, a deathbed scene that left audiences in tears, and courageous people struggling to rebuild lives and fortunes destroyed by war. Yet *Gone with the Wind* also offered an enduring image of life in the Old South and of Reconstruction's "dark days." On the O'Hara plantation, "chivalrous" whites and their loyal ex-slaves confronted "cruel and vicious" Yankee carpetbaggers in cahoots with "traitorous" scalawags. It was a theme that made sense to mostly white movie audiences in 1939. As early as 1912, D. W. Griffith's silent film *The Birth of a Nation* had told the story of the Ku Klux Klan's violent but "valiant" efforts to throw off "carpetbag" rule. Like Griffith's tale, *Gone with the Wind* found a sympathetic audience because it reflected their racial prejudices. As historical drama, it also fit comfortably with what they had learned in school, specifically, with interpretations imparted from history textbooks.

This chapter examines what some twentieth-century textbooks have taught Americans about Reconstruction. We will see if these books always contain the same past or if they, like such powerful movies as *The Birth of a Nation* and *Gone with the Wind,* reflect the biases of their producers. When done, you can judge how well *Gone with the Wind*'s picture of Reconstruction corresponds with those presented in textbooks today.

SETTING

Moviegoers in 1939 may have remembered producer David O. Selznick's name splashed across the screen. Far fewer recalled the author of their American history textbook. More likely than not it was David S. Muzzey, whose *American History* (1911) and *History of the American People* (1927) were best sellers by the 1930s. Among the most enduring American history textbooks, these books probably taught several generations of Americans more about their nation's past than any other book. If audiences had learned anything about Reconstruction before *Gone with the Wind*'s opening credits, it was probably Muzzey who had taught them.

Muzzey had plenty to say about Reconstruction, and in no uncertain terms. The Republican governments established under congressional Reconstruction he judged to be "sorry affairs." The government "of the negro [*sic*] and his unscrupulous carpetbagger and scalawag patrons was an orgy of extravagance, fraud, and disgusting incompetence." Muzzey, a New Englander, was sympathetic to the efforts of Southerners to "redeem" their states from "negro [*sic*] and carpetbagger rule." Although he called white Southerners' use of violence against black voters "exasperating," their response was understandable. "Congress," he asserted, "did [Southern states] an unpardonable injury by hastening to reconstruct them on the basis of negro [*sic*] suffrage."[1] In short, his view of Reconstruction was that of the white Redeemers themselves.

Muzzey, of course, did not invent this "Redeemer" view of Reconstruction. How, then, had he come to these conclusions? It is impossible to be certain about the intellectual influences on this Columbia University professor. Yet we do know that two other Columbia historians had already written sympathetically about the white South's plight under congressional Reconstruction. Ex-confederate John W. Burgess was an advocate of "Nordic" racial supremacy and the "white man's burden." In *Reconstruction and the Constitution* (1902), he declared that blacks failed to subject "passion to reason." Reconstruction thus put "barbarism in power over civilization."[2] William A. Dunning, a Northerner, agreed. His Reconstruction history was peopled with corrupt carpetbaggers and blacks pursuing "vicious" policies. White Southerners had little choice but to fight back. "All the forces [in the South] that made for civilization," Dunning asserted, "were dominated by a mass of barbarous freedmen."[3]

Burgess and Dunning played a crucial role in transmitting a Southern view of Reconstruction into classrooms nationwide. At Columbia they trained several generations of historians, who wrote more books and trained still other historians. By the time *Gone with the Wind* captivated many moviegoers, the struggle for the hearts and minds of high school and college students was already over. Although a few black historians dissented, most notably W. E. B. Du Bois, the South had triumphed in the historical battle over the theory of Reconstruction. Rather than a new view of the past, *Gone with the Wind* offered white audiences a reassuring version of the past that had been embedded in the popular mind for several decades. In 1939, Hollywood ensured that it would endure for several more.

INVESTIGATION

This chapter contains four selections from American history textbooks published in the twentieth century. The first was published in 1906 and the last in 1991. Your primary assignment is to determine how these accounts of Reconstruction differ from one another and which one is most accurate. As you read them, keep in mind the questions that the authors attempt to answer about Reconstruction.

These questions, mostly unstated, are not necessarily the same. Also, be careful to note the most important facts of Reconstruction that each presents and the meaning each assigns to them. To see more clearly how these textbook selections differ from one another, it would be helpful to write down brief answers to the following questions as you read each account:

1. **What is the author's view of the integrity and effectiveness of those involved in the Republican governments in the southern states?** Is the view of the "carpetbaggers" and scalawags positive, negative, or neutral?

2. **What is the author's view of blacks?** Is the author's analysis of Reconstruction based on racial assumptions about the character of the freedmen? Are blacks passive or active participants in shaping Reconstruction and their own lives?

3. **What is the author's view of the overturning of Reconstruction?** Is the seizure of power by white Southerners a welcome or regrettable development? What is the author's view of such terrorist organizations as the Ku Klux Klan?

Before you begin, read your own textbook's discussion of Reconstruction. When you are finished, you should be able to explain how these selections differ, which one is closest to the interpretation in your own text, and which one is most plausible.

SOURCES

SOURCE 1

Reconstruction (1906)

THOMAS W. WILSON

Adventurers swarmed out of the North to cozen, beguile, and use . . . them [negroes]. These men, mere "carpet baggers" for the most part, who brought nothing with them, and had nothing to bring, but a change of clothing and their wits, became the new masters of the blacks. They gained the confidence of the negroes, obtained for themselves the more lucrative offices, and lived upon the public treasury, public contracts, and their easy control of affairs. For

Source: Woodrow Wilson, *A History of the American People* (New York: Harper and Bros., 1906), V, 46, 47–49, 58, 59, 60, 62, 98, 99.

the negroes there was nothing but occasional allotments of abandoned or forfeited land, the pay of petty offices, a *per diem* allowance as members of the conventions and the state legislatures which their new masters made business for, or the wages of servants in the various offices of administration. Their ignorance and credulity made them easy dupes. . . .

. . . In Mississippi, before the work of the carpet baggers was done, six hundred and forty thousand acres of land had been forfeited for taxes, twenty *per cent,* of the total acreage of the State. The state tax levy for 1871 was four times as great as the levy for 1869 had been; that for 1873 eight times as great; that for 1874 fourteen times. The impoverished planters could not carry the intolerable burden of taxes, and gave their lands up to be sold by the sheriff. There were few who could buy. The lands lay waste and neglected or were parcelled out at nominal rates among the negroes. . . .

Taxes, of course, did not suffice. Enormous debts were piled up to satisfy the adventurers. . . . Treasuries were swept clean. . . .

. . . The white men of the South were aroused by the mere instinct of self-preservation to rid themselves, by fair means or foul, of the intolerable burden of governments sustained by the votes of ignorant negroes and conducted in the interest of adventurers: governments whose incredible debts were incurred that thieves might be enriched, whose increasing loans and taxes went to no public use but into the pockets of party managers and corrupt contractors. . . .

They took the law into their own hands, and began to attempt by intimidation what they were not allowed to attempt by the ballot or by any ordered course of public action. They began to do by secret concert and association what they could not do in avowed parties. Almost by accident a way was found to succeed which led insensibly farther and farther afield into the ways of violence and outlawry. In May, 1866, a little group of young men in the Tennessee village of Pulaski, finding time hang heavy on their hands after the excitements of the field, so lately abandoned, formed a secret club for the mere pleasure of association, for private amusement—for anything that might promise to break the monotony of the too quiet place. . . .

. . . Year by year the organization spread, from county to county, from State to State. Every country-side wished to have its own Ku Klux, founded in secrecy and mystery like the mother "Den" at Pulaski, until at last there had sprung into existence a great *Ku Klux Klan,* an "Invisible Empire of the South," bound together in loose organization to protect the southern country from some of the ugliest hazards of a time of revolution. . . .

It was impossible to keep such a power in hand. Sober men governed the counsels and moderated the plans of those roving knights errant; but it was lawless work at best. They had set themselves, after the first year or two of mere mischievous frolic had passed, to right a disordered society through the power of fear. Men of hot passions who could not always be restrained carried their plans into effect. . . .

The reconstruction of the southern States had been the undoing of the Republican party. The course of carpet bag rule did not run smooth. Every election fixed the attention of the country upon some serious question of fraud or violence in the States where northern adventurers and negro majorities were in control. . . . Before [Ulysses S. Grant's] term was out the white voters of the South had rallied strong enough in every State except South Carolina, Florida, and Louisiana to take their governments out of the hands of the men who were preying upon them.

◆

SOURCE 2

The Negro in Reconstruction (1922)

CARTER WOODSON

Reconstruction began in the schoolhouses not in the State houses, as uninformed persons often say. . . . As the Union armies gradually invaded that area the soldiers opened schools for Negroes. Regular teachers came from relief societies and the Freedmen's Bureau. These enlightened a fair percentage of the Negroes by 1870. The illiteracy of the Negroes was reduced to 79.9 by that time. When about the same time these freedmen had a chance to participate in the rehabilitation of State governments in the South, they gave that section of the first free public school system, the first democratic education it ever had. . . .

The [majority of] other States in the South, from 1868 to about 1872, became subjected to what is commonly known as "Negro carpet-bag rule."

To call this Negro rule, however, is very much of a mistake. As a matter of fact, most of the local offices in these commonwealths were held by the white men, and those Negroes who did attain some of the higher offices were usually about as competent as the average whites thereto elected. Only twenty-three Negroes served in Congress from 1868 to 1895. The Negroes had political equality in the Southern States only a few years, and with some exceptions their tenure in Congress was very short. . . .

The charge that all Negro officers were illiterate, ignorant of the science of government, cannot be sustained. In the first place, the education of the Negro by Union soldiers in the South began in spots as early as 1861. Many of the Negro leaders who had been educated in the North or abroad returned to the

Source: Carter G. Woodson and Charles H. Wesley, The Negro in Our History (Washington, D.C.: The Associated Publishers, Inc., 1962). Excerpted by permission of the Association for the Study of African American Life and History, Inc.

South after the war. Negro illiteracy had been reduced to 79.9 by 1870, just about the time the freedmen were actually participating in the reconstruction. The masses of Negroes did not take a part in the government in the beginning of the reconstruction.

It is true that many of them were not prepared to vote, and decidedly disqualified for the positions which they held. In some of the legislatures, as in Louisiana and South Carolina, more than half of the Negro members could scarcely read or write. They, therefore, had to vote according to emotions or the dictates of the demagogues. This, of course, has been true of legislatures composed entirely of whites. In the local and State administrative offices, however, where there were frequent chances for corruption, very few ignorant Negroes ever served. . . .

Most of the local, State and Federal offices, however, were held not by Negroes but by southern white men, and by others who came from the North and profited by the prostration of the South. They were in many respects selfish men, but not always utterly lacking in principle. The northern whites, of course, had little sympathy for the South. They depended for their constituency upon the Negroes, who could not be expected to placate the ex-slaveholders. Being adventurers and interested in their own affairs, the carpet-baggers became unusually corrupt in certain States. They administered affairs selfishly. Most Negro officers who served in the South came out of office with an honorable record. . . .

Reconstruction history, however, was distorted by J. W. Burgess, a slave-holder of Giles County, Tennessee, who was educated in the North and finally attained distinction as a teacher and writer at Columbia University; and by W. A. Dunning, the son of an industrialist of Plainfield, New Jersey, who became the disciple of Burgess. The two trained or influenced in the same biased way the sons and sympathizers of former slaveholders who prostituted modern historiography to perpetuate the same distortion. These pseudo-historians refused to use the evidence of those who opposed slavery, discredited the testimony of those who favored Congressional Reconstruction, and ignored the observations of travellers from the North and from Europe. These makers of history to order were more partial than required by the law of slavery, for they rejected the evidence from Negro sources and thus denied the Negro not only the opportunity to testify against the white man but even to testify in favor of himself. . . .

Wherever they could, the native whites instituted government by investigation to expose all shortcomings of Negro officials. The general charge was that they were corrupt. The very persons who complained of the corruption in the Negro carpet-bag governments and who effected the reorganization of the State governments in the South when the Negroes were overthrown, however, became just as corrupt as the governing class under the preceding régime. In almost every restored State government in the South, and especially in Mississippi, the white officers in control of the funds defaulted. These persons who had been so long out of office came back so eager to get the most out of it that they filled their own pockets from the coffers of the public. No exposure followed. . . .

The attack on the policies of the carpet-bag governments, moreover, had the desired effect among the poor and ignorant whites. Reared under the degrading influences of slavery, they could not tolerate the blacks as citizens. The Negroes thereafter were harassed and harried by disturbing elements of anarchy, out of which soon emerged an oath-bound order called the Ku Klux Klan, established to terrorize the Negroes with lawlessness and violence.

◆————————

SOURCE 3

The Ordeal of Reconstruction (1966)

THOMAS A. BAILEY

Enfranchised Freedmen

The sudden thrusting of the ballot unto the hands of the ex-slaves, between 1867 and 1870, set the stage for stark tragedy. As might have been foreseen, it was a blunder hardly less serious than thrusting overnight freedom upon them. Wholesale liberation was probably unavoidable, given the feverish conditions created by war. But wholesale suffrage was avoidable, except insofar as the Radicals found it necessary for their own ends, both selfish and idealistic.

The bewildered Negroes were poorly prepared for their new responsibilities as citizens and voters. Democracy is a delicate mechanism, which requires education and information. Yet about nine-tenths of the 700,000 adult Negro males were illiterate. When registering, many did not know their ages; and boys of sixteen signed the rolls. Some of these voters could not even give their last name, if indeed they had any. Bob, Quash, Christmas, Scipio, Nebuchadnezzar would take any surname that popped into their heads, often that of "massa." Sometimes they chose more wisely than they knew. On the voting lists of Charleston, South Carolina, there were forty-six George Washingtons and sixty-three Abraham Lincolns.

The tale would be amusing were it not so pathetic and tragic. After the Negroes were told to come in for registration, many appeared with boxes or

Source: Thomas A. Bailey, The American Pageant, 3rd ed., pp. 475, 476–478. Copyright © 1966 by D. C. Heath and Company. By permission of Houghton Mifflin Company.

baskets, thinking that registration was some new kind of food or drink. Others would mark their ballots and then carefully deposit them in mail boxes.

While these pitiable practices were going on, thousands of the ablest Southern whites were being denied the vote, either by act of Congress or by the new state constitutions. . . .

Enthroned Ignorance

Some of the new Southern legislatures created in 1867–1870, not unlike some Northern legislatures, presented bizarre scenes. They were dominated by newly arrived carpetbaggers, despised scalawags, and pliant Negroes. Some of the ex-bondsmen were remarkably well educated, but many others were illiterate. In a few of the states the colored legislators constituted a strong minority. In once-haughty South Carolina, the tally stood at 88 Negroes to 67 whites; and ex-slaves held offices ranging from speaker to doorkeeper. Negroes who had been raising cotton under the lash of the overseer were now raising points of order under the gavel of the speaker. As a Negro song ran:

> De bottom rail's on de top
> And we's gwine to keep it dar.

Greatly to their credit, these Negro-white legislatures passed much desirable legislation and introduced many overdue reforms. In some states a better tax system was created, state charities were established, public works were launched, property rights were guaranteed to women, and free public schools were encouraged—for Negroes as well as whites. Some of these reforms were so welcome that they were retained, along with the more enlightened state constitutions, when the Southern whites finally strong-armed their way back into control.

But the good legislation, unhappily, was often obscured by a carnival of corruption and misrule. Graft and theft ran wild, especially in states like South Carolina and Louisiana, where designing whites used naive Negroes as cats-paws. The worst black-and-tan legislatures purchased, under "legislative supplies," such items as hams, perfumes, suspenders, bonnets, corsets, champagne, and a coffin. One "thrifty" carpetbag governor in a single year "saved" $100,000 from a salary of $8000.

The public debt of the Southern states doubled and trebled, as irresponsible carpetbag legislatures voted appropriations and bond issues with lighthearted abandon. Burdensome taxes were passed in Mississippi, where some 6,000,000 acres were sold for delinquent taxes. The disfranchised and propertied whites had to stagger along under a tax burden that sometimes rose ten or fifteen-fold. . . .

One should also note that during this hectic era corruption was also rampant in the North, among Republicans as well as Democrats. The notorious Tweed Ring of New York City probably stole more millions, though with greater sophistication, than the worst of the carpetbag legislatures combined. And when the Southern whites regained the whip hand, graft by no means disappeared under Democratic auspices.

The Rule of Night Riders

Goaded to desperation, once-decent Southern whites resorted to savage measures against Negro-carpetbag control. A number of secret organizations blossomed forth, the most notorious of which was the Ku Klux Klan, founded in Tennessee in 1866. Besheeted night riders, their horses' hoofs muffled, would hammer on the cabin door of a politically ambitious Negro. In ghoulish tones one thirsty horseman would demand a bucket of water, pour it into a rubber attachment under pretense of drinking, smack his lips, and declare that this was the first water he had tasted since he was killed at the battle of Shiloh. If fright did not produce the desired effect, force was employed.

Such tomfoolery and terror proved partially effective. Many Negroes and carpetbaggers, quick to take a hint, were scared away from the polls. But those stubborn souls who persisted in their forward ways were flogged, mutilated, or even murdered. In one Louisiana parish in 1868, the whites in two days killed or wounded two hundred victims; a pile of twenty-five bodies was found half-buried in the woods. By such atrocious practices was the Negro "kept in his place."

SOURCE 4

Radical Reconstruction in the South (1991)

DAVID M. KENNEDY and THOMAS A. BAILEY

The Realities of Radical Reconstruction in the South

The blacks now had freedom, of a sort. Their friends in Congress had only haltingly and somewhat belatedly secured the franchise for them. Both Presidents Lincoln and Johnson had proposed to give the ballot gradually to selected blacks who qualified for it through education, property ownership, or military service. Moderate Republicans and even many radicals at first hesitated to bestow suffrage on the freedmen. The Fourteenth Amendment, in

Source: Thomas A. Bailey and David M. Kennedy, *The American Pageant,* 9th ed., pp. 490–493. Copyright © 1991 by D. C. Heath and Company. By permission of Houghton Mifflin Company.

many ways the heart of the Republican program for Reconstruction, had fallen short of guaranteeing the right to vote. (It envisioned for blacks the same status as women—citizenship without voting rights.) But by 1867 hesitation had given way to a hard determination to enfranchise the former slaves wholesale and immediately, while thousands of white Southerners were being denied the vote. By glaring contrast most of the Northern states, before ratification of the Fifteenth Amendment in 1870, withheld the ballot from their tiny black minorities. White Southerners naturally concluded that the Republicans were hypocritical in insisting that blacks in the South be allowed to vote.

In five states—Alabama, Florida, Louisiana, Mississippi, and South Carolina—the black voters enfranchised by the new state constitutions made up a majority of the electorate. But only in South Carolina did blacks predominate in the lower house of the legislature. No state senate had a black majority, and there were no black governors during what the whites called "black reconstruction." Many of the newly elected black legislators were literate and able; more than a few came from the ranks of the prewar free blacks who had acquired considerable education. More than a dozen black congressmen and two black United States senators, Hiram Revels and Blanche K. Bruce, both of Mississippi, did creditable work in the national capital.

Yet in many Southern capitals, former slaves held offices ranging from doorkeeper up to Speaker, to the bitter resentment of their one-time masters. Some untutored blacks fell under the control of white "scalawags" and "carpetbaggers," who used the blacks as political henchmen. The "scalawags" were Southerners, sometimes former Unionists and Whigs. By collaborating in creating the new regimes, they earned the undying enmity of the former Confederates, who accused them, often with wild exaggeration, of plundering the treasurers of the Southern states through their political influence in the radical governments. "Carpetbaggers" were mainly Northerners who supposedly had packed all their worldly goods into a single carpetbag suitcase at war's end and had come South to seek their fortune.

How well did the radical regimes rule? In many of them, graft did indeed run rampant. This was especially true in South Carolina and Louisiana, where conscienceless promoters and other pocket-padders used politically inexperienced blacks as cat's-paws. The worst "black-and-white" legislatures purchased, as "legislative supplies," such "stationery" as hams, perfumes, suspenders, bonnets, corsets, champagne, and a coffin. One "thrifty" carpetbag governor in a single year "saved" $100,000 from a salary of $8,000. Yet this sort of corruption was by no means confined to the South in these postwar years. The crimes of the Reconstruction governments were no more outrageous than the scams and felonies being perpetrated in the North at the same time, especially in Boss Tweed's New York.

The radical legislatures also passed much desirable legislation and introduced many badly needed reforms. For the first time in Southern history, steps were taken toward establishing adequate public schools. Tax systems were streamlined; public works were launched; and property rights were guaranteed to women. Many of these reforms were so welcome that they were retained by the all-white "redeemer" governments that later returned to power.

The Ku Klux Klan

Deeply embittered, some Southern whites resorted to savage measures against "radical" rule. Many whites resented the success and ability of black legislators as much as they resented alleged "corruption." A number of secret organizations mushroomed forth, the most notorious of which was the "Invisible Empire of the South," or Ku Klux Klan, founded in Tennessee in 1866. Besheeted night riders, their horses' hoofs muffled, would approach the cabin of an "upstart" black and hammer on the door. In ghoulish tones one thirsty horseman would demand a bucket of water. Then, under pretense of drinking, he would pour it into a rubber attachment concealed beneath his mask and gown, smack his lips, and declare that this was the first water he had tasted since he was killed at the Battle of Shiloh. If fright did not produce the desired effect, force was employed.

Such tomfoolery and terror proved partially effective. Many ex-bondsmen and white "carpetbaggers," quick to take a hint, shunned the polls. Those stubborn souls who persisted in their "upstart" ways were flogged, mutilated, or even murdered. In one Louisiana parish in 1868, the whites in two days killed or wounded two hundred victims; a pile of twenty-five bodies was found half-buried in the woods. By such atrocious practices were blacks "kept in their place"—that is, down.

CONCLUSION

These discussions of Reconstruction should make it clear that history textbooks contain interpretations. They are no different from other historical writing in that regard. Modern texts are also written by people with biases and opinions, although their interpretations may be as difficult to spot today as Muzzey's were for his students. In part that's because historians often do not reveal their most important assumptions, as the two selections from *The American Pageant*, another best-selling American history textbook, demonstrate. The original author, Stanford University historian Thomas A. Bailey, approached his task in much the same spirit as Muzzey; he wrote history as a lively story, with the accomplishments of prominent people giving direction to the narrative. Behind this approach was the unspoken assumption that the lives of people at the bottom of the society mattered less than the bold actions of diplomats, generals, and politicians. Moreover, Bailey wrote *The American Pageant* before the growing civil rights protests began to assault legal segregation and the racial attitudes that upheld it. Thus the earlier editions of *The American Pageant* reflect the continuing hold of the Dunning view of Reconstruction. On the other hand, Stanford historian and Bailey successor David M. Kennedy is of the generation of scholars who came of age in the 1960s. Not only do many of these historians incorporate ordinary people into their accounts, but their racial assumptions differ from those of most historians earlier in the twentieth century.

It is usually easier to spot interpretations in older textbooks because their authors do not share our premises. The first textbook selection, written with an unquestioned assumption of black inferiority, is a good example. Its author, Thomas W. Wilson, was probably as unfamiliar to you as were William Dunning and David Muzzey. He is better known today as Woodrow Wilson, the Princeton historian who later became the twenty-eighth president of the United States. If Wilson's text reflects the racist assumptions at the heart of the triumphant Southern view of Reconstruction, the second selection reveals that not all historians accepted this dominant view, even in the early twentieth century. Its author, Carter Woodson, was a Virginia-born African-American who earned a Ph.D. from Harvard University in 1912. Like the work of fellow Harvard-trained black historian W. E. B. Du Bois, Woodson's *The Negro in Our History* and his other Negro history textbooks were largely ignored by white historians and students. In its own way, of course, Woodson's text also demonstrates the importance of racial assumptions in shaping interpretations about Reconstruction. It also illustrates that historians are more than mouthpieces for the dominant views of their day.

Together, all of these texts remind us that Americans' social views have not remained frozen since the early twentieth century. And although the questions historians ask are not entirely dependent on whatever social views happen to be popular, historians are surely influenced by their times. However, these selections also make clear that historians do not simply mirror what happened in the past but instead give meaning to the "facts" of history. To do that, they study primary sources—the materials left to us by people in the past. We turn to them next.

FURTHER READING

W. E. B. Du Bois, *Black Reconstruction* (New York: Russell and Russell, 1935).
Frances FitzGerald, *America Revised: History Schoolbooks in the Twentieth Century* (New York: Random House, 1979).

Eric Foner, *A Short History of Reconstruction, 1863–1977* (New York: Harper and Row, 1990).

James W. Loewen, *Lies My Teacher Told Me: Everything Your American History Textbook Got Wrong* (New York: The New Press, 1995).

NOTES

1. David Saville Muzzey, *History of the American People* (New York: Ginn and Company, 1935), pp. 408, 410.
2. John W. Burgess, *Reconstruction and the Constitution, 1865–1876* (New York: De Capo Press, 1970; reprint of 1902 edition), p. viii.
3. William A. Dunning, *Reconstruction, Political and Economic* (New York: Harper and Brothers, 1907), p. 212.

Using Primary Sources: Industrialization and the Condition of Labor

This chapter introduces primary sources. The documents presented give information on nineteenth-century working conditions.

Sources

*I*n 1873 a financial panic sparked a severe depression. Four years later business was still stagnant, and, with unemployment at perhaps one million, working people grew restless. In Pennsylvania's coal mining regions the militia was called on repeatedly to keep order. Then in 1877 wage cuts and layoffs on the railroads exploded into a paralyzing railroad strike. After the violent confrontation was over, many people lay dead, millions of dollars of property had been destroyed, and dazed Americans stared at the specter of class warfare.

In 1878 Congress appointed a committee to investigate the causes of the "General Depression in Labor and Business." One of the witnesses called to testify was the Yale University professor William Graham Sumner. Sumner was a proponent of what would be known as Social Darwinism, a theory that applied Darwin's theories of evolution to society in an attempt to justify uncontrolled economic competition. Sumner later shared his views through books and a stream of popular magazine articles. Now, he responded to Congress with answers that many middle-class Americans found reassuring. When asked by one congressman what effect the spread of machinery had on workers, Sumner admitted that they suffered a loss of income and "a loss of comfort." Asked if there was any way to help, Sumner responded, "not at all." And when pressed to admit that there was "distress among the laboring classes," Sumner shot back, "I do not admit any such thing. I cannot see any evidence of it."[1]

Many of Sumner's contemporaries eagerly embraced his conclusion that industrialization caused no real suffering. Yet it would be foolish for us to do so. Instead, we can rely on a wide variety of primary sources—the historical evidence and artifacts that survive from the past—to understand the ways industrialization influenced the lives of workers. Without them, historians are at the mercy of other people's interpretations of the past. With them, they can make direct contact with the past. In this chapter, therefore, we turn to these sources to examine the same question about the "laboring classes" posed to William Graham Sumner in 1878.

SETTING

Historians who study workers in the late nineteenth century have a wealth of primary sources. They include "literary" or *written* sources, *statistical* sources relating to such information as wages and the cost of living, and such *nonwritten* sources as sketches and photographs. Many of these sources are available because a variety of bureaus, commissions, and committees in the late nineteenth century began to investigate the effects of industrial growth on labor. By the 1880s, for instance, a number of states had set up bureaus of labor statistics to assess the living and working conditions of wage earners. In 1884, Congress established the Bureau of Labor, which two years later began to issue annual reports related to the conditions of workers. At about the same time, the U.S. Senate issued a five-volume *Report upon the Relations Between Capital and Labor.* In addition, in 1901 and 1902 its Industrial Commission produced a massive report on the effects of industrial growth. Meanwhile, other investigators also began to produce valuable sources. Often armed with only pens and cameras, such reformers as Jacob Riis, Lewis Hine, John Spargo, and Upton Sinclair recorded the conditions in the industrial workplace at the turn of the century. The *Atlantic Monthly, Independent, Outlook,* and other popular magazines also published articles on the living and working conditions of laborers. Added to these sources are newspaper accounts, diaries, songs, and documents from such organizations as charities, labor unions, corporations, and business associations. In short, the sources reflecting the condition of labor in industrial America are as varied as they are numerous.

INVESTIGATION

The main problem we investigate in this chapter is the question posed to William Graham Sumner in the congressional investigation in 1878: Was there "distress" among the "laboring classes" as the United States industrialized in the late nineteenth century? That question is a very broad one, and, given the abundance of primary sources, it might seem easy to answer. Yet it is not. First, by 1900 there were more than 13 million nonagricultural wage earners in the United States, and their working conditions varied greatly. Second, we must define *distress* and determine whether our definition is the same as that of industrial wage earners themselves. We need to know the "objective" conditions as defined by wages, hours of labor, and cost of living, as well as what people at the time thought about them. That might depend, in turn, on workers' expectations. The question Sumner answered with such certainty is thus more complicated than it first appears. A good answer must be based on a careful consideration of the evidence. It should also address the following questions:

1. **Overall, do conditions appear to be improving or getting worse?** What important qualifications must be made to any generalizations about the conditions of workers? Do these qualifications involve certain groups or classes of workers?

2. **What do workers think about their conditions?** Which sources are especially valuable in understanding what it was like to be a wage earner in the late nineteenth century? Are some of the sources more biased than others?

3. **William Graham Sumner declared that schemes for "improving the conditions of the working classes" were "out of place" in American society. The claim of some writers that labor was treated "as a ware," he also asserted, was "ludicrous" in the "cold light of reason." Do you agree?** What does the "cold light" of your reason applied to this evidence suggest to you?

Before you begin, read the sections in your textbook on the condition of labor in the late nineteenth century and its response to industrial growth. See if you can detect a point of view regarding the living and working conditions of industrial workers.

SOURCES

---◆---

SOURCE 1   In 1878 the Massachusetts Bureau of the Statistics of Labor sent a questionnaire to workingmen and women throughout the state to solicit their opinions about their own work. According to the report, many of the respondents "expressed themselves at length upon some phase of the labor question."[2] Does this report show that workers were content or unhappy with their jobs? What were their primary complaints?

Testimony of Workingmen (1879)

Hours of Labor

From a Carpet-Mill Operative   I am satisfied with sixty hours a week: it is plenty time for any man, although there are some employed in the same place over that time, and get nothing extra for it. I know of one young man under age who was absent two Saturday afternoons, and his overseer gave him his bill on Monday morning when he went in. If there is any inspector of the ten-hour law, he would do well to call round, and see for himself.

From a Shoemaker   I think there ought to be an eight-hour law all over the country. There is not enough work to last the year round, and work over eight hours a day, or forty-eight hours a week. There can be only about so much work to do any way: and, when that is done, business has got to stop, or keep

Source: John A. Garraty, ed., *The Transformation of American Society, 1870–90* (Columbia, S.C.: University of South Carolina Press, 1968), pp. 88, 89–90, 91, 92, 94. Reprinted by permission of the University of South Carolina Press.

dragging the year round, so that a man has to work for almost any price offered; when, if there was an eight-hour law, things would be more even, and a man could get what his labor was worth, according to the price of living, and there would be plenty of work for all, and business would be good the year round. . . .

Overwork

From a Harness-Maker   In answer to the question, "Do you consider your-self overworked?" I answered, "Yes"; and it is my honest and firm conviction that I am, by at least two hours a day. With the great increase in machinery within the last fifteen or twenty years, I think, in justice, there ought to be some reduction in the hours of labor. Unless the hours of labor are shortened in proportion to the increase of machinery, I consider machinery an injury rather than a benefit to humanity. I tell you that ten hours a day, hard, steady work, is more than any man can stand for any length of time without injuring his health, and therefore shortening his life. For my own part, although my work is not very laborious, when I stop work in the evening, I feel completely played out. I would like to study some; but I am too fatigued. In fact it is as much as I can do to look over the evening paper; and I am almost certain that this is the condition of a majority of workingmen. . . .

From a Quarryman   In filling this blank, there are a good many questions which I did not answer relative to men with families; but, however, I would say, on behalf of married men in this locality, that they are poorly situated, working hard eleven and a half hours a day for $1.25 in summer, and 80 cents a day in winter, and obliged to purchase merchandise in company stores, and pay enormous rents for tenements. Merchandise being thirty per cent above market price, and being paid monthly, they are obliged to purchase at supply store; if not, they will be discharged, and starvation is the result. It is ridiculous in a free country that the laws are not more stringent, whereby the capitalist cannot rule and ruin his white slaves. I would draw your attention carefully to this matter, and I lay before you all truth, not hearsay, but from experience, I am a single man, and I would not be so if times were better than they are now. . . .

From a Machinist   In reply to your question concerning overwork, I wish to say, that, in employment requiring close application of mind or body, to be successful, the diligent and conscientious workman often, I might say always, finds his energy exhausted long before his ten hours are up. Then he is obliged to keep up an appearance to get the pay for his day's work, which he might do in eight hours as well as ten. If we are to have our pay by the hour, I should not advocate the eight-hour system. I think the employer would be the gainer, and the employé the loser. In the shop I work a little less than ten hours. To do that I have to leave home at 5:30 A.M., and arrive home again at 7 P.M.; so you see it makes a pretty long day. I travel not less than thirty-four miles daily, and pay $28.50 per quarter for car-fare. If I want to have a garden, I must do the work nights, or hire it done. I do not think I should be able to follow up work in this way until the age of sixty-five. Hope to find some way to avoid some of the long hours and some of the heavy work before then. I do not mean to complain; but it does seem as if the burdens and the pleasures of this world were very unequally divided. It is a hard matter to say what is right in every case. If my answers and statements should be of any service in improving the condition, prospects, or possibilities of the toiling thousands in our State, I shall be well paid for the same. . . .

The Use of Machinery

From a Boot and Shoe Cutter   Tax machinery. Bring it in common with hand labor, so a man can have twelve months' work in a year, instead of six or eight months. Protect hand labor, same as we protect trade from Europe, by tax or tariff.

From a Machinist   Machinery and the swarms of cheap foreign labor are fast rendering trades useless, and compelling the better class of mechanics to change their occupation, or go to farming. . . .

Habits of Industry

From a Shoe-Cutter   There is no way I think I could be paid more fairly than I now am. I do not consider that my employers profit unfairly by my labor. My labor is in the market for sale. My employers buy it just as they buy a side of leather, and expect, and I think are willing to pay, a fair market price for it. The miller who makes a grade of flour up to the very highest point in excellence will command the highest price for it in the market. The workingman who makes his labor of the most value will generally command the highest market price for it, and sharp business men are quick to discover its value. I consider all legislation in regard to any thing connected with labor as injurious. All trades-unions and combinations I also consider as injurious to the mass of working-people. A few profit by these associations, and the many pay the bills. If working-people would drop the use of beer, tobacco, and every thing else that is not of real benefit, and let such men as _____ and a host of others earn their own living, they would have far more money for the general expenses of a family than they now have. I live in a village of about two thousand inhabitants; and I do not know of a family in destitute circumstances which has let alone vicious expenditures, and been industrious. It is the idle, unthrifty, beer-drinking, don't-care sort of people, who are out at the elbows, and waiting for some sort of legislation to help them. The sooner working-people get rid of the idea that somebody or something is going to help them, the better it will be for them. In this country, as a general thing, every man has an equal chance to rise. In our village there are a number of successful business men, and all began in the world without any thing but their hands and a will to succeed. The best way for working-people to get help is to help themselves. . . .

◆

SOURCE 2   In 1884 the Illinois Bureau of Labor Statistics conducted an investigation of the standard of living of Illinois workers and their families. One result was a tabulation of the amount of money that 2,139 families in a number of communities actually earned and spent. As the bureau's report put it, "this minute catalogue of the details governing the life of each family portrays more vividly than any mere array of figures the common current of daily life among the people."[3] As you study these summaries, pay attention to the standard of living of families in this sample. Note the characteristics of the families who earned the most money or had the highest standard of living and of those who earned the least or had the lowest standard of living.

Earnings, Expenses and Conditions of Workingmen and Their Families (1884)

No. 35   LABORER   *Italian*

EARNINGS—Of father $270

CONDITION—Family numbers 5—parents and three children, all boys, aged one, three and five. Live in one room, for which they pay $4 per month rent. A very dirty and unhealthy place, everything perfectly filthy. There are

Source: Illinois Bureau of Labor Statistics, "Earnings, Expenses and Conditions of Workingmen and Their Families," *Third Biennial Report* (Springfield, Ill.: 1884), pp. 164, 267–271, 357–362, 365, 369–370, 373, 375, 383–385, 390–393, 395, 401–402, 404, 406–407, 410.

about fifteen other families living in the same house. They buy the cheapest kind of meat from the neighboring slaughter houses and the children pick up fuel on the streets and rotten eatables from the commission houses. Children do not attend school. They are all ignorant in the full sense of the word. Father could not write his name.

FOOD—*Breakfast*—Coffee and bread.
    Dinner—Soups.
    Supper—Coffee and bread.

COST OF LIVING—

Rent	$ 48
Fuel	5
Meat and groceries	100
Clothing, boots and shoes and dry goods	15
Sickness	5
Total	$173

No. 46	LABORER	*American*

EARNINGS—Of father	$360	
Of wife	100	
Total		$460

CONDITION—Family numbers 7—parents and five children, aged from six months to eight years. They live in a house which they rent, and pay rental of $10 per month. Two of the children attend school. House is situated in good, respectable neighborhood. The furniture and carpets are poor in quality, but substantial. The father is not a member of a labor organization, but subscribes for the labor papers. Their living expenses exceed their income.

FOOD—*Breakfast*—Salt meat, bread, butter and coffee.
    Dinner—Bread, meat and vegetables.
    Supper—Bread, coffee, etc.

COST OF LIVING—

Rent	$120
Fuel, meat and groceries	225
Clothing, boots and shoes and dry goods	85
Books, papers, etc.	2
Sundries	75
Total	$507

No. 47   LABORER   *Irish*

EARNINGS—Of father $343

CONDITION—Family numbers 5—parents and three children, two girls, aged seven and five, and boy, aged eight. They occupy a rented house of 4 rooms, and pay a rental, monthly of $7. Two of the children attend school. Father complains of the wages he receives, being but $1.10 per day, and says it is extremely difficult for him to support his family upon that amount. His work consists in cleaning yards, basements, out-buildings, etc., and is, in fact, a regular scavenger. He also complains of the work as being very unhealthy, but it seems he can procure no other work.

FOOD—*Breakfast*—Black coffee, bread and potatoes.
        Dinner—Corned beef, cabbage and potatoes.
        Supper—Bread, coffee and potatoes.

COST OF LIVING—

Rent	$ 84	
Fuel	15	
Meat and groceries	180	
Clothing, boots and shoes and dry goods	40	
Sundries	20	
Total		$339

No. 51   MACHINIST   *American*

EARNINGS—Of father	$540	
Of mother	255	
Of son, aged sixteen	255	
Total		$1,050

CONDITION—Family numbers 10—parents and eight children, five girls and three boys, aged from two to sixteen. Four of the children attend school. Father works only 30 weeks in the year, receives $3 per day for his services. They live in a comfortably furnished house, of 7 rooms, have a piano, take an interest in society and domestic affairs, are intelligent, but do not dress very well. Their expenditures are equal, but do not exceed their income. Father belongs to trades union, and is interested and benefited by and in it.

FOOD—*Breakfast*—Bread, meat and coffee.
        Dinner—Bread, meat, vegetables and tea.
        Supper—Bread, meat, vegetables and coffee.

COST OF LIVING—

Rent	$300
Fuel	50
Meat	100
Groceries	200
Clothing	160
Boots and shoes	50
Dry goods	25
Books, papers, etc.	15
Trades unions	10
Sickness	50
Sundries	90
Total	$1,050

No. 105	BRAKEMAN	*Irish*

EARNINGS—Of father $360

CONDITION—Family numbers 10—parents and eight children, six girls and two boys, aged one year to fifteen. Four of them attend public school. Family occupy a house of 3 rooms, for which they pay $5 per month rental. The house presents a most wretched appearance. Clothes ragged, children half dressed and dirty. They all sleep in one room regardless of sex. The house is devoid of furniture, and the entire concern is as wretched as could well be imagined. Father is shiftless and does not keep any one place for any length of time. Wife is without ambition or industry.

FOOD—*Breakfast*—Bread, coffee and syrup.
    Dinner—Potatoes, soup and bread, occasionally meat.
    Supper—Bread, syrup and coffee.

COST OF LIVING—

Rent	$ 60
Fuel	25
Meat	20
Groceries	360
Clothing	50
Boots and shoes	15
Dry goods	30
Books, papers, etc.	20
Sickness	5
Total	$585

No. 112   COAL MINER   *American*

EARNINGS—Of father $250

CONDITION—Family numbers 7—husband, wife, and five children, three girls and two boys, aged from three to nineteen years. Three of them go to the public school. Family live in 2 rooms tenement, in healthy locality, for which they pay $6 per month rent. The house is scantily furnished, without carpets, but is kept neat and clean. They are compelled to live very economically, and every cent they earn is used to the best advantage. Father had only thirty weeks work during the past year. He belongs to trades union. The figures for cost of living are actual and there is no doubt the family lived on the amount specified.

FOOD—*Breakfast*—Bread, coffee and salt meat.
         Dinner—Meat, bread, coffee and butter.
         Supper—Sausage, bread and coffee.

COST OF LIVING—

Rent	$72	
Fuel	20	
Meat	20	
Groceries	60	
Clothing	28	
Boots and shoes	15	
Dry goods	20	
Trades union	3	
Sickness	10	
Sundries	5	
Total		$252

No. 130   COAL MINER   *Irish*

EARNINGS—Of father $420
        Of son, twenty-one years of age   420
        Of son, eighteen years of age   420
        Of son, sixteen years of age   150
          Total $1,410

CONDITION—Family numbers 6—parents and four children, three boys and one girl. The girl attends school, and the three boys are working in the mine. Father owns a house of six rooms, which is clean and very comfortably furnished. Family temperate, and members of a church, which they attend with regularity. They have an acre of ground, which they work in summer, and raise vegetables for their consumption. They have their house about paid for, payments being made in installments of $240 per year. Father belongs to mutual assessment association and to trades union.

FOOD—*Breakfast*—Steak, bread, butter, potatoes, bacon and coffee.
    Dinner—Bread, butter, meat, cheese, pie and tea.
    Supper—Meat, potatoes, bread, butter, puddings, pie and coffee.

COST OF LIVING—

Rent	$240
Fuel	10
Meat	200
Groceries	700
Clothing	80
Boots, shoes and dry goods	70
Books, papers, etc.	15
Life insurance	18
Trades unions	3
Sickness	4
Sundries	75
Total	$1,415

No. 131	COAL MINER	*German*

EARNINGS—Of father $200

CONDITION—Family numbers 6—parents and four children, two boys and two girls, aged two, four, nine and eleven years. Two of them attend school. Family occupy a house containing 3 rooms, for which they pay $60 per annum. Father works all he can, and only receives $1 per day for his labor. He has only been in this country two and one half years and is anxious to get back to Germany. The house is miserably furnished, and is a wretched affair in itself. They have a few broken chairs and benches and a bedstead. Father is a shoemaker by trade, and does some cobbling which helps a little toward supporting his family. He receives the lowest wages in the shaft.

FOOD—*Breakfast*—Bread and coffee.
    Dinner—Bread, meat and coffee.
    Supper—Bread, meat, potatoes and coffee.

COST OF LIVING—

Rent	$60
Meat	36
Groceries	84
Clothing	12
Boots and shoes and dry goods	15
Sickness	1
Sundries	20
Total	$228

No. 137	IRON AND STEEL WORKER	*English*

EARNINGS—Of father $1,420
                   Of son, aged fourteen   300
                                   Total $1,720

CONDITION—Family numbers 6—parents and four children; two boys and two girls, aged from seven to sixteen years. Three of them attend school, and the other works in the shop with his father. Family occupy their own house, containing 9 well-furnished rooms, in a pleasant and healthy locality. They have a good vegetable and flower garden. They live well, but not extravagantly, and are saving about a thousand dollars per year. Father receives an average of $7 per day of twelve hours, for his labor, and works about thirty-four weeks of the year. Belongs to trades union, but carries no life insurance. Had but little sickness during the year.

FOOD—*Breakfast*—Bread, butter, meat, eggs, and sometimes oysters.
          Dinner—Potatoes, bread, butter, meat, pie, cake or pudding.
          Supper—Bread, butter, meat, rice or sauce, and tea or coffee.

COST OF LIVING—

Fuel	$ 55
Meat	100
Groceries	300
Clothing	75
Boots and shoes	50
Dry goods	50
Books, papers, etc.	10
Trades unions	6
Sickness	12
Sundries	50
Total	$708

No. 159   ROLLER BAR MILL   *American*

EARNINGS—Of father $2,200

CONDITION—Family numbers 5—parents and three children, two boys and one girl, aged four, six and eight years. Do not attend school. Family occupy house containing 3 rooms, well furnished in healthy locality, but the surroundings are not of the best. Family ordinarily intelligent. Father works eleven hours per day for 37 weeks in the year, and receives $10 per day for his labor; he saves about $1,400 per year, which he deposits in the bank. Family live well, but not extravagantly.

FOOD—*Breakfast*—Bread, meat, eggs, and coffee.
           Dinner—Bread, meat, vegetables, fruits and coffee.
           Supper—Bread, fruits, coffee and meat.

COST OF LIVING—

Rent	$120
Fuel	40
Groceries	200
Clothing	55
Boots and shoes	35
Dry goods	60
Books, papers, etc.	8
Sickness	50
Sundries	75
Total	$768

———◆———

SOURCE 3   The iron and steel industry was central to the economic growth of the United States in the late nineteenth century. The table on the following pages, from the United States Bureau of Labor Statistics, illustrates the wages of blast furnace keepers. Keeping in mind that workers often did not work full-time or year-round, note the general trend of their wages and hours. Were they better or worse off as time went on? Using information in the previous source, determine what living standard the average furnace keeper most likely had.

Wages in the Iron and Steel Industry, 1858–1900

Furnace keepers, pig-iron blast furnaces, 1858–1900, by year and state

| Year and State | Sex | Lowest, highest, and average— | | Year and State | Sex | Lowest, highest, and average— | |
		Hours per week	Rate per day (dollars)			Hours per week	Rate per day (dollars)
1858:				1866:			
Pennsylvania	M	(1)	1.70–1.70–1.70	Pennsylvania	M	(1)	2.41–2.41–2.41
1859:				1867:			
Pennsylvania	M	(1)	1.67–1.67–1.67	Pennsylvania	M	(1)	2.53–2.53–2.53
1860:				1868:			
Pennsylvania	M	(1)	1.85–1.85–1.85	Pennsylvania	M	(1)	2.53–2.53–2.53
1861:				1869:			
Pennsylvania	M	(1)	1.90–1.90–1.90	Pennsylvania	M	(1)	2.77–2.77–2.77
1862:				1870:			
Pennsylvania	M	(1)	1.68–1.68–1.68	Pennsylvania	M	(1)	2.77–2.77–2.77
1863:				1871:			
Pennsylvania	M	(1)	1.90–1.90–1.90	Pennsylvania	M	(1)	2.78–2.78–2.78
1864:				1872:			
Pennsylvania	M	(1)	2.70–2.70–2.70	Pennsylvania	M	(1)	3.15–3.15–3.15
1865:				1873:			
Pennsylvania	M	(1)	2.49–2.49–2.49	Pennsylvania	M	(1)	2.58–3.27–2.81

Source: United States Department of Labor, Bureau of Labor Statistics, *History of Wages in the United States from Colonial Times to 1928,* Revision of Bulletin No. 499 (Washington, D.C., 1934), pp. 247–248.

| Year and State | Sex | Lowest, highest, and average— | | Year and State | Sex | Lowest, highest, and average— | |
		Hours per week	Rate per day (dollars)			Hours per week	Rate per day (dollars)
1874:				1881:			
Pennsylvania	M	(1)	1.25–4.00–1.94	Ohio	M	70–84–77	1.00–2.65–1.65
1875:				Pennsylvania	M	84–84–84	1.78–1.90–1.84
Pennsylvania	M	(1)	1.60–1.94–1.71	1882:			
1876:				Pennsylvania	M	84–84–84	1.90–2.00–1.95
Pennsylvania	M	(1)	.85–2.37–1.67	1883:			
1877:				Pennsylvania	M	(1)	2.25–2.25–2.25
Ohio	M	60–84–77	.86–1.90–1.32	1884:			
Pennsylvania	M	(1)	1.56–1.56–1.56	Michigan	M	(1)	1.85–1.85–1.85
1878:				New Jersey	M	70–84–80	1.59–2.53–1.82
Ohio	M	(1)	.86–1.75–1.37	Ohio	M	(1)	1.00–2.25–1.64
Pennsylvania	M	67–84–82	.79–2.25–1.36	Pennsylvania	M	(1)	2.25–2.25–2.25
1879:				1885:			
Ohio	M	(1)	.86–2.80–1.51	Indiana	M	70–70–70	1.85–1.85–1.85
Pennsylvania	M	84–84–84	.79–2.50–1.59	Maryland	M	84–84–84	1.50–1.50–1.50
Do*	M	(1)	2.66– .66– .66	New York	M	84–84–84	1.67–1.85–1.79
1880:				Ohio	M	72–84–84	1.35–2.00–1.64
Ohio	M	60–84–78	1.07–2.50–1.63	Pennsylvania	M	84–84–84	1.80–2.25–2.02
Pennsylvania	M	84–84–84	1.30–1.78–1.62	Tennessee	M	84–84–84	1.80–1.80–1.80
				Virginia	M	84–84–84	1.50–2.30–1.93

Furnace keepers, pig-iron blast furnaces, 1858–1900, by year and state (continued)

Year and State	Sex	Lowest, highest, and average— Hours per week	Rate per day (dollars)	Year and State	Sex	Lowest, highest, and average— Hours per week	Rate per day (dollars)
1886:				1889 (con't):			
Pennsylvania	M	(1)	2.05–2.05–2.05	Illinois	M	84–84–84	3.10–3.25–3.21
1887:				Indiana	M	84–84–84	1.70–1.70–1.70
Ohio	M	70–84–74	1.40–2.25–1.91	Maryland	M	72–72–72	1.58–1.58–1.58
Pennsylvania	M	84–84–84	2.10–2.25–2.18	Michigan	M	84–84–84	2.00–2.00–2.00
Wisconsin	M	(1)	3.10–3.10–3.10	Missouri	M	84–84–84	1.70–1.70–1.70
1888:				New York	M	84–84–84	1.85–2.15–1.98
Illinois	M	84–84–84	3.25–3.25–3.25	Ohio	M	84–84–84	1.80–2.50–2.07
Michigan	M	84–84–84	1.80–2.00–1.90	Pennsylvania	M	56–84–83	1.08–3.00–1.91
New York	M	70–84–75	1.88–2.15–1.98	Tennessee	M	77–84–82	1.75–2.00–1.89
Ohio	M	84–84–84	2.40–2.40–2.40	Virginia	M	84–84–84	1.50–2.00–1.83
Pennsylvania	M	84–84–84	1.85–2.25–2.04	West Virginia	M	84–84–84	1.65–2.40–2.01
Tennessee	M	(1)	1.85–1.85–1.85	1890:			
Virginia	M	84–84–84	1.40–2.00–1.67	Alabama	M	84–84–84	2.00–2.00–2.00
West Virginia	M	84–84–84	2.40–2.40–2.40	New York	M	(1)	2.00–2.00–2.00
1889:				Ohio	M	72–84–76	1.00–2.30–1.43
Alabama	M	84–84–84	1.25–2.00–1.89	Pennsylvania	M	84–84–84	1.90–2.25–2.02
Georgia	M	84–84–84	1.65–1.65–1.65	Wisconsin	M	84–84–84	3.00–3.00–3.00

Year and State	Sex	Lowest, highest, and average—	
		Hours per week	Rate per day (dollars)
1891:			
New York	M	(1)	1.75–2.20–1.93
Pennsylvania	M	(1)	2.00–2.00–2.00
1892:			
Ohio	M	58–84–72	1.00–3.00–1.69
Pennsylvania	M	(1)	2.25–2.25–2.25
1893:			
New Jersey	M	84–84–84	1.75–1.75–1.75
1895:			
Ohio	M	84–84–84	.75–2.25–1.70
1896:			
Pennsylvania	M	84–84–84	1.68–1.69–1.69

Year and State	Sex	Lowest, highest, and average—	
		Hours per week	Rate per day (dollars)
1897:			
Ohio	(1)	84–84–84	.75–2.20–1.50
Pennsylvania	M	(1)	2.00–2.10–2.06
1898:			
Pennsylvania	M	(1)	2.10–2.20–2.17
1899:			
Alabama	M	84–84–84	1.75–1.85–1.82
Pennsylvania	M	(1)	2.40–2.50–2.47
1900:			
Alabama	M	84–84–84	1.80–1.85–1.83

[1]Not reported.
[2]And rent.
*Ditto.

◆

SOURCE 4   Prices did not remain stable in the late nineteenth century. Before concluding that wage earners' material conditions were improving or declining, it is necessary to determine if prices were rising (inflation) or declining (deflation). With inflation, the same wages purchase less over time; with deflation, the same wages purchase more. The indexes below reveal wholesale prices for basic

Price Indexes, 1866–1890

(1910–14 = 100)

Year	All com- modities	Farm products	Foods	Hides and leather products	Textile products	Fuel and lighting
	1	2	3	4	5	6
1890	82	71	86	74	103	72
1889	81	67	79	80	99	71
1888	86	75	86	86	98	72
1887	85	71	86	92	98	70
1886	82	68	78	101	100	70
1885	85	72	84	105	105	72
1884	93	82	93	111	109	77
1883	101	87	103	107	116	89
1882	108	99	114	108	119	92
1881	103	89	106	109	119	91
1880	100	80	96	113	128	92
1879	90	72	90	100	114	80
1878	91	72	93	95	115	93
1877	106	89	115	109	125	108
1876	110	89	113	104	138	127
1875	118	99	120	123	141	128
1874	126	102	126	128	151	135
1873	133	103	122	132	175	148
1872	136	108	121	130	177	153
1871	130	102	130	126	170	152
1870	135	112	139	128	179	134
1869	151	128	154	134	194	166
1868	158	138	171	126	197	149
1867	162	133	167	132	220	144
1866	174	140	173	146	245	160

Source: Historical Statistics of the United States: Colonial Times to 1957 (Washington, D.C.: Bureau of the Census, 1960), p. 115.

commodities between 1866 and 1890. They use the average wholesale prices between 1910 and 1914 as a base (100). A base is a convenient tool for determining how much prices rose above or fell below a fixed point. Note the general course of prices in the late nineteenth century—that is, whether commodities became more or less expensive. Consider how these price changes corresponded to the changes in workers' wages in the previous source. Taking into account the changes in prices, would you say that workers were better or worse off than they would have been if prices for major commodities had remained the same?

Metals and metal products	Building materials	Chemicals and drugs	House-furnish-ing goods	Spirits	Miscel-laneous
7	8	9	10	11	12
123	84	90	91	—	89
116	81	101	94	74	80
121	80	103	94	80	73
119	81	97	92	77	75
110	82	99	94	79	74
109	81	100	99	79	78
124	84	105	105	81	78
144	85	110	110	83	93
157	88	114	109	80	93
150	83	120	109	81	90
166	81	120	117	83	91
134	74	120	105	82	90
126	72	127	109	82	88
141	80	136	118	86	95
157	84	140	123	86	98
175	90	149	134	88	98
194	101	176	149	78	111
243	106	181	160	75	115
257	107	175	159	73	125
203	102	177	154	74	120
200	101	199	164	78	128
227	110	227	178	86	136
225	116	204	178	117	153
248	120	229	196	146	162
278	128	283	220	154	170

Workers Respond

Workers did not react passively to the conditions they confronted in the late nineteenth century. What do the following sources reveal about the conditions workers faced and what they thought about those conditions? What challenges did workers confront in attempting to improve their conditions?

◆

SOURCE 5   In 1894, workers at George Pullman's "model" company town went on strike. This is a statement of a Pullman striker at the Chicago convention of the American Railway Union.

Why We Struck at Pullman (1895)

We struck at Pullman because we were without hope. We joined the American Railway Union because it gave us a glimmer of hope. Twenty thousand souls, men, women, and little ones, have their eyes turned toward the convention today, straining eagerly through dark despondency for a glimmer of the heaven-sent message you alone can give us on this earth.

In stating to this body our grievances it is hard to tell where to begin. . . . Five reductions in wages, work, and in conditions of employment swept through the shops at Pullman between May and December 1893. The last was the most severe, amounting to nearly 30 percent and our rents had not fallen. . . . No man or woman of us all can ever hope to own one inch of George Pullman's land. Why even the streets are his. . . .

Pullman, both the man and the town, is an ulcer on the body politic. He owns the houses, the schoolhouses, the churches of God. . . . The revenue he derives from these, the wages he pays out with one hand—the Pullman Palace Car Company, he takes back with the other—the Pullman Land Association. He is able by this to bid under any contract car shop in the country. His competitors in business, to meet this, must reduce the wages of their men. . . . And thus the merry war—the dance of skeletons bathed in human tears—goes on, and it will go on, brothers, forever, unless you, the American Railway Union, stop it; end it; crush it out.

Source: Joshua Freeman et al., *Who Built America? Working People and the Nation's Economy, Politics, Culture, and Society* (New York: Pantheon Books, 1992), II, 140; originally from U.S. Strike Commission, *Report on the Chicago Strike of June–July 1894* (1895).

SOURCE 6   This letter was written by an African-American iron worker at the Black Diamond Steel Works.

Colored Workmen and a Strike (1887)

To the Editor:

As a strike is now in progress at the Black Diamond Steel Works, where many of our race are employed, the colored people hereabouts feel a deep interest in its final outcome. As yet few colored men have taken part in it, it having been thus far thought unwise to do so. It is true our white brothers, who joined the Knights of Labor and organized the strike without conferring with, or in any way consulting us, now invite us to join with them and help them to obtain the desired increase in wages and control by the Knights of Labor of the works. But as we were not taken into their schemes at its inception, and as it was thought by them that no trouble would be experienced in obtaining what they wanted without our assistance, we question very much the sincerity and honesty of this invitation. Our experience as a race with these organizations has, on the whole, not been such as to give us either great satisfaction or confidence in white men's fidelity. For so often after we have joined them, and the desired object has been attained, we have discovered that sinister and selfish motives were the whole and only cause that led them to seek us as members.

A few years ago a number of colored men working at this mill were induced to join the Amalgamated Association, thereby relinquishing the positions which they held at these works. They were sent to Beaver Falls, Pa., to work in a mill there controlled by said Association, and the men there, brothers too, mark you, refused to work with them because they were black. It is true Mr Jaret, then chairman of that Association, sat down upon those skunks, but when that mill closed down, and those men went out from there to seek employment in other mills governed by the Amalgamated, while the men did not openly refuse to work with them, they managed always to find some pretext or excuse to keep from employing them.

Now, Mr. Editor, I am not opposed to organized labor. God forbid that I should be when its members are honest, just and true! But when I join any

Source: Philip S. Foner and Ronald L. Lewis, eds., *Black Workers: A Documentary History from Colonial Times to the Present* (Philadelphia: Temple University Press, 1989), pp. 220–221; originally from *New York Freeman,* August 13, 1887.

society, I want to have pretty strong assurance that I will be treated fairly. I do not want to join any organization the members of which will refuse to work by my side because the color of my skin happens to be of a darker hue than their own. Now what the white men in these organizations should and must do, if they want colored men to join with and confide in them, is to give them a square deal—give them a genuine white man's chance—and my word for it they will flock into them like bees into a hive. If they will take Mr. B. F. Stewart's advice! "take the colored man by the hand and convince him by actual fact that you will be true to him and not a traitor to your pledge," he will be found with them ever and always; for there are not under heaven men in whose breasts beat truer hearts than in the breast of the Negro.

John Lucus Dennis
Colored Puddler at Black Diamond
Steel Works, Pittsburgh, Pa., Aug. 8.

Women at Work

By 1900 five million of the 25 million Americans in the work force were women, most of whom worked at wages far below those of male workers. Note what the following sources reveal about the conditions confronting many women wage earners. How do they compare to conditions confronting male workers?

◆

SOURCE 7   In 1869, a group of women petitioned the Massachusetts legislature to have the state help finance homes for them. Their demands were discussed in a meeting held in Boston. This account is from the *Workingman's Advocate,* an influential labor paper.

Women Make Demands (1869)

A convention of Boston work women was held in that city on the 21st ult. at which some extraordinary developments were made. We append some of the discussions:

Source: Rosalyn Baxandall et al., *America's Working Women: A Documentary History—1600 to the Present* (New York: Vintage Books, 1976), pp. 105–106; originally from *Workingman's Advocate* 5, No. 41 (May 8, 1869), 3.

Opening Address by Miss Phelps

Miss Phelps said: the subject of this meeting is to bring out the purpose of the petition just read, and the facts whereon it is based. We do not think the men of Massachusetts know how the women live. We do not think if they did they would allow such a state of things to exist. Some of us who signed the petition have had to work for less than twenty-five cents a day, and we know that many others have had to do the same. True, many get good wages comparatively for women. There are girls that get from $1 to $1.50 per day, either because they are superior laborers or have had unusual opportunities. But many of these poor girls among whom it has been my fortune to live and work, are not skilled laborers. They are incapable of going into business for themselves, or carrying on for themselves, and incapable of combination; they are uneducated, and have no resource but the system that employs them. There are before me now women who I know to be working at the present time for less than twenty-five cents a day. Some of the work they do at these rates from the charitable institutions of the city. These institutions give out work to the women with the professed object of helping them, at which they can scarcely earn enough to keep them from starving; work at which two persons, with their utmost exertions cannot earn more than forty-five cents a day. These things, I repeat, should be known to the public. . . .

SOURCE 8

Summary of Conditions Among Women Workers Found by the Massachusetts Bureau of Labor (1887)

. . . Feather-sorters, fur-workers, cotton-sorters, all workers on any material that gives off dust are subject to lung and bronchial troubles. In soap-factories the girls' hands are eaten by the caustic soda, and by the end of the day the fingers are often raw and bleeding. In making buttons, pins, and other manufactures . . . there is always liability of getting the fingers jammed or caught. For the first three times the wounds are dressed without charge. After that the person injured must pay expenses. . . .

In food preparation girls who clean and pack fish get blistered hands and fingers from the saltpetre. . . . Others in "working stalls" stand in cold water all day. . . .

Source: Barbara M. Wertheimer, *We Were There: The Story of Working Women in America* (New York: Pantheon Books, 1977), pp. 212–213.

In match-factories . . . necrosis often attacks the worker, and the jaw is eaten away. . . .

◆

SOURCE 9 A garment worker wrote this description for *The Independent* magazine.

Work in a Garment Factory (1902)

At seven o'clock we all sit down to our machines and the boss brings each one the pile of work that he or she is to finish during the day. . . . This pile is put down beside the machine and as soon as a skirt is done it is laid on the other side of the machine. Sometimes the work is not all finished by six o'clock and then the one who is behind must work overtime. . . . The machines go like mad all day, because the faster you work the more money you get. Sometimes in my haste I get my finger caught and the needle goes right through it. . . . The machines are all run by foot power, and at the end of the day one feels so weak that there is a great temptation to lie right down and sleep. But you must go out and get air, and have some pleasure. . . .

Source: Joshua Freeman et al., *Who Built America? Working People and the Nation's Economy, Politics, Culture, and Society* (New York: Pantheon Books, 1992), II, 173; originally from *The Independent* (1902).

Children at Work

Industrial growth in the late nineteenth century had an impact on working children. Note what these sources reveal about the numbers of children working full-time and about the conditions under which they labored.

SOURCE 10

Gainful Workers by Age, 1870–1920

(In thousands of persons 10 years old and over)

| Year | Total workers | Age (in years) | | | | |
		10 to 15	16 to 44	45 to 64	65 and over	Un-known
1930	48,830	667	33,492	12,422	2,205	44
1920	42,434	1,417	29,339	9,914	1,691	73
1910	37,371	1,622	26,620	7.606	1,440	83
1900	29,073	1,750	20,223	5,804	1,202	94
1890	23,318	1,504	16,162	4,547	1,009	97
1880	17,392	1,118		16,274		
1870	12,925	765		12,160		

Source: *Historical Statistics of the United States: Colonial Times to 1957* (Washington, D.C.: Bureau of the Census, 1960), p. 72.

SOURCE 11   Spargo was the author of *The Bitter Cry of the Children,* a major exposé of child labor.

Breaker Boys (1906)

JOHN SPARGO

According to the census of 1900, there were 25,000 boys under sixteen years of age employed in and around the mines and quarries of the United States. In the state of Pennsylvania alone,—the state which enslaves more children than any other,—there are thousands of little "breaker boys" employed, many of them not more than nine or ten years old. The law forbids the employment of children under fourteen, and the records of the mines generally show that the law is "obeyed." Yet in May, 1905, an investigation by the National Child Labor Committee showed that in one small borough of 7000 population, among the boys employed in breakers 35 were nine years old, 40 were ten, 45 were eleven, and 45 were twelve—over 150 boys illegally employed in one section of boy

Source: John Spargo, *The Bitter Cry of the Children* (New York: The Macmillan Company, 1915).

labor in one small town! During the anthracite coal strike of 1902, I attended the Labor Day demonstration at Pittston and witnessed the parade of another at Wilkesbarre. In each case there were hundreds of boys marching, all of them wearing their "working buttons," testifying to the fact that they were *bona fide* workers. Scores of them were less than ten years of age, others were eleven or twelve.

Work in the coal breakers is exceedingly hard and dangerous. Crouched over the chutes, the boys sit hour after hour, picking out the pieces of slate and other refuse from the coal as it rushes past to the washers. From the cramped position they have to assume, most of them become more or less deformed and bent-backed like old men. When a boy has been working for some time and begins to get round-shouldered, his fellows say that "He's got his boy to carry round wherever he goes." The coal is hard, and accidents to the hands, such as cut, broken, or crushed fingers, are common among the boys. Sometimes there is a worse accident: a terrified shriek is heard, and a boy is mangled and torn in the machinery, or disappears in the chute to be picked out later smothered and dead. Clouds of dust fill the breakers and are inhaled by the boys, laying the foundations for asthma and miners' consumption. I once stood in a breaker for half an hour and tried to do the work a twelve-year-old boy was doing day after day, for ten hours at a stretch, for sixty cents a day. The gloom of the breaker appalled me. Outside the sun shone brightly, the air was pellucid, and the birds sang in chorus with the trees and the rivers. Within the breaker there was blackness, clouds of deadly dust enfolded everything, the harsh, grinding roar of the machinery and the ceaseless rushing of coal through the chutes filled the ears. I tried to pick out the pieces of slate from the hurrying stream of coal, often missing them; my hands were bruised and cut in a few minutes; I was covered from head to foot with coal dust, and for many hours afterwards I was expectorating some of the small particles of anthracite I had swallowed.

I could not do that work and live, but there were boys of ten and twelve years of age doing it for fifty and sixty cents a day. Some of them had never been inside of a school; few of them could read a child's primer. True, some of them attended the night schools, but after working ten hours in the breaker the educational results from attending school were practically *nil*. "We goes fer a good time, an' we keeps de guys wots dere hoppin' all de time," said little Owen Jones, whose work I had been trying to do. How strange that barbaric patois sounded to me as I remembered the rich, musical language I had so often heard other little Owen Joneses speak in faraway Wales. As I stood in that breaker I thought of the reply of the small boy to Robert Owen. Visiting an English coal-mine one day, Owen asked a twelve-year-old lad if he knew God. The boy stared vacantly at his questioner: "God?" he said, "God? No, I don't. He must work in some other mine." It was hard to realize amid the danger and din and blackness of that Pennsylvania breaker that such a thing as belief in a great All-good God existed.

SOURCE 12

Night Shift in a Glass Factory (1906)

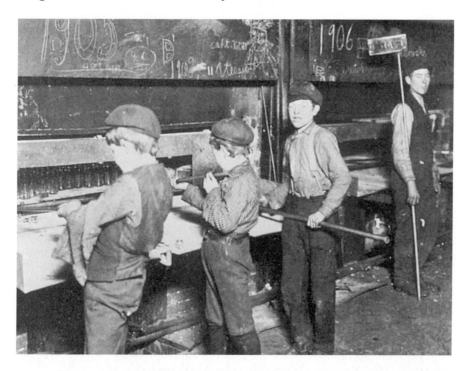

Source: From John Spargo, *The Bitter Cry of the Children,* 1906. Courtesy Harvard College Library.

CONCLUSION

When he was a graduate student, the future historian and president Woodrow Wilson protested that he had to learn "one or two hundred dates and one or two thousand minute particulars" about "nobody knows who." He took comfort in knowing that he would easily forget this "mass of information."[4] The sources in this chapter represent another set of "minute particulars." From them we can learn any number of forgettable facts, from the daily wage of steel workers to the amount of money a coal miner's family spent on rent. By themselves these facts are not useful; contrary to the cliché, they do not "speak for themselves." Rather, they have meaning and interest only when historians order and arrange them. Moreover, what they tell us is often influenced by contemporary concerns. Americans still debate the proper role of the government in their society, the regulation of business, the value of labor unions, the usefulness of "schemes" for helping people, and the desirability of letting people rise or fall on their own. Just as such debates help to frame the questions historians ask about the past, answers to these questions lend historical perspective to the debates. The questions in this chapter are thus part of the ongoing dialogue between the past and present. And if you compare your answers to this chapter's questions to those of your classmates, you will see that all of you did not come to the same conclusions. Historians do not always agree about the answers to their inquiries either. In fact, debate is at the heart of their discipline.

These sources further demonstrate that historians must do more than just select certain facts; they must also know what people in the past perceived and believed. In this case, we need to understand workers' circumstances as well as what they thought about those circumstances. In fact, as we shall see in the next chapter, primary sources are often more valuable to historians for the opinions and biases they reflect as for the facts that they contain.

FURTHER READING

Margaret F. Byington, *Homestead: The Households of a Mill Town* (Pittsburgh, Pa.: University Center for International Studies, 1974; originally published, 1910).

Lizabeth A. Cohen, "Embellishing a Life of Labor: An Interpretation of the Material Culture of American Working-Class Homes, 1885–1915," in *Common Places: Readings in American Vernacular Culture,* ed. Dell Upton and John Michael Vlach (Athens: University of Georgia Press, 1986).

Melvyn Dubofsky, *Industrialism and the American Worker, 1865–1920* (Arlington Heights, Ill.: AHM Publishing Corp., 1975).

Joshua Freeman et al., *Who Built America? Working People and the Nation's Economy, Politics, Culture, and Society* Vol. II (New York: Pantheon Books, 1992).

John Spargo, *The Bitter Cry of the Children* (London: Macmillan and Co., 1906).

NOTES

1. *Investigation by a Select Committee of the House of Representatives Relative to the Causes of the General Depression in Labor and Business,* 45th Cong., 3d sess., Misc. House Doc. No. 29 (Washington, D.C.: U.S. Government Printing Office, 1879), pp. 310–321.

2. *Massachusetts Bureau of the Statistics of Labor Reports* (1878, 1881), in *The Transformation of American Society, 1870–90,* ed. John A. Garraty (Columbia: University of South Carolina Press, 1968), p. 88.

3. *Illinois Bureau of Labor Statistics Report* (1884), in *The Transformation of American Society, 1870–90,* ed. John A. Garraty (Columbia: University of South Carolina Press, 1968), p. 120.

4. Quoted in James A. Henretta, *The Origins of American Capitalism* (Boston: Northeastern University Press, 1991), pp. xv, xvi.

Chapter 3

Evaluating Primary Sources:
The Populist Image in the 1890s

The primary sources by and about Populists in this chapter illustrate the biases often found in primary source material.

Sources

1. Platform of the People's Party (1892)
2. The Negro Question in the South (1892)
3. Financial Conspiracies (1888), SARAH E. V. EMERY
4. The Farmer's Troubles and Their Remedy (1891), WILLIAM ALFRED PEFFER
5. Cross of Gold Speech (1896), WILLIAM JENNINGS BRYAN
6. The English Octopus (1894)
7. Wall Street Milks the West and South (1894)
8. An Account of Mary Lease (1892)
9. James A. Troutman on the Populist Party (1894)
10. Description of the 1896 Populist Convention (1896)
11. What's the Matter with Kansas? (1896), WILLIAM ALLEN WHITE
12. William McKinley on the Bryan Democrats (1896)
13. Kansas Populists William Peffer and "Sockless Jerry" Simpson Take Their Seats in Congress (1891)
14. Bryan Blows Himself Around the Country (1896)
15. Urban and Rural Population, 1850–1900
16. Prices of Commodities, 1866–1890
17. Gross National Product, 1869–1901
18. Total Currency in the United States, 1866–1900

*I*n the 1890s the Populist movement often featured women speakers such as Mary Lease, who proclaimed that "Wall Street owns the country." She continued: "It is no longer a government of the people, for the people, by the people, but a government of Wall Street, for Wall Street, and by Wall Street." She told her audience that the "people" were dogged by the "blood hounds of money" and "robbed to enrich the masters."[1] By the time she had finished, she had cut into plutocrats, politicians, railroads, and bankers.

Such Populist rhetoric naturally aroused passionate responses. After listening to Lease, one Kansas Republican editor declared that she was "a miserable caricature upon womanhood, hideously ugly in feature and foul of tongue." Another insisted that Lease had "no figure, a thick torso . . . and no sex appeal—none!"[2] A clear image of the Populists soon emerged in the popular press: They were not just hicks, but dangerous crackpots. On the other side, of course, Populists had their own arsenal of powerful images: greedy Wall Street bankers, grasping monopolists, and jowly millionaires. In this chapter, we examine the images and rhetoric of the Populist campaigns in the 1890s to determine who the Populists were and what their movement represented. Perhaps even more than their creators realized, the primary sources from these campaigns reflect the ideas, beliefs, and fears of the Populists and their opponents.

SETTING

Political image making was practiced long before Populism arose. Earlier in the nineteenth century Andrew Jackson's supporters pictured John Quincy Adams as a spoiled aristocrat. Later the Whigs transformed presidential candidate William Henry Harrison into the "Log Cabin candidate." In the process they revealed more about a new age of democratic politics than about Harrison, who actually lived in a mansion. So when Populists caricatured their opponents in speeches and cartoons fifty years later, they were following a well-worn path. Populist images of overfed bankers and overdressed politicians were then countered by vivid anti-Populist images of deranged hayseeds. In fact, the Populists' opponents launched one of the most successful counterattacks in American political history. In the 1896 presidential campaign, when the Populist Party endorsed the populist Democrat William Jennings Bryan, the Republicans spent an unprecedented three and a half million dollars on William McKinley's campaign. Bryan went down to defeat and Populism never recovered as an organized political force.

It would be a long time before Populism regained its reputation. Long after 1896, the dominant historical view of these agrarian rebels remained unchanged: They were ill-tempered and misguided. Not until the publication of John D. Hicks's *The Populist Revolt* (1931) did their image change. Hicks argued that Populism was a democratic and rational response to the oppressive conditions confronting Western and Southern farmers. His view gained popularity during the Great Depression, when big business and Wall Street were out of favor, but by the 1950s the Populists were once again under assault. The rise of fascism and later anticommunism had made many historians suspicious of popular movements. In *The American Political Tradition* (1948), *The Age of Reform* (1955), and *Anti-Intellectualism in American Life* (1963), Richard Hofstadter argued that Populists were bigoted, ignorant, anti-Semitic, and anti-intellectual. Hofstadter claimed that Populists romanticized the nation's agrarian past and failed to see themselves as commercial farmers. Blinded by a nostalgic haze, they also failed to offer realistic solutions to their economic ills.

Later, other historians challenged this negative assessment, arguing that Populists were tolerant and insightful reformers. Lawrence Goodwyn's *Democratic Promise* (1976), for example, pictured Populists as radical reformers who offered a democratic vision to counter the abuses of late nineteenth-century capitalism. Meanwhile Michael Paul Rogin and other historians argued that Populists were neither irrational nor bigoted. Rogin's *The Intellectuals and McCarthy* (1967) also questioned the connection between Populism and such twentieth-century mass movements as fascism and McCarthyism. As historians continue to debate the nature of the Populist movement, it is clear that Populists have lost none of their ability to summon powerful images or elicit strong feelings.

INVESTIGATION

This chapter contains a variety of primary sources from the Populist campaigns of the 1890s and the presidential campaign of 1896. Some of the sources illustrate the conservative counterattack on Populism and on the Bryan campaign. Others illustrate the Populists' attack on their opponents. For additional perspective, several sources also illustrate social and economic conditions facing farmers in the late nineteenth century. As you analyze these sources, your main job is to determine whether the Populists were visionaries who proposed logical solutions to their problems or misguided reactionaries. A good analysis of the Populists will address these questions:

1. **What were the Populists' main demands?** Did they effectively address the problems facing farmers in the late nineteenth century?

2. **Do the images of the Populists created by their opponents accurately portray their program?** What biases and fears do they appeal to? What do they reveal about the changing status of farmers in the late nineteenth century?

3. **What biases and fears do the images created by the Populists reveal?** Were Populists backward-looking bigots or enlightened reformers?

As you evaluate the sources in this chapter, remember that they may not support only one conclusion. Before you begin, read the sections in your textbook on the condition of farmers in the late nineteenth century, the rise of agrarian unrest, and the political campaigns of the 1890s. Note its interpretation of these developments.

SOURCES

Populist Rhetoric

This section contains excerpts from the writings and speeches of Populists and of the Populist-backed Democratic presidential candidate William Jennings Bryan. Note who or what Populists thought was responsible for the economic and social ills they confronted. Why were they so concerned with cheap money? Did they offer sound analyses of their problems, or were they guilty of a conspiratorial view of the world?

◆

SOURCE 1   Adopted by the Omaha convention, this was the first platform of the Populist Party.

Platform of the People's Party (1892)

Preamble

The conditions which surround us best justify our co-operation; we meet in the midst of a nation brought to the verge of moral, political, and material ruin. Corruption dominates the ballot-box, the Legislatures, the Congress, and touches even the ermine of the bench. The people are demoralized; most of the States have been compelled to isolate the voters at the polling places to prevent universal intimidation and bribery. The newspapers are largely subsidized or muzzled, public opinion silenced, business prostrated, homes covered with mortgages, labor impoverished, and the land concentrating in the hands of capitalists. The urban workmen are denied the right to organize for self-protection, imported pauperized labor beats down their wages, a hireling standing army, unrecognized by our laws, is established to shoot them

Source: The World Almanac, 1893 (New York, 1893), pp. 83–85.

down, and they are rapidly degenerating into European conditions. The fruits of the toil of millions are boldly stolen to build up colossal fortunes for a few, unprecedented in the history of mankind; and the possessors of those, in turn, despite the Republic and endanger liberty. From the same prolific womb of governmental injustice we breed the two great classes—tramps and millionaires.

The national power to create money is appropriated to enrich bondholders; a vast public debt payable in legal tender currency has been funded into gold-bearing bonds, thereby adding millions to the burdens of the people.

Silver, which has been accepted as coin since the dawn of history, has been demonetized to add to the purchasing power of gold by decreasing the value of all forms of property as well as human labor, and the supply of currency is purposely abridged to fatten usurers, bankrupt enterprise, and enslave industry. A vast conspiracy against mankind has been organized on two continents, and it is rapidly taking possession of the world. If not met and overthrown at once it forebodes terrible social convulsions, the destruction of civilization, or the establishment of an absolute despotism. . . .

Platform

We declare, therefore—

First.—That the union of the labor forces of the United States this day consummated shall be permanent and perpetual; may its spirit enter into all hearts for the salvation of the Republic and the uplifting of mankind.

Second.—Wealth belongs to him who creates it, and every dollar taken from industry without an equivalent is robbery. "If any will not work, neither shall he eat." The interests of rural and civic labor are the same; their enemies are identical.

Third.—We believe that the time has come when the railroad corporations will either own the people or the people must own the railroads, and should the government enter upon the work of owning and managing all railroads, we should favor an amendment to the Constitution by which all persons engaged in the government service shall be placed under a civil-service regulation of the most rigid character, so as to prevent the increase of the power of the national administration by the use of such additional government employés.

Finance   We demand a national currency, safe, sound, and flexible, issued by the general government only, a full legal tender for all debts, public and private, and that without the use of banking corporations, a just, equitable, and efficient means of distribution direct to the people, at a tax not to exceed 2 per cent, per annum, to be provided as set forth in the sub-treasury plan of the Farmers' Alliance, or a better system; also by payments in discharge of its obligations for public improvements.

1. We demand free and unlimited coinage of silver and gold at the present legal ratio of 16 to 1.
2. We demand that the amount of circulating medium be speedily increased to not less than $50 per capita.
3. We demand a graduated income tax.
4. We believe that the money of the country should be kept as much as possible in the hands of the people, and hence we demand that all State and national revenues shall be limited to the necessary expenses of the government, economically and honestly administered.
5. We demand that postal savings banks be established by the government for the safe deposit of the earnings of the people and to facilitate exchange.

Transportation   Transportation being a means of exchange and a public necessity, the government should own and operate the railroads in the interest of the people. The telegraph, telephone, like the post-office system, being a necessity for the transmission of news, should be owned and operated by the government in the interest of the people.

Land   The land, including all the natural sources of wealth, is the heritage of the people, and should not be monopolized for speculative purposes, and alien ownership of land should be prohibited. All land now held by railroads and other corporations in excess of their actual needs, and all lands now owned by aliens should be reclaimed by the government and held for actual settlers only.

SOURCE 2   Watson served as a congressman from Georgia from 1891 to 1893 and ran as the Populist candidate for vice president in 1896. (In later years, Watson reversed the position expressed here and led the movement to disenfranchise blacks in Georgia.)

The Negro Question in the South (1892)

TOM WATSON

The People's Party will settle the race question. First, by enacting the Australian ballot system. Second, by offering to white and black a rallying point which is free from the odium of former discords and strifes. Third, by presenting a platform immensely beneficial to both races and injurious to neither.

Source: Thomas E. Watson, "The Negro Question in the South," *The Arena,* 6 (October 1892), 510–550.

Fourth, by making it to the *interest* of both races to act together for the success of the platform. Fifth, by making it to the *interest* of the colored man to have the same patriotic zeal for the welfare of the South that the whites possess. . . .

The white tenant lives adjoining the colored tenant. Their houses are almost equally destitute of comforts. Their living is confined to bare necessities. They are equally burdened with heavy taxes. They pay the same high rent for gullied and impoverished land.

They pay the same enormous prices for farm supplies. Christmas finds them both without any satisfactory return for a year's toil. Dull and heavy and unhappy, they both start the plows again when "New Year's" passes.

Now the People's Party says to these two men, "You are kept apart that you may be separately fleeced of your earnings. You are made to hate each other because upon that hatred is rested the keystone of the arch of financial despotism which enslaves you both. You are deceived and blinded that you may not see how this race antagonism perpetuates a monetary system which beggars both."

This is so obviously true it is no wonder both these unhappy laborers stop to listen. No wonder they begin to realize that no change of law can benefit the white tenant which does not benefit the black one likewise; that no system which now does injustice to one of them can fail to injure both. Their every material interest is identical. The moment this becomes a conviction, mere selfishness, the mere desire to better their conditions, escape onerous taxes, avoid usurious charges, lighten their rents, or change their precarious tenements into smiling, happy homes, will drive these two men together, just as their mutually inflamed prejudices now drive them apart.

———————◆———————

SOURCE 3   Emery, a Michigan Populist, wrote this widely read discussion of the causes of deflation.

Financial Conspiracies (1888)

SARAH E. V. EMERY

[T]he busy brain of avarice is ever reaching out—not after new truths—but for gain, *gain*, GAIN; and we next find these civilized brigands have consummated a scheme for the *demonetization of silver*. This act, passed in 1873, destroyed the money quality of silver, and thus produced a farther contraction of the cur-

Source: Mrs. Sarah E. V. Emery, *Seven Financial Conspiracies Which Have Enslaved the American People,* 2nd ed. (Lansing, Mich.: Launt Thompson, 1888), pp. 69–81.

rency. The object of this act was first to prevent the payment of the bonds, and second, to increase their value.

Never in this country had there been an investment so safe and yet so reliable. Shylock, with his hoarded millions, could rest on beds of down. Neither fire, flood, mildew nor blight brought anxiety to him. He seemed to rest in assurance of the Divine favor, having obeyed the injunction to "lay up his treasure where moth and rust could not corrupt, nor thieves break through and steal." Indeed, the entire country had become sponsor for his wealth, for under the law every producer and millions of wage-workers had been instituted a vigilance committee to look after his welfare. Why should he not be opposed to having his bond investment disturbed? The government held that property in safe keeping, and did not charge a cent for the favor; it collected his interest and paid it over to him free of charge; it paid his gold interest in advance and exempted him from taxation; the insurance agent and tax gatherer were strangers to him, they did not molest or make him afraid, and being thus fortified, he was content to let the producers of wealth eke out a miserable existence while he fared sumptuously every day. But it was not the American capitalist alone who entered into this murderous scheme for demonetizing silver. In the *Banker's Magazine* of August, 1873, we find the following on this subject:

> In 1872, silver being demonetized in France, England and Holland, a capital of $500,000 was raised, and Ernest Seyd of London was sent to this country with this fund, as agent of the foreign bond holders and capitalists, to effect the same object (demonetization of silver), which was accomplished.

There you have it, a paid agent of English capitalists sent to this country with $500,000 to buy the American Congress and rob the American people. . . .

◆

SOURCE 4   Peffer was a Populist United States Senator from Kansas. His book on the plight of farmers was a popular Populist tract.

The Farmer's Troubles and Their Remedy (1891)

WILLIAM ALFRED PEFFER

The most pressing want of the farmer is to get rid of debts for which his home is mortgaged. It was not generally believed until recently that the clamor about

Source: William Alfred Peffer, *The Farmer's Side, His Troubles and Their Remedy* (New York: D. Appleton and Co., 1891), pp. 179–184.

individual indebtedness of our people had much foundation in truth. The most extravagant guesses upon the subject came short of the cold facts, which Mr. Porter, of the Census Bureau, is giving to us. The writer of this made an investigation of the subject, examining such sources of information as were within his reach, and came to the conclusion that $1,000,000,000 would about cover the entire indebtedness of the people in town and country for which their homes were mortgaged; but enough has already been shown by the Census Bureau to make it probable that the estimate is too short by at least 60 per cent. . . .

And, as shown further by the census report, the interest on this indebtedness is exorbitant—three, four, five times, even twenty times the average increase of wealth produced by labor in the ordinary form, which is about 3 per cent. Farmers find that difficulties in the way of payment of their debts are increasing from year to year, that it is growing constantly harder to meet their obligations. . . .

. . . How is he to obtain money at anything less than he is paying now? How is he to renew his loan except at the discretion of the owner of the money which he borrowed, or of the agent who negotiated the loan? He is at the mercy of his creditor, and that being true he is practically powerless, for the creditor is not a man to be trifled with. That brings us up to the question whether money can be obtained at lower rates of interest, and if so, how? For it may as well be admitted now as at any other time, the plain, naked truth is, that unless lower rates of interest can be obtained, one half of our farmers will be renters within the next ten years, and one half of the remainder in another ten years, and by the time the nineteenth century is ten years past the occupied lands of the country will be owned almost wholly by a comparatively few wealthy men.

———◆———

SOURCE 5   Bryan, a spellbinder on the stump, secured his party's nomination with this rousing speech at the Democratic convention in Chicago.

Cross of Gold Speech (1896)

WILLIAM JENNINGS BRYAN

I would be presumptuous, indeed, to present myself against the distinguished gentlemen to whom you have listened if this were a mere measuring of

Source: Thomas A. Bailey and David M. Kennedy, eds., *The American Spirit* (Lexington, Mass.: D. C. Heath and Company, 1994), II, pp. 155–156.

abilities. But this is not a contest between persons. The humblest citizen in all the land, when clad in the armor of a righteous cause, is stronger than all the hosts of error. I come to speak to you in defense of a cause as holy as the cause of liberty—the cause of humanity.

We [silverites] do not come as aggressors. Our war is not a war of conquest. We are fighting in the defense of our homes, our families, and posterity. We have petitioned, and our petitions have been scorned. We have entreated, and our entreaties have been disregarded. We have begged, and they have mocked when our calamity came. We beg no longer; we entreat no more; we petition no more. We defy them! . . .

There are two ideas of government. There are those who believe that, if you will only legislate to make the well-to-do prosperous, their prosperity will leak through on those below. The Democratic idea, however, has been that if you legislate to make the masses prosperous, their prosperity will find its way up through every class which rests upon them.

You come to us and tell us that the great cities are in favor of the gold standard. We reply that the great cities rest upon our broad and fertile prairies. Burn down your cities and leave our farms, and your cities will spring up again as if by magic. But destroy our farms, and the grass will grow in the streets of every city in the country. . . .

Populist Image Making

Populists also spread their message with powerful visual images in newspapers, popular magazines, and Populist publications. One of those publications was *Coin's Financial School,* a call for the coining of silver published by William H. "Coin" Harvey. Sources 6 and 7 are from Harvey's book, which became a Populist bible. As you examine these images, keep in mind the main targets in these Populist cartoons. What attributes did Populists assign to their opponents? What do these drawings reveal about the Populists' view of the world?

SOURCE 6

The English Octopus (1894)

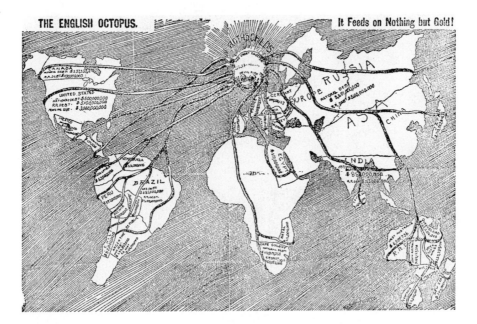

Denver Road.
"The Rothschilds own 1,600,000,000 in gold."—*Chicago Daily News*. This is nearly one-half the gold in the Chicago wheat pit.

Source: From *Coin's Financial School* 1894, Boston Athenaeum.

SOURCE 7

Wall Street Milks the West and South (1894)

Source: From *Coin's Financial School* 1894, Boston Athenaeum.

Anti-Populist Rhetoric

The Populists and silver-Democrat William Jennings Bryan came under scathing attack in the press and on the campaign trail. In the following excerpts from editorials and speeches of Republican candidates, what characteristics do these writers and speakers assign to Populists? How do these traits make Populists different and disreputable? Also look for how female Populists are portrayed. What images of the Populists reveal fears that have little to do with the Populist program?

SOURCE 8   This description was published in the *Salina* (Kansas) *Weekly Republican*.

An Account of Mary Lease (1892)

Well, boys, she is a plumb sight. If I had a hound dog that would bark at her as she passed by the gate I'd kill him before night. She could set on a stump in the shade and keep the cows out of a 100 acre corn field without a gun. She's got a face that's harder and sharper than a butcher's cleaver. I could take her by the heels and split an inch board with it. She's got a nose like an ant-eater, a voice like a cat fight and a face that is rank poison to the naked eye.

Source: Salina Weekly Republican, October 28, 1892.

SOURCE 9   Troutman was the Republican candidate for lieutenant governor in Kansas in 1894.

James A. Troutman on the Populist Party (1894)

[The Populist Party] has crucified upon the altar of personal ambition and aggrandizement the distinctive claims of every form of industrial toil, and elevated to exalted places a class of nondescripts having no visible means of support. This party, organized as it maintains, to subserve the interest of the toiling masses, is dominated by lawyers without clients, by doctors without patients, by preachers without pulpits, by teachers without schools, by soldiers without courage, by editors without papers, by bankers without money, by financiers without credit, by moralists without morals, by farmers without farms, by women without husbands, and by statesmen out of a job.

Source: From a speech entitled "The First (And Last) People's Party Government on Earth," delivered on January 9, 1894 as part of *The Kansas Day Club Addresses* (Hutchinson, 1901).

SOURCE 10   This account was printed in a Kansas newspaper.

Description of the 1896 Populist Convention (1896)

The Calamity Convention at St. Louis last week, pretending to represent a great national party, was the most disgraceful aggregation that ever got together in America. Anarchists, howlers, tramps, highwaymen, burglars, crazy men, wild-eyed men, men with unkempt and matted hair, men with long beards matted together with filth from their noses, men reeking with lice, men whose feet stank, and the odor from under whose arms would have knocked down a bull, brazen women, women with beards, women with voices like a gong, women with scrawny necks and dirty fingernails, women with their stockings out at the heels, women with snaggle-teeth, strumpets, rips, and women possessed of devils, gathered there, and sweltered and stank for a whole week, making speeches, quarrelling, and fighting like cats in a back yard. Gray-haired, scrawny, yellow-skinned women appeared upon the stage, dressed in hideous or indecent costumes, and gave performances that disgusted the most hardened Calamityites, until even Jerry Simpson gagged, and protested that the Convention was too much of a circus. . . . The gathering was so outlandish that each delegate imagined that the others were burlesquing him. To wind up the whole thing, delegates were bought up like the hogs they were.

Source: From *The Weekly Kansas Chief,* Troy, July 3, 1896.

SOURCE 11   White was the editor of the *Emporia* (Kansas) *Gazette.* This anti-Populist editorial gained him nationwide attention.

What's the Matter with Kansas? (1896)

WILLIAM ALLEN WHITE

Go east and you hear them laugh at Kansas; go west and they sneer at her; go south and they "cuss" her; go north and they have forgotten her. Go into any

Source: Emporia Gazette (Weekly), October 1, 1896.

crowd of intelligent people gathered anywhere on the globe, and you will find the Kansas man on the defensive. The newspaper columns and magazines once devoted to praise of her, to boastful facts and startling figures concerning her resources, are now filled with cartoons, jibes and Pefferian speeches. Kansas just naturally isn't in it. She has traded places with Arkansas and Timbuctoo.

What's the matter with Kansas?

We all know; yet here we are at it again. We have an old mossback Jacksonian who snorts and howls because there is a bathtub in the State House; we are running that old jay for Governor.* We have another shabby, wild-eyed, rattlebrained fanatic who has said openly in a dozen speeches that "the rights of the user are paramount to the rights of the owner": we are running him for Chief Justice, so that capital will come tumbling over itself to into the state. We have raked the old ash heap of failure in the state and found an old human hoop skirt who has failed as a businessman, who has failed as an editor, who has failed as a preacher, and we are going to run him for Congressman-at-Large. He will help the looks of the Kansas delegation at Washington. Then we have discovered a kid without a law practice and have decided to run him for Attorney General. Then, for fear some hint that the state had become respectable might percolate through the civilized portions of the nation, we have decided to send three or four harpies out lecturing, telling the people that Kansas is raising hell and letting the corn go to weed.

Oh, this is a state to be proud of! We are a people who can hold up our heads! What we need is not more money, but less capital, fewer white shirts and brains, fewer men with business judgment, and more of those fellows who boast that they are "just ordinary clodhoppers, but they know more in a minute about finance than John Sherman"; we need more men who are "posted," who can bellow about the crime of '73, who hate prosperity, and who think, because a man believes in national honor, he is a tool of Wall Street. We have had a few of them—some hundred fifty thousand—but we need more. . . .

"There are two ideas of government," said our noble Bryan at Chicago. "There are those who believe that if you legislate to make the well-to-do prosperous, this prosperity will leak through on those below. The Democratic idea has been that if you legislate to make the masses prosperous their prosperity will find its way up and through every class and rest upon them."

That's the stuff! Give the prosperous man the dickens! Legislate the thriftless man into ease, whack the stuffing out of the creditors and tell the debtors

---

*White was referring to John W. Leedy, the successful Populist candidate who also had the backing of Democrats.

who borrowed the money five years ago when money "per capita" was greater than it is now, that the contraction of currency gives him a right to repudiate.

Whoop it up for the ragged trousers; put the lazy, greasy fizzle, who can't pay his debts, on the altar, and bow down and worship him. Let the state ideal be high. What we need is not the respect of our fellow men, but the chance to get something for nothing.

Oh, yes, Kansas is a great state. Here are people fleeing from it by the score every day, capital going out of the state by the hundreds of dollars; and every industry but farming paralyzed, and that crippled, because its products have to go across the ocean before they can find a laboring man at work who can afford to buy them. Let's don't stop this year. Let's drive all the decent, self-respecting men out of the state.

◆

SOURCE 12

William McKinley on the Bryan Democrats (1896)

Let us settle once for all that this government is one of honor and of law and that neither the seeds of repudiation* nor lawlessness can find root in our soil or live beneath our flag. That represents all our aims, all our policies, all our purposes. It is the banner of every patriot, it is, thank God, today the flag of every section of our common country. No flag ever triumphed over it. It was never degraded or defeated and will not now be when more patriotic men are guarding it than ever before in our history.

Repudiation is a reference to Bryan's and the Populists' demand to inflate the currency by coining silver. Opponents to silver charged that this would represent a repudiation of debt contracted with creditors.
Source: Lawrence Goodwyn, *Democratic Promise: The Populist Movement in America* (New York: Oxford University Press, 1976), p. 528.

Anti-Populist Images

What traits do these cartoons assign to the Populists and to Bryan and his supporters? In what ways do they make the Populists' and Bryan's demands unappealing?

SOURCE 13   The departing Republican congressmen are Senator George Edmunds of Vermont and Congressman William McKinley of Ohio.

Kansas Populists William Peffer and "Sockless Jerry" Simpson Take Their Seats in Congress (1891)

Source: From *Judge* magazine, April 5, 1891. Courtesy *Populism: Its Rise and Fall: William A. Peffer,* University Press of Kansas, 1992.

SOURCE 14

Bryan Blows Himself Around the Country (1896)

"BLOWING" HIMSELF AROUND THE COUNTRY.

Source: Courtesy Harvard College Library.

Statistical Indexes

This section contains several tables indicating changes in prices, production, population, and money in circulation. Pay particular attention to changes in the amount of currency in circulation compared to the nation's economic growth as indicated by the gross national product. If the money supply does not increase as fast as the growth of the economy, a dollar will buy more as time goes on. In other words, there will be deflation. Declining prices are especially hard on debtors, who must pay back loans with money that is both increasingly scare and valuable. What do these sources reveal about the social and economic problems facing farmers? Do these tables indicate that the Populist analysis of farmers' problems was misguided or correct?

SOURCE 15

Urban and Rural Population, 1850–1900

Class and Population Size	1900	1890	1880	1870	1860	1850
Urban territory	30,159,921	22,106,265	14,129,735	9,902,361	6,216,518	3,543,716
Places of 1,000,000 or more	6,429,474	3,662,115	1,206,299	—	—	—
Places of 500,000 to 1,000,000	1,645,087	806,343	1,917,018	1,616,314	1,379,198	515,547
Places of 250,000 to 500,000	2,861,296	2,447,608	1,300,809	1,523,820	266,661	—
Places of 100,000 to 250,000	3,272,490	2,781,894	1,786,783	989,855	992,922	659,121
Places of 50,000 to 100,000	2,709,338	2,027,569	947,918	768,238	452,060	284,355
Places of 25,000 to 50,000	2,800,627	2,268,786	1,446,366	930,119	670,293	611,328
Places of 10,000 to 25,000	4,333,250	3,451,258	2,189,447	1,709,541	884,433	560,783
Places of 5,000 to 10,000	3,204,195	2,383,685	1,717,146	1,278,145	976,436	596,086
Places of 2,500 to 5,000	2,899,164	2,277,007	1,617,949	1,086,329	594,515	316,496
Places under 2,500	—	—	(1)			
Rural territory	45,834,654	40,841,449	36,026,048	28,656,010	25,226,803	19,648,160
Places of 1,000 to 2,500	3,298,054	2,508,642	(1)			
Places under 1,000	3,003,479	2,249,332	(1)			
Other rural territory	39,533,121	36,083,475	(1)			

[1]Not available.

Source: Historical Statistics of the United States: Colonial Times to 1957 (Washington, D.C.: Bureau of the Census, 1960), p. 14.

SOURCE 16

Prices of Commodities, 1866–1890

Year	Wheat	Wheat flour	Sugar	Cotton, raw
	101	102	103	104
	Bu.	*100 lb.*[1]	*Lb.*	*Lb.*
1900	.704	3.349	.053	.096
1899	.711	3.382	.049	.066
1898	.885	4.145	.050	.060
1897	.795	4.361	.045	.072
1896	.641	3.620	.045	.079
1895	.600	3.231	.042	.073
1894	.559	2.750	.041	.070
1893	.677	3.283	.048	.083
1892	.788	4.122	.044	.077
1891	.962	4.905	.047	.086
1890	{ .893 / *.865* }	4.652 / *6.039*	.062 / *.063*	.111 / *.115*
1889	.895	6.540	.080	.107
1888	.886	6.120	.071	.103
1887	.769	5.817	.059	.103
1886	.797	6.119	.062	.094
1885	.864	6.275	.064	.105
1884	.913	7.043	.068	.106
1883	1.038	7.735	.087	.106
1882	1.198	9.020	.095	.122
1881	1.154	8.895	.097	.113
1880	{ 1.057 / 1.253 }	8.895	.099	.120
1879	1.223	8.632	.086	.104
1878	1.252	9.101	.092	.113
1877	1.685	10.806	.111	.117
1876	1.320	9.898	.106	.130

Source: Historical Statistics of the United States: Colonial Times to 1957 (Washington, D.C.: Bureau of the Census, 1960), p. 123.

Year	Wheat	Wheat flour	Sugar	Cotton, raw
	101	102	103	104
	Bu.	*100 lb.*[1]	*Lb.*	*Lb.*
1875	1.403	10.218	.107	.150
1874	1.517	10.728	.106	.170
1873	1.787	11.498	.112	.182
1872	1.780	12.141	.124	.205
1871	1.581	10.245	.131	.170
1870	1.373	{ 9.281 / 5.029 }	.135	.240
1869	1.651	5.725	.162	.290
1868	2.541	7.912	.163	.249
1867	2.844	9.164	.159	.316
1866	2.945	7.920	.166	.432

In dollars per unit. Where 2 prices are shown for a single year, those in italic are comparable to preceding years, and those in regular type comparable with following years.

———◆———

SOURCE 17

Gross National Product,* 1869–1901

[In billions of dollars. 5-year periods are annual averages]

1897–1901	35.4	1877–1881	16.1
1892–1896	28.3	1872–1876	11.2
1887–1891	24.0	1869–1873	9.1
1882–1886	20.7		

*The value of the total output of goods and services.

Source: Historical Statistics of the United States: Colonial Times to 1957 (Washington, D.C.: Bureau of the Census, 1960), p. 144.

♦

SOURCE 18

Total Currency in the United States, 1866–1900

Year	Total currency in U.S.	Year	Total currency in U.S.
1900	2,366,220	1880	1,185,550
1899	2,190,094	1879	1,033,641
1898	2,073,574	1878	984,225
1897	1,906,770	1877	916,548
1896	1,799,975	1876	905,238
1895	1,819,360	1875	925,702
1894	1,805,079	1874	950,116
1893	1,738,808	1873	903,316
1892	1,752,219	1872	900,571
1891	1,677,794	1871	894,376
1890	1,685,123	1870	899,876
1889	1,658,672	1869	873,759
1888	1,691,441	1868	888,413
1887	1,633,413	1867	1,020,927
1886	1,561,408	1866	1,068,066
1885	1,537,434		
1884	1,487,250		
1883	1,472,494		
1882	1,409,398		
1881	1,349,592		

Source: Historical Statistics of the United States: Colonial Times to 1957 (Washington, D.C.: Bureau of the Census, 1960), p. 647.

CONCLUSION

The sources in this chapter demonstrate that historians' primary material is often biased, reflecting not only objective conditions but also what people thought about them. Yet these biases and views are as important as historical facts. They reveal a great deal about the nature of Populism because they reveal the beliefs and perceptions of Populists and of their opponents.

Similarly, historians' writings—called secondary sources—contain different views of the past even when they rely upon the same primary sources. Thus historians' debates hinge less on matters of fact than on their own assumptions and values. Remembering that will make it easier in the following chapters to evaluate both primary and secondary sources and to use one kind of historical source to appraise the other.

FURTHER READING

Gene Clanton, *Populism: The Humane Preference in America, 1890–1900* (Boston: Twayne Publishers, 1991).

Lawrence Goodwyn, *Democratic Promise: The Populist Movement in America* (New York: Oxford University Press, 1976).

Richard Hofstadter, "The Folklore of Populism" in Hofstadter, *The American Political Tradition* (New York: Alfred A. Knopf, 1948).

Richard Stiller, *Queen of the Populists: The Story of Mary Elizabeth Lease* (New York: Thomas Y. Crowell Company, 1970).

George Brown Tindall, ed., *A Populist Reader: Selections from the Works of Populist Leaders* (New York: Harper and Row, 1966).

NOTES

1. O. Gene Clanton, *Kansas Populism: Ideas and Men* (Lawrence: University of Kansas Press, 1969), pp. 77–78.
2. Ibid., pp. 75, 76.

Evaluating a Historical Argument: The "Yellow Press" and the Spanish-American War

This chapter presents one secondary source, an argument concerning the cause of the Spanish-American War, and several primary sources that can be used to evaluate that argument.

Secondary Source

1. McKinley, the Press, and the Decision for War (1990), RICHARD J. BARNET

Primary Sources

2. Chicago *Tribune* Editorial on Public Opinion and Cuba (October 10, 1895)
3. The Case of Evangelina Cisneros (1897)
4. Our Country (1885), JOSIAH STRONG
5. The Expansion of the United States (1895), HENRY CABOT LODGE
6. William McKinley on Overseas Trade (1898)
7. Some Time in the Future (1895)
8. The White Man's Burden (ca. 1900)
9. A Policy of Murder and Starvation (February 1898), WILLIAM E. MASON
10. Conditions Are Unmentionable (March 1898), REDFIELD PROCTOR
11. McKinley's War Message (1898)
12. The *New York Times* Reports on Preparations for War (May 4, 1898)
13. Value of Manufactured Exports, 1866–1900

*I*n 1896 the most popular boy in New York was an insolent street urchin named the Yellow Kid, a cartoon character in the New York *World*'s comic strip "Hogan's Alley." This gang leader gave his name to the newspaper's sensational headlines and entertaining stories. By 1896, readers were calling newspapers' simplified approach to the news the "yellow press." No paper practiced it better than Joseph Pulitzer's *World*, which screamed "HOW BABIES ARE BAKED" after 392 children died in a heat wave. Pulitzer soon had competition. In 1895, William Randolph Hearst bought the rival New York *Journal* and then raided the *World*'s staff, including the creator of "Hogan's Alley." Before long the *Journal*'s circulation had soared and it was Hearst himself who was known as the "Yellow Kid."

The competition between Pulitzer and Hearst reflected the transformation of American society in the late nineteenth century. Cities like New York teemed with immigrants, and Pulitzer and Hearst understood the importance of large circulations rather than discriminating readers. Championing the underdog was an obvious way to attract readers. In 1897 the *Journal* hired an attorney for a drunken woman who had allegedly assaulted a policeman. Then the paper rounded up seventeen witnesses who testified that she was poor but respectable. By 1897, the *Journal* discovered an even bigger underdog. In 1895 Cubans had begun a guerrilla war to throw off Spanish rule. Brutality was inevitable, especially when the Spanish countered by waging war against the Cuban population. The Hearst and Pulitzer papers embellished and even manufactured accounts of Spanish atrocities. By 1898, the yellow press had whipped up a war fever that soared even higher when the battleship *Maine* blew up in Havana harbor. Unenthusiastic about war with Spain, President McKinley encouraged negotiations. When diplomatic efforts failed, however, McKinley asked Congress for a declaration of war against Spain, pointing to the "barbarities, bloodshed, starvation, and horrible miseries" in Cuba.

The war that followed was a little conflict that had big consequences. The United States easily defeated Spain's forces in Cuba and Puerto Rico and destroyed Spain's fleet at Manilla Harbor in the Spanish-controlled Philippines. McKinley then announced that the United States should take all of the Philippines. Early the next year, the Senate ratified a treaty with Spain that granted independence to Cuba and that ceded Puerto Rico, Guam, and the Philippines to the United States. The Spanish-American War thus left America with an overseas empire.

Nearly a century later, the reasons for the Spanish-American War remain far less clear than its results. Historians continue to debate why the United States went to war and what, if anything, the yellow press had to do with it. Examining this war is thus a good way to encounter conflict about the past. In this chapter, we evaluate one historian's argument about the American decision for war in 1898.

SETTING

The war with Spain produced some of American history's most enduring images: the sinking of the *Maine* and the Rough Riders' charge up San Juan Hill. At the center of historians' debates about the Spanish-American War is another powerful image: the sensational headlines of the yellow press. For a long time the hysteria whipped up by the yellow press offered a simple explanation for this war. One historian in 1934 said that "the public, aroused by the press, demanded it."[1] According to this view, political leaders were influenced by public opinion, and the decision for war was an irrational, unthinking response to popular passion. Moreover, William McKinley was a weak president who succumbed to popular emotions and even had to consult a globe at war's end to determine the location of the Philippines. The nation had stumbled blindly into both war and empire at the end of the century.

That interpretation did not go unchallenged. Progressive historian Charles Beard, for example, argued that McKinley's decision for war reflected his close ties to expansionist business leaders, not the influence of the yellow press. That view was popular in the 1930s, when many Americans held business responsible for the country's economic ills and when "war profiteers" were under investigation by the U.S. Senate for their role in World War I. Nevertheless, Beard's conclusions were not accepted by all historians. In *Expansionists of 1898* (1936), historian Julius Pratt concluded that many prominent business leaders opposed war. A generation later, historian Ernest May also disputed business leaders' influence with McKinley. In *Imperial Democracy* (1961), May argued that McKinley was unable to withstand the tide of public opinion and thus "led his country unwillingly toward a war that he did not want for a cause in which he did not believe."[2]

It was not long before some historians questioned these conclusions too. By the 1960s the Vietnam War had created doubts among many Americans about the motives of elite policymakers. At the same time, "New Left"* historians began to emphasize the economic influences in American foreign policy and the expansionist nature of capitalism. These historians downplayed the role of the yellow press and public opinion, pointing instead to the desire of American leaders to expand abroad. In *The New Empire* (1963), for instance, Walter LaFeber argued that although the business community did not have direct influence in the McKinley administration, American leaders concluded that expansion would relieve the country's economic ills. The nation was led into war not by an inflamed public, but by elites who welcomed war as an opportunity to build an American commercial empire. Moreover, McKinley knew exactly where the Philippines were because he discussed the possibility of

---

*The label was applied to distinguish these historians from the "Old Left" of the 1930s.

military operations there months before the outbreak of war. In short, the results of the Spanish-American War were related to its causes.

More recently, historians have argued that the Spanish-American War and overseas expansion had as much to do with culture as with economics. Unlike many "New Left" historians, these scholars emphasize the ideological rather than the purely economic motives of American expansionists. They maintain that American expansion was driven by economic motives *and* by a powerful belief in the duty of the "Anglo-Saxon race" to uplift "uncivilized" peoples. They also argue that the Spanish-American War was not the result of popular passions aroused by the yellow press, but the natural outcome of an expansionist vision dating at least from the Monroe Doctrine. In *Spreading the American Dream* (1982), for instance, Emily Rosenberg argued that a powerful ideology combining assumptions about the superiority of the "Anglo-Saxon race" and of American political, religious, and economic institutions propelled American expansion at the turn of the century.

The question about the impact of the yellow press in 1898 demonstrates how a narrow question may yield answers to broad historical questions. Does elite or public opinion matter more in the American political system? How much are political decisions influenced by the needs of business? Is American expansion rooted in idealistic assumptions about America's mission in the world or in the needs of the American economic system? By providing answers to these questions, the Spanish-American War may reveal much about our society. Thus a war usually remembered only by vivid images can also provide a mirror to observe America's own image.

INVESTIGATION

If historians often ask small questions to understand large issues, they also use small pieces of evidence to construct big arguments. In this chapter you will use evidence from primary sources to evaluate one historian's argument about why the United States went to war in 1898. The main question presented by the secondary and primary sources is what role the yellow press played in the decision to go to war with Spain. First determine the author's conclusions about the role of the yellow press. Then assess what the primary sources reveal about the reasons for the Spanish-American War. A good discussion of this problem will address the following questions:

1. **What are the author's conclusions about the role of the yellow press in the decision for war?** Does he see it or other factors as primarily responsible?

2. **Do the primary sources indicate that public opinion or an expansionist-minded elite played a greater role in the decision for war?** What is the main

evidence that public opinion was influenced by the yellow press? What is the most important evidence that McKinley and Congress were influenced by public opinion? What is the evidence that they were influenced by other factors? Is there evidence that elite groups manipulated public opinion?

3. **Do you agree with the author's conclusions about why the U.S. went to war with Spain? Do you agree with his conclusion about the relationship between war and a desire for the Philippines?** Was the decision to take the Philippines a cause or a consequence of the war?

Before you begin, read the sections in your textbook on American overseas expansion in the late nineteenth century and on the Spanish-American War. Note its conclusions about the role of the yellow press in the decision for war. When you are finished with this assignment you will be able to compare your text's interpretation with the one in this chapter's main essay.

SECONDARY SOURCE

◆

SOURCE 1   In this selection, Richard Barnet discusses America's decision to go to war with Spain. What role does he assign the press in the decision for war? Look for his evidence that McKinley or Congress was influenced by the press, public opinion, or business and other leaders. Determine whether the author thinks McKinley was weak and indecisive or in command. According to Barnet, what role did a belief in America's cultural superiority play in the decision for war? Finally, what is his view of the relationship between the cause of the war and the decision to take Spanish possessions at its end?

McKinley, the Press, and the Decision for War (1990)

RICHARD J. BARNET

William McKinley scarcely looked like the public relations pioneer he actually was. No one would have accused this Republican politician who had risen to prominence by dutifully serving the ironmongers and sheep raisers of Ohio of having an ounce of charisma. Yet from the neck up he looked every inch a president. His dark eyes were famous for their kindly twinkle. He wore a

Source: Reprinted with the permission of Simon & Schuster from *The Rockets' Red Glare* by Richard Barnett. Copyright © 1990 by Policy Research, Inc.

carnation in his lapel, and on at least one occasion presented it to a petitioner as he turned down his request, thus earning his eternal gratitude. He would countenance no unseemly language in his presence, would jump up from the cabinet table to perform little errands of mercy for his invalid wife, and in general behaved, as the historian Ernest May puts it, like a character out of Louisa May Alcott. He invariably insisted upon being photographed in what he considered his presidential pose, always affecting the same austere look. An enigmatic figure who left little trace in a hundred volumes of personal papers of his real feelings or the evolution of his thought, McKinley remains a puzzle to historians. Was he the passive instrument of the imperialists? Was he, as others argue, an exceedingly cunning politician with an imperial vision no less grand than Theodore Roosevelt's who preferred to dissemble rather than to exhort? Or was he a weak man who was pushed into a war he did not want by the hysteria of the people? . . .

When he came into office in March 1897, Cuba was not yet a burning issue. The latest insurrection against Spanish rule had been going on for two years. Filibustering activities were flourishing despite their being officially discouraged as violations of the U.S. Neutrality Act. The Coast Guard succeeded in stopping most of the expeditions, but there were more than thirty vessels that were regularly supplying the insurgents from Florida. When the Spanish fired on what they believed to be one of these ships, the newspapers began their cry for war. The American flag had been insulted, said the New York *Sun,* and the Spanish government "requires a sharp and stinging lesson at the hands of the United States."

For most Americans the insurrection in Cuba became a compelling emotional issue because of Spanish violations of human rights on the island. A Spanish force of 150,000 troops rounded up Cuban civilians by the thousands and put them behind barbed wire in concentration camps. Because of this brutal policy perhaps as many as a quarter million Cubans died. For two hundred years foreign oppression has aroused American sympathies and anger. Appeals to American public opinion because of human rights violations in foreign countries began . . . with the French Revolution. In the Greek War of Independence in the 1820s Harvard and Yale students collected money for the rebels. American citizens protested the pogroms of czarist Russia. Just as the crisis over Cuba was about to heat up, American outrage reached new heights because of the massacre of some ten thousand Armenians by the Ottoman Empire. William Lloyd Garrison, Julia Ward Howe, and the Congregational Church launched a successful campaign to arouse public opinion in behalf of the Armenians. At public meetings jingoist speakers cried out that the United States had a Christian obligation to use its power to promote justice—by the sword if necessary. As Ernest May argues, Armenia was a dress rehearsal for Cuba. The popular outcry demonstrated "that public opinion could be mobilized . . . for a moral crusade."

A crusade for human rights in Cuba involved no great risks, for Spain was a tottering empire, even weaker than when it was stripped of its continental possessions in North America almost one hundred years earlier. Americans treated the Spanish with undisguised contempt. They were, as the early American historian Jedidiah Morse had put it, "naturally weak and effeminate." Encouraged by the jingoist press and by the adroit propaganda efforts of the junta, or central committee, of the Cuban rebels, demonstrations and rallies denouncing the Spanish and raising money for the insurrection were held in Chicago, Kansas City, Cleveland, Providence, and many other cities and towns. William James, trying to understand the surge of interest in Cuba, doubted whether the average person was all that excited by the fiery preachers. Nor was all the pious talk about "raising and educating inferior races" anything more than "mere hollow pretext." Imperialism, he finally decided, was catching on because it had become a "peculiarly exciting kind of *sport*."

The philosopher's intuition was shared by the great press lords of New York. William Randolph Hearst's legendary promise to his illustrator, Frederic Remington—immortalized in *Citizen Kane*—that if he would produce the pictures, the publisher would produce the war, was more self-promotion than history. Neither Hearst nor his archrival, Joseph Pulitzer, publisher of the New York *World*, produced the war, but they tried. No question, they used the war to build empires of their own. . . .

. . . Hearst's New York *Journal* had a circulation of 150,000 in 1896. Over the next two years, during which the paper played up the insurrectionary war in Cuba and agitated for the United States to intervene, the circulation climbed to more than 800,000, and this phenomenal growth was almost entirely attributable to the sensational coverage of events in Cuba. In the race for readers the *World* kept pace. Pulitzer, according to his biographer, "rather liked the idea of war, not a big one, but one that would arouse interest and give him a chance to gauge the reflex in his circulation figures."

The other New York dailies and major papers across the country like the Chicago *Tribune* and Hearst's San Francisco *Examiner* joined in the drumbeat for war. They carried huge banner headlines denouncing the Spanish and ran human-interest stories of Americans—often their own correspondents— caught in the war. (The Spanish executed one reporter and threatened to try another.) Spanish attacks on American ships suspected of supplying the guerrillas were featured. While editorials sounded the war cry, the front page featured atrocity stories. "The skulls of all were split down to the eyes. Some of these were gouged out. . . . The bodies had almost lost semblance of human form." For more than three years "eyewitness accounts" like these by James Creelman of the *World* or those by the *Journal*'s Richard Harding Davis describing the cruelties visited on the island by the Spanish were spread across the front pages, accompanied by Remington's lurid sketches, and denounced in shrieking headlines. The Spanish were indeed carrying out a cruel pacification campaign, pioneering counterinsurgency techniques that the U.S. Army itself would use in the Philippines a few years later. But liberties were taken with the facts in virtually every news story out of Cuba and some of the accounts were outright fakes. Terrorist acts of the *insurrectos,* who were extorting protection money from American plantation owners in Cuba, were glossed over or not reported.

Not content with reporting the news, the *Journal* made news. A young woman by the name of Evangelina Cisneros, whose father had been sent to the Spanish prison colony on the Isle of Pines for some modest complicity with the insurgents, was also arrested, allegedly because she defended her virtue against a lecherous Spanish officer. "Enlist the women of America," William Randolph Hearst is reported to have cried as he launched a public relations crusade to free Señorita Cisneros. The publisher induced Mrs. Jefferson Davis to sign an appeal to the queen regent of Spain and persuaded Julia Ward Howe, famous for writing the words to "The Battle Hymn of the Republic," to send off a letter to the pope. The *Journal* was able to persuade twenty thousand women to join its crusade, including President McKinley's mother. Hearst then dispatched one of his correspondents to rescue the señorita, which he did by climbing the roof of the house next to the ancient jail, taking a crowbar to the rotting window bars, and lifting the young woman out. "The Rescued Martyr in her Prison Garb" was spread across the front pages, and *Journal* headlines took credit for what months of diplomacy had "FAILED UTTERLY TO BRING ABOUT." Send five hundred reporters and free the whole island, the governor of Missouri suggested. . . .

William McKinley did not want war with Spain. He feared that the cost of war would undermine the dollar and stall the economy just as the twenty-year depression appeared to be ending. He did not want to annex Cuba; the country needed no more blacks. He was enough of a traditionalist to believe that the Constitution followed the flag. The United States should annex no territory which it was unwilling to grant statehood. His interest was to protect American property on the island and exert American influence without taking responsibility for a miserably poor country. His strategy was to use the threat of war to persuade the Spanish to put down the rebellion and to grant reforms. In his secret negotiations with the Spanish the president emphasized the pressure of Congress and public opinion, which were forcing him to take stern measures. But actually when his ultimatum was delivered to the Spanish on September 18, 1897—the Spanish had until November 1 to give the American minister in Madrid "such assurance as would satisfy the United States that early and certain peace can be promptly secured"—neither his scrapbooks of newspaper articles nor his personal mail revealed that he was under any such pressure. He was in fact deliberately protected from the "yellow press" by his press secretary, who considered these "products of degenerate minds" unworthy of presidential attention. In the last six months of 1897, according to one scholar who went through the presidential files, McKinley received exactly three letters from the public on Cuba. "The impression I got on crossing the continent," the publisher Whitelaw Reid wrote McKinley a little more than a month before war was declared, "was that the more intelligent classes are not greatly affected by the sensational press; . . . I have never seen a more profound or touching readiness to trust the President, and await his word."

McKinley knew that powerful interests in the country divided on the issue. When he took office, magnates such as John D. Rockefeller, J. P. Morgan, and George Pullman were against risking war. So were most business organizations, from the Boston Merchants Association to the Baltimore Board of Trade. But the people seemed more jingoist than the bankers and the railroad barons who bankrolled the Republican Party. In 1896 there had been rallies in small towns from New Jersey to Iowa where the Spanish general in command in Cuba, "Butcher" Weyler, was burned in effigy. Civil War veterans in GAR posts throughout the North were aching to send the next generation to war. The Cigarmakers' Union, to which many Cubans belonged and from whose ranks had come Samuel Gompers, head of the American Federation of Labor, was equally ready to take on Spain. Blacks were sympathetic to their brothers fighting in Cuba, and the organization of white upper-middle-class Americans that had been formed to carry forward the spirit of Lincoln, the Union League Club, considered it a duty to fight for the Negroes in Cuba. The Cubans themselves energetically marketed atrocity stories, collected millions of dollars, and lobbied for votes.

With the country divided, the president decided to say almost nothing about Cuba and let public opinion develop on its own. The cry in Congress to recognize the belligerent status of the rebels and even to intervene militarily was increasing. The atrocity reports were beginning to be read on the Senate floor. In just three weeks "American Friends of Cuba" gathered 300,000 signatures for recognizing Cuba. More mass meetings were held around the country, and by the end of 1897 young men were enlisting to fight in Cuba. Of course, only a small part of the population took part in these activities, and their importance was exaggerated by the newspapers pressing for war.

McKinley delivered an "appeal to the people" for patience while he waited for the concession he still hoped to extract from Spain, the granting of "autonomy" for the island. The president was neither concerned that the public would push him into war—he believed that the expansionists in Congress did not have broad public backing—nor worried that the public would shrink from war if he sounded the call. But he wanted such overwhelming public support that if war broke out he would be free to conduct it without criticism or controversy.

By January 1898, it was evident that the Spanish would not, probably could not, meet the American terms, for when they offered to give the Cubans autonomy, there were riots in Havana, instigated by Spanish army officers. On January 20 the Senate passed a resolution recognizing the Cuban rebels as having the status of a belligerent under international law, a declaration without legal effect but clearly a hostile message. About forty or fifty Republican members of the House threatened to turn on the president if he did not move to war. Republican politicians worried that William Jennings Bryan would campaign against him two years later for not rallying to the banner of human rights in Cuba. The president in fact was deeply moved by the plight of the Cubans and sent an anonymous gift of $5,000 to a humanitarian organization working for the victims in Cuba, but it still appeared that he wished to avoid war. Assistant Secretary of the Navy Theodore Roosevelt let his friends know that he considered the president to be a "white-livered cur" with "no more backbone than a chocolate eclair."

On February 9, 1898, the *Journal* succeeded in raising the temperature further. The paper procured a confidential letter from the Spanish minister to Washington recounting his hostility to the negotiations and published it. The minister called McKinley a "low politician catering to the rabble," an indiscretion that may have had as much to do with making war inevitable as the blowing up of the battleship *Maine* in Havana harbor six days later.

The explosion and the loss of 253 Americans was the biggest single news event since President Garfield's assassination eighteen years before. McKinley had the secretary of the navy announce that there was no "cause for alarm" and "no indication of anything but an accident." A Court of Inquiry was appointed, which deliberated in secret, while the *Journal* and the *World* conducted their own investigations, which resulted, not unexpectedly, in "proof" of Spain's responsibility. (TR was of course totally convinced. "I would give anything," he wrote in a private letter, "if President McKinley would order the fleet to Havana tomorrow. . . . The *Maine* was sunk by an act of dirty treachery on the part of the Spaniards.") But the Court of Inquiry was unable to fix blame and most historians doubt that the Spanish, who had every interest in not provoking the United States, were behind the explosion. The captain of the *Maine* himself considered it an accident. Many contemporary newspapers came to the same conclusion but said the Spanish were "responsible" anyway since the ship was in their harbor.

McKinley used the Court of Inquiry to focus public attention and to deflect some of the pressure from the newspapers and from Congress to go to war. He kept hinting about the imminent release of the court's finding and teased the press into reporting it as less than the anticlimax it actually was. He made a point of giving small scoops to the wire services, and was rewarded by their almost consistent support. His scrapbook began to fill with laudatory editorials approving his prudence and diplomatic skill, and 90 percent of his correspondence, according to his press secretary, was "an endorsement of the President's course." The public favored war, his press secretary reported, only "as a necessity and for the upholding of the national honor."

On March 17, 1898, McKinley's close friend Senator Redfield Proctor of Vermont, who had opposed going to war, made a speech shortly after returning from a visit to Cuba in which he announced that he had changed his mind. War was now the only way to protect American property and to keep leftist revolutionaries from taking over. A week later the president received a telegram from W. C. Reick, a political confidant in New York: "Big corporations here now believe we will have war. Believe all would welcome it as a relief to suspense." McKinley now knew that the "business pacifism," which so infuriated Roosevelt, had weakened, and that indeed no substantial segment of public opinion would oppose him, whatever he did. He set April 6 as the date for sending his war message to Congress, then waited five more days to permit Americans to evacuate Cuba. Meanwhile, the Spanish offered concessions, and the president in a more or less parenthetical sentence said he hoped Congress would give them "just and careful attention." But the mood in Congress was now more in keeping with the advice of the New York *World*, which suggested, "Negotiate afterward if negotiation is necessary."

In the cloakroom and lobby, Congressmen were singing "Dixie" and "The Battle Hymn of the Republic" as the heated debate on the war resolution proceeded on the floor. Books were thrown, reported the London *Times*. "Members rushed up and down the aisles like madmen, exchanging hot words, with clenched fists and set teeth." Eight days later Congress passed a joint resolution directing the president to use armed force to free Cuba. Any intention to annex the island was specifically disclaimed. The Senate had wanted the president to recognize the revolutionaries, but McKinley did not want to commit himself to support of the *insurrectos*, whom he distrusted. He insisted on maintaining presidential control of foreign policy and faced the Senate down. Because McKinley, in William Allen White's words, combined "the virtues of the serpent, the shark, and the cooing dove," he was able to carve out for himself more freedom to set his own foreign policy than his immediate predecessors had enjoyed. He was strengthened greatly by the fact that the generation-long economic crisis was coming to an end.

The war was short, spectacular, and victorious. "Divine favor seemed manifest everywhere," McKinley declared when it was over. Five days after the declaration of war Commodore George Dewey sailed into Manila Bay and destroyed the Spanish fleet. On February 25, almost two months before the president's war message, Acting Secretary of the Navy Theodore Roosevelt had cabled secret orders to Dewey to begin "offensive operations in Philippine Islands" in the event of war with Spain. (The secretary of the navy was away for the afternoon. "Do not take any such step . . . without consulting the President or me," he admonished his subordinate upon his return. "I am anxious to have no occasion for a sensation in the papers.") The president later claimed that when he received word that Dewey had taken the Philippines, he could not have located "those darned islands" on a map. But the secretary of the navy had on two occasions discussed with the president the orders that his brash assistant had sent to Dewey in February.

Roosevelt's ideological friends knew exactly where the islands were and how important they could be. On the day war was declared Albert Beveridge of Indiana, a leading expansionist, cried, "The Philippines are logically our first target." Roosevelt had written his friend Senator Lodge the previous September, "Our Asiatic squadron should blockade, and if possible, take Manila." Cuba, not the Philippines, was in the headlines. Most Americans had never heard of Manila, although the New York *Sun,* a strongly expansionist paper, kept mysteriously predicting that an American attack would soon take place there.

It is now clear that the imperial strategists like Roosevelt and his friend Captain Mahan saw the Philippines as crucial to the expansion of American power in the Far East. The American minister to China, a railroad lawyer by the name of Charles Denby, saw the Philippines as a stepping-stone to the markets of China. These men had a clear-eyed view of the war against Spain, and they saw themselves as guardians of the American national interest. But the war they sought and the war they succeeded in winning had almost nothing to do with the cause in the Caribbean that had aroused popular feelings. It was once said that France had its conquests and Napoleon his. The United States had also had the experience of the people's representatives declaring one war and the nation fighting another as well.

PRIMARY SOURCES

The primary sources in this chapter fall into several categories: news accounts, editorials, cartoons, speeches by McKinley and members of Congress, diplomatic communications, and statements of prominent expansionists. All of these sources may not support the same conclusion. Although not all of them relate directly to the Spanish-American War, they may help explain why it was fought. One approach to help assess the evidence in this section is to complete a chart like the one below. As you finish evaluating each source, note which influence it represents. The sources may not be equally important in assessing the reasons for war, and they may illustrate more than one influence.

	Public Opinion	Economic Concerns	Desire to "Civilize"
Source #			

When you are finished evaluating these sources, you should be able to rank the importance of each of these factors. You can then use this evidence to assess the author's argument and, of course, come to your own conclusion about the importance of the yellow press in explaining the American decision for war.

The Press Reports on Cuba

Much of the sensational press coverage of Cuba involved accounts of Spanish atrocities against Cubans. What do these sources reveal about the impact of such reporting on the public? Do any of the sources reveal that the press or public opinion influenced McKinley?

◆

SOURCE 2

Chicago *Tribune* Editorial on Public Opinion and Cuba (1895)

Whatever may be the feeling of the rest of the country in regard to the Cuban struggle for independence there can hereafter be no doubt that the citizens of Chicago are heartily in sympathy with the brave people who are struggling to free themselves from the yoke of Spain. Central Music Hall, commodious as it is, proved much too small to hold the mass meetings a few earnest men had arranged for them last night, and the hundreds who were unable to obtain admittance gathered in another room to join in voting stirring resolutions and to listen to the eloquence of chosen speakers.

Chicago, represented by its mayor, by its Common Council, and by hundreds of its foremost citizens, has spoken—first of all the communities of the republic. Now let other cities follow the example and roll up to Washington a tide of public opinion that shall sweep the sluggish men in the seats of Congress toward liberty.

Source: From Chicago *Tribune,* October 10, 1895.

◆

SOURCE 3   Evangelina Cisneros, the daughter of a Cuban insurgent, was charged with rebellion and imprisoned in 1895. In 1897, the New York *Journal* discovered her story. It charged that "this tenderly nurtured girl was imprisoned at eighteen among the most depraved negresses of Havana." Later that year, the

Journal announced that one of its own reporters had made a daring rescue of Cisneros by sawing through the bars of her cell. Her arrival in the United States was big news, as indicated by this report in the *New York Times.*

The Case of Evangelina Cisneros (1897)

Evangelina Cossio y Cisneros, the young Cuban girl whose escape from a prison in Havana was attended with so much daring, was formally welcomed to freedom last night at Delmonico's, and afterward in Madison Square.

It was estimated that nearly 75,000 people swarmed in the park on Broadway as far up as Twenty-seventh Street, and as far down as Twenty-third Street. Even Madison Avenue was packed, and when four searchlights shot their white rays upon the nervous, shrinking girl and her stalwart rescuer the roar of greeting began at the stand and thundered to the furthest limits of the crowd.

The receptions, for there were two, were under the auspices of The New York Journal, the correspondent of which, Karl Decker, effected the rescue. The one at Delmonico's was private, for which invitations were issued. There the large banquet hall and the Red Room had been handsomely decorated with flowers, potted plants, and ropes of evergreens. Upon the walls were American and Cuban flags entwined, while streamers of the two colors hung everywhere. . . .

Senator Thurston of Nebraska, ex-Ambassador James B. Eustis, Congressman William Sulzer, and Dr. Lincoln de Zayas made short congratulatory speeches, and then, while another was speaking, there came the sharp commands of a policeman clearing a passageway, and the sound of cheering from Twenty-sixth Street. The speaker finished quickly, and all upon the stand arose. The crowd could not see what was going on, but they whispered to one another that the girl rescued from prison was there. Then fell that strange hush upon them all that indicates intense curiosity. . . .

Source: "Ovation to Miss Cisneros," *New York Times,* October 17, 1897, p. 5.

Expansionist Sentiment

In the late nineteenth century, there were a growing number of outspoken advocates of American overseas expansion. As you read these sources, note the reasons these spokesmen offer for overseas expansion. Consider whether there was a connection between such sentiments and the American decision for war in 1898.

———————◆———————

SOURCE 4   Strong, the author of *Our Country: Its Possible Future and Its Present Crisis,* proclaimed that Anglo-Saxons were particularly suited to spread Western civilization throughout the world.

Our Country (1885)

JOSIAH STRONG

Then this race of unequaled energy, with all the majesty of numbers and the might of wealth behind it—the representative, let us hope, of the largest liberty, the purest Christianity, the highest civilization—having developed peculiarly aggressive traits calculated to impress its institutions upon mankind, will spread itself over the earth. If I read not amiss, this powerful race will move down upon Mexico, down upon Central and South America, out upon the islands of the sea, over upon Africa and beyond. And can any one doubt that the result of this competition of races will be the "survival of the fittest"?

Source: Pratt, *Expansionists of 1898: The Acquisition of Hawaii and the Spanish Islands* (New York: Quadrangle Books, 1964), p. 6; originally from Josiah Strong, *Our Country: Its Possible Future and Its Present Crisis* (1885).

———————◆———————

SOURCE 5   A senator from Massachusetts, Lodge wrote this call for expansion for *Forum* magazine.

The Expansion of the United States (1895)

HENRY CABOT LODGE

There is a very definite policy for American statesmen to pursue . . . if they would prove themselves worthy inheritors of the principles of Washington and Adams. We desire no extension to the south, for neither the population nor the lands of Central or South America would be desirable additions to the United States. But from the Rio Grande to the Arctic Ocean there should

Source: Robert A. Divine, ed., *American Foreign Policy,* World Publishing Company, 1960.

be but one flag and one country. Neither race nor climate forbids this extension, and every consideration of national growth and national welfare demands it. In the interests of our commerce and of our fullest development we should build the Nicaragua canal, and for the protection of that canal and for the sake of commercial supremacy in the Pacific we should control the Hawaiian Islands and maintain our influence in Samoa. England has studded the West Indies with strong places which are a standing menace to our Atlantic seaboard. We should have among those islands at least one strong naval station, and when the Nicaragua canal is built, the island of Cuba, still sparsely settled and of almost unbounded fertility, will become to us a necessity.

SOURCE 6   This is an excerpt from a speech McKinley delivered to the National Association of Manufacturers in early 1898.

William McKinley on Overseas Trade (1898)

Much profitable trade is still unenjoyed by our people because of their present insufficient facilities for reaching desirable markets. Much of it is lost because of a lack of information and ignorance of the conditions and needs of other nations. We must know just what other people want before we can supply their wants. We must understand exactly how to reach them with least expense if we would enter into the most advantageous business relations with them. The ship requires the shipper; but the shipper must have assured promise that his goods will have a sale when they reach their destination. It is a good rule, if buyers will not come to us, for us to go to them. It is our duty to make American enterprise and industrial ambition, as well as achievement, terms of respect and praise, not only at home, but among the family of nations the world over.

Source: Speeches and Addresses of William McKinley (New York: Doubleday and McClure Co., 1900), pp. 62–63.

Cartoons from the Popular Press

As you examine these sources, note what they reveal about America's self-image in the late nineteenth century and whether it might have helped propel the United States into the Spanish-American War.

SOURCE 7

Some Time in the Future (1895)

Source: The Granger Collection, New York.

SOURCE 8

The White Man's Burden (ca. 1900)

Source: From the Detroit *Journal,* n.d., Courtesy Harvard College Library.

Speeches in Congress

By 1898, the situation in Cuba was intensely debated in Congress. Do the following speeches reveal that the yellow press's emphasis on atrocities in Cuba had an influence in Congress?

---◆---

SOURCE 9   Mason was a Republican senator from Illinois.

A Policy of Murder and Starvation (February 1898)

WILLIAM E. MASON

Mr. Mason. In order to lay the foundation for what I have to say and what I have said, I wish to have read from the Secretary's desk a part, at least, of a communication, showing that it is . . . not the destruction of the battle ship *Maine*, but that it is the continued policy of murder and starvation that is being pursued on this continent, the same as yesterday, and yesterday the same as last week, last month, and last year. I want to have read the letter, or a part of it, so that it may be printed in the RECORD. I do not know whether I ought to take the time of the Senate to have read more than a little of it. I do not care to have the headlines read, as they are not written or signed.

The Secretary read as follows:

> No one can see Habana and its surroundings without feeling that so much beauty should be the frame and background of whatever in human relations is delightful and of good repute. The island is an earthly paradise, and the climate the most exquisite and caressing that I, in a tolerably wide experience of climate, have ever known. There is no richer soil in the world. Nature has withheld nothing that could make man happy or serve to render him prosperous. She has given all and produced an Eden, but man, who takes all, has transformed it into a hell.

Mr. Mason. I hope you will pardon me, but I should have stated that this letter was written by Mr. Julian Hawthorne,* well known to many of us personally, and a man who has a national reputation. I believe, as a man of high character, and one who does not exaggerate for newspaper notoriety.

The Secretary continued the reading, as follows:

> Not in this age, certainly, has a crime been perpetrated more revolting to humanity than Weyler† committed when he forced the women and children of the patriots in

*Julian Hawthorne was a New York *Journal* correspondent.
†General Valeriano Weyler was in charge of Spanish forces in Cuba and began a "reconcentration" policy that resulted in Cubans being herded into concentration camps.
Source: Congressional Record, 55th Cong., 2nd Sess., 31, pt. 2, p. 1875, February 18, 1898.

the Cuban army to come within the Spanish lines and then deliberately starved them there.

His ostensible purpose was to weaken the heart of resistance by attacking its tenderest point, but his real aim was the literal extinction of the Cuban race, and he has so far succeeded that out of the million and a half inhabitants of this island when the war began, 600,000 at least, by far the most of them women and children, have been destroyed, either by direct murder or by the slower and more agonizing torture of famine and of disease caused by famine. The Cuban soldiers fighting to save their country have not been met and defeated in the field. They have been barbarously robbed of their mothers, wives, sisters, and offspring. When their independence is won, they will have no families to return to.

◆

SOURCE 10   Proctor, a Vermont Republican, had just returned from Cuba. In this dramatic speech, he described some of the conditions there.

Conditions Are Unmentionable (March 1898)

REDFIELD PROCTOR

Outside Havana all is changed. It is not peace, nor is it war. It is desolation and distress, misery and starvation. Every town and village is surrounded by a *trocha* (trench), a sort of rifle pit, but constructed on a plan new to me, the dirt being thrown up on the inside and a barbed-wire fence on the outer side of the trench. . . .

The purpose of these *trochas* is to keep the *reconcentrados* in as well as to keep the insurgents out. From all the surrounding country the people have been driven into these fortified towns and held there to subsist as they can. . . .

Their huts are about 10 by 15 feet in size, and for want of space are usually crowded together very closely. They have no floor but the ground, no furniture, and, after a year's wear, but little clothing except such stray substitutes as they can extemporize; and with large families, or more than one, in this little space, the commonest sanitary provisions are impossible. Conditions are unmentionable in this respect. Torn from their homes, with foul earth, foul air, foul water, and foul food or none, what wonder that one-half have died and that one-quarter of the living are so diseased that they cannot be saved? A form of dropsy is a common disorder resulting from these conditions. Little children are still walking about with arms and chests terribly emaciated, eyes swollen,

Source: Robert A. Divine, ed., *American Foreign Policy,* World Publishing Company, 1960.

and abdomen bloated to three times the natural size. The physicians say these cases are hopeless.

Deaths in the streets have not been uncommon. I was told by one of our consuls that they have been found dead about the markets in the morning, where they had crawled, hoping to get some stray bits of food from the early hucksters and that there had been cases where they had dropped dead inside the market surrounded by food.

SOURCE 11   When diplomatic efforts did not bring timely Spanish concessions, McKinley requested war from Congress. As you read McKinley's war statement, note the reasons he offers for war with Spain. Can these reasons be taken at face value when trying to understand why the United States went to war?

McKinley's War Message (1898)

Executive Mansion, April 11, 1898

To the Congress of the United States:

* * *

Since the present revolution began, in February, 1895, this country has seen the fertile domain at our threshold ravaged by fire and sword in the course of a struggle unequaled in the history of the island and rarely paralleled as to the numbers of the combatants and the bitterness of the contest by any revolution of modern times where a dependent people striving to be free have been opposed by the power of the sovereign states.

Our people have beheld a once prosperous community reduced to comparative want, its lucrative commerce virtually paralyzed, its exceptional productiveness diminished, its fields laid waste, its mills in ruins, and its people perishing by tens of thousands from hunger and destitution. We have found ourselves constrained, in the observance of that strict neutrality which our laws enjoin and which the law of nations commands, to police our own waters and watch our own seaports in prevention of any unlawful act in aid of the Cubans.

Source: Richard B. Morris, ed., *Great Presidential Decisions: State Papers That Changed the Course of History* (New York: Harper and Row, Publishers, 1973), pp. 307–309, 318, 322.

Our trade has suffered, the capital invested by our citizens in Cuba has been largely lost, and the temper and forbearance of our people have been so sorely tried as to beget a perilous unrest among our own citizens, which has inevitably found its expression from time to time in the National Legislature, so that issues wholly external to our own body politic engross attention and stand in the way of that close devotion to domestic advancement that becomes a self-contained commonwealth whose primal maxim has been the avoidance of all foreign entanglements. . . .

The grounds for such intervention may be briefly summarized as follows:

First. In the cause of humanity and to put an end to the barbarities, bloodshed, starvation, and horrible miseries now existing there, and which the parties to the conflict are either unable or unwilling to stop or mitigate. It is no answer to say this is all in another country, belonging to another nation, and is therefore none of our business. It is specially our duty, for it is right at our door.

Second. We owe it to our citizens in Cuba to afford them that protection and indemnity for life and property which no government there can or will afford, and to that end to terminate the conditions that deprive them of legal protection.

Third. The right to intervene may be justified by the very serious injury to the commerce, trade, and business of our people and by the wanton destruction of property and devastation of the island.

Fourth, and which is of the utmost importance. The present condition of affairs in Cuba is a constant menace to our peace and entails upon this Government an enormous expense. With such a conflict waged for years in an island so near us and with which our people have such trade and business relations; when the lives and liberty of our citizens are in constant danger and their property destroyed and themselves ruined; where our trading vessels are liable to seizure and are seized at our very door by war ships of a foreign nation; the expeditions of filibustering that we are powerless to prevent altogether, and the irritating questions and entanglements thus arising—all these and others that I need not mention, with the resulting strained relations, are a constant menace to our peace and compel us to keep on a semi war footing with a nation with which we are at peace. . . .

. . . The only hope of relief and repose from a condition which can no longer be endured is the enforced pacification of Cuba. In the name of humanity, in the name of civilization, in behalf of endangered American interests which give us the right and the duty to speak and to act, the war in Cuba must stop.

In view of these facts and of these considerations I ask the Congress to authorize and empower the President to take measures to secure a full and final termination of hostilities between the Government of Spain and the people of Cuba, and to secure in the island the establishment of a stable government, capable of maintaining order and observing its international obligations, insuring peace and tranquillity and the security of its citizens as well as our own, and to use the military and naval forces of the United States as may be necessary for these purposes.

◆

SOURCE 12   The United States went to war with Spain in April 1898. Does this news item support the view that the McKinley administration stumbled into the Spanish-American War or that it engaged in advanced planning for war?

The *New York Times* Reports on Preparations for War (May 4, 1898)

CINCINNATI, Ohio. May 4—Mr. Byron Williams, whose son is a Lieutenant on the Baltimore, has received a letter from the latter, posted at Honolulu March 22, which tells of the stores of munitions laid in by the Asiatic Squadron prior to the attack on Manila.

Lieut. Williams wrote as follows: "Before the bubbles from the wrecked Maine ceased to rise, ammunition that could not be duplicated in all America was ordered on to trains that had the right of way over all that came before and rushed to San Francisco. There these explosives, that must be handled as carefully as the mother holds a babe, were tenderly transported to the slow but steady old warship Mohican and started for Honolulu. At Honolulu they were again as hastily as possible unloaded and placed on the Baltimore.

"Every solid foot of the Baltimore's magazines was filled, and 400 tons more of modern munitions were secured on her decks. She was also filled to the utmost with coal. On March 22 the officers and crew of the Baltimore mailed their farewell letters and started on the long sail of 5,000 miles to Yokohama and thence to Hong Kong, where Dewey and his intrepid bluejackets were waiting for the 'food of war.'"

Source: New York Times, May 4, 1898, p. 1.

◆

SOURCE 13   In the table on the next page, note the trend in manufactured exports in the late nineteenth century. Is this trend relevant in understanding the desires of expansionists or the decision for war in 1898?

Value of Manufactured Exports, 1866–1900

[in millions of dollars]

Year	Manufactured foodstuffs	Semi manufactures	Finished manufactures
1900	320	153	332
1899	305	118	263
1898	285	102	223
1897	235	98	213
1896	219	76	182
1895	219	62	144
1894	250	67	136
1893	247	49	130
1892	250	50	133
1891	226	48	140
1890	225	46	133
1889	175	43	123
1888	170	40	114
1887	176	37	112
1886	163	34	112
1885	202	39	111
1884	195	38	118
1883	186	38	122
1882	178	37	125
1881	226	33	102
1880	193	29	93
1879	174	30	103
1878	170	29	110
1877	150	32	113
1876	122	31	74
1875	110	27	75
1874	114	26	81
1873	101	25	76
1872	84	21	65
1871	67	14	76
1870	51	14	56
1869	44	14	47
1868	42	17	43
1867	34	15	44
1866	41	12	39

Source: Historical Statistics of the United States: Colonial Times to 1957 (Washington, D.C.: U.S. Bureau of the Census, 1960), pp. 544–545.

CONCLUSION

Whatever your conclusions about the role of the yellow press in starting the Spanish-American War, you have probably discovered that it is not easy to prove broad assertions. McKinley and Congress, of course, made the ultimate decision for war, but not in a vacuum. They may have been subject to numerous influences, including an ideology of "manifest destiny," an assessment of the needs of American business, a concern for the fate of the Cuban people, or the sentiments of voters. The sources here suggest that these and other influences were present in 1898.

The sources also illustrate some important axioms of historical inquiry. First, historians seek the causes of things. They do not just want to know when the Spanish-American War was fought, but why. The search for causes often leads historians to consider the influence of ideology, in this case an American sense of mission. It also requires them to ask whether history is better written "from the top down" or "from the bottom up," that is, from the point of view of leaders or followers. Thus historians attempt to determine if ideas of elite groups or the emotions of the public were more important in explaining the Spanish-American War. In addition, as historians explain the causes of things, they often point to unique circumstances and to general forces. Thus some see McKinley's personality as an important factor in the decision for war; others think an expanding capitalist economy was far more important. Finally, the sources in this chapter make clear that the question of motivation is central to historical inquiry. Your conclusion about the role of the yellow press in this war will involve a corresponding view about the motives of McKinley and other leaders. The chapters that follow will consider these problems: historical causation, ideology and history, history written from the top and bottom of society, and, as we will see next, motivation in history.

FURTHER READING

John Dobson, *Reticent Expansionism: The Foreign Policy of William McKinley* (Pittsburgh, Pa.: Duquesne University Press, 1988).

Lloyd C. Gardner, ed., *A Different Frontier: Selected Readings in the Foundations of American Economic Expansion* (Chicago: Quadrangle Books, 1966).

Walter LaFeber, *The New American Empire: An Interpretation of American Expansion, 1860–1898* (Ithaca: Cornell University Press, 1963).

Joyce Milton, *The Yellow Kids: Foreign Correspondents in the Heyday of Yellow Journalism* (New York: Harper and Row, 1989).

H. Wayne Morgan, *America's Road to Empire: The War with Spain and Overseas Expansion* (New York: Alfred A. Knopf, 1965).

NOTES

1. Joseph E. Wisan, "The Cuban Crisis as Reflected in the New York Press" in *American Imperialism in 1898,* ed. Theodore P. Greene (Lexington: D. C. Heath, 1955), p. 51.
2. Ernest R. May, *Imperial Democracy: The Emergence of America as a Great Power* (New York: Harcourt, Brace and World, 1961), p. 159.

Chapter 5

The Problem of Historical Motivation: The Bungalow as the "Progressive" House

The documents in this chapter present various kinds of information on the craze for the bungalow style in the Progressive era.

Secondary Source

1. The Progressive Housewife and the Bungalow (1981), GWENDOLYN WRIGHT

Primary Sources

2. A Craftsman Cottage (1909)
3. *The Craftsman* Contrasts Complexity and Confusion with Cohesion and Harmony (1907)
4. Gustav Stickley on the Craftsman Home (1909)
5. Edward Bok on Simplicity (1900)
6. Conspicuous Consumption and the Craftsman Style (1899), THORSTEIN VEBLEN
7. Cover from *The Bungalow Magazine* (1909)
8. Putting the American Woman and Her Home on a Business Basis (1914), CHRISTINE FREDERICK
9. The Efficient and Inefficient Kitchen (1920)
10. Domestic Economy (1904), CHARLOTTE PERKINS GILMAN
11. Double Bungalow Plan, Bowen Court
12. Average Daily Servants' Wage Rates, Chicago, 1890–1910
13. Female Servants by Regions, per 1,000 Families, 1880–1920
14. Clerical Workers in the United States, by Sex, 1870–1920

*I*n the first decades of the twentieth century, the bungalow transformed the appearance of neighborhoods throughout the United States. With its wide, low-pitched roof, overhanging eaves, prominent front porch, straight lines, "modern" kitchen, and economical use of space, it was the new ideal home for middle-class Americans. In drawings and photographs, it filled the pages of *Architectural Record, Ladies' Home Journal, Good Housekeeping,* and other magazines. One book on bungalows published in 1908 went through five editions in two years. To Progressive-era critics, the older Victorian house was now "aesthetically repulsive," an "architectural atrocity," "hideous," and a reflection of a "fatuous craze for the crudely ornate."[1] Suddenly nineteenth-century styles were out of date.

The bungalow was more than a fad. Many housing crusaders—architects, craftsmen, social reformers, home economists, feminists, and home builders—promoted this architectural style as a powerful means to transform American society. What exactly did the bungalow promoters hope to achieve with new designs and furnishings? What motivated them to assault older "Victorian" aesthetic standards? What values did they seek to promote? In this chapter, we examine the motives of the early twentieth-century housing reformers and the middle-class Americans whose tastes they influenced.

SETTING

The bungalow craze did not arise in a cultural vacuum, but was one expression of a broader artistic movement at the turn of the century known as Arts and Crafts. English Arts and Crafts enthusiasts in the late nineteenth century promoted simple architectural styles and handicraft production. In response to the spread of the factory, they drew inspiration from Oxford artist John Ruskin and his student William Morris, who argued that machines robbed work of its creativity and pleasure. By the early twentieth century the Arts and Crafts movement had come to America. It was taken up by a number of influential reformers, including Jane Addams, labor reformer Ellen Gates Starr, architect Frank Lloyd Wright, and naturalist Charles Keeler.

Middle-class magazines also popularized the bungalow. *Ladies' Home Journal* editor Edward Bok campaigned relentlessly to replace the "repellently ornate" Victorian home and its "machine-made ornamentation" with simplified home designs and decorations.[2] So did Gustav Stickley, founder of *The Craftsman* magazine, which published dozens of bungalow plans and promoted the Arts and Crafts style as the key to "right living." Other magazines, including *House Beautiful, House and Garden,* and *Country Life in America,* also publicized the Arts and Crafts style. As one observer put it, the nation seemed to have been swept by a "craftsman craziness."[3]

Although craftsmen promoters helped to popularize the bungalow, "craftsman craziness" was not foisted on an unsuspecting public by a cultural elite. Influenced by a variety of social and economic trends, an expanding middle class was very receptive to the new style. For instance, as the army of white-collar workers swelled between 1860 and 1900, so did the anxiety about loss of independence and masculinity. One popular magazine observed in 1903 that "the middle class is becoming a salaried class, and rapidly losing the economic and moral independence of former days."[4] Promoters of Arts and Crafts associated its rugged style with creative manual work, independence, and "the return of manhood to common work."[5] Theodore Roosevelt, who fretted about the decline of America's virility, was an enthusiastic supporter of the new style and called for "the overcivilized man" to cultivate "hardy virtues." Gustav Stickley was in turn an ardent supporter of Roosevelt and reprinted Roosevelt's "The Strenuous Life" in *The Craftsman*.

The bungalow's appeal was also related to dramatic changes overtaking women in the late nineteenth century. By the turn of the century the weight of household chores had been lightened by such technological innovations as water heaters, running water, and washing machines. Moreover, urbanization had led to both lower middle-class birthrates and the ability to purchase more household goods outside the home. Gradually, the housewife's role had been transformed from producer to consumer. At the same time, smaller families and labor-saving products created greater opportunities for women to work outside the home. As work at typewriters and telephone switchboards drew the daughters of the middle class out of the house, the supply of domestic servants declined and fears about a household "crisis" rose.

These changes in women's roles stimulated varied responses, from alarm about the fate of the family to proposals for completely reorganizing the family. Some commentators called on housewives to become experts in spending. The new profession of home economics moved to transform housekeeping into a profession, a domestic science requiring special training in household and scientific management. Settlement house pioneer Jane Addams advocated public kitchens for working mothers. Feminist Charlotte Perkins Gilman, who believed that domestic architecture kept women enslaved, proposed new living arrangements involving cooperative housekeeping and homes without kitchens to free women to pursue careers outside the home.

To many Progressive-era Americans, however, the bungalow was the answer to the "woman question." Within its walls they could project their ideal middle-class woman and family. It was not an accident that bungalow "craziness" swept Americans in the midst of a discussion about work, families, and the role of women in society. Progressive-era Americans, from Edward Bok and Gustav Stickley to Theodore Roosevelt and Charlotte Perkins Gilman, had a deep desire to reshape institutions and values and an enormous faith in the power of the domestic environment to reform people. As one commentator put it: "Our works and our surroundings corrupt or refine our souls. The dwelling, the walls, the windows, the roof, the furniture, the pictures, the ornaments . . . all act constantly upon the imagination and determine its contents."[6] Like the tenement house movement, bungalow "craziness" reflected a Progressive impulse to view the home as an instrument of uplift. Examining this infatuation with the bungalow is thus a good way for historians to understand one generation's domestic hopes and fears.

INVESTIGATION

Americans embraced the bungalow for many reasons. Examining the ideas and designs of its promoters can reveal what they thought about family life and what they hoped to achieve by adopting this new style. One of their concerns was the changing status of women. The essay in this chapter examines the relationship between the popularity of the bungalow and changing gender roles. It is accompanied by a variety of primary sources, including house plans, illustrations of home decorations, and the writings of Progressive-era housing reformers. As you read the essay and study the primary sources, your main task is to determine what motivated Americans to adopt the bungalow style in the early twentieth century. To complete this assignment, use the secondary and primary sources to answer the following main questions:

1. **According to the essay, why were many Americans receptive to the bungalow style at the turn of the century?** What social and economic developments influenced their tastes in housing?

2. **Is the author's argument supported by the primary sources?** What evidence do the primary sources provide about the motives of bungalow promoters? What family problems do they identify, and how do they think the bungalow would solve them?

3. **Was the bungalow craze prompted mostly by radical or conservative motives?** Did the bungalow hold out the promise of revamping domestic life completely, or of solving social problems without drastic change?

Before you begin, read the sections in your textbook on Progressive reform and cultural changes at the turn of the century. Although these sections may not mention the bungalow, they will provide additional background on the economic, social, and cultural trends in the Progressive era and about the goals of Progressive reformers.

SECONDARY SOURCE

◆————————————

SOURCE 1   In *Building the Dream: A Social History of Housing in America* (1981), from which the following selection was drawn, Gwendolyn Wright argues that Americans have long used domestic architecture to encourage certain kinds of family and home life and that the bungalow was no exception. As you read this excerpt, note Wright's argument about the impact of changing gender roles on the popularity of the bungalow. What kind of home life did bungalow enthusiasts envision? Were they motivated by a desire to keep women in the home or to free her from it? How did their house plans reflect their desires?

The Progressive Housewife and the Bungalow (1981)

GWENDOLYN WRIGHT

In the early twentieth century, many different groups were campaigning for what they called a progressive approach to house design and upkeep. While their social goals often were based on conflicting values, public-health nurses, arts and crafts advocates, feminists, domestic scientists, and settlement-house workers favored the same simplified, standardized home to represent those values. . . .

In the arts and crafts movement of the early 1900s, architects and designers mixed with poets and writers, housewives and reformers, combining a sentimental reverence for hand-crafted goods with a more up-to-date endorsement of simplified, wholesome environments. Some designers acclaimed a self-consciously rustic aesthetic for the home, using massive tree trunks and uncut stone for structural elements, which they left exposed. While the fashionable family might display Indian handicrafts or folk art in the living room, most American arts and crafts enthusiasts simply called for "good taste" through quiet lines and minimal ornament. In contrast to their English counterparts who had initiated the arts and crafts movement as a reaction against the abuses of industrialization, most members of the numerous American organizations claimed that it was possible to produce pleasing forms in a factory as well as in a crafts workshop. They focused predominantly on the final product rather than on the actual conditions of making that product.

One of the most prominent popularizers of the arts and crafts movement in the United States was Gustav Stickley of Syracuse, New York. A furniture

Source: From *Building the Dream: A Social History of Housing in America* by Gwendolyn Wright. Reprinted by permission of Pantheon Books, a division of Random House, Inc.

maker, Stickley had first redesigned the practices in his shop so that all work was done with hand tools. Simple, rectilinear lines and unvarnished oak became characteristic of his "Craftsman" furniture. In 1901 Stickley began publication of a magazine, *The Craftsman*, hoping to lead a social and artistic revolution in America. The journal featured articles on tenements in New York City, . . . utopian anarchism, factory working conditions, flower arranging, and glass blowing. The following year, Stickley began to offer his readers model house designs, and continued to feature both interior and exterior plans until the magazine's demise in 1916. In 1903 he established the Craftsman Home Builder's Club, which gave free advice on "well-built, democratic, well-planned homes."

According to Stickley, "The Craftsman type of building is largely the result not of elaboration, but of elimination." The houses in his magazine had simple, rectilinear, built-in furniture, plain surfaces of native stone or wood, unpretentious plans and elevations. Stickley did not insist that every dwelling be a highly personalized design, even though he clearly enjoyed experimenting with the texture and variety of materials. To him, "democratic architecture" meant good homes available to all Americans through economy of construction and materials, together with necessary standardization. Though Craftsman designs suggested time-consuming construction techniques, the exposed beams were often simply tacked on under the eaves and the rough "clinker brick," produced in a factory to look like hand-molded brick.

Stickley claimed that his approach to design could remedy almost every problem facing the middle-class family, from lack of servants to the increased divorce rate. He also saw the well-crafted home as a key to solving larger social problems, such as crime and civil disorder. Small, inexpensive versions of the Craftsman house would make working-class families homeowners. Apprentice training programs in house construction and furniture making, run by the state and by private business, would provide uplifting employment for young men. The pages of *The Craftsman* carried the message that housing and social issues were related in their need for good design. Though Stickley's expectations of immediate, lasting social harmony through aesthetic reform were obviously unrealistic, he found a sizable audience that regarded residential architecture as the preferred American approach to reform.

Other magazines also offered detailed specifications for modern model houses, as well as more general advice on decoration and domesticity. By the time Edward Bok retired in 1919 as editor of *Ladies' Home Journal*, this magazine had a circulation of 2 million largely because of Bok's crusade for "model *Journal* houses." Bok wanted to encourage middle-class women to become more involved with the home, thereby relinquishing their recent tendencies to abandon domestic duties for jobs or women's club activities. He was emphatic about architectural standards for the modern home. The house should be free from "senseless ornamentation"; it should be equipped with the latest sanitary fixtures; it should be decorated with unpretentious furnishings and a few handmade niceties. These dicta did not, by any means, imply a spartan setting. The *Journal's* 1901 series of room designs by the St. Louis artist Will Bradley were opulent Art Nouveau décors. Yet Bok's taste was not all-embracing. He laid down exacting specifications for every detail, from pillows to room dimensions, often showing comparisons of "Good Taste vs. Bad Taste" in furnishings.

At first, no architects would deign to accept Bok's offer to design "model *Journal* houses," but with the depression of the 1890s, they became more willing. Beginning in 1895, suburban dwellings in Colonial Revival, Elizabethan, and Queen Anne styles, costing between $3,500 and $7,000, regularly appeared. In 1901, Bok launched the first of a series of modern model dwellings by Frank Lloyd Wright and his associates in Chicago. Thousands of readers sent in $5 for a complete set of plans and specifications, which would enable them to build duplicates of these model houses. As Theodore Roosevelt supposedly said of the *Journal's* editor "Bok is the only man I ever heard of who changed, for the better, the architecture of an entire nation, and he did it so quickly and yet so effectively that we didn't know it was begun before it was finished."

While there were many words for the new house of the early twentieth century, "bungalow" was certainly the most widely used. It usually referred to a relatively unpretentious small house, although more exotic, expansive, hand-crafted dwellings created by architects like Charles and Henry Greene in southern California were also called bungalows. In general, though, the term implied a one-story or story-and-a-half dwelling of between six hundred and eight hundred square feet. Bedrooms were only bunk spaces. The kitchen, fitted like a ship's galley, accommodated a single person, and she (it was assumed) had a squeeze, . . .

. . . The kitchen replaced the parlor as the focus of attention in many builders' pattern books, and certainly in domestic science textbooks and women's magazines. Isabell McDougall, describing "An Ideal Kitchen" for readers of *The House Beautiful* in 1902, evoked the by-now familiar metaphors of impeccable laboratory order to be enforced by the housewife, or household administrator. "Everything in her temple is clean," she explained, "with the scientific cleanliness of a surgery, which we all know to be far ahead of any mere housewifely neatness."

The average kitchen in the turn-of-the-century bungalow or larger house was compact and carefully planned. It measured approximately 120 square feet, and everything had its place. The commodious Hoosier cabinet, with numerous wooden drawers and bins, stood against one wall. Wooden worktables were positioned to cut down on unnecessary steps—a principle that domestic scientists borrowed from Taylorism. By 1910, the built-in breakfast nook had become popular; and in many houses, the kitchen had been reduced to a Pullman kitchen, or "kitchenette."

New appliances held center stage. The sink and drainboard were of shiny white porcelain or enameled iron. An automatic pump supplied hot and cold running water. If there was no brine-cooled or ammonia-cooled icebox on the back porch, where the iceman had easy access, a metal basin in one corner sufficed. A hood hung over the gas range to cut smells, and porcelain-enameled cookware hung on wall hooks. Unfortunately, the new appliances were not necessarily reliable. As one textbook on domestic architecture admitted, most laundry machines "are not economical on account of the severity of the process on the clothes being washed." Most households still used a washboard and hung the clothes in the yard to dry.

To many Americans, mechanical devices for the home were the essence of progressive improvements and a bright future. Writing in the *Congregationalist*, Henry Demarest Lloyd, the Chicago muckraking journalist, extolled the benefits he envisioned:

> Equal industrial power will be as invariable a function of citizenship as the equal franchise. Power will flow in every house and shop as freely as water. All men will become capitalists and all capitalists co-operators. . . . Women, released from the economic pressure which has forced them to deny their best nature and compete in unnatural industry with men, will be re-sexed. . . . Every house will be a center of sunshine and scenery.

According to Lloyd, technology promised individual freedom and social equality. Men and women of all classes would share the infinite power of electricity, the "modern servant." Lloyd envisioned women returning to their homes, leaving their jobs because of increased economic abundance brought about by electrical power. But other reformers, especially feminists, foresaw a future wherein more women would be able to take on jobs outside the home because electricity had freed them from household drudgery. . . .

In more and more cases, the housewife worked alone in her kitchen. Between 1900 and 1920, the number of domestic servants in the United States declined by half—from eighty per thousand families to thirty-nine. (Most of these were day workers, usually black married women rather than live-in servants.) Yet no builders considered opening up the kitchen and ending the housewife's isolation there. Rather, they praised the smaller, better-equipped kitchen, planned for the domestic scientist who had no need of a servant, since she had learned the most efficient techniques for housework. The kitchen was not to be a place for playing with children or visiting with neighbors but a modern "home laboratory."

One of the principal justifications for the smaller kitchen and the minimum-upkeep materials of the progressive house was the middle-class woman's demand for more time of her own outside the house. By 1900, women held jobs in almost every occupation listed in the census. Although most of these women were unmarried, and a quarter of them domestics or factory workers, college-educated women did enter the professions. Other young women donned the starched shirtwaist and ankle-length skirt of the Gibson girl and entered offices as receptionists, clerical workers, and typewriters (the same word was used for the machine and the person working at it).

Middle-class women who did not hold regular jobs often worked as volunteers in charity or civic organizations, promoting the numerous improvement campaigns of the National Consumers' League or their local women's club, lobbying for reform legislation or neighborhood parks. These women still considered domestic issues their primary concern, but now the entire city was their home. In 1910, the president of the General Federation of Women's Clubs declared that their platform was based on protecting "women and children, and the home, the latter meaning the four walls of the city as well as the four walls of brick and mortar."

Private homes were often the focus of debate, all the same. In order for women to have time for their non-domestic activities, they wanted both simpler houses that were easier to keep clean and more labor-saving appliances. The single-family dwelling was condemned in the pages of *Harper's Bazaar* as "a prison and a burden and a tyrant." The Philadelphia economist Robert E. Thompson and Charlotte Perkins Gilman and other radical feminists demanded kitchenless houses and public childcare facilities to ease the domestic demands on women.

There was some reservation about architectural changes that were tied to new sex roles. The restlessness that characterized "the modern woman" caused a stir among many conservatives. Journalists, physicians and politicians raised the issues of "race suicide" and "desexualization," which they connected to the declining birth rate among white women. In *The Foes of Our Own Household* (1917) and in articles for *Ladies' Home Journal*, Theodore Roosevelt spoke about the dangers of women abandoning the traditional roles of wife and mother for more exciting challenges outside the home. Higher education for women came under attack, since college-educated women often did not marry, and when they did, they had one or two children at most. The modern home and, even worse, the apartment, requiring as little time as they did, seemed to encourage these tendencies.

Despite their misgivings, architects, builders, and the editors of women's magazines recognized the growing market of working women. Even the married woman who worked was not necessarily considered a pariah. *Ladies' Home Journal* carried several articles on ways to earn one's living both inside and outside the home; and a full-page color spread in February 1911 considered the best house plan for a woman with a family and a career at home. Her bungalow had two separate entrances, a living room that doubled as a reception room for clients, and many built-in conveniences to accelerate housekeeping chores. Bungalows designed for single "business-girls" or "girl-bachelors" were featured in magazines and home-economics texts in the 1910s. Space allotted for cooking and laundering was minimal, for it was assumed that such tasks were done commercially, outside the private home. . . .

An elaboration of this model was the bungalow court—a group of ten or twenty almost identical dwellings, first designed as winter housing in southern California—which appeared in all parts of the country in the 1910s. Since the bungalows were quite small, there was usually a community "playhouse," where residents entertained guests and organized evening entertainments. Those who promoted the bungalow court as a modern living environment suggested that it could domesticate single working women, demonstrating to them the progressive side of home life. According to many advocates, this setting also represented "The Community Problem Solved." The harmonious uniform aesthetic and the shared outdoor spaces, playhouse, and garages were evidence that the residents had established strong social ties among themselves. . . .

While more than half the nation's farmers owned their homes in 1910, only one third of non-farm households did. . . . It was increasingly difficult for Americans to afford to become homeowners. In particular, the growing number of unmarried women and men usually rented rather than owned. The smaller, plainer dwelling, especially one set on a common court rather than on a large private yard, was an attempt to find a solution to the economic problem and to the seemingly related problem of a growing population of unmarried persons. Participants at the annual National Conference on City Planning, whose meetings began in 1909, and the National Conference on Housing, which commenced in 1911, hoped to find innovative ways to increase homeownership without moving toward any sort of federal subsidies. They endorsed architectural solutions to economic and social dilemmas. The Model Street display at the St. Louis Exposition of 1904, the Model Bungalow installed at the Indiana State House for the 1913 National Conservation Congress, and the flurry of competitions for model suburban developments were all expressions of a nationwide enthusiasm for the "progressive house," which began to look much the same, wherever it appeared.

The uniform image appealed to a range of people who hoped that domestic architecture would encourage social cooperation. The Victorian suburb was branded as a "labyrinth of unreason," reflecting a time of "rabid democracy," of social and aesthetic license. Settlement workers Jane Addams and Graham R. Taylor, Jr., the domestic scientist Marion Talbot, the statistician Adna Weber, and the political journalist Herbert Croly concurred: houses conceived as individualistic display encouraged class differences and competition among neighbors. They argued for common architectural standards that would visually reinforce their ideal of a balanced, egalitarian social life for women and men. Both feminists and conservatives asserted that it was possible to solve "the woman question" through a more rational approach toward living environments. In 1912, Grosvenor Atterbury, who designed the model suburb of Forest Hills Gardens in Queens and championed planned industrial towns, wrote an appeal for progressive residential planning in *Scribner's*. He too argued that domestic architecture could reinforce the higher social values of residents, subordinating individual desires to the general good. "[T]he truth is that with any kind of control anarchy ceases," Atterbury claimed. "With the elimination of lawless eccentricity and disregard of architectural decency, the good elements begin to count."

PRIMARY SOURCES

There are several types of primary sources in this chapter: sketches and floor plans of Progressive-era bungalows, illustrations of old and new styles of household furnishings, and the writings of housing reformers and others. They may reflect a variety of motives for embracing a new architectural style.

Craftsman Home Designs

The Craftsman magazine offered house plans and suggestions for home decorations to "simplify the work of home life." What features of these houses and their interiors might Progressive-era Americans have found especially appealing? *The Craftsman* magazine publisher Gustav Stickley suggested that his own home reflected the personality of a man, in contrast to "the majority of modern houses . . . built to meet the ideas of women."[7] Why may this have been one of the appealing features of the Craftsman house?

SOURCE 2

A Craftsman Cottage (1909)

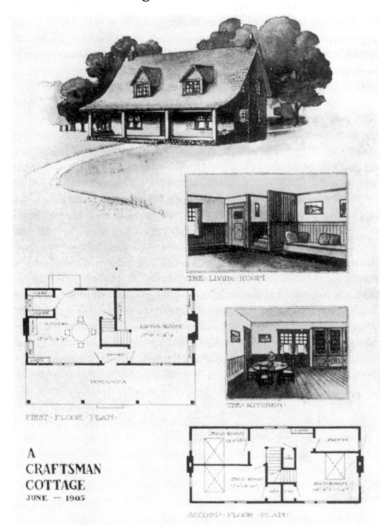

Note the division of space so that the greatest amount of freedom and convenience is obtained within a small area. The illustrations of the interior serve to show how the structural features, although simple and inexpensive, give to each room an individual beauty and charm. The kitchen is arranged to serve also for a dining room.

Source: Gustav Stickley, *Craftsman Homes.* Courtesy Harvard College Library.

SOURCE 3

The Craftsman Contrasts Complexity and Confusion with Cohesion and Harmony (1907)

Source: Gustav Stickey, *The Craftsman,* 1907. Courtesy Harvard College Library.

◆

SOURCE 4   Stickley was one of the most influential promoters of the bungalow. Note the social ills that Stickley suggests will be solved by the adoption of
this simple home style.

Gustav Stickley on the Craftsman Home (1909)

That the influence of the home is of the first importance in the shaping of
character is a fact too well understood and too generally admitted to be
offered here as a new idea. One need only turn to the pages of history to find
abundant proof of the unerring action of Nature's law, for without exception
the people whose lives are lived simply and wholesomely, in the open, and
who have in a high degree the sense of the sacredness of the home, are the
people who have made the greatest strides in the development of the race.
When luxury enters in and a thousand artificial requirements come to be
regarded as real needs, the nation is on the brink of degeneration. . . . Even in
the rush and hurry of life in our busy cities we remember well the quality given
to the growing nation by such men and women a generation or two ago and,
in spite of the chaotic conditions brought about by our passion for money-get-
ting, extravagance and show, we have still reason to believe that the dominant
characteristics of the pioneer yet shape what are the salient qualities in
American life.

To preserve these characteristics and to bring back to individual life and
work the vigorous constructive spirit which during the last half-century has
spent its activities in commercial and industrial expansion, is, in a nut-shell,
the Craftsman idea. We need to straighten out our standards and to get rid of
a lot of rubbish that we have accumulated along with our wealth and commercial supremacy. It is not that we are too energetic, but that in many ways
we have wasted and misused our energy precisely as we have wasted and
misused so many of our wonderful natural resources. All we really need is a
change in our point of view toward life and a keener perception regarding the
things that count and the things which merely burden us. This being the case,
it would seem obvious that the place to begin a readjustment is in the home,
for it is only natural that the relief from friction which would follow the
ordering of our lives along more simple and reasonable lines would not only
assure greater comfort, and therefore greater efficiency, to the workers of the

Source: Excerpted from Gustav Stickley, *Craftsman Homes: Architecture and Furnishings of the
American Arts and Crafts Movement* (Mineola, NY: Dover Publications, 1979) by permission of
Dover Publications.

nation, but would give the children a chance to grow up under conditions which would be conducive to a higher degree of mental, moral and physical efficiency.

Therefore we regard it as at least a step in the direction of bringing about better conditions when we try to plan and build houses which will simplify the work of home life and add to its wholesome joy and comfort. We have already made it plain to our readers that we do not believe in large houses with many rooms elaborately decorated and furnished, for the reason that these seem so essentially an outcome of the artificial conditions that lay such harassing burdens upon modern life and form such a serious menace to our ethical standards. Breeding as it does the spirit of extravagance and of discontent which in the end destroys all the sweetness of home life, the desire for luxury and show not only burdens beyond his strength the man who is ambitious to provide for his wife and children surroundings which are as good as the best, but taxes to the utmost the woman who is trying to keep up the appearances which she believes should belong to her station in life. Worst of all, it starts the children with standards which, in nine cases out of ten, utterly preclude the possibility of their beginning life on their own account in a simple and sensible way. Boys who are brought up in such homes are taught, by the silent influence of their early surroundings, to take it for granted that they must not marry until they are able to keep up an establishment of equal pretensions, and girls also take it as a matter of course that marriage must mean something quite as luxurious as the home of their childhood or it is not a paying investment for their youth and beauty. Everyone who thinks at all deplores the kind of life that marks a man's face with the haggard lines of anxiety and makes him sharp and often unscrupulous in business, with no ambition beyond large profits and a rapid rise in the business world. Also we all realize regretfully the extravagance and uselessness of many of our women and admit that one of the gravest evils of our times is the light touch-and-go attitude toward marriage, which breaks up so many homes and makes the divorce courts in America a by-word to the world. But when we think into it a little more deeply, we have to acknowledge that such conditions are the logical outcome of our standards of living and that these standards are always shaped in the home.

That is why we have from the first planned houses that are based on the big fundamental principles of honesty, simplicity and usefulness,—the kind of houses that children will rejoice all their lives to remember as "home," and that give a sense of peace and comfort to the tired men who go back to them when the day's work is done. Because we believe that the healthiest and happiest life is that which maintains the closest relationship with out-of-doors, we have planned our houses with outdoor living rooms, dining rooms and sleeping rooms, and many windows to let in plenty of air and sunlight.

◆

SOURCE 5   As the editor of the *Ladies' Home Journal,* Edward Bok promoted a variety of Progressive causes. He also used the magazine to publicize the simple bungalow style. Note the ills Bok hoped to cure with the reform of home design, especially for women.

Edward Bok on Simplicity (1900)

There are no people on the face of the earth who litter up the rooms of their homes with so much useless, and consequently bad, furnishing as do the Americans. The curse of the American home to-day is useless bric-a-brac. A room in which we feel that we can freely breathe is so rare that we are instinctively surprised when we see one. It is the exception, rather than the rule, that we find a restful room.

As a matter of fact, to this common error of overfurnishing so many of our homes are directly due many of the nervous breakdowns of our women. The average American woman is a perfect slave to the useless rubbish which she has in her rooms. This rubbish, of a costly nature where plenty exists, and of a cheap and tawdry character in homes of moderate incomes, is making housekeeping a nerve-racking burden. A goodly number of these women are conscious of their mistakes. Others, if not absolutely conscious, feel that something is wrong in their homes, yet they know not exactly what it is. But all are loath, yes, I may say afraid, to simplify things. They fear the criticism of the outside world that their homes are sparsely furnished; they dread the possibility that their rooms may be called "bare." They fear to give way to common-sense. It is positively rare, but tremendously exhilarating, to find a women, as one does now and then, who is courageous enough to furnish her home with an eye single to comfort and practical utility, and who refuses to have her home lowered to a plane of mediocrity by filling it with useless bric-a-brac and jimcracks, the only mission of which seems to be to offend the eye and accumulate dust. . . .

More simplicity in our homes would make our lives simpler. Many women would live fuller lives because they would have more time. As it is, hundreds of women of all positions in life are to-day the slaves of their homes and what they have crowded into them. Instead of being above inanimate objects of wood and clothes and silks, their lives are dominated by them. They are the slaves of their furniture and useless bric-a-brac. One hears men constantly complain of this. The condition is not a safe one for wives. No woman can

Source: Reprinted from David E. Shi, *In Search of the Simple Life* (Layton, Utah: Gibbs M. Smith, 1986), by permission of the author.

afford to allow a lot of unnecessary furnishings to rule her life. . . . We need only to be natural: to get back to our real, inner selves. Then we are simple. It is only because we have got away from the simple and the natural that so many of our homes are cluttered up as they are, and our lives full of things that are not worth the while. We have bent the knee to show, to display, and we have lowered ourselves in doing it: surrounded ourselves with the trivial and the useless: and filling our lives with the poison of artificiality and the unnatural, we have pushed the Real: the Natural: the Simple: the Beautiful—the best and most lasting things—out of our lives. Now, I ask, in all fairness: Is it worth while?

◆————————

SOURCE 6   Economist Thorstein Veblen wrote a biting critique of "conspicuous consumption" in his *Theory of the Leisure Class* (1899). Veblen argued that "ostentatious display" was the means by which the wealthy established social status and that their spending patterns became the standard for the rest of society. Although Veblen denied any intention of passing judgment on upper- or middle-class spending, his message was clear. In the passage below, Veblen analyzes the appeal of items produced in the Arts and Crafts style. As you read, note what Veblen thought motivated people to embrace simple designs.

Conspicuous Consumption and the Craftsman Style (1899)

THORSTEIN VEBLEN

As has already been pointed out, the cheap . . . articles of daily consumption in modern industrial communities are commonly machine products; and the generic feature . . . of machine-made goods as compared with the hand-wrought article is their greater perfection in workmanship and greater accuracy in the detail execution of the design. Hence it comes about that the visible imperfections of the hand-wrought goods, being honorific, are accounted marks of superiority . . . Hence has arisen that exaltation of the defective, of which John Ruskin and William Morris were such eager spokesmen in their time; and on this ground their propaganda of crudity and wasted effort has been taken up and carried forward since their time. And hence also the propaganda for a return to handicraft and household industry. So much of the work and speculations of this group of men . . . would have been impossible at a time when the visibly more perfect goods were not the cheaper.

Source: Thorstein Veblen, *Theory of the Leisure Class* (New York: The Macmillan Company, 1912, originally published 1899), pp. 126–127, 161–162.

◆

SOURCE 7   *The Bungalow Magazine* provided readers with plans for inexpensive bungalows. What does this cover illustration suggest about the benefits of a simpler home style?

Cover from *The Bungalow Magazine* (1909)

Source: From *The Bungalow Magazine* (October 1909). Courtesy Harvard College Library.

Christine Frederick on the Efficient Homemaker

Frederick was one of the leaders of the home economics movement at the turn of the century. In numerous articles and books she preached the need to apply the principles of scientific management to housekeeping. She was a vocal advocate of simple designs, and her ideal home closely resembled the Arts and Crafts bungalow. As you read and examine these selections, note what Frederick hoped to achieve by applying the principles of efficiency and simplicity to the home. Did she advocate a change in gender roles?

◆

SOURCE 8

Putting the American Woman and Her Home on a Business Basis (1914)

Is the American housewife facing a great revolution? Is the efficiency idea, which has already revolutionized many industrial plants, now going to attack that last stronghold of tradition—the American Home?

Signs point that way. The ideas of motion study, standardized conditions of work, scientific management of servants, had simply to be announced to strike a responsive chord among intelligent home-makers. Efficiency is in the air, and has permeated to the kitchen no less than to the counting-room, and to general homemaking—even to woman herself. . . .

The most serious evidences of decay of the home such as it used to be are seen on every side. From scores of points the home has been, and is being attacked. The chief of these are:

1. Decided drift to large cities, where more and more of the original functions of the home, even to cooking, are being diminished.
2. Increasing demands of sanitation and modern ideas in homemaking, which compel progress upward with, or downward from, accepted standards.
3. Greatly increased cost of living, compelling either disastrous extravagances or lowered standards, or increased brain management on the part of housewives to meet the situation.
4. General broadening of woman's horizon and making the entire line of human endeavor her sphere, with the home becoming more incidental, as with men. . . .

If the home is to survive it must do so on a reorganized basis. No industry founded upon admittedly unwilling, uninterested millions can continue to

Source: The American Review of Reviews, 64 (February 1914), pp. 199, 200.

operate; yet everybody admits the tremendous discontent among home women. As at present operated, American housekeeping is distasteful to admittedly the livest and most intelligent portion of housekeepers, and is only endured in a dull way by the masses of women. Its grave faults have been that it lacked mental interest, that it was without the spur of competition, and that it did not possess the dignity of a serious profession. Degradation has more and more attached itself to housework as ambition has raised other standards of living. Every other member of the family hastened to rise from the drudgery state of his chosen work, but the woman who merely "kept house" has felt her wings clipped.

◆

SOURCE 9

The Efficient and Inefficient Kitchen (1920)

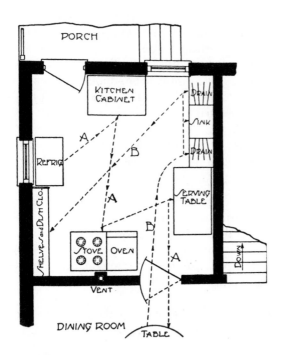

"Badly Grouped Kitchen Equipment." A: preparation route; B: clearing-away route. A and B intersect with no apparent order.

Source: Household Engineering, 1920. Courtesy Harvard College Library.

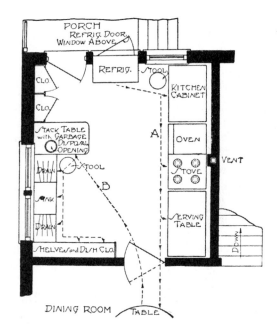

"Efficient Grouping of Kitchen Equipment." Preparing and clearing away do not intersect; each activity is clearly organized.

Charlotte Perkins Gilman and the Bungalow

Feminist Charlotte Perkins Gilman wrote extensively on the need to revamp domestic architecture. She advocated the replacement of traditional household arrangements so that women could enjoy work outside the home and the economic independence it would bring. Gilman called for the replacement of the traditional home with its isolated kitchen by kitchenless houses and apartments connected to central kitchens staffed by paid professionals. She also suggested the advantages of husbands and wives living in "separate establishments" such as those at Bowen Court, constructed in Pasadena, California, in 1910. Known as a bungalow court, Bowen Court contained twenty-two bungalows bordering a center garden. It also featured a sewing room and laundry for women tenants. Some of the units were double bungalows "planned for two or more persons who may wish to live under the same roof, but desire separate establishments."[8] Bowen Court was designed by architects who had been influenced by Gilman. As you read and examine these sources, note Gilman's response to the home economists' solution to the problem of "domestic economy." How do the motives behind the bungalow court compare to those of Stickley, Bok, and other bungalow promoters?

SOURCE 10

Domestic Economy (1904)

One of the strongest intrenchments of our piously defended system of household industry is its supposed economy. "The careful housewife" is our ideal of a wise and judicious expender of money, some even going so far as to call her a "partner" in the business of housekeeping. . . .

Let us give a fair examination to this particular point, the economy of domestic industry. . . .

Merely as a matter of business, is it good business?

What is, exactly, the business we are to study?

It is that of catering to the personal physical needs of the human animal, caring for the health of the body, providing shelter, warmth, food and cleanliness. . . .

The home is intended to furnish shelter and protection to the family—sleeping accommodations, food, and those cleansing processes so essential to all civilized life. The business of the home is in the rent or purchase and replenishment of the place and plant; the provision of supplies for consumption; the preparation and service of food, and all kinds of cleaning. What is commonly called "housekeeping" really embraces this group of industries, arbitrarily connected by custom, but in their nature not only diverse, but grossly incompatible. . . .

Yet we carry on all these contradictory trades in one small building, and also live in it!

Not only do we undertake to have all these labors performed in one house, but by one person.

In full ninety per cent of our American homes there is but one acting functionary to perform these varied and totally dissimilar functions—to be cook, laundress, chambermaid, charwoman, seamstress, nurse and governess. . . .

The person who is expected to achieve this miracle is not some specially selected paragon of varied ability, but merely the average woman; neither is she prepared for her herculean tasks (Hercules was never required to perform his twelve labors all at once!) by a rigorous course of training, but is supposed to be fitted by nature for their successful achievement, aided perhaps by instruction from a similarly well prepared predecessor. Under these circum-

Source: Charlotte Perkins Gilman, "Domestic Economy," *The Independent,* June 16, 1904, pp. 1359–63.

stances the wonder is that even half of us live to grow up, that our average of intelligence and ability is so good, and that our common standard of comfort and cleanliness, of health, vigor and peace of mind is as high as it is; that any degree of family happiness remains to us; and it is no wonder whatever, but an inevitable consequence, that the waste and incompetence manifested in this pitiful business constitute so huge a loss and injury. . . .

SOURCE 11

Double Bungalow Plan, Bowen Court

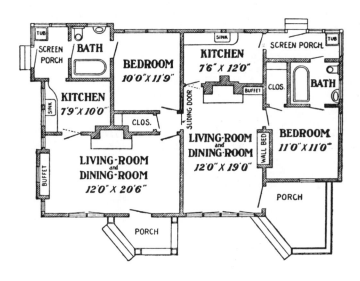

Source: Ladies' Home Journal 30 (April 1913).

Changes in Middle-Class Life

By the turn of the century industrial growth had had a profound impact on middle-class life. What changes do these tables reveal that may have made the bungalow more attractive to middle-class Americans?

SOURCE 12

Average Daily Servants' Wage Rates, Chicago, 1890–1910

Year	Wage	Year	Wage	Year	Wage
1890	$3.82	1897	$3.60	1904	$5.10
1891	4.15	1898	4.12	1905	5.08
1892	4.23	1899	4.08	1906	5.36
1893	4.50	1900	4.28	1907	5.77
1894	3.99	1901	4.40	1908	5.60
1895	4.16	1902	4.57	1909	5.68
1896	3.83	1903	4.93	1910	6.16

Source: From *Seven Days a Week: Women and Domestic Service in Industrializing America,* edited by David M. Katzman. Copyright © 1988 by David M. Katzman. Used by permission of Oxford University Press.

SOURCE 13

Female Servants by Regions, per 1,000 Families, 1880–1920

	Per 1,000 families		
United States	1880	1900	1920
The North	92	80	39
New England	105	96	45
Middle Atlantic	121	99	49
Eastern North Central	74	68	32
Western North Central	61	61	32
The South	78	63	46
Northern South Atlantic	131	104	64
Southern South Atlantic	70	59	51
Eastern South Central	68	61	42
Western South Central	51	43	36
The West	43	49	28
Mountain, Basin, and Plateau	33	43	25
Pacific	49	53	29

Source: From *Seven Days a Week: Women and Domestic Service in Industrializing America,* edited by David M. Katzman. Copyright © 1988 by David M. Katzman. Used by permission of Oxford University Press.

SOURCE 14

Clerical Workers in the United States, by Sex, 1870–1920

Job Category	1870	1880	1890	1900	1910	1920
Bookkeepers, cashiers, and accountants						
Total	38,776	74,919	159,374	254,880	486,700	734,688
Male	37,892	70,667	131,602	180,727	299,545	375,564
Female	884	4,252	27,772	74,153	187,155	359,124
% Female	2.0	5.7	17.4	29.1	38.5	48.4
Office clerks						
Total	29,801	59,799	187,969	248,323	720,498	1,487,905
Male	28,878	59,484	163,686	229,991	597,833	1,015,742
Female	923	315	24,283	18,332	122,665	472,163
% Female	3.1	.5	12.9	7.4	17.0	31.7
Messenger, errand, and office boys/girls						
Total	8,046	12,818	47,183	66,009	108,035	113,022
Male	7,967	12,421	44,294	59,392	96,748	98,768
Female	79	397	2,889	6,617	11,287	14,254
% Female	.9	3.1	6.1	10.0	10.4	12.6
Stenographers and typists						
Total	154	5,000	33,418	112,364	316,693	615,154
Male	147	3,000	12,148	26,246	53,378	50,410
Female	7	2,000	21,270	86,118	263,315	564,744
% Female	4.5	40.0	63.6	76.6	83.1	91.8

Source: Alba M. Edwards, *Comparative Statistics for the United States, 1870 to 1940*. Part of the *Sixteenth Census of the United States: 1940* (Washington, D.C.: U.S. Government Printing Office, 1943), Tables 9 and 10.

CONCLUSION

As the bungalow craze illustrates, historians must often sort out a variety of motives. Housing reformers expressed fears about inflation, declining middle-class birthrates, rising divorce rates, women leaving the home, and the confinement of women in the home. They saw new housing styles as a way to reform domestic life. Because their views about domestic problems varied, so too did their motives for promoting the bungalow.

The sources in this chapter also illustrate that we cannot escape the influence of ideas. The bungalow reflected the influence of a Progressive ideology characterized by a belief in efficiency, faith in the power of the environment to transform people, and a distrust of concentrated wealth, class divisions, and urban life. It led Progressive reformers to take up such diverse causes as trust busting, housing reform, and conservation. It also led them to see common solutions for social problems. It was no coincidence, for instance, that Progressive conservationists promoted contact with nature at the same time that Progressive-era bungalow designers found rugged, natural houses aesthetically pleasing. As we shall see next, historians cannot fully understand motivations or any historical change without reference to ideologies.

FURTHER READING

Polly Wynn Allen, *Building Domestic Liberty: Charlotte Perkins Gilman's Architectural Feminism* (Amherst: University of Massachusetts Press, 1988).

Eileen Boris, "The Gendered Meaning of Arts and Crafts," in *The Ideal Home, 1900–1920: The History of Twentieth-Century American Craft,* ed. Janet Kardon (New York: H. N. Abrams, 1993).

Clifford Edward Clark, Jr., *The American Family Home, 1800–1960* (Chapel Hill: The University of North Carolina Press, 1986).

David E. Shi, "Progressive Simplicity," in *The Simple Life: Plain Living and High Thinking in American Culture* (New York: Oxford University Press, 1985).

Gustav Stickley, *Craftsman Homes: Architecture and Furnishings of the American Arts and Crafts Movement* (New York: Dover Publications, 1979; reprint of 1909 edition).

NOTES

1. Quoted in Clifford Edward Clark, Jr., *The American Family Home* (Chapel Hill: University of North Carolina Press, 1986), pp. 132, 144.
2. Quoted in David E. Shi, *The Simple Life: Plain Living and High Thinking in American Culture* (New York: Oxford University Press, 1985), p. 186.
3. Quoted in Eileen Boris, *Art and Labor: Ruskin, Morris, and the Craftsman Idea in America* (Philadelphia: Temple University Press, 1986), p. 75.
4. Quoted in Eileen Boris, "Crossing Boundaries: The Gendered Meaning of Arts and Crafts," in *The Ideal Home: The History of Twentieth-Century American Craft,* ed. Janet Kardon (New York: Harry N. Abrams, 1993), p. 35.

5. Quoted in ibid., p. 36.
6. Quoted in Clark, *American Family Home,* p. 153.
7. Quoted in Eileen Boris, "The Gendered Meaning of Arts and Crafts," in Kardon, *The Ideal Home,* p. 44.
8. Quoted in Dolores Hayden, *The Grand Domestic Revolution: A History of Feminist Designs for American Homes, Neighborhoods, and Cities* (Cambridge, Mass.: MIT Press, 1981), p. 239.

Chapter 6

Ideology and History:
Closing the "Golden Door"

The sources in this chapter offer information on the attitude of Americans toward immigrants at the turn of the century.

Secondary Source

1. Racism and Immigration Restriction (1984) JOHN HIGHAM

Primary Sources

2. The Passing of the Great Race (1916), MADISON GRANT
3. Whose Country Is This? (1921), CALVIN COOLIDGE
4. The Klan's Fight for Americanism (1926), HIRAM W. EVANS
5. Because You're a Jew (1908)
6. Her Father's Daughter (1921), GENE STRATTON-PORTER
7. A Congressman Calls for Restriction (1921)
8. The Bootleggers (1925)
9. Immigrant Occupation Groups, 1899–1924
10. Unemployment Rates, 1900–1924

*"G*ive me your tired, your poor,
Your huddled masses yearning to breathe free,
The wretched refuse of your teeming shore.
Send these, the homeless, tempest tossed to me,
I lift my lamp beside the golden door!"
                    —Emma Lazarus

The majestic statue commemorated in Emma Lazarus's poem was the first glimpse many immigrants had of their new home. Despite its welcoming words, many of the newcomers were also aware of other attitudes in their new country, since news, letters, and even immigrants traveled both ways across the Atlantic. They might not know that native-born Americans did not see the Statue of Liberty as a national symbol of refuge, yet some of them surely suspected that they might not be welcome.

Their suspicions were well founded. Growing numbers of Americans at the turn of the century were convinced that there was too much "wretched refuse" pouring in from the Old World's "teeming shores." Such sentiments had already led Congress to exclude Chinese immigrants and soon thereafter led it to restrict Japanese immigration. The doors to European immigration—through most of the nineteenth century white, overwhelmingly Christian, and mostly Protestant—remained wide open. Yet that too would change when Congress severely restricted European immigration in the early 1920s.

Although restrictions on immigration and hostility toward immigrants remain today, by World War II intense hostility toward European immigrants had subsided. Only then did Lazarus's poem, engraved on Lady Liberty's pedestal and in the minds of countless schoolchildren, help to transform the Statue of Liberty into an enduring symbol of asylum. Today the national self-image embodied in the statue still obscures other images Americans have had of immigrants. We often forget that in the early twentieth century many Americans looked at newcomers through a powerful ideological filter of beliefs, values, fears, and prejudices that prevented them from seeing America as a haven for all of the oppressed. In this chapter we examine the nature this ideology and its role in closing the "golden door" after World War I.

SETTING

America had never experienced the sheer numbers of immigrants that arrived in the first fifteen years of the twentieth century. Between 1900 and 1914, more than 13 million immigrants arrived, mostly from Europe. Yet this European immigration was changing. Since the mid-1880s, the percentage of southern and eastern European immigrants had risen steadily, from about 16 percent of total immigration in 1885 to 75 percent in 1914. This dramatic shift alarmed many observers, especially after the U.S. Immigration Commission concluded in 1911 that the "new" southern and eastern European immigrants differed from the "old" northern European immigrants. The commission declared that the old immigrants had "entered practically every line of activity" and had "mingled freely" with native-born Americans. On the other hand, the new immigrants were mostly unskilled laborers who "congregated together in sections apart from native Americans."[1] They seemed unable to become American.

Doubts about the ability or willingness of immigrants to assimilate were nothing new. Nativism—hostility to groups because of their foreignness—had a long history in the United States. In the 1790s Federalists pointed to foreign radicals as a threat to the republic. When Irish immigrants fled oppression and famine in their homeland a half century later, many Americans flocked into the Know-Nothing party to battle the "menace" of Catholicism. In 1882, a growing fear of a "yellow menace" on the West Coast led Congress to exclude the Chinese from further entry. A Gentleman's Agreement between the United States and Japan denied entry to Japanese laborers in 1907. Asian immigrants were also denied the benefits of citizenship.

Meanwhile European immigration policy reflected a demand for cheap labor and optimism about America's ability to absorb white newcomers. But here too doubts were growing at the end of the century. In 1894, the Immigration Restriction League began a campaign to close America's doors even to European immigrants. The league's immediate goal was to impose a literacy test on immigrants, a goal it achieved in 1917. Then in 1921 Congress enacted a provisional measure that established annual quotas on European immigration, and in 1924 it passed the Johnson-Reed Act, which set a total annual limit of European immigrants at 150,000. The act distributed annual quotas on the basis of the proportion of each nationality in the existing American population, and it also banned Japanese immigration entirely, making Asian exclusion virtually complete. Since southern and eastern European nationalities made up far smaller percentages of the population than northern European groups, their quotas were tiny. At the same time, the larger quotas of more prosperous northern European countries went mostly unfilled. By closing the doors to the worrisome Asians and "new" immigrants, restrictionists had ended a century of massive immigration to America.

INVESTIGATION

Historians point to many reasons for growing hostility to immigrants in the first decades of the twentieth century: fears about radical influence, the fact that most new immigrants were Catholics or Jews, a perception that they took jobs from native-born Americans, and the general hostility to foreigners aroused by the loyalty campaigns during World War I. Others insist that immigration restriction cannot be understood apart from a nativist ideology that led many Americans to see racial distinctions among immigrant groups. Your main job in this chapter is to explain why the United States ended Japanese and unrestricted European immigration after World War I. To do that, you must analyze the role that ideology—a complex of values, fears, interests, and prejudices—played in immigration restriction. Answering the following questions will make it easier to assess this ideology:

1. **What is the main essay's explanation for the restriction of European immigration?** What role did a racist ideology play in closing the doors? What does the author mean when he says that race was a "vehicle for thinking about culture"?

2. **What do the primary sources reveal about the racial differences many native-born Americans saw among immigrants?** What qualities did nativists assign to "racially inferior" groups? What other factors contributed to restrictionist sentiment after World War I?

3. **Were the fears about "inferior racial stock" deeply held or simply a convenient weapon for nativists who were interested in closing the doors for other reasons?** Do you agree that the "race-menace" argument actually reflected deeper fears about maintaining cultural homogeneity?

Before you begin, read the sections in your textbook on immigration. Pay special attention to the role it assigns to racial thought in the restriction of immigration.

SECONDARY SOURCE

◆

SOURCE 1   John Higham is a leading immigration scholar. In the following essay, he discusses the role that racial theory in the early twentieth century played in defining a nativist ideology and in closing the gates to unrestricted European immigration. Note how ideas about race change in the late nineteenth century, according to Higham. What influences transformed the concept of race from a simple notion of white supremacy to something much more elaborate? What is Higham's evidence that Americans became increasingly concerned about the "unity of their culture" after World War I?

Racism and Immigration Restriction (1984)

JOHN HIGHAM

In the decade from 1905 to 1914 an average of more than a million people annually crowded past the immigration inspectors. After 1896 the great majority derived from southern and eastern Europe. Thereafter, the outflow from the more highly developed countries of northwestern Europe declined as the movement from distant lands increased. . . . Whereas nativists in the nineties had very generally disliked the foreigner as such, the "new immigration" now stood out sharply as the heart of the problem. All of the regressive and antisocial qualities once imputed to the immigrants in general could now be fixed upon this more specific category. In fact, the major theoretical effort of restrictionists in the twentieth century consisted precisely in this: the transformation of relative cultural differences into an absolute line of cleavage, which would redeem the northwestern Europeans from the charges once leveled at them and explain the present danger of immigration in terms of the change in its sources. . . .

. . . The earliest attacks stressed a social and economic peril. Pennsylvania coal miners denounced the Italian, Hungarian, and Polish labor arriving among them as a degraded, servile class whose presence frustrated efforts to improve wages and conditions. Economists and a growing number of labor leaders generalized the argument into a plea for saving "the American standard of living." The economic case was systematized by the United States Immigration Commission of 1907–11, whose forty-two-volume report comprised the most massive investigation of immigration ever made. The Commission worked out, in vast detail, an unfavorable contrast between the northwestern and southeastern Europeans in the United States *at that time.* The latter were more highly concentrated in cities and in unskilled jobs and were more inclined to return to Europe. These figures obscured significant differences between particular nationalities and did not take account of a marked improvement in the social-economic caliber of northwestern European immigration since the time when it had led the way. Other critics, beginning with the Immigration Restriction League, produced even more misleading figures, correlating the new immigration with the growth of slums and with a high incidence of crime, disease, and insanity.

A second line of argument concerned a racial menace. Here, the case against the new nationalities was harder to build. In popular parlance, race meant color. Since no very clear-cut difference of complexion was apparent between native Americans and any European group, the old instincts of white suprem-acy did not extend to the new immigration as easily as they did to the Chinese. To a large extent, race lines would have to be manufactured. Their construction was a gradual process, long impeded by the democratic tradition. Ultimately, however, the racial attack on the new immigration emerged as a powerful ideological weapon of the restriction movement.

For a starting point, restrictionist intellectuals had a romantic, traditionalist concept of race that was different from the popular spirit of white supremacy. Throughout the nineteenth century patrician writers often acclaimed the American people as the finest branch of the Anglo-Saxon race. The Anglo-Saxon myth was somewhat inconsistent with the cosmopolitan ideal of na-tionality; but originally no race feelings (in the sense of biological taboos) were involved. In the Anglo-Saxon sense "race" meant essentially the persistence of national character; it expressed a cultural nationalism. In time, however, Anglo-Saxonism expanded and sharpened. It became permeated with race feelings. Increasingly, Anglo-Saxon culture seemed to depend on the persist-ence of a physical type. Nationalism was naturalized; and "race" in every sense came to imply a biological determinism.

Darwinism was a preliminary influence in the confusion of natural history with national history. By suggesting that a biological struggle underlies all of life, Darwinism encouraged Anglo-Saxon theorists to think of nations as species engaged in a desperate battle for survival. Toward the end of the nineteenth century, a number of patrician intellectuals turned the Anglo-Saxon tradition into a defensive attack on immigrants and an aggressive doctrine in foreign policy. They summoned Anglo-Saxon America to protect herself at home and to demonstrate her mastery abroad. Consequently, the victory of imperialism in 1898 gave racial nationalism an unprecedented vogue. Ideas that had been the property of an intellectual elite permeated public opinion.

Yet, race thinking still did not satisfactorily define the danger of the new immigration. Why would they or their children not respond favorably to the American environment? Indeed, what were the racial differences between southeastern Europeans and old-stock Americans? Darwinism was little help in answering these questions. Answers came only in the early twentieth century through new scientific and pseudoscientific ideas imported from Europe. The dazzling development of modern genetics around 1900 revealed principles of heredity that seemed entirely independent of environmental influences. Genetics inspired many scientists, led by Sir Francis Galton in England and Charles B. Davenport in the United States, to hope for the improvement of society by preventing the inheritance of bad traits. Under the banner of "eugenics," these biological reformers gave a presumably scientific validation to immigration restriction; for how could a nation protect and improve its genes without keeping out "degenerate breeding stock"?

Simultaneously, a new school of anthropology was reeducating Anglo-Saxon nationalists on the racial composition of European man. William Z.

Ripley's *The Races of Europe* (1899) conveyed to American readers a tripartite classification of white men recently developed by European scholars. The new race lines conformed not to national groups, but to physical types: the Nordics of northern Europe, the Alpines of central Europe, and the Mediterraneans of southern Europe. The latter two corresponded roughly to the new immigration. A number of writers combined the new anthropology with eugenics to produce a racist philosophy of history. Probably the most influential of these was Madison Grant, whose pretentious tract, *The Passing of the Great Race* (1916), delivered a solemn warning that the Nordics were making their last stand against the inferior races pouring in from southern and eastern Europe.

These ideas did not develop autonomously. Their importance was chiefly in giving clarity, definition, and some intellectual substance to fears and anxieties that were much more broadly based. The new racism seems to have reflected a wider tendency to make racial categories ever more rigid and impermeable; for this was also the period when lynchings and other measures to degrade and isolate southern Negroes reached an all-time high. Moreover, allegations of a racial peril in the new immigration rationalized an underlying concern about cultural homogeneity. At the deepest level, what impelled the restriction movement in the early decades of the twentieth century was the discovery that immigration was undermining the unity of American culture and threatening the accustomed dominance of a white Protestant people of northern European descent. The science of the day, together with America's traditional susceptibility to race feelings, made the language of race an impelling vehicle for thinking and talking about culture.

The mounting sense of danger—even dispossession—among millions of native-born white Protestants in the period 1910–30 is not hard to understand. A people whose roots were in the towns and farms of the early republic saw great cities coming more and more under the control of strangers whose speech and values were not their own. A people who unconsciously identified Protestantism with Americanism saw Catholic voters and urban bosses gaining control of the industrialized states. A people whose religion was already badly damaged by modern ideas saw the compensating rigors of their lifestyle flouted in the saloons and cabarets of a more expressive, hedonistic society. In reaction, the older America mounted a cultural counteroffensive through the prohibition movement, immigration restriction, and a sharpened racism.

At first the counteroffensive made headway slowly. Statewide prohibition took hold in the South after 1907 but spread widely in the Midwest only after 1912. In Congress an effort to pass the literacy test failed in 1906. No further attempt was made until six years later. Not until 1914 did the restriction movement regain the momentum it had in the mid-nineties. The main reason for this slow recovery was the generally optimistic spirit of the first years of the twentieth century—an optimism reflected in the progressives' absorption with internal reform and the industrialists' unconcern with foreign radicalism. Another constraint was imposed by the ballots of the new immigrants. By the early twentieth century their voting strength in northeastern industrial areas was attracting Republican as well as Democratic politicians. Republicans could sometimes offset Democratic strength in the big cities by appealing to Jews, Slavs, Italians, and French Canadians who fell out with the Irish. Consequently, the G.O.P. could not afford to identify itself with restriction as openly as it had in the nineties. The immigrants made use of their growing influence whenever restriction bills came up. No legislative issue was closer to their hearts, and congressional committees had to face troops of immigrant representatives whenever hearings opened. Jews generally took the lead; a National Liberal Immigration League under Jewish auspices did much to rally the opposition to the literacy bill in 1906 and in succeeding years.

Against this opposition, the restrictionist forces drew on three centers of strength. Patrician race thinkers supplied intellectual leadership. A stream of books and articles urged the eugenic implications of immigration policy and the danger of "race suicide." Meanwhile, a second group, the trade unions, lobbied energetically against the business apologists for immigration. The American Federation of Labor had moved far enough from its immigrant past by the early twentieth century to adopt an uncompromisingly restrictionist position. But its agitation did not count for much in actuality. The Congressmen who might have done labor's bidding were swayed by the stronger pressure of the immigrants; the big cities and industrial centers voted regularly and overwhelmingly against restriction.

Most of the support for restriction in Congress came from a third sector. From 1910 to 1952, the common people of the South and West formed a massive phalanx in favor of rigid legislation. This regional grouping represented a major shift in the alignment of forces. Initially, restriction sentiment had congealed in the Northeast, where the impact of immigration was most quickly and directly felt. In the 1890's the South and West had responded to the issue slowly and uncertainly. But in the twentieth century, while industrial and immigrant opposition thwarted northeastern restrictionists, the South and West emerged into the forefront of the movement. Appropriately, the political leadership passed from Henry Cabot Lodge of Massachusetts, who retired into the background after 1906, to more demagogic men like "Cotton Ed" Smith of South Carolina, Albert Johnson of Washington, and Pat McCarran of Nevada.

The essential explanation is to be found in racial and cultural defensiveness. The Deep South and the Far West, where the new regional lineup started, had long been the areas of most intense race feelings. Even without the sophisticated rationale of the new racial science, southerners and westerners could regard the unfamiliar peoples of southeastern Europe as less than completely white. Moreover, the Deep South and the western frontier had long been the sections with the most militant consciousness of having to fight to maintain a culture against external enemies. As racial lines hardened in the early twenti-eth century and the torrent of immigration mounted, community leaders from Seattle to Savannah raged at the great alien cities of the East and Midwest for polluting the purity of an Anglo-Saxon country and corrupting an individu-alistic, Protestant culture.

The first operative demonstration of the new racial emphasis came in 1905 with the outbreak of an anti-Japanese movement on the West Coast. Restric-tionist leaders sensed that the Japanese issue might enable them to get the kind of general legislation they wanted. As matters turned out, the immigration law enacted in 1907 began the process of Japanese exclusion but otherwise con-tained only administrative reforms. Nevertheless, it was significant that Asi-atic and European immigration were now, and would henceforth be, treated as different phases of a single question, not as entirely separate from one another. . . .

From 1911 (when the United States Immigration Commission made its report) to 1917, a general bill that included a watered-down literacy test was continually before an increasingly race-conscious Congress. Despite vocifer-ous support from the South and West, the bill did not become law until the eve of America's entry into the war. In even years, Congress stalled for fear of antagonizing the foreign vote in the November elections. In odd years, the bill passed by large majorities but succumbed to a presidential veto. Taft, in 1913, argued that America needed the immigrants' labor and could supply the literacy. Wilson, in 1915 and 1917, appealed to the cosmopolitan ideal of America as a haven for the oppressed.

Enacted finally over Wilson's second veto, the immigration law of 1917 was the first general and sweeping victory for the restrictionists in their thirty-five-year crusade. . . .

Though the whole law grew out of prewar trends, the First World War created the extra margin of support that carried it past a veto. And before long, the war generated a climate of opinion that made these restrictions seem perilously inadequate. Although the war temporarily deferred further action by interrupting migration automatically, the European holocaust unleashed the forces that brought immigration restriction to its historic culmi-nation.

The struggle with Germany stirred public opinion like a cyclone. America's isolation from European affairs, taken for granted in 1914, dissolved. Though statesmen tried to restore it after the war, henceforth it would have to be a deliberate contrivance rather than a natural condition. No longer could the American people feel providentially exempted from any international crisis. The new sense of danger came with such devastating force that it produced very little of the caution and restraint that had marked Roosevelt's Japanese policy. Instead, in every section of the country, men reacted toward all ethnic minorities as Californians had reacted toward the Japanese. Suddenly con-scious of the presence of millions of unassimilated people in their midst,

Americans quaked with fear of their potential disloyalty. Roosevelt himself signalized the change; for now he led the clamor for repressing any kind of divided loyalty.

The chief victims during the war years, the German-Americans, were soon thereafter restored to public favor, but the new emotional climate was not a passing phenomenon. Other minorities inherited the hysteria because it arose from a structural change in American nationalism. Known at the time as 100-percent Americanism, the new spirit demanded an unprecedented degree of national solidarity; loyalty and social conformity became virtually synony-mous. The slack and gradual processes of assimilation characteristic of the past no longer seemed tolerable. Thus the war destroyed most of what remained of the old faith in America's capacity to fuse all men into a "nation of nations." The development of social stratification had weakened that faith; racial and cultural cleavage had narrowed it; and international stresses dealt it a final blow.

Once immigration revived in 1920, stringent restrictions seemed instantly imperative. Outside of immigrant groups and a few sympathetic social work-ers, the question no longer concerned the desirability of restriction, but simply the proper degree and kind. Even big business conceded the value of a "selective" policy. Furthermore, the 100-per-cent-American impulse created by the war greatly intensified the racial attitudes evolved in earlier years. For the first time the demand for Japanese exclusion met a general sympathy in eastern opinion; and everywhere a large sector of both the public and the intelligentsia echoed Madison Grant's pleas for preserving Nordic America from the mongrel hordes of southeastern Europe.

Two laws resulted. The first of them, though frankly a makeshift designed to hold the gate while a permanent plan was worked out, established the underlying principle of national quotas based on the preexisting composition of the American population. The law of 1921 limited European immigration to 3 per cent of the number of foreign-born of each nationality present in the United States at the time of the last available census, that of 1910. This would hold the transatlantic current to a maximum of 350,000 and assign most of that total to northwestern Europe. Ethnic affiliation became the main determinant for admission to the United States.

Restrictionists remained dissatisfied, partly because of administrative snarls in the law but chiefly because it was not sufficiently restrictive. In fact, a good many people were pressing for complete suspension of immigration. After three years of bickering, a permanent law passed on a landslide of southern, western, and rural votes. The only opposition came from industrial areas in the Northeast and Midwest. Owing to considerations of Pan-Ameri-can goodwill and to the southwestern desire for Mexican "stoop-labor," the act of 1924 left immigration from the western hemisphere unrestricted; but it perfected the structure of Oriental exclusion and drastically tightened the quota system for the rest of the world.

PRIMARY SOURCES

The primary sources in this section illustrate nativism in the late nineteenth and early twentieth centuries. They also reflect developments that may have influenced perceptions of immigrants. As you analyze these sources, keep in mind the argument you just read about the role of racial thought as an "ideological weapon" to restrict immigration. One approach is to make a brief list of the most important immigrant characteristics that the primary sources mention, and then determine if nativists saw them as racial traits. What evidence is there that a racist ideology helped to define deeper fears among many Americans?

◆

SOURCE 2   Grant's book, which helped popularize turn-of-the-century theories about "race suicide," went through four editions by 1921. His discussion is based on the assumption that "Nordics" or northern Europeans were racially superior to other "racial stocks." What fears about immigrants does Grant reveal?

The Passing of the Great Race (1916)

MADISON GRANT

The prosperity that followed the [Civil War] attracted hordes of newcomers who were welcomed by the native Americans to operate factories, build railroads and fill up the waste spaces—"developing the country" it was called.

These new immigrants were no longer exclusively members of the Nordic race as were the earlier ones who came of their own impulse to improve their social conditions. The transportation lines advertised America as a land flowing with milk and honey and the European governments took the opportunity to unload upon careless, wealthy and hospitable America the sweepings of their jails and asylums. The result was that the new immigration . . . contained a large and increasing number of the weak, the broken and the mentally crippled of all races drawn from the lowest stratum of the Mediterranean basin and the Balkans, together with hordes of the wretched, submerged populations of the Polish Ghettos. Our jails, insane asylums and almshouses are filled with this human flotsam and the whole tone of American life, social, moral and political has been lowered and vulgarized by them.

With a pathetic and fatuous belief in the efficacy of American institutions and environment to reverse or obliterate immemorial hereditary tendencies,

Source: Excerpted from Madison Grant, *The Passing of the Great Race,* third edition (New York: Charles Scribner's Sons, 1916) as in Oscar Handlin, ed., *Immigration as a Factor in American History* (Englewood Cliffs: Prentice-Hall, Inc., 1959), pp. 184–185.

tal reasons. Biological laws tell us that certain divergent people will not mix or blend. The Nordics propagate themselves successfully. With other races, the outcome shows deterioration on both sides. Quality of mind and body suggests that observance of ethnic law is as great a necessity to a nation as immigration law. . . .

———————◆———————

SOURCE 4   By 1923, the Ku Klux Klan had attracted millions of members. Hiram Evans's article, published in the *North American Review* in 1926, offers some clues about the fears of many of them. Does his article support the main essay's contention that race was only a "vehicle" for expressing anxieties about culture?

The Klan's Fight for Americanism (1926)

HIRAM W. EVANS

. . . The Klan, therefore, has now come to speak for the great mass of Americans of the old pioneer stock. We believe that it does fairly and faithfully represent them, and our proof lies in their support. To understand the Klan, then, it is necessary to understand the character and present mind of the mass of old-stock Americans. The mass, it must be remembered, as distinguished from the intellectually mongrelized "Liberals."

These are, in the first place, a blend of various peoples of the so-called Nordic race, the race which, with all its faults, has given the world almost the whole of modern civilization. The Klan does not try to represent any people but these. . . .

[T]hese Nordic Americans for the last generation have found themselves increasingly uncomfortable, and finally deeply distressed. There appeared first confusion in thought and opinion, a groping and hesitancy about national affairs and private life alike, in sharp contrast to the clear, straightforward purposes of our earlier years. There was futility in religion, too, which was in many ways even more distressing. Presently we began to find that we were dealing with strange ideas; policies that always sounded well but somehow always made us still more uncomfortable.

Finally came the moral breakdown that has been going on for two decades. One by one all our traditional moral standards went by the boards or were so disregarded that they ceased to be binding. The sacredness of our Sabbath, of our homes, of chastity, and finally even of our right to teach our own children

Source: Hiram W. Evans, "Klan's Fight for Americanism," from *North American Review* (March/April/May 1926), pp. 37–63. Reprinted by permission of the University of Northern Iowa.

in our own schools fundamental facts and truths were torn away from us. Those who maintained the old standards did so only in the face of constant ridicule. . . .

One more point about the present attitude of the old-stock American: he has revived and increased his long-standing distrust of the Roman Catholic Church. It is for this that the native Americans, and the Klan as their leader, are most often denounced as intolerant and prejudiced. . . .

There are three of these great racial instincts, vital elements in both the historic and the present attempts to build an America which shall fulfill the aspirations and justify the heroism of the men who made the nation. These are the instincts of loyalty to the white race, to the traditions of America, and to the spirit of Protestantism, which has been an essential part of Americanism ever since the days of Roanoke and Plymouth Rock. They are condensed into the Klan slogan: "Native, white, Protestant supremacy."

SOURCE 5   The author of this article, published in *The Independent* magazine, asked several Gentiles why anti-Semitism existed. What stereotypes are evident in the responses? How do the stereotypes here compare to group stereotypes in the other sources?

Because You're a Jew (1908)

It was not easy to get frank testimony. Merchants, officials, hotel men, did not care to speak out. When they spoke at all they stipulated that their names should not be mentioned. It was only by putting many testimonies together that one was enabled to get the Gentile side of the case, which may be fairly presented in this manner:

"We have no prejudice against the Jews. We do dislike them but it is dislike based on knowledge and evidence which is so widespread and so general that it has resulted in an instinctive dislike. It is because of qualities which are manifested by Jews. The dishonest among them are out of all proportion to their numbers. No other people so persistently, shrewdly, cunningly, constantly, skim the very verge of crime, and many go over the verge." . . .

"There is another thing against the Jew. They are too prosperous. Where they contest they win. Five or six years ago, after the French Ball, there was a fight and the victor stood over the body of his antagonist and proudly proclaimed: 'The Jew is always on top.' The fact that the man whom he had defeated was also a Jew did not affect the truth he had uttered. The Jew is

Source: Lewis H. Carlson and George A. Colburn, *In Their Place: White America Defines Her Minorities, 1850–1950* (New York: John Wiley & Sons, Inc., 1972), pp. 255, 256–257.

winning everywhere. By fair means or by foul means he wins. He has the commerce of the city in his hands now, and the signs on Broadway make one think of the main street in New Jerusalem and make Gentiles curse Titus and wish that he had never been born. Why couldn't he leave them alone in Judea? Perhaps he might have stayed there? As to the possibility of a great Zionist movement, it's too good to be true!

"One tentacle of the Hebrew octopus has caught our newspapers now, and we also see Jews running our theaters and giving us a drama that never before was so low. We see the Hebrew octopus seizing one enterprise after the other, and we can't stop it. They are beating us. . . ."

"Two or three Jews at a summer resort utterly spoil the place for the Gentiles. The first thing that the Jew does when he gets in a hotel is to bribe the head waiter. He must have the best steak, the best of everything, and be served first, and he is so persistent, so acute, so eager and so willing to resort to anything to get his way that he does get his way and makes every less strenuous person about him so uncomfortable that they'd sooner leave the place than contend. If he sits at a table near you and you have secured something especially good, his greedy eyes boring into you utterly spoil your repast. If you give your children new toys and send them out to play you will find in half an hour that the Jew children have the new toys while your youngsters are looking on. The young Jews are not violent, but they get what they want by reason of their greater appetite for it. They're insatiable and can only be repressed by force. . . ."

"How foolish, then, to associate with these people when there can by no means be any real assimilation."

◆

SOURCE 6   Stratton-Porter's novels were popular with young readers in the early twentieth century. In this selection from *Her Father's Daughter,* Linda advises a fellow student at a Los Angeles high school how to overtake a Japanese-American student at the head of the class. How does the fear of the Japanese compare to the fear of Jews in the previous source?

Her Father's Daughter (1921)

GENE STRATTON-PORTER

An angry red rushed to the boy's face. It was an irritating fact that in the senior class of that particular Los Angeles high school a Japanese boy stood at the head. This was embarrassing to every senior.

Source: Lewis H. Carlson and George A. Colburn, *In Their Place: White America Defines Her Minorities, 1850–1950* (New York: John Wiley and Sons, Inc., 1972), pp. 225–227.

Shortly after this, Sweet Linda is discussing the problem with a fellow student:

"I am getting at the fact that a boy as big as you and as strong as you and with as good brain and your opportunities has allowed a little brown Jap to cross the Pacific Ocean and in a totally strange country to learn a language foreign to him, and with the same books and the same chances, to beat you at your game. You and every other boy in your class ought to be thoroughly ashamed of yourselves. Before I would let a Jap, either boy or girl, lead in my class, I would give up going to school and go out and see if I could beat him growing lettuce and spinach." . . .

"For God's sake, Linda, tell me how I can beat that little coconut-headed Jap."

Linda slammed down the lid to the lunch box. Her voice was smooth and even but there was battle in her eyes and she answered decisively: "Well, you can't beat him calling him names. There is only one way on God's footstool that you can beat him. You can't beat him legislating against him. You can't beat him boycotting him. You can't beat him with any tricks. He is as sly as a cat and he has got a whole bag full of tricks of his own, and he has proved right here in Los Angeles that he has got a brain that is hard to beat. All you can do, and be a man commendable to your own soul, is to take his subject and put your brain on it to such purpose that cut pigeon wings around him. . . . There is just one way in all this world that we can beat Eastern civilization and all that it intends to do to us eventually. The white man has dominated by his color so far in the history of the world, but it is written in the Books that when the men of colour acquire our culture and combine it with their own methods of living and rate of production, they are going to bring forth greater numbers, better equipped for the battle of life, than we are. When they have got our last secret, constructive or scientific, they will take it, and living in a way that we would not, reproducing in numbers we don't, they will beat us at any game we start, if we don't take warning while we are in the ascendency, and keep there." . . .

"I'll do anything in the world if you will only tell me how," said Donald. "Maybe you think it isn't grinding me and humiliating me properly. Maybe you think Father and Mother haven't warned me. Maybe you think Mary Louise isn't secretly ashamed of me. How can I beat him, Linda?" . . .

"I have been watching pretty sharply," she said. "Take them as a race, as a unit—of course there are exceptions, there always are—but the great body of them are mechanical. They are imitative. They are not developing anything great of their own in their own country. They are spreading all over the world and carrying home sewing machines and threshing machines and automobiles and cantilever bridges and submarines and aeroplanes—anything from eggbeaters to telescopes. They are not creating one single thing. They are not missing imitating everything that the white man can do anywhere else on earth. They are just like the Germans so far as that is concerned." . . .

Donald started up and drew a deep breath.

"Well, some job I call that," he said. "Who do you think I am, The Almighty?"

"No," said Linda quietly, "you are not. You are merely His son, created in his own image, like Him, according to the Book, and you have got to your advantage the benefit of all that has been learned down through the ages. . . . All Oka Sayye knows how to do is to learn the lesson in his book perfectly, and he is 100 per cent. I have told you what you must do to add the plus, and you can do it if you are that boy I take you for. People have talked about the 'yellow peril' till it's got to be a meaningless phrase. Somebody must wake up to the realization that it's the deadliest peril that ever has menaced white civilization. Why shouldn't you have your hand in such wonderful work?"

◆

SOURCE 7   Speeches by members of Congress often reflected popular attitudes toward immigrants. In this selection, Representative Lucian W. Parish, a Democrat from Texas, compares old and new immigrants. How does he compare them? Look for evidence of anxieties about postwar American society.

A Congressman Calls for Restriction (1921)

We should stop immigration entirely until such a time as we can amend our immigration laws and so write them that hereafter no one shall be admitted except he be in full sympathy with our Constitution and laws, willing to declare himself obedient to our flag, and willing to release himself from any obligations he may owe to the flag of the country from which he came.

It is time that we act now, because within a few short years the damage will have been done. The endless tide of immigration will have filled our country with a foreign and unsympathetic element. Those who are out of sympathy with our Constitution and the spirit of our Government will be here in large numbers, and the true spirit of Americanism left us by our fathers will gradually become poisoned by this uncertain element.

The time once was when we welcomed to our shores the oppressed and downtrodden people from all the world, but they came to us because of

Source: Congressional Record, April 20, 1921, p. 450.

oppression at home and with the sincere purpose of making true and loyal American citizens, and in truth and in fact they did adapt themselves to our ways of thinking and contributed in a substantial sense to the progress and development that our civilization has made. But that time has passed now; new and strange conditions have arisen in the countries over there; new and strange doctrines are being taught. The Governments of the Orient are being overturned and destroyed, and anarchy and bolshevism are threatening the very foundation of many of them, and no one can foretell what the future will bring to many of those countries of the Old World now struggling with these problems.

Our country is a self-sustaining country. It has taught the principles of real democracy to all the nations of the earth; its flag has been the synonym of progress, prosperity, and the preservation of the rights of the individual, and there can be nothing so dangerous as for us to allow the undesirable foreign element to poison our civilization and thereby threaten the safety of the institutions that our forefathers have established for us.

Now is the time to throw about this country the most stringent immigration laws and keep from our shores forever those who are not in sympathy with the American ideas. It is the time now for us to act and act quickly, because every month's delay increases the difficulty in which we find ourselves and renders the problems of government more difficult of solution. We must protect ourselves from the poisonous influences that are threatening the very foundation of the Governments of Europe; we must see to it that those who come here are loyal and true to our Nation and impress upon them that it means something to have the privileges of American citizenship. We must hold this country true to the American thought and the American ideals. . . .

SOURCE 8   As you examine this cartoon, pay attention to the fears about immigrants that it reflects. What developments after World War I reinforced the fear of immigrants?

The Bootleggers (1925)

Source: From *The Independent,* March 14, 1925. Courtesy Harvard College Library.

Tables on Unemployment and Immigrant Occupations

Do these tables provide evidence for additional reasons why many Americans, including organized labor, supported immigration restriction after World War I?

◆

SOURCE 9

Immigrant Occupation Groups, 1899–1924

Year	Total	Professional, technical, and kindred workers	Farmers and farm managers	Managers, officials, and proprietors, exc. farm	Clerical, sales, and kindred workers
1924	706,896	20,926	20,320	15,668	27,373
1923	522,919	13,926	12,503	12,086	17,931
1922	309,556	9,696	7,676	9,573	10,055
1921	805,228	12,852	22,282	18,286	18,922
1920	430,001	10,540	12,192	9,654	14,054
1919	141,132	5,261	3,933	4,247	6,524
1918	110,618	3,529	2,583	3,940	4,239
1917	295,403	7,499	7,764	8,329	10,554
1916	298,826	9,024	6,840	8,725	9,907
1915	326,700	11,453	6,518	10,728	9,377
1914	1,218,480	13,454	14,442	21,903	17,933
1913	1,197,892	12,552	13,180	19,094	15,173
1912	838,172	10,913	7,664	14,715	13,782
1911	878,587	11,275	9,709	15,416	14,723
1910	1,041,570	9,689	11,793	14,731	12,219
1909	751,786	7,603	8,914	11,562	8,467
1908	782,870	10,504	7,720	16,410	11,523
1907	1,285,349	12,016	13,476	20,132	12,735
1906	1,100,735	13,015	15,288	23,515	12,226
1905	1,026,499	12,582	18,474	27,706	12,759
1904	812,870	12,195	4,507	26,914	11,055
1903	857,046	6,999	13,363	15,603	7,226
1902	648,743	2,937	8,168	9,340	3,836
1901	487,918	2,665	3,035	8,294	3,197
1900	448,572	2,392	5,433	7,216	2,870
1899	311,715	1,972	3,973	6,815	2,473

Source: "Occupations," *Historical Statistics of the United States: Colonial Times to 1957* (Washington, D.C.: U.S. Bureau of the Census, 1960), p. 60.

Craftsmen, foremen, operatives, and kindred workers	Private household workers	Service workers, exc. private household	Farm laborers and foremen	Laborers, exc. farm and mine	No occu- pation
123,923	51,680	29,261	27,492	112,344	277,909
87,899	52,223	22,244	25,905	86,617	191,585
40,309	44,531	12,340	10,529	33,797	131,050
109,710	102,478	24,298	32,400	162,859	301,141
55,991	37,197	18,487	15,257	83,496	173,133
21,671	6,277	11,571	4,412	18,922	58,314
17,501	7,816	6,367	4,538	15,142	44,963
38,660	31,885	11,784	22,328	52,182	104,418
36,086	29,258	10,989	26,250	56,981	104,766
45,591	39,774	11,976	24,723	49,620	116,940
149,515	144,409	19,621	288,053	228,935	320,215
139,091	140,218	17,609	320,105	223,682	297,188
107,893	116,529	13,580	184,154	137,872	231,070
128,717	107,153	11,051	176,003	158,518	246,022
121,847	96,658	8,977	288,745	216,909	260,002
75,730	64,568	5,849	171,310	176,490	221,293
106,943	89,942	10,367	138,844	147,940	242,677
169,394	121,587	13,578	323,854	293,868	304,709
156,902	115,984	10,439	239,125	228,781	285,460
159,442	125,473	5,849	142,187	290,009	232,018
133,748	104,937	6,400	85,850	212,572	214,692
110,644	92,686	11,482	77,518	321,824	199,701
71,131	69,913	6,298	80,562	243,399	153,159
57,346	42,027	5,352	54,753	162,563	148,686
54,793	40,311	4,406	31,949	164,261	134,941
38,608	34,120	4,580	17,343	92,452	109,379

SOURCE 10

Unemployment Rates, 1900–1924

Year	Unemployed*	Percent of civilian labor force
1924	2,440	5.5
1923	1,380	3.2
1922	3,220	7.6
1921	5,010	11.9
1920	1,670	4.0
1919	950	2.3
1918	560	1.4
1917	1,920	4.8
1916	1,920	4.8
1915	3,840	9.7
1914	3,110	8.0
1913	1,680	4.4
1912	1,960	5.2
1911	2,290	6.2
1910	2,150	5.9
1909	1,870	5.2
1908	2,960	8.5
1907	600	1.8
1906	280	0.8
1905	1,000	3.1
1904	1,490	4.8
1903	800	2.6
1902	800	2.7
1901	710	2.4
1900	1,420	5.0

*In thousands.

Source: "Unemployment," *Historical Statistics of the United States: Colonial Times to 1957* (Washington, D.C.: U.S. Bureau of the Census, 1960), p. 73.

CONCLUSION

Like the newcomers sailing through the Golden Gate, steaming by the Statue of Liberty, or crossing the Rio Grande, historians often find themselves strangers in the land. As we saw in the last chapter, houses and furniture in the past were often different from ours. More important, the ideological "filter"—the complex of beliefs, values, fears, prejudices, and interests that people in the past used to make sense of their world—was also different from ours. Because these differences make the past a foreign place for us, we cannot expect to get very far without understanding what people thought—their ideology. Although that alone may not make their motives clear, no explanation of motivation is complete without it. And when historians know the motives of people in the past they can better comprehend historical causes—the subject of the next chapter.

FURTHER READING

Leonard Dinnerstein and David Reimers, *Ethnic Americans and Assimilation* (New York: Harper and Row, 1975).

Maldwyn A. Jones, *American Immigration* (Chicago: University of Chicago Press, 1960).

Alan M. Kraut, *The Huddled Masses: The Immigrant in American Society, 1880–1921* (Arlington Heights, Ill.: Harlan Davidson, 1982).

Wayne Moquin, ed., *Makers of America—Hyphenated Americans, 1914–1924* (Chicago: Encyclopaedia Britannica Educational Corp., 1971).

Dale Steiner, *Of Thee We Sing: Immigrants and American History* (San Diego: Harcourt Brace Jovanovich, 1987).

NOTE

1. Maldwyn Allen Jones, *American Immigration* (Chicago: University of Chicago Press, 1960), p. 177.

The Problem of Historical Causation:
The Election of 1928

The documents in this chapter relate to the causes of Herbert Hoover's victory over Al Smith in the 1928 presidential election.

Secondary Source

Primary Sources

$\mathscr{T}$he election in 1928 promised to be as dull and forgettable as the other presidential contests of the 1920s. In 1920, the likeable poker-playing Ohio Republican Warren Harding offered the electorate "not nostrums but normalcy" and swamped the lackluster Ohio Governor James Cox. Four years later Calvin Coolidge said almost nothing during the campaign. The Republicans virtually ignored Democratic candidate John W. Davis, a dignified corporation lawyer, and spent their time attacking Progressive Party candidate Robert LaFollette as a "socialist." When it was over, "Silent Cal" rolled up more votes than Davis and LaFollette combined. Then in 1928 the Republican favorite was Herbert Hoover. During the campaign he delivered eight leaden campaign addresses in a monotone voice, his eyes rarely raised from the text. In the other corner stood the Democratic underdog, New York Governor Al Smith. Smith campaigned with gusto, but his campaign also lacked punch. He attempted to counter the Republican theme of prosperity, for instance, by having a General Motors vice president run his campaign. Pointing to Hoover's wartime efforts to feed Europe and to the prospect of four more years of "Republican prosperity," most observers predicted a Hoover landslide.

The differences between the candidates turned this campaign into one of the most acrimonious in American history. Born on New York's rough-and-tumble Lower East Side, Smith was a "wet" on Prohibition, a Catholic, and a product of Tammany Hall, the New York Democratic party machine. He spoke in a heavy East-Side accent, often ungrammatically. Befitting his image as a big city politician, he was fond of derbies, cigars, and a crowd. In contrast, Hoover advocated rugged individualism and traditional values. Born in America's rural heartland, he was a "dry" on Prohibition, a Protestant, and a Stanford graduate. His speeches were laden with abstract ideas. He detested backslapping and even wore a starched collar. Although Hoover and Smith hardly bloodied each other in the campaign, many Americans were impassioned by these obvious differences. Today historians are still intrigued by the 1928 election because of the emotions that it aroused and the divisions in American society that it reveals.

SETTING

For nearly seven decades, historians have sparred over the causes of Hoover's victory in 1928. Some argue that Hoover symbolized traditional values, while Al Smith represented ethnic and cultural diversity and "cosmopolitan" values. In this view, this election contest reflected a cultural fault line dividing "old" and "new" America, country and city, and native-born Americans and immigrants. Other historians concede that the election reflected a conflict over values, but insist that it was really a referendum on alcohol. They contend that the main reason for Hoover's victory was the candidates' stands on prohibition. Still other historians argue that religion was the main fault line in 1928. In this interpretation, anti-Catholicism rather than a conflict between new and old values was the dominant cause of the campaign's bitterness and of Smith's defeat. Meanwhile, some historians maintain that the economy determined the election's outcome. They point to the New Era's economic expansion and to the widespread belief that Republican policies were responsible for never-ending prosperity. As one assessment of the 1928 election concluded: "The Democrats probably would have lost with any nominee—even a polished Protestant of English stock, college-bred, farm-domiciled, bone-dry, Boston-accented, and descended from old Plymouth Rock."[1]

Such conflicting views make it tempting to conclude that Hoover's election can be explained by combining all these factors. That approach avoids a monocausal explanation, one of the fallacies historians sometimes commit. Because few historical events or developments have a single cause, the ability to see multiple influences is one mark of a critical approach. Yet there is also a danger in this approach. Because historical causes rarely exert equal weight, historians must also be discriminating. Otherwise their histories lose their explanatory power.

Conclusions about Hoover's election are good examples of the relationship between the ability to discriminate and the power to explain. Scholars who trace this campaign's passions to a cultural division between an "older" rural, provincial society and a "newer" urban, cosmopolitan one see this election as a significant turning point in the nation's political history. Although Smith lost, they point to new urban voters—often Jewish and Catholic immigrants and their children—who began to vote Democratic. Joined by labor union members and African-Americans, these voters formed a powerful coalition that would soon elect Franklin Roosevelt president and keep Democrats in power for years to come. Thus these scholars see the harsh attacks of the campaign as the birth pangs of a new political order. For them, the 1928 election illustrates that American society is not riven by deep discord because its political system accommodates numerous outside groups.

On the other hand, historians who attribute the campaign's bitterness and Hoover's election to religious and racial bigotry see little evidence of accommodation to outsiders. They argue that this election points to the existence of deep-seated prejudice, not the birth of a new political alignment. For them, the main cause of Hoover's victory reflects deep and persistent divisions within American society.

INVESTIGATION

The sources in this chapter deal with the issues in the bitter 1928 election. Your main task is to determine the most important reasons for Hoover's victory and what they tell us about America in the "New Era." Carefully evaluate the main essay's conclusions about Hoover's victory and what it reveals about American society, and then determine what the primary sources suggest about the reasons for the election's outcome. As you evaluate the sources in this chapter, answer the following main questions:

1. **According to the main essay, did one factor override all others in determining the outcome of this election, or were various factors somehow interrelated?** Were some of the reasons for voting actually substitutes for concealed reasons?

2. **Do the primary sources support or contradict the main essay's conclusions about why Hoover won?** What do they reveal as the most important reasons for Hoover's victory? Were the causes of the campaign's animosity the same as the causes of Hoover's victory?

3. **Could Smith have conducted his campaign in a way that could have brought him victory?** If so, how?

Before you begin, read the sections in your textbook on the 1920s, especially on politics. They will provide useful background that will help you assess the sources in this chapter.

SECONDARY SOURCE

◆

SOURCE 1   In this selection, Allan Lichtman takes issue with the views of many historians regarding the Smith-Hoover contest. Lichtman uses a statistical technique known as multivariate analysis to discover the primary characteristics that divided Hoover's and Smith's supporters. Historians often employ this type of analysis to assess the influence on behavior of such separate factors as religion, race, ethnicity, gender, or place of residence. Catholics, for instance, may have been more likely to vote for Smith than for Hoover. But if they were also more likely to be urban residents or immigrants, a simple comparison of how Catholics and Protestants voted may reflect influences other than religion. Multivariate analysis attempts to weigh the influence of each variable. Using this method, Lichtman concludes that one factor was more important than any other in explaining voters' behavior in 1928. Note Lichtman's explanation for Hoover's victory and his conclusion about the basic division in the electorate. What is his evidence regarding the causes of each? Does it support his conclusions? What role does Lichtman attribute to an "ideology of prosperity" in determining the outcome of this election? Finally, look for his view of Hoover and whether he blames Hoover for the Republican party's effort to exploit prejudice for political gain.

Prejudice and the Election of 1928 (1979)

ALLAN J. LICHTMAN

For residents of America's West Coast, suspense created by the presidential contest of 1928 scarcely outlasted an early dinner on election night. At his home in Palo Alto, California, Herbert Hoover, the Republican nominee, gathered with a small group of friends to follow the election returns. By 7:30, Pacific Coast time, the candidate's own carefully kept scorecard already showed a majority of electoral votes safely in the Republican column. Hoover flashed a rare grin, then retired to the privacy of his study, while his guests savored films of his campaign speeches. About an hour and forty-five minutes later, they were interrupted by the arrival of a twenty-seven-word telegram of concession from Al Smith, the Democratic candidate.

The Wednesday morning papers reported that Hoover probably would garner about 60 percent of the popular vote and over 80 percent of the electoral returns. They noted that the most tempestuous campaign in recent memory had produced a record tally, large enough to net the defeated Al Smith more popular votes than any previous candidate, regardless of party. Prepared for a Republican triumph, journalists readily supplied instant explanations. Some commentators stressed the nation's devotion to the GOP, the achievements of the Coolidge administration, the booming national economy, the qualifications of Herbert Hoover, and his dazzling record as secretary of commerce. Other scribes pointed to the reaction against Al Smith—he was not only the first Catholic nominated by a major party, but also an opponent of prohibition and a leader of Tammany Hall, the notorious Democratic machine of New York County. A few observers focused on dissension within the ranks of Democrats and Smith's allegedly blundering campaign. . . .

Interest in the presidential election of 1928 has continued despite general agreement that the Democrats had no chance to score an upset and turn the dominant party out of power. In this view, Herbert Hoover, the legatee of Republican prosperity and a formidable candidate in his own right, would have thrashed any nominee of the Democratic party. Given the health of the national economy, scholars have likewise concluded that the class standing of voters was not a central determinant of their choice between the two candidates. Attention has centered instead on social and cultural divisions engendered by the presidential contest and on its meaning for later shifts in the balance of political power.

Although they have eliminated economic class as a primary concern, historians have been reluctant to assess the independent importance of other

Source: Excerpted from *Prejudice and the Old Politics: The Presidential Election of 1928,* by Allan Lichtman. Copyright © 1979 by the University of North Carolina Press. Used by permission of the publisher.

potential cleavages within the electorate. The main line of scholarship, . . . suggests that the encounter between Hoover and Smith tapped a fault line in the structure of American society. Pressure on the fault neatly cleaved the polity into two sets of antagonists: Catholic-wet-foreign-urban Americans versus Protestant-dry-native-rural Americans. Voters on each side of the divide responded to multiple cues suggested by each candidate. Democrats who turned against Smith, for example, did not separate fear of his Catholicism from revulsion to his wetness or from alarm at his associations with the metropolis and the immigrant masses. To isolate particular variables would be to destroy the unity of the images projected by the two candidates and to obscure the division of America into two discrete cultures.

An interpretation combining sources of electoral cleavage into a single dimension of conflict appeals to our sense that behavior springs from a plurality of motives that cannot properly be teased apart. To insist that several factors interacted to sway the voters of 1928 seems more sophisticated and subtle than to isolate a single factor—be it religion, prohibition, or ethnic heritage. For historians relying on traditional methods, a unidimensional model becomes a way around the problem of determining the independent effects of attributes that obviously are correlated with one another. . . .

This interpretation of the struggle between Smith and Hoover also conforms to a synthesis of social conflict in which strife between an "old" and a "new" America culminated in the 1920s. The old America, located squarely in the countryside, was peopled by Protestants of native stock. Its denizens sought to defend America's traditional values and beliefs from the alien culture and religion of the immigrant and from the cosmopolitan ethos of the city. According to this account, the boundary between the two Americas was formed by distinctions between the nation's rural and urban traditions. A contemporary observation by Walter Lippmann is the favorite clincher of those endorsing this conclusion: "The Governor's more hasty friends show an intolerance when they believe that Al Smith is the victim of purely religious prejudice. Quite apart even from the severe opposition of the prohibitionists, the objection to Tammany, the sectional objection to New York, there is an opposition to Smith which is as authentic, and, it seems to me, as poignant as his support. It is inspired by the feeling that the clamorous life of the city should not be acknowledged as the American ideal." . . .

Historians who maintain that two American traditions collided in 1928 identify this election as one of those rare turning points in national history that mark the end of one political era and the beginning of another. Ironically, the resounding triumph of Herbert Hoover was the denouement of an age dominated by the old America. Samuel Lubell, in his seminal work *The Future of American Politics*, wrote in 1952, "Before the Roosevelt Revolution there was an Al Smith Revolution. . . . Smith's defeat in 1928, rather than Roosevelt's 1932 victory, marked off the arena in which today's politics are being fought. . . . It was Smith who first slashed through the traditional alignments that had held so firmly since the Civil War, clearing the way for the more comprehensive realignment which came later." The presidential election of 1928 thus becomes a prelude to the New Deal coalition that dominated American politics in the next decade and survived innumerable predictions of its imminent demise. Al Smith, this view suggests, represented the rising underclass of American politics—the Catholic, foreign-stock workers who thronged to the nation's great cities. Although defeated in 1928, the Happy Warrior of New York is said to have generated alliances and antagonisms whose influence is still felt. Following his bid for the presidency, the values of rural America would no longer control the political agenda or guide the cultural life of the nation. . . .

The present study disputes these overlapping interpretations of the encounter between Al Smith and Herbert Hoover. It denies that prosperity per se guaranteed a Hoover victory, that the class standing of voters had little effect on their choice of candidates, or that voter reaction to social issues can be fused into a single dimension of conflict between two American cultures. . . .

Senator George W. Norris of Nebraska bolted his party in 1928 to support Al Smith. He later reflected that "close friends of years standing were so bitter" about his defection "that some of them would have delighted to cast me into the bottomless pit if the opportunity had presented itself." Religion, Norris concluded, "was the dominant thing that brought about this bitterness. Religious grievances always do bring bitterness—unreasonable, illogical bitterness. Prohibition brings pointed disagreement, but men do not turn their love of years into hatred because their friends do not agree with them regarding it." Religion was undoubtedly the most sensitive emotional issue of 1928. The nomination of a Catholic by one of the nation's two major parties rekindled religious strife in the United States. Conflicts over the legitimacy of parochial education still smoldered in 1928; the Scopes "monkey" trial had ended just three years before; and at its zenith in 1924, the Ku Klux Klan had claimed several million members. In 1928, Americans avidly followed every twist and turn of what the media dubbed the "religious issue."

Despite the storm and stress produced by religion during the campaign, most historians have not considered it an especially significant influence on the vote for president. . . .

Contradicting these conclusions, the presidential tally of 1928 mirrors profound differences in the preferences of Catholic and Protestant voters. For all 2,058 counties outside the South, [the table below] displays the influence of the percentage of Catholic residents on various measures of voter choice, when controlling for the influence of other variables included in the regression analysis. The coefficients of the table disclose that an increase in the percentage of Catholics from one county to another produces a substantial increase in Al Smith's percentage of . . . the presidential vote cast in each county. . . .

Influence of Percentage of Catholics on
Measures of the Vote for President:
2,058 Counties (in percent)*

	Regression Coefficient b
Dem 1928	.37
Rep 1928 total	−.12

*Controlling for percentages of Urban, Foreign
stock, Owners, Negro, Female, Under 35, Pop
change, Jewish, Prot church, and for Economic
status.

A coefficient of .37, . . . obtained for the influence of a county's percentage
of Catholics on Al Smith's percentage of the presidential vote, would indicate
that for every increase of 1 percent in a county's percentage of Catholics, its
percentage of Smith voters should increase by .37 percent, controlling for the
effects of such variables as the percentage of home owners and the percentage
of urban dwellers. Assume, for example, that two counties were identical in
demographic composition; if one has 1 percent more Catholics, it should have
.37 percent more Democratic voters; if it has 10 percent more Catholics, it
should have 3.7 percent more Democratic voters; if it has 100 percent more
Catholics, it should have 37 percent more Democratic voters. Thus a regression
coefficient of .37 means that when adjusting for the influence of other explanatory variables, the percentage of Catholics voting for Al Smith is 37 percentage
points greater than the percentage of non-Catholics opting for his candidacy.

But a historian need not travel so far afield for survey evidence relevant to
deciding how religion affected voting decisions in 1928. The results of small-
group surveys roughly contemporary with the election also sustain the conclusion that religion skewed the vote for president in 1928. Moreover, when,
in 1940, the Gallup Poll asked a national cross section of likely voters if they
would support a qualified Catholic candidate for president, 33 percent said
they would not.

Pundits from both parties also testified to the importance of religious
differences in 1928. . . . Many Democratic politicians insisted that anti-Catholicism robbed Smith of a likely victory in their states and localities. . . .

Several of the Democratic leaders writing to Roosevelt expressed shock at
finding that religious opposition to Smith was not confined to strains of
Protestantism traditionally associated with anti-Catholic agitation. W. H.
O'Keefe, for example, editor of the *Democratic-Sun* of Greenville, Tennessee,
was amazed to find religious prejudice surfacing among members of the more
tolerant Protestant sects: "It is our conviction that Governor Smith's prohibi-

tion views cut no ice in his defeat, that the objection was solely on account of his religion. This fact was verified through thousands of instances. . . . I was literally knocked flat to find that Episcopalians, of whom I had expected better things, were just as prejudiced and bitter as any Methodist or Baptist could be." . . .

Public statements by Republican politicians, including their presidential candidate, seem to reflect a strategic decision to risk only mild repudiations of religious bigotry, while shifting the onus of intolerance to the opposition party. In his acceptance speech, Herbert Hoover endorsed religious tolerance in the following terms: "In this land dedicated to tolerance we still find outbreaks of intolerance. I come of Quaker stock. My ancestors were persecuted for their beliefs. Here they sought and found religious freedom. By blood and conviction I stand for religious tolerance both in act and in spirit. The glory of our American ideals is the right of every man to worship God according to the dictates of his own conscience." Although Hoover may have been personally tolerant, this general statement only minimally expressed the political necessity to oppose religious bigotry. . . .

Policies of the Republican campaign raise further questions about the sincerity of Herbert Hoover's attempt to dampen the flames of intolerance. Despite the lack of detailed records relating the closed-door activities of Republican strategists, some conclusions can be extracted from available information. The evidence suggests that Hoover and the Republican leadership did not shrink from sponsoring personal attacks on Al Smith and probably took part in efforts to gain anti-Catholic votes.

Although Hoover insisted that the national leadership of the GOP should not be associated with personal innuendo directed against Smith, he did not hesitate to vilify the governor through ostensibly independent spokesmen. Hoover, for instance, ordered that a twelve-thousand-word pamphlet on Tammany Hall prepared by the Republican National Committee be issued instead by a group of bolting Democrats. According to Henry J. Allen, publicity director of the Republican campaign, Hoover had decided that "it would be better to let the attack on Tammany originate elsewhere." Similarly, at Hoover's direction, the national committee provided information and encouragement for William Allen White's attempt to portray Smith as a friend of gambling and prostitution. Publicly, the committee disclaimed "any relationship between the Republican National Committee and the charges levelled against him by William Allen White." . . . . White, however, had specifically informed Hoover of his success at "pulling Smith over the first pages by his pants." White disclosed in his private correspondence that "I have a letter from Hoover written after my first blast obviously approving it. . . ."

The national committee also sponsored the political sorties of Mabel Walker Willebrandt, assistant attorney general for prohibition enforcement. In 1928, Willebrandt was the highest ranking woman official in the executive branch of the federal government. She had been recommended for placement in the attorney general's office in 1921 by Senator Hiram Johnson of California. After becoming an assistant attorney general, Willebrandt joined forces with Herbert Hoover, helping to manage his campaign for the Republican nomination and serving as a political operative in both official and unofficial capacities. In the summer of 1928, for example, Willebrandt traveled to Mississippi to obtain a federal indictment for corruption against Percy Howard, one of the black Republican leaders Hoover sought to purge from the GOP. Some male politicians felt that the assistant attorney general's ambition and political activism were unseemly for a member of her sex. In 1928, her erstwhile benefactor Senator Johnson wrote that "she is the perfect type of woman as I have found woman in politics—ambitious, mad for publicity, bitter, deceitful, utterly without principle and wholly treacherous." During the 1928 campaign, Willebrandt appeared before Protestant church groups raising a hue and cry against the election of Al Smith. Although she indicted Smith for his wetness rather than his Catholicism, she reviled the governor for cooperating with the underworld, flouting federal law, and nullifying the Constitution. . . .

Anti-Catholic attitudes were not manufactured during the presidential election of 1928. That the campaign newly awakened American Protestants to the menace posed by a Roman Catholic president is unlikely. Rather, hostility to Catholics became politically salient as a consequence of Al Smith's nomination. Anti-Catholicism in the United States was a widespread phenomenon with multiple causes; it was neither the product of a single viewpoint, nor confined to dry, rural, native-stock Protestants. The fading of religious agitation after the 1928 contest did not herald a victory for the spirit of religious tolerance, but only an ebbing of the salience of anti-Catholicism for the behavior of most Americans. . . .

Although accounts of the presidential election do not emphasize the behavior of black voters or strategies followed on racial issues, both parties ardently played the politics of race in 1928, and ripples of political change spread across black communities. Seizing the opportunity offered by a Democratic candidate who was both Catholic and wet, Herbert Hoover sought to purge the black leadership of his party's southern wing and fashion a lily-white organization that could compete for the votes of white supremacists. The Democrats responded in kind, seeking to stave off defeat in southern states by reminding voters that their party remained the most sturdy and reliable bulwark against changes in race relations. Abandoning traditional allegiances, prominent blacks defected from the Republican camp in 1928, urging voters to follow their lead. Republican performance during their years of dominance and the campaign strategies of 1928 convinced black leaders that the GOP was no longer a champion of black aspirations. Despite the unabated racism of the southern Democracy, they reasoned that it was better to support a candidate from another minority group than cling to faded memories of Republican benevolence. Only a modest percentage of black voters, however, heeded this call, and blacks were an even smaller proportion of the Democratic coalition four years later. The pull of old loyalties seemed stronger for ordinary blacks than for black elites. Not until 1936 did black voters shift their preferences to become stalwarts of the Democratic party. . . .

Historians seem convinced beyond reasonable doubt that national prosperity guaranteed a Republican victory in the presidential election of 1928. Yet scholars have failed to reconcile this conviction with the undercurrent of poverty that flowed beneath the gilded surface of the 1920s. Greater attention must be paid to the means by which an ideology of prosperity was developed and maintained. The brief account offered in this study suggests that the schools, business, labor, media, and government all fostered public faith in the availability of economic opportunity and pinned responsibility for failure on the individual. Democrats throughout the nation reported to FDR that, in 1928, potential constituents of their party were mesmerized by the promise of Republican prosperity. Neither of the major political parties challenged the ideology of prosperity or sought to muster support for programs aimed at redistributing resources. Nor did other organized groups offer a strong institutional base for dissent from the prevailing order. Al Smith, tabbed by some as the workingman's candidate, firmly believed that America offered ample opportunity to the talented, the thrifty, and the industrious. His notion of social justice embraced only amelioration of the excesses of free enterprise and recognized no conflict of class interests. In 1928, he advanced policies designed to placate business and relied on his personal appeal to those who labored for a meager income. . . .

Al Smith did not emerge in the campaign of 1928 as an exemplar of the need to reform American society. His positions on national issues failed to challenge the status quo. Despite the governor's humble origins, his progressive record in state politics, his Catholicism, and his associations with the new immigrant, his policy proposals were scarcely more venturesome than those of Herbert Hoover. Smith never sought to offer the politics of redistribution as an alternative to Hoover's politics of distribution. His candidacy did not promise to improve the lives of ordinary Americans by altering the nation's lopsided distribution of wealth and power. Yet lower-class Catholics and members of some nationality groups believed that Smith was their champion because they could identify with the image he projected. He appealed to their longing to enter the mainstream of national life regardless of the terms. From this perspective, Smith's bid for the presidency was a conservative influence on American life.

Although Al Smith addressed himself specifically to the farmer and the worker, he did not define coherent and persuasive alternatives to Republican policies of the past eight years. Relying on his personal appeal to ordinary Americans, Al Smith never sought to develop issues that could forge a broad-based coalition of minority interests. From the first stages of platform building to the final orations of early November, the governor and other leading Democrats behaved more like front runners than longshots. They obfuscated or dodged issues that could conceivably have brought together a coalition of minorities and sought to dampen conflict and controversy. Although Al Smith was undoubtedly an underdog in 1928, the tactics he followed seemed most appropriate for a candidate who did not wish to burst the bubble of a majority coalition. . . .

The Republican presidential campaign of 1928 relied upon moralistic appeals to the mass of American voters. Not only did the Republicans appeal to the optimism of Americans and their faith in the economic system, but they also played upon the fear that a Democratic victory would destroy the nation's booming prosperity. They attempted to associate Al Smith with dangerous and un-American schemes for reconstructing society. And they exploited Protestant fears about the consequences of electing a Catholic president. In later campaigns, Republicans continued to rely on issues that cut across interest groups. During the New Deal, for example, the party unsuccessfully sought to counter FDR's welfare liberalism by invoking traditional values of American democracy.

Herbert Hoover directed the strategies and tactics of his presidential campaign of 1928. A diverse group of historians including William Appleman Williams, Donald R. McCoy, David Burner, Ellis M. Hawley, Joan Hoff Wilson, and Edgar Eugene Robinson have favorably reinterpreted Hoover's career—his leadership of the Commerce Department, his campaign for the presidency in 1928, his tenure as president, and his later years as dedicated public servant. One aspect of the new Hoover scholarship is an affirmation of the former president's integrity, his devotion to principle, and his unwillingness to engage in petty politics. Recent studies of the campaign of 1928 implicitly or explicitly exonerate Hoover from responsibility for either anti-Catholicism or white racism. These historians have mistakenly placed Hoover on a pedestal above the turmoil of presidential politics. In 1928, Hoover responded as a politician to the dictates of political advantage. He was a presidential candidate intent upon his own election, concerned with the fine details of his campaign, and willing to exploit the tensions of his society.

PRIMARY SOURCES

The primary sources in this chapter reflect a variety of issues in the 1928 campaign. As you read and analyze them, determine the most important causes of Hoover's victory. One approach is to use a chart like the one below. Fill in the appropriate squares with the number of each source. Keep in mind that some sources may reflect more than one factor and some sources may contain arguments for support of a candidate that mask other reasons.

Prohibition	Religion	"Ideology of Prosperity"	Urban/Rural Values	Other Factors

◆

SOURCE 2   Cannon was a southern bishop of the Methodist Episcopal Church and a prominent prohibition advocate. As you read this selection, note whether Cannon's primary concern was Smith's position on prohibition or his Catholicism.

Al Smith—Catholic, Tammany, Wet (1928)

JAMES CANNON, JR.

If it were necessary to explain this in a single sentence, I should say: Governor Smith is personally, ecclesiastically, aggressively, irreconcilably Wet, and is ineradicably Tammany-branded, with all the inferences and implications and objectionable consequences which naturally follow from such views and associations. In the issue of *The Nation* of November 30, in an article discussing Governor Smith as a "Presidential possibility," Mr. [Oswald Garrison] Villard said:

> Do you believe in electing to the Presidency a man who drinks too much for his own good, and is politically a rampant Wet? . . . Does "Al" drink and does he drink too much? Well, I am reliably informed that he drinks every day, and the number of his cocktails and highballs is variously estimated at from four to eight. It is positively denied that he is ever intoxicated, much gossip to the contrary notwith-

Source: James Cannon, Jr., "Al Smith—Catholic, Tammany, Wet" from *The Nation,* July 4, 1928. Reprinted with permission from *The Nation* magazine. © The Nation Company, L.P.

standing. He is a Wet, and he lives up to it, and for that consistency he is to be praised. ... One may regret with all one's heart, as does the writer of these lines, that, being in an exalted position, he cannot set an example of abstinence to the millions whose State he governs, but at least one knows where he stands.

It is now over six months since that statement concerning Governor Smith's personal habits was printed and quoted, and there has been no official denial of its accuracy. It coincides with the private statements of other reliable persons. The facts certainly appear to warrant the asking of this question: Shall Dry America, a country with prohibition imbedded in its Constitution, elect a "cocktail President"? ...

Moreover, Governor Smith is ecclesiastically Wet. There was published in the secular press on January 2, 1928, a quotation which has not been denied from the *Osservatore Romano,* the official organ of the Vatican, stating that "the attempt to enforce prohibition in America has become so useless, not to say dangerous, that it would be better to abolish it, especially since unbridled passion is always more rampant as soon as there is an attempt to enforce complete abstinence." This attack upon the prohibition law of the United States by the Vatican organ is in full agreement with the open criticism of that law by the Cardinal Archbishop of New York and Boston and other Roman Catholic dignitaries.

I concede the right of the Pope, cardinals, archbishops, and other Roman Catholics to declare their attitude as freely as Methodist, Baptist, Presbyterian, or other Protestant bodies or ministers or laymen upon this question. Nor would I even intimate that these Roman Catholic leaders are not sincere in their opposition to the prohibition law. But it is not surprising, indeed it is to be expected, that this position of high dignitaries of the Roman church will be reflected in the attitude of many loyal Catholics who are members of legislatures, or of Congress, or who hold other official positions. It is a fact that the attacks in Congress upon the prohibition law are made chiefly by men who are themselves Roman Catholics or who represent constituencies with large Roman Catholic populations. Certainly it is likely that Governor Alfred E. Smith is influenced by the views of the Pope and the cardinals on the subject of prohibition.

◆

SOURCE 3   Willebrandt was an assistant attorney general of the United States who was assigned to prohibition enforcement. She spoke to numerous church meetings and conferences during the campaign. In this speech, what targets besides antiprohibitionism does Willebrandt attack?

Speech to the Ohio Methodist Conference (1928)

MABEL WALKER WILLEBRANDT

"Scattered over the United States were members of the intelligentsia who organized the Association Against the Prohibition Amendment. . . .

"Certain leaders in the Association Against the Prohibition Amendment saw the importance of securing as spokesman of their cause so powerful a leader as the Governor of New York.

"Thus the wealthy groups of antiprohibitionists and Tammany, symbol of predatory politics, and Governor Smith were found in early alliance.

"They have prepared well for this critical hour. Newspapers in rural and Southern communities were bought by New York money and have switched from a long-settled dry policy to preaching the doctrine of 'It can't be enforced.' At the same time there have been insinuated into strategic positions in dry enforcement men who were members of the Association Against the Prohibition Amendment. They have left office proclaiming from the lecture platform and through the press one general chorus that 'prohibition can never be enforced.' . . .

"Of course the law is not being enforced in New York; it is being evaded and nullified; a few hundred Federal agents and thirteen Federal Judges with four United States Attorneys cannot alone cope successfully with so much lawlessness.

"There are 2,000 pastors here. You have in your churches more than 600,000 members of the Methodist Church in Ohio alone. That is enough to swing the election. The 600,000 have friends in other States. Write to them. Every day and every ounce of your energy are needed to rouse the friends of prohibition to register and vote.

"The Eighteenth Amendment is new in politics. You did not put it there. The Republican Party did not put it there.

"Neither did the rank and file of the loyal constitutional Democrats. Neither did the National Democratic Convention put it there. It was put there by its enemies; and Governor Smith by a formal act as ruthless as was ever recorded in American politics became their leader. You have a chance to prove by electing Herbert Hoover that obedience to law can be secured and that America does not retreat before organized crime."

Source: New York Times, September 8, 1928, p. 3.

SOURCE 4   Conservative Protestant denominations and the Ku Klux Klan openly attacked Smith's Catholicism. Yet liberal Protestants also expressed doubts about electing a Catholic president. In 1927, the *Atlantic Monthly* published a widely read open letter to Governor Smith written by an Episcopalian lawyer. Note the author's concerns about electing a Catholic president. Why might some voters have found this article reassuring?

An Open Letter to Governor Smith (1927)

CHARLES C. MARSHALL

SIR:—

. . . American life has developed into a variety of religious beliefs and ethical systems, religious and nonreligious, whose claims press more and more upon public attention. None of these presents a more definite philosophy or makes a more positive demand upon the attention and reason of mankind than your venerable Church. . . . Is not the time ripe and the occasion opportune for a declaration, if it can be made, that shall clear away all doubt as to the reconcilability of her status and her claims with American constitutional principles?

It is indeed true that a loyal and conscientious Roman Catholic could and would discharge his oath of office with absolute fidelity to his moral standards. As to that in general, and as to you in particular, your fellow citizens entertain no doubt. But those moral standards differ essentially from the moral standards of all men not Roman Catholics. They are derived from the basic political doctrine of the Roman Catholic Church, asserted against repeated challenges for fifteen hundred years, that God has divided all power over men between the secular State and that Church. . . .

The deduction is inevitable that, as all power over human affairs, not given to the State by God, is given by God to the Roman Catholic Church, no other churches or religious or ethical societies have in theory any direct power from God and are without direct divine sanction, and therefore without natural right to function on the same basis as the Roman Catholic Church in the religious and moral affairs of the State. The result is that the Church, if true to her basic political doctrine, is hopelessly committed to that intolerance that has disfigured so much of her history. This is frankly admitted by Roman Catholic authorities.

Furthermore, the doctrine of the Two Powers, in effect and theory, inevitably makes the Roman Catholic Church at times sovereign and paramount over the State. It is true that in theory the doctrine assigns to the secular State jurisdiction over secular matters and to the Roman Catholic Church jurisdiction over

Source: Charles C. Marshall, "An Open Letter to Governor Smith," from *Atlantic Monthly,* April 1927. Reprinted with permission.

matters of faith and morals, each jurisdiction being exclusive of the other within undisputed lines. But the universal experience of mankind has demonstrated, and reason teaches, that many questions must arise between the State and the Roman Catholic Church in respect to which it is impossible to determine to the satisfaction of both in which jurisdiction the matter at issue lies.

Here arises the irrepressible conflict. Shall the State or the Roman Catholic Church determine? The Constitution of the United States clearly ordains that the State shall determine the question. The Roman Catholic Church demands for itself the sole right to determine it, and holds that within the limits of that claim it is superior to and supreme over the State. . . .

Thus the Constitution declares the United States shall hold in equal favor different kinds of religion or no religion and the Pope declares it is not lawful to hold them in equal favor. Is there not here a quandary for that man who is at once a loyal churchman and a loyal citizen?

SOURCE 5   This exposé of Tammany Hall was published on the eve of the election. What does Tammany Hall represent?

Al Smith's Tammany Hall (1928)

WILLIAM H. ALLEN

Tammanyism in New York is like Tammanyism anywhere else but more so. It is larger. It is richer. It has more sources of revenue. It is older. It is bolder. It has more affiliations that bribe and paralyze the forces of righteousness and uplift. It is more versatile. It uses specialists in exploiting to the public's limit of endurance.

Tammanyism in New York has more to offer, therefore it recruits faster and miseducates in more subtle ways. It can intimidate more and bribe more without running into the penal law.

Tammanyism menaces democracy not so much because of its unlawful corruption as because of the lawful corruption which its appetite, its promises, its examples of success and its methods can spread in the body politic. Its wasting is worse than its stealing. Its not studying is worse than its deceiving. Its not planning is worse than its obstructing. The crooked thinking it grafts onto public opinion and youthful aspiration is infinitely more costly than the dollar grafting it chaperones.

Source: William H. Allen, from *Al Smith's Tammany Hall: Champion Political Vampire* (New York: Institute for Public Service, 1928), pp. 328, 329, 334.

Tammanyism's miseducation is worse than its neglect of schools because its glorification of private favor at public expense works upon private and public morals the way meningitis paralyzes the spine and tuberculosis deadens the lungs. . . .

Like the tiger after which it is named, it is tame when on show; will take all the rope allowed; is ferocious when the trainer is scared; grows ravenous when it tastes the blood of a profit. . . .

Al Smith reformed because away from his Tammany Hall, surrounded by anti-Tammany legislators and responsible to anti-Tammany voters, is a reality that promises much for democracy everywhere.

Tammanyism reformed by Al Smith is a myth and a myth of mighty menace to municipal management everywhere.

SOURCE 6   Shortly after the election, the Republican National Committee asked state and local politicians around the country to estimate the Republican vote among various groups, including women. As you read these responses, note whether women were more likely to support Hoover because of his stands on certain issues.

The Women's Vote (1928)

Chicago   It is estimated here that 65 percent of the women voted the Republican ticket; and that we received many votes from Democratic women—possibly 25 percent; and that their reasons for affiliating themselves with the Republican party this time was on account of both the religious and prohibition issues.

Cincinnati   The majority of women were for Hoover and the increase in voting from Cincinnati was largely represented by the registration and voting of women voters. The women were for Hoover because he was dry, because he represented prosperity and better living conditions to them, and because of his work in the food relief problem. The women were original Hoover boosters. A part of the women were for Hoover because they were opposed to Governor Smith, to Tammany Hall and to the wet platform, and a small majority we believe, were for Hoover because they admired Mrs. Hoover and thought that she would make a fitting "First Lady of the Land"

Source: Excerpted from *Prejudice and the Old Politics: The Presidential Election of 1928* by Allen Lichtman. Copyright © 1979 by the University of North Carolina Press. Used by permission of the publisher.

and were opposed to the Smith's because of their supposed lack of cultural attainments.

Cleveland   The women, except Catholic women, were very definitely aligned with the Republicans. The increase in the womens' vote was approximately 15 percent. We obtained the vote of perhaps 5 percent of normally Democratic women. Religion was the cause.

Connecticut   The work of the women contributed largely to the success of the campaign. . . . I think this was for two reasons, the wet and dry issue and the feeling that the Democratic candidate and his family did not represent a proper class to occupy the White House. In addition to this the Republican candidate was very strong with them.

Indiana   The increase in the women vote this year totaled 153,000 while the men vote was substantially the same as in 1924 and also in 1920.

The support of women was almost exclusively due to the wet and dry issue though of course there was to some degree a support of our candidate because of his policies as well as the dislike for the Democratic candidate and his policies.

Los Angeles   It is my belief that the women's vote almost neutralized the loss among the Republican men on the wet issue. I believe that the Democratic women stepped aside from their party affiliation primarily because of the personality of the candidate, strengthened in their views by their fears of the personality and policies of the Democratic candidate.

Maryland   We gained very decidedly by the women's vote. Probably 50,000 more women voted than in 1924. We got probably from 15 to 20 percent of the Democratic women. They supported our candidate for two reasons: Dislike of the opposition candidate and like for a humanitarian, like Hoover.

Massachusetts   Some normally Democratic women voted Republican this year—perhaps 5 percent. This was on the prohibition issue partly and partly on the particular appeal that Mr. Hoover makes to the women voters.

Among the so-called intelligent people, normally Republican, a great many husbands voted for Smith on the prohibition issue and their wives for Hoover. . . .

New Jersey   We made a gain of over 30 percent to 40 percent in the women's vote. Women were with us to a very large degree. Many Democratic women voted for Hoover. Women who never voted before could not support Smith, some because of his stand on prohibition and some for other reasons.

Oregon   I should say that the increased registration was very marked among the women voters. While the women of our state held Mr. Hoover in very high regard, I think this applied also to the men. The personality of Governor Smith and his religious and wet and Tammany affiliations had a marked effect on the voters of the state.

Rhode Island   It is apparent that the Catholic women voted for Smith and the Protestants came out strongly for Hoover. I do know that our women vote was large and also influenced to a great extent by the religious question.

◆

SOURCE 7   W. E. B. Du Bois was the editor of *The Crisis* and a prominent advocate for the rights of African-Americans in the first decades of the twentieth century. What is Du Bois's criticism of Smith and Hoover? For what reasons might Smith have avoided making appeals to African-Americans, besides a fear of losing the South? Does Du Bois support Lichtman's argument about the role of prejudice in the 1928 campaign?

Is Al Smith Afraid of the South? (1928)

W. E. B. Du BOIS

Mr. Smith is silent about the Negro. Why? Certainly it is not because he has no need of the Negro vote. Migration from South to North, and from country to city, has increased the effective vote which Negroes cast very appreciably over 1916, and considerably over 1920 and 1924. We must, of course, depend upon estimates instead of actual figures, but in States where the real battles of this campaign are apparently being fought, there is a large Negro vote. . . . Of course, in the Southern hinterland, there is little chance that any appreciable Negro vote will be cast or counted. And yet in Virginia, South Carolina, Georgia, Florida, Texas, and Oklahoma the Negro vote of 100,000 might conceivably be of importance if any real rift were made in the governing oligarchy.

   This is an asset that no astute politician—and no one has accused Mr. Smith of not being astute—would ordinarily neglect. Moreover, the Negroes are incensed against the Republican Party and against Mr. Hoover as never before. . . .

Source: W. E. B. Du Bois, "Is Al Smith Afraid of the South?" from *The Nation,* October 17, 1928. Reprinted with permission from *The Nation* magazine. © The Nation Company. L.P.

. . . If Al Smith would raise a finger to assure American Negroes that, while he was not necessarily a warm friend, at least he could not be classed as an enemy, he would receive more Negro votes than any Democrat has ever received. . . .

. . . Hoover has joined openly with the "Lily Whites" of the South,—that is, with those active Southern politicians who propose, not simply to keep the Southern Negro disfranchised, but to prevent the organization of any effective minority party in which the Negro has representation. Hoover knows perfectly well that the disfranchisement of the better class Negroes in the South delivers them into the hands of venal politicians, black and white. . . .

Here, then, was a chance and an unusual chance for Al Smith, and not simply a chance for political maneuvering. It was a chance to attack in its stronghold the central danger of American democracy; the thing that makes it impossible for the American people today to vote logically or coherently on any subject whatsoever; and that incubus is the bloc of 114 to 139 electoral votes which are out of politics in the sense that no political discussion, no appeal to intelligence or justice, has any influence on them. This was the time for a really great statement. The Governor of New York might have stepped into the arena and said: "I believe in democracy. I believe that poverty and misfortune, even if coupled with slavery and color, are in themselves no reason for caste and disfranchisement. If in spite of misfortune, poverty, and handicap a man meets the qualifications laid down for voting, he ought to vote and to be protected in his vote. He and his ought not to be interfered with by lawlessness and lynching. Education and encouragement ought freely to be offered, and every opportunity for development placed before such people." . . .

Now why should a man otherwise in many respects liberal and likable, who has himself come up from the common people, show himself so illiberal and petty toward the Negro? It is because Smith has been afraid of the South, and is so today. He probably first ignored the Negro because, with East Side ignorance, he knew nothing about him, and shared the East Side's economic dislike of Negro labor competition: a dislike which was back of the Irish anti-Negro riots before and during the war, in Philadelphia and New York. As Smith began to develop in political power and ambition, he recognized that if he wanted to carry the South he must be orthodox on the Negro according to Southern traditions. He has been so, and, in the future, according to Congressman Hill of Alabama, "Governor Smith says he will let us handle the Negro problem as we see fit. What more could we ask?" Then, again, his liquor program and his religion have stirred up enough trouble and revolt south of the Mason and Dixon line. Smith is determined, therefore, not to say a single word that will enable his enemies and the Ku Klux Klan to fasten the title "Nigger-lover" upon him.

◆

SOURCE 8   Hoover delivered his speech accepting the Republican presidential nomination in August 1928. As you read these excerpts, note what issues Hoover emphasizes. Were voters likely to credit the Republicans for the decade's prosperity?

Acceptance Speech (1928)

HERBERT HOOVER

. . . [I]t is not through the recitation of wise policies in government alone that we demonstrate our progress under Republican guidance. To me the test is the security, comfort, and opportunity that have been brought to the average American family. During this less than eight years our population has increased by eight percent. Yet our national income has increased by over thirty billions of dollars per year or more than forty-five percent. Our production—and therefore our consumption—of goods has increased by over twenty-five percent. It is easily demonstrated that these increases have been widely spread among our whole people. Home ownership has grown. While during this period the number of families has increased by about 2,300,000, we have built more than 3,500,000 new and better homes. In this short time we have equipped nearly nine million more homes with electricity, and through it drudgery has been lifted from the lives of women. The barriers of time and distance have been swept away and life made freer and larger by the installation of six million more telephones, seven million radio sets, and the service of an additional fourteen million automobiles. Our cities are growing magnificent with beautiful buildings, parks, and playgrounds. Our countryside has been knit together with splendid roads.

We have doubled the use of electrical power and with it we have taken sweat from the backs of men. The purchasing power of wages has steadily increased. The hours of labor have decreased. The twelve-hour day has been abolished. Great progress has been made in stabilization of commerce and industry. The job of every man has thus been made more secure. Unemployment in the sense of distress is widely disappearing. . . .

One of the oldest and perhaps the noblest of human aspirations has been the abolition of poverty. By poverty I mean the grinding by undernourishment,

Source: Aaron Singer, ed., *Campaign Speeches of American Presidential Candidates 1928–1972* (New York: Frederick Ungar Publishing Co., 1976), pp. 6–7, 13–14.

cold, and ignorance, and fear of old age of those who have the will to work. We in America today are nearer to the final triumph over poverty than ever before in the history of any land. The poorhouse is vanishing from among us. We have not yet reached the goal, but, given a chance to go forward with the policies of the last eight years, we shall soon with the help of God be in sight of the day when poverty will be banished from this nation. There is no guarantee against poverty equal to a job for every man. That is the primary purpose of the economic policies we advocate. . . .

I recently stated my position upon the Eighteenth Amendment, which I again repeat:

"I do not favor the repeal of the Eighteenth Amendment. I stand for the efficient enforcement of the laws enacted thereunder. Whoever is chosen President has under his oath the solemn duty to pursue this course.

"Our country has deliberately undertaken a great social and economic experiment, noble in motive and far-reaching in purpose. It must be worked out constructively."

Common sense compels us to realize that grave abuses have occurred—abuses which must be remedied. An organized searching investigation of fact and causes can alone determine the wise method of correcting them. Crime and disobedience of law cannot be permitted to break down the Constitution and laws of the United States.

Cartoons from the 1928 Campaign

Cartoons from the popular press reveal a good deal about intolerance in the 1928 campaign. As you examine the illustrations on the following pages, note what issues they use to attack Smith. Do these cartoons support the view that a number of associations regarding Smith were intertwined in the minds of voters?

SOURCE 9

A Heavy Load for Al (1928)

The traditional symbol for Tammany Hall was a tiger.
Source: Courtesy Harvard College Library.

SOURCE 10   This cartoon was from *The Fellowship Forum,* a Ku Klux Klan publication.

The Wet "Hope" (1928)

Source: The Fellowship Forum, November 3, 1929. Courtesy Harvard College Library.

CONCLUSION

The controversy about the 1928 election illustrates the importance of causal explanations in historical inquiry. It also shows that the search for causes inevitably raises questions about historians' assumptions and methods. Some historians try to understand behavior in the past by using quantitative analyses.

Others believe that human behavior is too complicated for such precise quantitative measurement and rely more on the analysis of speeches, letters, cartoons, or other "literary" sources to understand behavior in the past. Historians also debate the usefulness of "counterfactual" history, in which the importance of a single factor is judged by imagining events if it were removed or changed. Historians might ask, for instance, what it would have taken for Al Smith to win the election. Unfortunately, such a hypothetical question can quickly lead from conclusions based on facts to mere speculation.

The exercise in this chapter is also a reminder that historians cannot establish causes without considering the subjects of the two previous chapters: motivation and ideology. Obviously, one cannot separate conclusions about Hoover's victory from views about the motives of voters. Likewise, any explanation for the cause of Hoover's victory must assess the power of what Lichtman calls "an ideology of prosperity," not to mention the nativist ideology we examined in the previous chapter.

Finally, by focusing so much attention on two political leaders, the Hoover-Smith contest highlights the question of the role of the individual in history. Some historians examine historical change by looking at the top of society—that is, by concentrating on the actions and ideas of prominent and powerful people. Other historians see more change at the bottom of society and argue that it is more rewarding to concentrate on the actions and ideas of many ordinary and often obscure people. In the next two chapters we will look at both ways to the past: from the "top down" and from the "bottom up."

FURTHER READING

Paula Eldot, *Governor Alfred E. Smith: The Politician as Reformer* (New York: Garland Publishing, 1983).

Oscar Handlin, *Al Smith and His America* (Boston: Little, Brown, 1958).

William E. Leuchtenburg, *The Perils of Prosperity, 1914–1932* (Chicago: University of Chicago Press, 1958).

Donald J. Lisio, *Hoover, Blacks, and Lily Whites: A Study in Southern Strategies* (Chapel Hill: University of North Carolina Press, 1985).

Joan Hoff Wilson, *Herbert Hoover: Forgotten Progressive* (Boston: Little, Brown, 1975).

NOTE

1. Thomas A. Bailey, *The American Pageant*, 4th ed. (Lexington: D. C. Heath, 1971), II, 845.

Chapter 8

History "From the Top Down": Eleanor Roosevelt, Reformer

The sources in this chapter enable the reader to evaluate the activities of Eleanor Roosevelt and to assess their relevance to the times.

Secondary Source

1. Eleanor Roosevelt and the Great Depression (1987), Lois Scharf

Primary Sources

2. This I Remember (1949), Eleanor Roosevelt
3. Transcripts of Eleanor Roosevelt's Press Conferences (1933–1938)
4. Letter to Her Daughter (1937)
5. My Parents: A Differing View (1976), James Roosevelt
6. Excerpts from Letters to Franklin Roosevelt (1935)
7. Letter from Barry Bingham to Marvin McIntyre (1934)
8. News Item, "Definition of Feminism" (1935)
9. News Item, "Opposes Amendment" (1938)
10. It's Up to the Women (1933)

$\mathscr{D}$uring the Great Depression in 1932, unemployed World War I veterans marched on Washington, D.C., to demand early payment of their service bonuses. In response Herbert Hoover called out the army, which routed the desperate marchers out of their shantytown and then burned it down. Shortly after Franklin Roosevelt took office in 1933, a second "bonus army" descended on Washington. This time the First Lady drove out to talk to them. When she arrived, they asked her who she was and what she wanted. She told them her name and that she wanted to see how they were doing. "I did not spend as much as an hour there; then I got into my car and drove away," she said. "Everyone waved and I called, 'Good luck,' and they answered, 'good-by and good luck to you.' "[1]

Before the Depression was over, Eleanor Roosevelt had visited coal miners, Civilian Conservation Corps boys, women in Works Progress Administration sewing rooms, tenant farmers, and many others. As she traveled around the country, the First Lady gave a human face to numerous New Deal relief programs. At the same time she was her paralyzed husband's eyes and ears, reporting to him Americans' struggles to survive the Depression. She was also his conscience, fighting amid much criticism to extend the boundaries of the New Deal to blacks and women.

By sharing the public spotlight with her husband, Eleanor Roosevelt was the first "modern" First Lady. As a political activist, she redefined the role of the president's wife. At the same time, there was also something old-fashioned about her. A Victorian upbringing gave her what one historian called "an uncynical sense of duty and moral purpose."[2] It also left her with a traditional view of women as mothers and wives. Eleanor believed that women were agents of moral good and needed protection more than equality. She never went to college or pursued a career. Self-reliance grew only slowly, nurtured by the pain of rejection.

Eleanor Roosevelt's struggle for independence is a compelling story for biographers, but there is another reason to examine her life. Like her, there is something "old-fashioned" about biography itself. Traditionally it was written about people at the "top" of their society, wealthy and influential people like Eleanor. Moreover, as one writer put it, biography "moves to the pace and powers of individual human beings and not to the impersonal dictates of markets and masses."[3] During the Depression, of course, few Americans had escaped the dictates of either. FDR was president because markets had collapsed and the "masses" had chosen him to lead the nation. At first glance, biography's personal approach to history might seem ill-suited to a time dominated by such impersonal forces. Yet the Depression era is actually a good time to see how one person's life illuminates the past, because biographers deal with the important historical developments as well as with individual lives. Biographies show us the forces that shaped their subjects' lives and how, in turn, their lives influenced history. This chapter, therefore, examines how one exceptional woman both reflected and affected her times.

SETTING

Anna Eleanor Roosevelt was born in 1884 into a world of privilege. The daughter of two families that could trace their wealth to colonial times, she grew up sheltered from both the masses and the marketplace. Yet her childhood was hardly blissful. Eleanor's mother was cold, distant, and disappointed by her only daughter's plain appearance. As Eleanor later realized, she grew up shy and lonely, "entirely lacking in the spontaneous joy and mirth of youth."[4] Her affectionate but alcoholic father was the one bright spot in her childhood. Unfortunately, he died when she was ten, two years after diphtheria had claimed her mother. Eleanor and her younger brother lived with their grandmother, who reared them "on the principle that 'no' was easier to say than 'yes.' "[5]

Escape came in the form of an English finishing school. There Eleanor learned more than the social graces that upper-class Americans considered "education" for their daughters. Headmistress Marie Souvestre encouraged her students to think critically and to challenge conventional ideas. Souvestre took special interest in Eleanor, who seemed burdened with a sense of inferiority. She taught her to champion the underdog. Together they traveled through Europe. "Whatever I have become since," Eleanor later confided, "had its seeds in those three years of contact with a liberal mind and strong personality."[6]

Still, exposure to Madame Souvestre's "liberal" ideas did not prevent Eleanor from becoming a New York society debutante when she returned home, or from being depressed about her appearance. "I was the first girl in my mother's family who was not a belle," she confessed, "and . . . I was deeply ashamed."[7] Eleanor had not forgotten Souvestre's lessons, however. After her debut, she joined the National Consumers' League, which fought for better conditions for female workers in sweatshops and clothing factories. She also joined the Junior League, recently founded by charity-minded socialites. She taught classes at a community center on the Lower East Side, where she was at first terrified at the sight of "foreign-looking people, crowded and dirty."[8] In time, however, Eleanor discovered she preferred social work to the social whirl.

Marriage to distant cousin Franklin in 1905 ended Eleanor's trips to the tenements. For the next fifteen years she was occupied with her five children and her husband's budding political career. Gradually, though, she was again drawn out of her private sphere. After World War I, Eleanor joined the League of Women Voters and the Women's Trade Union League, which fought for legislation regulating women's wages and hours of labor. Personal shocks furthered a growing sense of independence and self-confidence. In 1918 she discovered Franklin's affair with her personal secretary. "The bottom dropped out of my . . . world and I faced myself, my surroundings, my world honestly for the first time," she later wrote.[9] Their marriage continued, but marital relations did not. Eleanor began to spend more time in reform causes and discovered her own political skills. Franklin's paralyzing bout with polio four years later further encouraged her independence.

Eleanor began to represent her husband in public and became active in New York Democratic party politics. She organized women voters, fought for numerous social reforms, and developed associations with many female reformers. In 1928, while teaching part-time at a private girls' school in New York City, Eleanor worked for Al Smith's unsuccessful campaign for the presidency, running the New York headquarters of the Democratic Party's National Women's Committee. When Franklin was elected governor of New York the same year, Eleanor decided to keep her teaching job and be First Lady in Albany only part-time.

Eleanor nevertheless played an influential role as the governor's wife, advising him on policies and appointments, and when FDR ran for the presidency four years later she put her experience to work campaigning around the country. It was on the campaign that she also began an intimate friendship with reporter Lorena Hickok. During Eleanor's years in the White House, the two women sustained a furtive relationship that was both passionate and romantic. To Hickok, Eleanor shared her fears about becoming First Lady. Eleanor was fearful for her husband and children, but mostly she was worried about her own fate. She knew that, far more than in the governor's mansion, she would have to sacrifice her autonomy and tend to social obligations as the nation's First Lady. Right after FDR's sweeping victory in 1932, Eleanor confided to Hickok that she was "sincerely" glad for her husband. "Now," she added, "I shall have to work out my own salvation."[10]

INVESTIGATION

This chapter examines Eleanor Roosevelt's efforts to "work out" her "salvation" as First Lady. Thus your main task is to evaluate Eleanor Roosevelt as an activist First Lady during the Depression. Your evaluation should address the following main questions:

1. **What do Eleanor Roosevelt's activities reveal about the limitations on women in the early twentieth century?** Do the sources reveal that she had power, or only influence with other people?

2. **Do the sources reveal that Eleanor challenged or reinforced traditional conceptions of women's proper role?** Did she challenge her role as helpmate to her husband or channel her energies in only socially acceptable directions?

3. **In what ways was Eleanor Roosevelt's struggle unique and how did it reflect the situation of women generally?** What do the sources reveal about the influence of Eleanor's social background on her attitudes?

4. **Do you agree with the main essay's conclusions about Eleanor's achievements?** What were her greatest achievement and biggest failure as First Lady? Was she able to change the lives of women and blacks, or only her own?

Before you begin, review the sections in your textbook on the status and role of women in American society in the first decades of the twentieth century, as well as the chapter on the New Deal. Although Eleanor Roosevelt may not be mentioned, these sections will provide useful background for evaluating her activities and achievements.

SECONDARY SOURCE

◆

SOURCE 1   In this selection, historian Lois Scharf examines Eleanor Roosevelt's role as First Lady during the 1930s. Note Eleanor's position on female equality and how it differed from that of "radical" feminists, who advocated the passage of an equal rights amendment. Also notice how Scharf uses Eleanor's life to examine important social issues during the Depression. What does Eleanor's life reveal about them? Do you think a biography of an exceptional, upper-class woman like Eleanor Roosevelt reveals a lot or a little about historical developments and the lives of ordinary Americans in the early twentieth century?

Eleanor Roosevelt and the Great Depression (1987)

LOIS SCHARF

. . . The winter of Eleanor Roosevelt's discontent was mirrored by an American economy limping toward paralysis. All the standards of measure signaled disaster as the interregnum dragged on. Initial efforts of industrial leaders to maintain wage levels had collapsed. Manufacturing and mining production levels followed suit, increasing the numbers of jobless and reducing the pay scales of those who hung on to their jobs. . . .

As a female journalist, Lorena Hickok was acutely aware of the price depression was exacting. She was particularly sensitive to the precarious professional circumstances of her colleagues. "People were losing their jobs on every hand, and unless the women reporters could find something new to write about, the chances were that some of them would hold their jobs a very short time," she told her friend. Hickok suggested that Eleanor hold press conferences for the women. Louis Howe approved the idea, and Eleanor Roosevelt met thirty-five "press girls" for the first time just two days after the inauguration.

The press conferences proved mutually beneficial. By limiting the session to female reporters, the wire services and Washington bureaus of leading newspapers had little choice but to hire, retain, and even promote women at a time when so many female professionals in nontraditional occupations were losing ground. . . .

The press forums also provided a stage on which Eleanor Roosevelt introduced women officeholders who helped direct the New Deal programs she supported. As historian Susan Ware has demonstrated, during the first Roosevelt term, more women were engaged in administrative positions than had ever worked in Washington before. These women, many of whom had cemented ties with Eleanor and Franklin Roosevelt during the previous decade, formed a political and social network rooted in shared educational attainments and social reform endeavors. . . .

The women who served in the administration brought to their posts a commitment to the broad-based relief and reform that marked the New Deal generally. Within that framework Eleanor Roosevelt added special concerns for women, whose problems were usually slighted by policy planners and program administrators. With the White House as her bully pulpit, she adopted a watchdog stance and publicized projects that ignored women or discriminated against them. Her efforts brought mixed results. . . .

The first lady worked as effectively and sympathetically with the capable women who served the New Deal as she worked with and in front of the "press girls." Yet there was one important issue that created a gulf between the social reformers and the professional journalists that even she could not and would not bridge. Issues of legal equality for women, definitions of womanhood, and strategies for achieving political and economic equity divided the two groups. The passage of the Fair Labor Standards Act highlighted this schism, but it also held out the possibility of healing it.

Protective legislation for working women had galvanized women reformers from the beginning of the twentieth century. Their determination to have women's hours, wages, and types of employment regulated by law was unshakable. Eleanor Roosevelt had honed her skills as a lobbyist and witness by working on behalf of hours legislation in New York. The appeal of these laws was both expedient and ideological. Attempts by states to establish work guidelines for men and women, or in some cases for specific classes of workers like miners or bakers, had been struck down repeatedly by the courts. Only legislation that focused on the most vulnerable workers, women and children, sometimes stood the test of judicial scrutiny. In the well-known Brandeis brief of 1909, compiled to support an Oregon maximum hour law for women, the legislation was defended on the basis of female social roles as mothers and their physical vulnerability as women.

Once the Supreme Court upheld the Oregon hours bill, the reformers rigidly adhered to this rationale. They sincerely believed that the biological differences between women and men underlay different social expectations. As the mothers of the next generation, the young single women who composed the majority of the female work force should not share identical workplace conditions and experiences with men. The reformers' arguments brought slow but tangible legislative results. Through the 1920s, maximum hour laws spread among states, minimum wage lobbying became more extensive, night work was widely prohibited, and employment in seemingly dangerous occupations was outlawed. After 1923 a threat to these apparent advances came from an unexpected quarter.

In the aftermath of the suffrage victory, militant feminists of the National Woman's party (NWP) realized that the right to vote did not automatically guarantee legal equality. The small group of women proposed a constitutional amendment to achieve that goal. Reformers immediately understood that a blanket guarantee of equality between the sexes would destroy the gender-based protective legislation for which they had worked and continued to work so hard. Their opposition to the proposed Equal Rights Amendment (ERA) was implacable, and Eleanor Roosevelt stood firmly with the reformers.

... At an early press conference, a question about the proposed ERA brought a negative response from the first lady. "I think that the National Woman's Party ignores the fact that there is a fundamental difference between men and women," she told the reporters. "I don't mean by that women can't make as great a contribution, nor if they do the same work they not be paid the same wages. The mere fact that women basically are responsible for the future physical condition of the race means for many restrictions," she insisted, trying to justify protective and restrictive legislation.

In *It's Up to the Women,* which Eleanor wrote late in 1933, she restated her position, in the process exposing its many underlying contradictions. On the one hand, she extolled the special qualities and responsibilities women brought to their families and communities especially during the perilous conditions brought on by the depression. She encouraged women to become involved in local politics and to strive for the appointed and elected positions attained by the competent women in her husband's administration. But she also reaffirmed her belief that "women are different from men, their physical functions are different, and the future of the race depends upon their ability to produce healthy children." Extolling the virtues and primacy of mother-hood, she harked back to traditional ideals of feminine goals and behavior strangely at odds with her own growing influence and the life-style of the coterie of activist women around her.

The movement for a constitutional amendment challenged her to reconcile her belief in women's "specialness" with the principle of legal equity and she could not do so. Protection was necessary for women workers because they were different, but constraints, she insisted, were not synonymous with inferiority. In certain instances, women excelled. When a dramatist insisted women could never be great writers because they lacked the knowledge and experience of men, Eleanor Roosevelt drew on her own experience to reply that "as a rule women know not only what men know, but much that men will never know. For how many men really know the heart and soul of a woman?" The personally revealing remark underscored her belief in the unique qualities of women. She refused to distinguish between her applause for the achievements of strong, capable women as individuals and her insistence that women as a class needed special treatment. . . .

The reporters who covered the White House and accompanied her marveled at her indefatigable pace. Her schedule was unlike anything veterans of the Washington social and political scene had ever encountered. . . .

. . . Some Americans were offended by the unconventional nature and scope of her activities, complaining that "because I make speeches, I am more in the press, I'm not dignified, I do something that isn't the proper thing to do." She answered simply that she was sorry she offended these critics but that she was determined to follow her inclinations. "Everyone must live their own life in their own way and not according to anybody else's ideas."

On the other hand, criticism came from readers who found "My Day" banal.* "Why don't you make your daily column a constant appeal to individuals and organizations to do their part—instead of filling it up with inane chatter about your family affairs—words, words, words, which are of very little interest to anyone and only once in a blue moon of any value whatsoever," wrote a woman who was undoubtedly astonished to find her letter printed verbatim in a column shortly after the first lady had received it. There seemed to be no way to satisfy the expectations of those who wanted a traditional hostess and helpmate and others who wanted an effective agent of social change.

The fact that her activities also earned income made her vulnerable to charges that she commercialized her honorific position. When her earnings became a campaign issue, she responded frankly that she "made a great deal. Now it has not all gone into charity. It has gone into wages to a certain extent. It has gone into many charitable things." And furthermore, "I pay income tax

*"My Day" was Eleanor Roosevelt's syndicated column.

on everything." Her earnings were important to her, for they made it possible to adopt an independent stance and give financial support to projects about which she cared deeply. . . .

On behalf of distressed Americans who wrote her to ask for a job, a way to save their home, or just some cast-off clothing, she took personal action. Pleas for employment or complaints about relief administrators were forwarded to the appropriate agencies with a cover letter signed by the first lady herself. Officials were seldom shaken loose from their accepted procedures even by Eleanor Roosevelt, but her correspondents believed that she truly cared and a note by return mail confirmed their confidence in her. "You have saved my life. I would have killed myself if I would have lost my house," a grateful woman wrote the first lady after she advised the woman to consult the local office of the Federal Home Loan Agency. . . .

During the 1936 reelection campaign, her columns were as effective as any Democratic party literature. In simple, clear—and mawkish—ways, she translated experiences along the campaign trail into glowing praise for FDR's presidency and its achievements. She described her encounter with a waiter in a Detroit restaurant who told her, "I'm for Mr. R. He saved my home and my family." What a responsibility for a president to know the impact of his policies on "the lives and hopes of so many people," she concluded. And she recounted the story of a three-year-old girl who prayed that "the president be fat" because, the child explained, "then he won't be hungry the way we were before he helped Daddy get a job."

The first lady also lent credence to Republican attacks on FDR and his New Deal. A vote for Alf Landon would not only send Roosevelt packing, according to GOP faithful, but would also remove his busybody wife from the national scene. Political cartoonists discovered a windfall in her unattractive appearance. Lack of beauty was equated with renunciation of conservative verities, with a women who did not know her place and posed as a do-gooder. But for all the bluster, Eleanor Roosevelt could not be turned into a political liability. Wherever crowds gathered to see their president and listened to his appeals for support, people called for a glimpse of their first lady, too.

The 1936 campaign concluded with a resounding victory for FDR. It also marked a turning point in the voting patterns of significant sectors of the American electorate. A tenuous but enduring coalition that had been building for several years finally emerged and made Democrats the majority party for decades thereafter. Tensions would surface among conflicting elements, and parts of the coalition would fall away. But one group held tenaciously to the partisan revolution wrought by Franklin Roosevelt. As historian Nancy Weiss had demonstrated, black Americans in the North bid "farewell to the party of Lincoln" during the 1930s, not because the administration supported civil rights for the racial minority but because New Deal policies—although discriminatory in their application—prevented the unraveling of the economic fabric of black lives. If there was any perception in black communities, however, that this federal government did care about racial justice, that notion stemmed from the ideas and actions of Eleanor Roosevelt.

Overcoming her inbred prejudices and stereotypes was an arduous and incomplete process. In 1937, one of her daily columns retold a tactless joke in tasteless dialect because many Americans "do not appreciate what we owe the colored race for its good humor and its quaint ways of saying and doing things." But the pleas and complaints she received by mail and during on-site visits to black communities convinced her that Negro problems not only mirrored other Americans' need for relief and reform but also extended beyond those needs. Pervasive racism compounded economic distress and political liabilities. She addressed these issues with her usual fervor. Letters pleading for aid or complaining about prejudicial treatment at the hands of local relief officials were forwarded to the appropriate agencies. Unfortunately, the letters often made their way back to the local agencies in spite of the first lady's good intentions and her correspondents' pleas for anonymity.

She addressed the call from black leaders for more voice in administrative posts by pressing for the appointment of black educator Mary McLeod Bethune to the National Youth Administration. Efforts to place other capable blacks were less successful. Even as close a colleague as Frances Perkins refused to name a black to one of the bureaus in the Department of Labor, claiming social and personnel difficulties would undermine efficiency. When otherwise liberal government officials backed away from integrating their staffs, they were reflecting prevalent American attitudes toward racial minorities.

Eleanor Roosevelt was not intimidated. Tours of black schools, churches, and relief projects were constant items on her busy schedule. She spoke at conventions of black organizations, appeared at interracial gatherings, and invited black leaders to White House receptions. Not only prominent blacks saw the executive mansion firsthand. In May 1936, she inspected the National Training School for Girls, the District of Columbia reformatory for black girls. She was appalled at the conditions and described the visit in great detail at her next press conference. She also invited the inmates to a garden party at the White House. "I feel if these girls are ever to be rehabilitated and, as far as possible, returned into community living prepared to meet the difficulties of life, they need much more than they are getting. Therefore, it seems to me, as every young person enjoys an occasional good time, these youngsters should have an occasional good time." . . .

Her stress on individual opportunities for blacks precluded an assault on social arrangements like racial segregation. Although Eleanor Roosevelt personally protested the forced separation of the races at a public assembly by deliberately moving her chair to the middle of the aisle that separated blacks from whites when she attended a conference in Atlanta, she did not attack Jim

Crow laws in the South or more subtle forms of discrimination elsewhere. Her gradualist approach to social welfare and justice applied to racial policies. Opportunities for advancement could best be promoted within existing structures: blacks must respect the limits of the possible and not overextend their reach; patience was the ultimate virtue and most effective strategy. In this respect her stance, while far ahead of her progressive cohorts in so many respects, appeared painfully shortsighted when civil rights became a major liberal aim a generation later.

In the 1930s more dramatic issues than legal segregation highlighted black disabilities in American society. No threat was more menacing than the possibility of physical violence and death through lynching. Social segregation, disenfranchisement in the South, and lack of economic opportunities everywhere encumbered black Americans. But mob violence was the ultimate assault on the body of the victims and the minds of all those who identified with their fate. The number of these atrocities increased during the early 1930s as economic hardship compounded interracial tension. Leaders of black organizations like Walter White of the NAACP hoped that a new administration would support efforts to criminalize lynching.

White personally gained the support of two Democratic senators, Robert F. Wagner of New York and Edward P. Costigan of Colorado, who agreed to sponsor an antilynching bill. The proposed legislation was introduced in the Senate at the beginning of 1934. The campaign to arouse public sentiment on behalf of the bill included efforts to enlist the backing of the president. Roosevelt was hesitant. He finally agreed to meet with White only because his wife personally intervened to schedule the appointment. Sara* joined the three conferees, agreeing with White and her daughter-in-law that they should all stick to the subject whenever her son engaged in good-natured, evasive banter.

But even his mother's uncharacteristic interest could not convince FDR that support for the Costigan-Wagner bill was worth alienating the southern wing of the Democratic party. Whether his position was entirely expedient or reflected, in part, his personal lack of concern is uncertain. The extent to which he used his wife's good standing to deflect criticism in the black community is also difficult to measure. But she continued to act behind the scenes as conduit between White and FDR and in full public view, to move comfortably, if controversially, with and among black citizens. Blacks therefore were convinced that they had at least one friend in high circles, and "at a time when there had previously been neither positive symbol nor substance, the First Lady helped significantly to shape the black response to the New Deal." She was considerably less effective in shaping her husband's attitudes and priorities. . . .

---

*Eleanor Roosevelt's mother-in-law.

Franklin Roosevelt respected his wife's opinions. He was not adverse to using her position as a highly visible and admired first lady to test the political waters on sensitive issues. She understood that for all her independence of action and frank criticism of shortcomings in New Deal programs as she saw them, there were boundaries beyond which she could not move. FDR made the decisions about political feasibility on the basis of his own judgments, and if his assessments clashed with Eleanor's proposals, her influence was negligible. And if her actions threatened to stir public controversy beyond the scope he would tolerate, then she curtailed them at his request. Bowing to FDR's wishes, she did not attend a rally protesting a particularly brutal lynching although she was appalled at the murder and at the inaction of the government.

When the Daughters of the American Revolution (DAR) barred well-known black singer Marian Anderson from performing at Constitution Hall in 1939, Eleanor Roosevelt resigned from the organization. Her action spoke eloquently about her attitude toward racial discrimination. Her explanation to "My Day" readers was thoughtful and straightforward, for she had pondered her decision carefully. Usually she belonged to organizations in which she could work for ideas and positions with which members might disagree. She might be defeated, but at least she had had her say and perhaps she would prevail in the future. But the inflexibility with which the DAR declared its determination to adhere to its racist policies convinced her that change was impossible. Remaining as a member implied approval of that action, and so she resigned. Secretary of Interior Harold Ickes stepped into the public furor over the DAR prohibition and the first lady's reply and scheduled a free open-air concert at the Lincoln Memorial. It was a moving event. Over 75,000 people gathered to hear the magnificent voice of contralto Anderson and to give some semblance of recognition to the indignities of discrimination. Although she had played a central role in the events surrounding the public uproar, Eleanor Roosevelt did not attend the concert.

The occasions of cautious, imposed reticence were hardly noted by Americans who had grown accustomed to this most energetic and outspoken of first ladies. There seemed to be no end to the causes she espoused or the platforms from which she pronounced her opinions. She sometimes worried that she might focus on one issue and that her role as publicist for Americans—minorities, tenant farmers, the hungry and homeless—who had no platform or spokesperson of their own would be diminished. On one lecture tour in 1937 she had seen the physical and human toll of the Dust Bowl. Instead of speaking on the prearranged topics, she described what she had seen to her audiences and pleaded for support for programs to address soil erosion. "I have talked about it to so many people," she wrote, "I feel a little afraid they will think I am interested in only one subject." She need not have worried. If there was a serious criticism of her wide-ranging interests and outspoken ideals, it centered on the impression she created of a ubiquitous meddler whose activities and postures had no coherent pattern and whose opinions rested on insufficient information and analysis.

Eleanor Roosevelt's actions and visions did have focus and definition. She espoused the basic tenets of American liberalism as it came to be redefined in the 1930s, and she even anticipated planks that would become central to the liberal platform during the decades that followed. She believed that human welfare and social justice should be encouraged and protected under the auspices of an enlightened, caring government. Midway in the first Roosevelt administration, she addressed the issue of the public role in securing a more humane and just society. "The big achievement of the past two years is the great change in the thinking of the country," she told the "press girls" in 1935. "Imperceptibly we have come to recognize that government has a responsibility to defend the weak." In anticipation of contemporary and later attacks on bureaucratic management of programs as well as the programs themselves, she added, "I also think that in spite of criticism, the administration of relief has been a great achievement." Government-supported and administered assistance for those who could not help themselves was the common thread that bound her vision to her seemingly feverish activities. . . .

In enacting the legislation that created the American welfare state, the Roosevelt administration legislated the social agenda Eleanor Roosevelt's female colleagues had advocated since the turn of the century. Civil rights for minorities and attacks on persistent poverty would become liberal priorities in the future.

PRIMARY SOURCES

Many of the sources in this section are the kinds of evidence that biographers often use to learn about people's lives: personal letters, autobiographies, memoirs, and speeches or transcriptions. They will help you evaluate Eleanor Roosevelt's effectiveness as a reformer and the challenges she faced as First Lady.

◆

SOURCE 2   *This I Remember,* the second volume of Eleanor Roosevelt's autobiography, deals with her life from the early 1920s until her husband's death in 1945. In the following selections, she discusses the nature of her influence on FDR and her interest in several reforms. How much influence did Eleanor appear to have with FDR?

This I Remember (1949)

ELEANOR ROOSEVELT

Always, when my husband and I met after a trip that either of us had taken, we tried to arrange for an uninterrupted meal so that we could hear the whole story while it was fresh and not dulled by repetition. That I became, as the years went by, a better reporter and a better observer was largely owing to the fact that Franklin's questions covered such a wide range. I found myself obliged to notice everything. For instance, when I returned from a trip around the Gaspé, he wanted to know not only what kind of fishing and hunting was possible in that area but what the life of the fisherman was, what he had to eat, how he lived, what the farms were like, how the houses were built, what type of education was available, and whether it was completely church-controlled like the rest of the life in the village.

When I spoke of Maine, he wanted to know about everything I had seen on the farms I visited, the kinds of homes and the types of people, how the Indians seemed to be getting on and where they came from.

Franklin never told me I was a good reporter nor, in the early days, were any of my trips made at his request. I realized, however, that he would not question me so closely if he were not interested, and I decided this was the only way I could help him, outside of running the house, which was soon organized and running itself under Mrs. Nesbitt.

In the autumn I was invited by the Quakers to investigate the conditions that they were making an effort to remedy in the coal-mining areas of West Virginia. My husband agreed that it would be a good thing to do, so the visit was arranged. I had not been photographed often enough then to be recognized, so I was able to spend a whole day going about the area near Morgantown, West Virginia, without anyone's discovering who I was.

The conditions I saw convinced me that with a little leadership there could develop in the mining areas, if not a people's revolution, at least a people's party patterned after some of the previous parties born of bad economic conditions. There were men in that area who had been on relief for from three to five years and who had almost forgotten what it was like to have a job at which they could work for more than one or two days a week. There were children who did not know what it was to sit down at a table and eat a proper meal.

One story which I brought home from that trip I recounted at the dinner table one night. In a company house I visited, where the people had evidently seen better days, the man showed me his weekly pay slips. A small amount had been deducted toward his bill at the company store and for his rent and for oil for his mine lamp. These deductions left him less than a dollar in cash each week. There were six children in the family, and they acted as though they were afraid of strangers. I noticed a bowl on the table filled with scraps, the kind that you or I might give to a dog, and I saw children, evidently looking for their noonday meal, take a handful out of that bowl and go out munching. That was all they had to eat.

As I went out, two of the children had gathered enough courage to stand by the door, the little boy holding a white rabbit in his arms. It was evident that it was a most cherished pet. The little girl was thin and scrawny, and had a gleam in her eyes as she looked at her brother. She said, "He thinks we are not going to eat it, but we are," and at that the small boy fled down the road clutching the rabbit closer than ever.

It happened that William C. Bullitt was at dinner that night and I have always been grateful to him for the check he sent me the next day, saying he hoped it might help to keep the rabbit alive.

This trip to the mining areas was my first contact with the work being done by the Quakers. I liked the theory of trying to put people to work to help themselves. The men were started on projects and taught to use their abilities to develop new skills. The women were encouraged to revive any household arts they might once have known but which they had neglected in the drab life of the mining village.

This was only the first of many trips into the mining districts but it was the one that started the homestead idea. The University of West Virginia, in Morgantown, had already created a committee to help the miners on the Quaker agricultural project. With that committee and its experience as a nucleus, the government obtained the loan of one of the university's people, Mr. Bushrod Grimes, and established the Resettlement Administration. Louis Howe created a small advisory committee on which I, Mr. Pickett, and others served. It was all experimental work, but it was designed to get people off relief, to put them to work building their own homes and to give them enough land to start growing food.

It was hoped that business would help by starting on each of these projects an industry in which some of the people could find regular work. A few small industries were started but they were not often successful. Only a few of the resettlement projects had any measure of success; nevertheless, I have always felt that the good they did was incalculable. Conditions were so nearly the kind that breed revolution that the men and women needed to be made to feel their government's interest and concern. . . .

Franklin did not talk a great deal about the work he was doing, either at meals or in private family conversations. Most of us felt that when he was with his family he should have a respite from the concerns of his office.

When an administration bill was up before Congress, we often found that the number of Congressmen coming to his study in the evenings increased. I learned that I must make an evaluation of the bills on which he had to get support. He calculated votes closely on what was known as the administration policy, and considered "must" legislation.

Only bills that were "must" legislation got full administration support. In the first years these were largely economic measures; later on, they were measures for defense. While I often felt strongly on various subjects, Franklin frequently refrained from supporting causes in which he believed, because of political realities. There were times when this annoyed me very much.

I also remember wanting to get all-out support for the anti-lynching bill and the removal of the poll tax, but though Franklin was in favor of both measures, they never became "must" legislation. When I would protest, he would simply say: "First things first. I can't alienate certain votes I need for measures that are more important at the moment by pushing any measure that would entail a fight." And as the situation in Europe grew worse, preparations for war had to take precedence over everything else. That was always "must" legislation, and Franklin knew it would not pass if there was a party split.

Often people came to me to enlist his support for an idea. Although I might present the situation to him, I never urged on him a specific course of action, no matter how strongly I felt, because I realized that he knew of factors in the picture as a whole of which I might be ignorant.

One of the ideas I agreed to present to Franklin was that of setting up a national youth administration. Harry Hopkins, then head of the WPA, and Aubrey Williams, his deputy administrator and later head of the National Youth Administration, knew how deeply troubled I had been from the beginning about the plight of the country's young people. One day they said: "We have come to you about this because we do not feel we should talk to the President about it as yet. There may be many people against the establishment of such an agency in the government and there may be bad political repercussions. We do not know that the country will accept it. We do not even like to ask the President, because we do not think he should be put in a position where he has to say officially 'yes' or 'no' now."

I agreed to try to find out what Franklin's feelings were and to put before him their opinions and fears. I waited until my usual time for discussing questions with him and went into his room just before he went to sleep. I described the whole idea, which he already knew something of, and then told him of the fears that Harry Hopkins and Aubrey Williams had about such an agency. He looked at me and asked: "Do they think it is right to do this?" I said they thought it might be a great help to the young people, but they did not want him to forget that it might be unwise politically. They felt that a great many people who were worried by the fact that Germany had regimented its youth might feel we were trying to do the same thing in this country. Then Franklin said: "If it is the right thing to do for the young people, then it should be done. I guess we can stand the criticism, and I doubt if our youth can be regimented in this way or in any other way."

I went back to Harry Hopkins and Aubrey Williams the next day with Franklin's message. Shortly after, the NYA came into being and undoubtedly benefited many young people. It offered projects to help high school and college youngsters to finish school, and provided training in both resident and nonresident projects, supplementing the work of the Civilian Conservation Corps in such a way as to aid all youth.

It was one of the occasions on which I was proud that the right thing was done regardless of political considerations. As a matter of fact, however, it turned out to be politically popular and strengthened the administration greatly.

◆

SOURCE 3   In 1933, Eleanor Roosevelt began to hold regular press conferences limited to female reporters. What do Eleanor's answers to reporters' questions reveal about her efforts to change the role of women during the Depression?

Transcripts of Eleanor Roosevelt's Press Conferences (1933–1938)

June 15, 1933

TOPIC: Need for women to understand news.
Mrs. Roosevelt: "It is an awfully good thing to stress that this is a time when women have a special stake in watching national and international news. Every woman should have a knowledge of what is going on in economic conferences. It does affect the future amicable relations between the nations of the world. It has been stated the debt question is not to be discussed. But whatever does come out will be vitally important to every woman in her own home. Very few women know how to read newspapers and they miss what could give a new point of view. If more women would get in the habit of reading first the headlines, then the first paragraph,—often the whole gist of the article is in the first paragraph—that way a busy woman can count on keeping track at a time when every one of us ought to be on our toes to get what is happening every minute of time.

"The average woman today ought to read one paper that gives her point of view and two opposing points of view to draw her own conclusions. One's own prejudices and own ideas go into interpretation of public events.

Women should train themselves to see both sides, then decide what they really think.

"Many people will never read editorials at all. It is grand to read editorials and opinion but not to accept without thought. All writing and all opinion is only good when you make it your own."

July 6, 1933

TOPIC: National Woman's Party and the Equal Rights Amendment.
Mrs. Roosevelt: "I think the National Woman's Party ignores the fact that there is a fundamental difference between men and women. I don't mean by that women can't make as great a contribution, nor if they do the same work they not be paid the same wages. The mere fact that women basically are responsible for the future physical condition of the race means for many restrictions. It is a physical difference, not a mental.

"In my mail the most violent protestation against employment of married women comes from women themselves."

May 15, 1936

TOPIC: Garden party at the White House for inmates of the National Training School for Girls, a District of Columbia reformatory for Negroes. [Note by Strayer*] Mrs. Roosevelt went alone [on a visit to the reformatory] and told her press conference about it after her visit.
Mrs. Roosevelt: "I know of no place else where conditions exist like I found there. They have no psychiatrist. I think Dr. [Carrie] Smith [superintendent] said two girls were locked in cells when she came to the institution. I think she said 26 of the girls had syphilis and almost every girl had gonorrhea.

"There are no facilities to separate them from each other in cottages, each with one type of disease, but Dr. Smith separates them as far as possible. Every possible precaution is taken, but in those circumstances, what can you do? That is why Judge [Fay] Bentley [of the District of Columbia Juvenile Court] hasn't been willing to send any girls out there. She hasn't sent any girls there for a year.

"There was no teacher when Dr. Smith came. They now have one teacher that they are going to get a government appropriation for. Most of these girls are still school age. The youngest is 14. They go up to 21. Some of them have been there five years. The school has discarded library books that are falling to pieces.

"The girls have to be taken to Juvenile Court three times before they are committed out there. This is because of the physical conditions. The place has

---

*Martha Strayer was one of the reporters.

had no program to fit the girls to earn a living except doing the work of the institution, which, of course, is some preparation.

"They were making dresses to wear to the [White House] party when I was there the other day. They have always done the mending and sewing and made their own clothes because they always have to. They also were making gym suits of different colors for the different cottages. That, I thought, was beginning to give them a little more interest in life."

June 16, 1938

TOPIC: Married women in the labor force.
. . . **Mrs. Weed:** "Do you think there is a greater moral obligation on women to give up their work, when they have other means of support, than there is on men in the same circumstances, married or single?"

Mrs. Roosevelt: "I think if the single woman has to support herself, the question does not arise if she is under more moral obligation than a man.

"So I think it boils down to a married woman, and then comes the question whether the man or woman should be the main support in a family. My own instinct is a feeling that most women, if it comes to a decision, have more ability to find employment for themselves than most men have. But that doesn't always hold true.

"I happen to know of a couple where the woman earns money and the man runs a farm. It's the kind of work which doesn't bring in a large amount of income but which makes living a very pleasant, happy thing, and he is happy and does the kind of thing he enjoys. It's a happy family. My instinct is to say that, as a rule, a woman is more adjustable."

May [Craig?]: "What is a woman's duty? Her first duty is to stay home and take care of her family, and the other is to take a job in the economic situation when jobs are scarce."

Mrs. Roosevelt: "Who is going to be the person to decide whether it is a woman's duty to stay at home and take care of her family?

"Second, who should say that where the skills of the woman were such that she could do that particular job better than anybody else, better than she could do any other, probably it would be economically sound as well as spiritually a good thing? On the other hand, there may be a great many people for whom it would neither be spiritually or economically the best thing for their children or for that individual."

◆

SOURCE 4   Eleanor Roosevelt and Anna, her first child and only daughter, corresponded regularly. What does the letter on the following page reveal about the difficulties Eleanor had as First Lady?

Letter to Her Daughter (1937)

20 East 11th Street
New York City
March 3d [1937]

Darling,

. . . Pa is both nervous & tired. The court hue & cry [the Supreme Court packing controversy] has got under his skin. I thought stupidly his little outburst of boredom on meals was amusing & human & used it in my column & it was taken up by papers & radio & over the ticker & Steve [Early, press secretary] & Jimmy got hate letters & were much upset & Pa was furious with me. James came & reproved me & said I must distinguish between things which were personal & should not be said or none of them would dare to talk to me & he thought I should apologize to Father. I did before McDuffie [FDR's valet] Monday night before leaving as I couldn't see him alone & Pa answered irritably that it had been very hard on him & he would certainly say nothing more to me on any subject! So it has become a very serious subject & I am grieved at my poor judgment & only hope it won't be remembered long. Will I be glad when we leave the W.H. & I can be on my own!

A world of love to you all & much to you darling.

Mother

Source: Bernard Asbell, ed., *Mother and Daughter: The Letters of Eleanor and Anna Roosevelt* (New York: Coward, McCann and Geoghegan, 1982), p. 79.

◆———

SOURCE 5   James Roosevelt was Franklin and Eleanor's oldest son. What does he reveal about his mother's struggle for independence?

My Parents: A Differing View (1976)

JAMES ROOSEVELT

After [FDR's 1932] election, mother also confided to her friend Lorena Hickok that she never wanted to be a president's wife. And yet she may have been the best. She was the first First Lady to hold press conferences. In fact she held her first press conference two days before father held his first as president. She did

Source: From James Roosevelt, *My Parents: A Differing View,* p. 179. Playboy Press, a division of the Berkley Publishing Group, 1976.

so to ease the demand on her for individual interviews, but she avoided discussion of directly political topics. However, from the time beer was made legal again—the first of the thrusts that would lead to the repeal of Prohibition—and she announced at her regular press conference that she would serve it in the White House, hard news with a political angle began to emerge from these sessions.

Later she began to do magazine articles, magazine and newspaper columns ("My Day") and even books. While these were not purely political, they had a political impact. Father was aware of this. He edited her book *This Is My Story* rather ruthlessly and would have edited, or had written for her, the columns and articles in his favor if she had given him the opportunity. But she was becoming independent. When there were complaints about her receiving $1000 an article, she ignored them because she did not consider the complaints justified. I doubt that today a president's wife would be permitted to receive pay for articles unless she donated the cash to charity, but mother treasured her private income. She did give much of it away, but only as she wished.

Attacks on Eleanor Roosevelt

As Eleanor Roosevelt began to champion a variety of reforms, she was assaulted by critics.

◆

SOURCE 6

Excerpts from Letters to Franklin Roosevelt (1935)

From Fort Wayne, Indiana

[The First Lady] "would be rendering her country a far greater service if she would but uphold the dignity of the White House," . . .

From a New York woman

". . . is it not humanely [sic] possible to muzzle that female creature, known to the world as your wife?"

Source: James R. Kearney, *Anna Eleanor Roosevelt: The Evolution of a Reformer* (Boston: Houghton Mifflin Company, 1968), pp. 228–229; originally from "President's Personal File #2," Box 1, Franklin D. Roosevelt Library.

From a Philadelphia man

Mrs. Roosevelt should cease "gadding about the country and butting into matters that are no concern of hers. . . . My God, what a woman!"

◆

SOURCE 7   Bingham was the son of Robert W. Bingham, the publisher of the Louisville *Courier-Journal* and FDR's ambassador to Great Britain; McIntyre was FDR's appointments secretary.

Letter from Barry Bingham to Marvin McIntyre (1934)

The old propaganda story is being passed around in Louisville to the effect that Mrs. Roosevelt has made herself offensive to Southerners by a too great affection for Negroes. The tale is that she was visiting in South Carolina recently, and was scheduled to make a speech in one of the larger towns. She is said to have ridden to the auditorium, through the streets of the town, in an open car in which she sat next to a Negro woman, with whom she conversed sociably all the way.

Source: From *Eleanor and Franklin* by Joseph P. Lash. Copyright © 1971 by Joseph P. Lash. Reprinted by permission of W. W. Norton and Company.

Eleanor Roosevelt on Feminism

Eleanor Roosevelt was frequently asked about her stands on equality for women and the proposed equal rights amendment, which the National Women's Party lobbied Congress to pass every year starting in 1923. What are her positions on these issues? Do these sources reveal contradictions in her views about female equality? Do they reveal attitudes shaped by class as well as gender?

SOURCE 8

News Item, "Definition of Feminism" (1935)

SPECIAL TO THE NEW YORK TIMES

Washington, May 7.—Mrs. Roosevelt gave today "by request" her definition of feminism as follows:

"Fundamentally, the purpose of feminism is that a woman should have an equal opportunity and equal rights with any other citizen of the country.

"I believe the desire of women for equality of opportunity and of recognition is just as alive, certainly in this country, and in fact more so, than it was ten years ago," she told her press conference.

"I may be wrong," she added. "I am conscious that I know very little, and I don't want to argue with anybody."

Source: New York Times, May 8, 1935, p. 2. Copyright © 1935 by the New York Times Co. Reprinted by permission.

SOURCE 9

News Item, "Opposes Amendment" (1938)

SPECIAL TO THE NEW YORK TIMES

Washington, Feb. 7.—Opposition to the proposed equal-rights amendment and the tipping system, and approval of special laws for women in industry, were reiterated today by Mrs. Roosevelt.

"There is no question that professional people and people who work with their heads should be on the same basis, regardless of sex," she said.

"But I still believe in protective legislation for women in industrial groups and shall continue to believe in it until the whole situation in industry changes."

In regard to tipping, a live issue here in a controversy on whether tips should be included in estimating the minimum wage to be fixed for waitresses,

Source: New York Times, February 8, 1938, p. 7. Copyright © 1938 by the New York Times Co. Reprinted by permission.

Mrs. Roosevelt said she "disliked the whole idea of tipping," regarding it as an outgrowth of a less-than-living wage.

"However," she said, "if tips must be relied on for part of the income of waiters, then I think they might better be included in the bill and the total pooled and distributed among the employes on payday."

◆

SOURCE 10   Eleanor Roosevelt addressed this advice book to women coping with the Depression.

It's Up to the Women (1933)

If a woman does her own work, the vital thing for her to do is to organize it so well that when her husband returns home she is not an exhausted human being, but can still meet him with a smile and enter into whatever interests he may wish to discuss with her.

If she has a domestic helper in her household, she must remember that she is dealing with a human being, and it is well for her to try everything herself before she lays down her rules for any one else. I have a theory that, under our modern system in which it is rare for any one to have more than one maid in the house, if a young woman will systematize her own work, she can greatly assist whoever is working for her. For instance, if when she gets up she immediately puts her bedclothes to air, it will save either her or her maid the necessity of coming up to do it later on, or of making up the bed without airing. Habits of neatness can be formed by the mistress so that she keeps her own part of the house tidy, and when she enters the kitchen to give an order, or to do some piece of work, she does not leave behind her a trail of work for somebody else to do. Then the household will run smoothly, the maid will come to her for advice and she will soon find if she does her own part of the work, that there is no shirking on the part of those who work with her. . . .

. . . I have often thought that it sounded so well to talk about women being on an equal footing with men and sometimes when I have listened to the arguments of the National Woman's Party and they have complained that they could not compete in the labor market because restrictions were laid upon women's work which were not laid upon men's, I have been almost inclined to agree with them that such restrictions were unjust, until I came to realize that when all is said and done, women *are* different from men. They are equals in many ways, but they cannot refuse to acknowledge their differences. Not

Source: From Eleanor Roosevelt, *It's Up to the Women,* Frederick A. Stokes Company, 1933, pp. 25–26, 201–202.

to acknowledge them weakens the case. Their physical functions in life are different and perhaps in the same way the contributions which they are to bring to the spiritual side of life are different. It may be that certain questions are waiting to be solved until women can bring their views to bear upon those questions. . . .

CONCLUSION

Few students would disagree with one historian's claim that "the behavior of . . . individuals is more interesting . . . than their behavior as groups or classes."[11] Maybe that is why the biographical approach to history remains popular, even though historians today reject the idea that history is merely the biography of great people. Yet Eleanor Roosevelt's life demonstrates that biography does more than create an enjoyable path to the past. Rather, it shows the power of individuals to move at great odds against impersonal forces. As First Lady, Eleanor struggled against the social and economic forces that shaped the lives of people who had no biographers. As she sought her own "salvation," she also struggled with the cultural forces influencing her own life. Her successes and failures as a reformer thus reveal as much about her times as they do about her life.

Still, neither Eleanor Roosevelt's background nor her public activities made her typical. Few girls had the opportunity to grow up in late nineteenth-century high society. Far fewer had the opportunity to become First Lady. In the past, that did not matter to most historians, who were more interested in people at the top of society than at the bottom. Today, however, many historians are interested in the lives of ordinary people. By writing history "from the bottom up," they reveal the historical significance of people who traditionally have lacked distinct voices. So in the next chapter, we turn to people whose lives were a world removed from Eleanor Roosevelt's.

FURTHER READING

Blanche Wiesen Cook, *Eleanor Roosevelt, 1884–1933* (New York: Viking, 1992).

Tamara K. Hareven, *Eleanor Roosevelt: An American Conscience* (Chicago: Quadrangle Books, 1968).

Stella K. Hershan, *The Candles She Lit: The Legacy of Eleanor Roosevelt* (Westport, Conn.: Praeger Publishers, 1993).

Joseph P. Lash, *Eleanor and Franklin: The Story of Their Relationship, Based on Eleanor's Private Papers* (New York: W. W. Norton and Company, 1971).

Eleanor Roosevelt, *The Autobiography of Eleanor Roosevelt* (New York: Harper and
Brothers, 1961).

NOTES

1. Eleanor Roosevelt, *This I Remember* (New York: Harper and Brothers, 1949), p. 113.
2. Doris Kearns Goodwin, "The Home Front," *The New Yorker,* August 15, 1994, p. 51.
3. Nelson W. Aldrich, *Old Money: The Mythology of America's Upper Class* (New York: Vintage Books, 1989), p. 212.
4. Quoted in William H. Chafe, "Biographical Sketch," in Joan Hoff-Wilson and Marjorie Lightman, eds., *Without Precedent: The Life and Career of Eleanor Roosevelt* (Bloomington: Indiana University Press, 1984), p. 4.
5. Eleanor Roosevelt, *This Is My Story* (New York: Harper and Brothers, 1937), p. 24.
6. Quoted in William H. Chafe, "Biographical Sketch," in Hoff-Wilson and Lightman, *Without Precedent,* p. 5.
7. Quoted in Lois Scharf, *Eleanor Roosevelt: First Lady of American Liberalism* (Boston: Twayne, 1987), p. 28.
8. Eleanor Roosevelt, *This Is My Story,* p. 40.
9. Quoted in Joseph P. Lash, *Eleanor and Franklin: The Story of Their Relationship, Based on Eleanor Roosevelt's Private Papers* (New York: W. W. Norton, 1971), p. 220.
10. Quoted in ibid., p. 355.
11. Quoted in Edward H. Carr, *What Is History?* (New York: Alfred A. Knopf, 1962), p. 56.

Chapter 9

History "From the Bottom Up":
The Detroit Race Riot of 1943

The documents in this chapter offer facts and theories about the participants of the Detroit race riot of 1943.

Secondary Source

1. The Detroit Rioters of 1943 (1991), DOMINIC J. CAPECI, JR., and MARTHA WILKERSON

Primary Sources

2. A Handbill for White Resistance (1942)
3. Black Employment in Selected Detroit Companies, 1941
4. An Explanation for Strikes (1943)
5. Black Workers Protest Against Chrysler (1943)
6. A Complaint About the Police (1939)
7. Changes in White and Black Death Rates, 1910–1940
8. A Profile of the Detroit Rioters

*A*t 6:30 P.M. Monday June 21, 1943, Moses Kiska, a 58-year-old African-American, waited for a streetcar at Mack Avenue and Chene Street in Detroit. Kiska may have noticed a car drive by him and then turn around. Inside the car were four white youths, aged 16 to 20. Earlier, they had been looking for something to do and decided to drive around to see the fighting between blacks and whites that was turning Detroit into a bloody racial battleground. Late the night before, black and white youths had clashed on Belle Isle, a public park in the Detroit River. Less than a day later, rampaging African-American and white mobs were assaulting one another, beating innocent motorists, pedestrians, and streetcar passengers, burning cars, destroying storefronts, and looting businesses.

As the four whites youths drove around, one of them said, "Let's go out and kill us a nigger."[1] They continued to drive, but they couldn't find a target. They saw a lot of blacks, but they were in groups. They wanted someone by himself. Then on Mack Avenue they saw what they were looking for. The driver of the car grabbed his companion's gun, turned the car around, pulled up to the lone man, and pulled the trigger. As Moses Kiska fell to the ground, the car carrying the four boys sped off. "We didn't know him," one of the youths later testified. "He wasn't bothering us. But other people were fighting and killing and we felt like it, too."[2]

Moses Kiska was one of 34 people who lay dead after three days of rioting in Detroit. The riot was a brutal reminder to Americans in 1943 of deep racial divisions in their society. Today it reminds historians that they must know something about the lives of ordinary people in places like Detroit if they are to understand fully the impact of World War II on American society.

Before the mid-twentieth century, historians usually did not write such "grassroots" history. They relied mostly on written sources produced by an educated elite, and their histories were written without reference to the lives of people at society's bottom. When historians did examine ordinary people, it was usually within the context of movements or organizations. If they studied labor history, for instance, they focused on unions, not the lives of workers. Of course, there is much more to the lives of common people than their involvement in political or labor organizations. By the 1950s, such scholars as George Rudé, Eric Hobsbawm, and Christopher Hill began to explore "an unknown dimension of the past," that is, the lives of ordinary people.[3] These historians had been influenced by the Great Depression and World War II, powerful examples of the masses' involvement in history. They were often guided as well by the Marxist conviction that history was made in the peasant's hut as well as in the castle.

Unfortunately, these historians did not have a ready-made body of sources at hand. Since people at the bottom of society rarely leave written records to explain their lives, much of their history was initially restricted to riots and revolutions. Such events as European peasant revolts or the French and American revolutions brought to public notice many people who rarely attracted attention. These uprisings left historians with documentation of otherwise obscure lives.

Today, historians with tape recorders and computers can preserve the memories of ordinary people and analyze massive amounts of data from a census or legal documents. Such technology helps them explore "bottom up" history far removed from riots or revolutions. As a result, many scholars are now interested in the lives of everyone from seventeenth-century slaves to late twentieth-century migrant farm workers. At the same time, historians have not abandoned the study of civil disturbances such as the Detroit riot. Like other social upheavals, this riot thrust people at the bottom of the society into the public arena. For that reason it remains a good place to explore the lives of people mostly absent from the pages of history.

SETTING

In the months after Pearl Harbor, many observers saw trouble ahead on the home front. As black, white, and Hispanic workers converged on booming defense plants, racial and ethnic tensions began to rise. In 1943, more than 200 riots and racial conflicts had erupted across the country. In Los Angeles, a large war production center, sailors on leave attacked Mexican-American youths who had embraced the zoot suit, a style characterized by baggy pants tied in at the ankle. The fighting lasted four days and ended only when military authorities intervened. In May, black and white workers clashed in a Mobile, Alabama, shipyard. Several weeks later, a white mob attacked the black section of Beaumont, Texas, leaving two dead. Then in August, a race riot in New York City resulted in five deaths and millions of dollars in property damage.

Before 1943, however, many observers had predicted that the greatest racial strife would be in Detroit. As automobile and other factories converted to defense production, thousands of Depression-ravaged people descended on the Motor City. Many were from the South, and most were poor. Eighteen months after Pearl Harbor, Detroit's population had surged by 350,000 people, 50,000 of them black. They joined the 160,000 African-Americans already living in the city's slums. "Detroit," declared *Life* magazine, "is dynamite." The city, it predicted, "can either blow up Hitler or it can blow up the U.S."[4]

In June America's greatest "Arsenal of Democracy" exploded. After three days of rioting state and federal troops finally restored order. By then, property damage had run into the millions of dollars and war production had been halted for days. But the greatest toll was that suffered by African-Americans. Twenty-five blacks had lost their lives, 17 of them killed by police. Blacks made up more than 75 percent of the approximately 600 injured people and 85 percent of the roughly 1,800 people arrested.

When the riot was over, Detroiters joined other Americans in the search for explanations. There were plenty of convenient targets: "thugs," Axis agents, the Ku Klux Klan, the police, Polish-Americans, Italian-Americans, Syrian-Americans, and "hillbillies." One Mississippi newspaper even blamed Eleanor Roosevelt. The most popular scapegoat, however, was the African-American. The lure of wartime jobs had drawn large numbers of southern blacks to northern cities like Detroit, where they were often scorned by longtime residents. Many observers thought that they were unable to adjust to northern life. Franklin Roosevelt's attorney general, for instance, recommended that the president limit the migration of blacks into cities that could not "absorb" them for "cultural" reasons. "It would seem pretty clear," he declared, "that no more Negroes should move to Detroit."[5]

After the riot, Detroit's white city leaders were also quick to point fingers. The mayor declared that the riots were started by young African-American hoodlums. The Wayne County prosecutor charged that the leaders of the National Association for the Advancement of Colored People "were the biggest instigators of the race riot" and "would be the first indicted" if a grand jury were called.[6] A committee of city, county, and state law enforcement officials agreed with that assessment. It concluded that the "exhortation by many Negro leaders to be 'militant' in the struggle for racial equality played an important part in exciting the Negro people to violence."[7] Just as quickly, black leaders pointed to other causes: job discrimination in Detroit's booming defense plants, housing discrimination that forced blacks into expensive but run-down housing, police brutality, and the daily animosity of Detroit's white residents. Explanations of the riot revealed battle lines that were as clearly drawn as those in the riot itself.

INVESTIGATION

If Detroiters had ready answers to the causes of the riot, the sources in this chapter offer some as well. Your main assignment, therefore, is to determine who the Detroit rioters were and why they rioted. A good analysis of the riot should address the following questions:

1. **What is the main essay's explanation for the riot?** Was the riot an irrational act or a form of protest?

2. **How would you characterize the rioters?** Do the characteristics of the rioters contradict contemporary observers' explanations for the riot?

3. **Was the Detroit riot for revenge or personal gain, or was it an ideological protest?** What is the authors' evidence for the motive of the rioters? Do the characteristics of the rioters reveal their motives?

4. **Do the primary sources support the essay's conclusions?** Do they offer evidence that World War II changed the expectations of African-Americans? What role should those expectations play in accounting for the riot?

SECONDARY SOURCE

◆

SOURCE 1   In this essay, Dominic Capeci and Martha Wilkerson examine who rioted in Detroit and offer an explanation for their behavior. They rely on evidence from Detroit's criminal court records to study the background and assess the actions of some of the rioters. Their work reflects the challenge that historians often face when trying to establish the motives of people who leave few written records to explain their behavior. Your analysis of the Detroit riot should begin with a careful reading of the authors' argument. Pay particular attention to their explanation for the behavior of the rioters, and look for evidence for the motives of the rioters. Also note whether the authors offer evidence that World War II changed the attitudes of Detroit's black and white residents. Do you agree with the authors' characterization of rioters or with the assessment of Gustave Le Bon and other European scholars of collective violence?

The Detroit Rioters of 1943 (1991)

DOMINIC J. CAPECI, JR., AND MARTHA WILKERSON

To Charles "Little Willie" L.—and, no doubt, to many others who rose on Sunday morning to clear, sunny skies, summerlike temperatures, and a day free from monotonous work, the tension that made Detroit "dynamite" seemed ever-present. Twenty years old and single, L. lived with his brothers and sisters at 5815 Brush Street (see Detroit map). His apartment sat in the east side, black Detroit's oldest, most congested, run-down community, one extending from downtown Adams Street north to Leicester Court, bounded by Woodward Avenue on the east and St. Aubin Street on the west. His world, like that of most of the city's 185,000 black residents, consisted of dilapidated accommodations rendered "almost intolerable" by time and in-migration. Since his arrival from Brookhaven, Mississippi, five years earlier, Charles L.

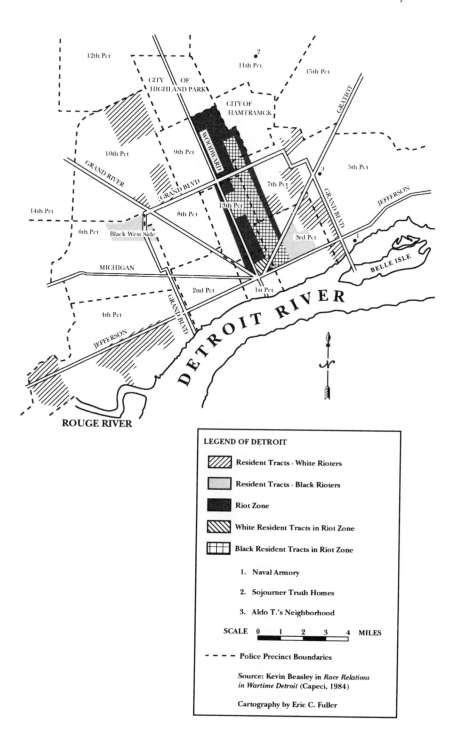

LEGEND OF DETROIT

▨	Resident Tracts - White Rioters
▨	Resident Tracts - Black Rioters
■	Riot Zone
▨	White Resident Tracts in Riot Zone
▦	Black Resident Tracts in Riot Zone

1. Naval Armory

2. Sojourner Truth Homes

3. Aldo T.'s Neighborhood

SCALE   0   1   2   3   4   MILES

- - - -   Police Precinct Boundaries

Source: Kevin Beasley in *Race Relations in Wartime Detroit* (Capeci, 1984)

Cartography by Eric C. Fuller

had witnessed an enormous influx of black newcomers, which had swelled to 2,100 per month since the previous year and increased the black population by 24 percent.

Packed into a ghetto three-and-one-half miles square, which contained several viable institutions, diverse classes, and close-knit families, Charles L. and his neighbors found employment in the war-boom economy. He had worked as a laborer in grocery stores and factories for the past two years, no doubt denied access to well-paying defense jobs because of low skills, limited education, and "marked racial feelings." "Little Willie," who stood 5 feet 4 inches, weighed 140 pounds, and appeared dark-skinned, was considered "aggressive" and "antisocial"—perhaps the result of his diminutive size and ghetto experience. He seemed "criminalistic" to the Recorder's Court psychiatrist, although he boasted no arrest record. He knew discrimination firsthand, however, and had clashed recently with white youths and lawmen.

Seeking escape from the east side's confines, where the temperature broke 90 degrees on Sunday afternoon, Charles L. headed for Belle Isle. Perhaps he brooded along the way, angered by Detroit's inadequate recreation area and agitated by memories of Eastwood Park six days earlier. On Tuesday evening, he was one of fifty black teenagers and zoot suiters accosted by nearly 200 white high school students and servicemen at the privately owned amusement park in East Detroit. He lost the fight, as policemen arrested several whites and ejected all blacks. Charles L. had traveled over seven miles from his home to this amusement park, deep into lily-white territory. Consciously or otherwise, he also did so to protest the restrictive and humiliating conditions placed upon him—upon all black Detroiters. He embodied the "zoot effect," adopting expressive dress—broad shouldered, long-waisted coats, and bloused, pegged pants—behavior, and language that stroked his ego, parried racism, and affronted many of both races, who labeled such antics as abnormal, even gangsterlike, and mocked them in caricatures.

Small wonder that today Charles L. ventured more than three miles to Belle Isle—an island park in the Detroit River connected to the mainland by the Jefferson Avenue bridge—where 100,000 Detroiters converged to escape sultry weather and, ironically, wartime tensions. He arrived in midafternoon, one of many blacks who made up fully 80 percent of the crowd that jammed the isle's 985 acres of ball fields, beaches, and boardwalks, hiking trails and canoe livery, playgrounds and picnic areas. The large proportion of blacks present may have emboldened him, or the growing resentment of many whites, who objected to close racial associations, may have raised his own bitterness. In any event, around 3:30 P.M. he led a milling crowd of blacks in a series of altercations with whites, which officials said "fanned the flame of hatred" and led ultimately to the death of thirty-four persons.

Charles L. shot craps with several youths, both black and white, before a fight broke out over the question of crooked dice. The white cheaters fled the scene, and Charles L. and his friends were unable to catch them. Frustrated, he exhorted seven teenagers to avenge their humiliation in Eastwood Park and "take care of the Hunkies." Quickly he led them in a series of forays, assaulting whites, breaking up their picnics, and consuming their food. In thus evening the score, L. and his marauders reflected the racial tone of other confrontations that began to break out with increasing regularity (blacks and whites scuffling for pony rides or picnic grills). By 9:30 P.M. the exchange of blows and epithets escalated, recording the first hospital casualty—a white teenager assaulted three times within twenty minutes—and Charles L. surfaced again. At the playground, he and his pack attacked fourteen-year-old Gus Niarhos and stole his carfare. Failing to hail a homeward bus or chase down another white target, they headed across the crowded bridge to Detroit. It was now 10:45 P.M. Soon L. brushed against thirty-eight-year-old Joseph B. Joseph, called him a "white mother-fucking son of a bitch," and slammed him to the pavement, where other black youths kicked him and suggested hurling him into the river. As the victim struggled to his feet and raced into the path of two white sailors and their dates at the island end of the bridge, L. and his cohorts moved toward Jefferson Avenue.

Pushing and name calling—"black bitch," "white bastard"—turned to mayhem as one of the sailors blew his whistle and rallied some fifty bluejackets stationed at the armory on Jefferson Avenue. Fighting broke out all along the bridge and spilled onto the thoroughfare, where one of Charles L.'s gang unsuccessfully urged blacks to enter the fray, claiming, "a colored woman and her baby had been drowned." By 11:30, however, white numbers had soared and comprised most of the 5,000 persons in the area. Sailors, still smarting from a racial brawl the previous morning, bridge crossers, and nearby residents fought to reclaim the park and reestablish social distance: "We don't want any niggers on Belle Isle." They beat and chased blacks, spreading their vengeance one block either side of Jefferson Avenue and four blocks north on Grand Boulevard. During the next two and a half hours, the crowd dispersed as police officers flooded the intersection and took control without serious loss of life. They handled the disorder, said blacks, by "beating and arresting Negroes while using mere persuasion on whites."

Charles L. was neither among the twenty-eight blacks arrested nor the five injured. He made his way back to the east side and, along with several witnesses frightened by the crazed-looking white toughs, alerted others in the black community. He, or someone else, arrived at the east-side Forest Club at 12:30 A.M. and informed Leo T. of the fighting across-town on Jefferson Avenue.

Thirty-five-year-old T. lived with his wife at 976 Wilkins Street. A resident of Detroit since the age of three, he was familiar with past racial conflicts—the Ossian Sweet incident (1925), the Black Legion terrorism (1930s), and the Sojourner Truth housing disorder (1942). He had brushed with the law as a way of life: thirteen arrests for unarmed robbery, breaking and entering, disturbing the peace, frequenting a gambling place, destruction of property, and, as recently as May 1941, carrying concealed weapons; four convictions, two prison terms, and one probation violation. He had worked as a handy man at the Forest Club, a popular recreation center, since his last police encounter, operating a sound truck, selling dance tickets, and manning the coat room. Literate but crime-prone, he doubtlessly experienced alienation toward white society and especially its gendarmes. His victims, however, had hitherto been fellow blacks.

At the Forest Club that night, Leo T. made his way through the crowd of 700 dancers, climbed atop the bandstand, and stopped the music. Dressed in a dark suit and carrying a briefcase, he identified himself as Sergeant Fuller and announced that a riot was in progress on the island, where whites had thrown "a colored lady and her baby" off the bridge. Everyone "get your guns" and "go out there," he instructed; free transportation awaited outside. Then, having directed his anger against whites, he disappeared, and pandemonium broke out.

Leo T.'s shocking news stampeded Forest Club patrons into the street, but no vehicles idled at the curb for their convenience. Their numbers were unusually large because the night spot, which contained a bowling alley, dance floor, and skating rink, provided one of the few recreational outlets for blacks, and, on June 20, was holding a "big dance" that drew several hundred youths. Galvanized by the rumor of whites killing a black woman and child, which linked a specific violation of sacred mores with general hostile beliefs in white violence, dancers and pedestrians became vengeance-seeking mobs. They filled the intersection of Forest Avenue and Hastings Street, stoning white motorists and trolley passengers while taunting policemen who came to rescue them. One thousand persons of both sexes and various classes struck human targets and overwhelmed lawmen, whose depleted wartime ranks and Belle Isle emergency assignments made answering 500 east-side calls impossible. Unchecked, blacks beat, hit, and stabbed whites who crossed their path, sending one injured person every minute to Receiving Hospital.

Soon rioters roamed throughout "the colored district," flush with victory and, like counterparts of a later generation, "commonality of purpose." South of Canfield on Brush, they knocked unconscious a twenty-seven-year-old white man, who became the first fatality when crushed accidentally by a cab. North of Grand Boulevard on Holbrook, they fought fifty Chevrolet Gear and Axle shift workers, and created disturbances along Oakland Avenue at Owen and Westminster. In this section, a mile above the boulevard, black residents like John T. clashed with police and forced them to detour streetcars. Most in their early twenties, married, and employed as laborers—and well aware of the "hate strikes" that had rocked Detroit for the previous six months, denying promotion of blacks to more skilled, better paying jobs—they might have been pursuing white workers out of revenge.

As police sealed the ghetto and whites avoided it, rioters turned their attention to stores, and, sometime before dawn of June 21, began to loot them. In fact, within one hour of Leo T.'s announcement, they were smashing windows on Hastings Street. Their fury now spread out of control along all the major commercial streets: St. Antoine, Beaubien, Brush, and John R, east to Hastings; Rivard, Russell, Riopelle, and Dequindre, west to St. Aubin. From Adams Street north to Grand Boulevard and ultimately beyond, residents shifted from an interracial or communal upheaval to a riot against property. Hemmed in by physical boundaries, they concentrated on symbols of white domination—lawmen, property, and goods— as white citizens, absentee landlords, and shop owners slept beyond their reach. They confronted officers, injured several, and killed one, but drew deadly, often indiscriminate gunfire, which would ultimately claim seventeen black lives. More often, rioters demolished store fronts and showcases, strewed mannequins and merchandise around the streets in the midst of broken glass, and left large segments of the business district looking as if it "had been bombed from the air with block busters." Looters, in turn, swept through drug and grocery stores, haberdasheries, pawnshops and taverns, confiscating everything from aspirin to liquor. Some stole alone, others in groups; some acted crazy, others deliberate; some targeted any store, but a great majority spared known "colored" establishments or those later identified by hastily painted signs.

At 4:00 A.M., whites began to retaliate along Woodward Avenue, probably having heard of the upheaval from escaping passersby and laborers. Adolescents and young men gathered about the Roxy and Colonial theaters, stoning the cars of blacks that passed along the thoroughfare, which separated black ghetto and white west side, itself characterized by substandard dwellings and transient populations. They also assaulted black patrons exiting from the all-night cinemas and tried to push their way into the black community at Alfred, but were driven back by police officers. In close residential proximity to east siders and competing with them for jobs and status, white assailants, like their predecessors in earlier interracial riots, sought to kick blacks back into their place. And, despite a lull in their activities around 6:30 A.M., they—again like earlier rioters—seemed proud of themselves and threatened further bloodshed. . . .

. . . White gangs controlled Woodward Avenue, halting traffic to drag blacks from trolleys and automobiles, beat them viciously, sometimes senseless, overturn and incinerate their cars—all pay-back for east-side attacks. They roamed about, with little interference from bluecoats, whose numbers never exceeded 1,000, were divided between two war zones, and generally harbored racial prejudice. Inside the ghetto, where most officers found themselves assigned, blacks continued to break into stores, forage for possessions, and run afoul of patrolmen. Looters represented older, more mature residents, albeit no less resentful than the ruffians led by Charles L.

Rudolph M. certainly would have fought at Belle Isle. A twenty-three-year-old native of Louisiana, who had come to Detroit only thirteen months before the disturbance, he lived with his wife on Edmund Place, two blocks east of Woodward Avenue and midway between Forest Avenue and downtown. He worked in a store stocking shelves for wages far below those paid in the defense industry. Perhaps angered by his environment—slums largely built before 1915, often lacking indoor plumbing, and cruelly dubbed "Paradise Valley"—he turned his anger against absentee owners responsible for his plight. Rather than destroy his own dwelling, however, he selected a more practical target over a half mile from home: Paul's Drug Store at Hastings and Leland. He hurled first a brick and then, moments later, a bottle through the plate-glass window. He was only one of many in the missile-throwing crowd, but he alone drew the attention of police officers, who apprehended him after a short chase. He was found to be carrying a 7-inch butcher knife, a concealed weapon. Though he made no effort to slash his captors, his possession of the blade indicated fear and possibly Southern tradition. Significantly, his presence on the street and repeated attacks on the pharmacy revealed deep alienation and purposeful protest—the combination of ghetto isolation, oppression, numbers, and solidarity with wartime opportunities and anxieties.

Looters carried this racial complaint further. Their early morning plunder seemed symbolically defiant, and soon became wholesale theft by usually law-abiding citizens. Roy S., for instance, watched as several people tossed armfuls of merchandise out of a grocery store at 4717 St. Antoine, half a mile from his home on East Ferry. He and a companion were loading several pounds of pork loins, smoked ham, canned salmon, and cheese—then rare and rationed items—into their car, when police arrested them for larceny. Born in Gregory, Arkansas, but a Detroit resident for the past five years, S. lived with his wife and child and earned good money at Ford Motor Company. Approaching thirty years of age, seeming less disaffected and more established than window smashers like Rudolph M., he nonetheless helped himself to food thrown into the street. Possibly he considered such actions righteous redistribution and redefinition of property—as would some ghetto rioters a generation later. Yet S. never hinted at motivation; he told officers only that he had picked up the goods and indicated which store they came from. That a man like this should engage in behavior normally unlawful—but momentarily acceptable by many in the community—disclosed the drawing power and the grievance of mob activity; that he should collect mostly perishables that would have spoiled if left in the gutters and could have been purchased in the expensive but equitable rationing system, exhibited the ambivalence of moral standards and the anomie among oppressed people. Experiencing mixed emotions and motives in a wholly unregulated and opportunistic setting, Roy S. stole, but he did so for much more than "fun and profit."

Neither Rudolph M. nor Roy S. knew the proprietors of the stores they sacked, despite later contentions by observers that such actions manifested anti-Semitism. Living half a mile away and possessing little if any knowledge of which stores were Jewish-owned, they delivered symbolic attacks on "the white caste." They probably knew that German and, more recently, Russian Jews had occupied the east side before them and still controlled many of its apartments and businesses, yet the antagonisms that fueled the violence were customer-merchant rather than ethnic. They believed themselves exploited by all shopkeepers, not simply the white druggist and the Russian Jewish grocer. Certainly black anti-Semitism—growing out of socioeconomic competition and cultural conflict, which enjoyed a long tradition in the ghetto, and intensified in the face of Nazi propaganda—heightened tensions, but M. and S. reacted as opportunists seizing the moment rather than as ideologues punishing Semites. They struck at accessible, safe targets, emblems of white exploitation and black humility, and they struck as everyday residents, who had neither police records nor apparently political doctrines. . . .

. . . Concentrated in an enormous rectangle, stretching from downtown Detroit north to the city of Highland Park, running through the heart of the 1st, 13th, and 9th precincts and spilling over east and west into adjacent zones, upheaval also occurred in the black west side and above the Polish city of Hamtramck. Approximately three miles west of Woodward Avenue at Ironwood and Tireman, deep in the black middle-class community to which those who escaped the ghetto had moved, Thomas H. disturbed the peace. Like many living in this stable, upwardly mobile area of homeowners, he was married and employed in a skilled job; unlike most of those milling in the street, he had brushed with the police once before. He might have been displaying anger over reports of DPD brutality in the east side and indifference to white assaults downtown. At thirty-nine years of age, H. and his cohorts were older than most rioters elsewhere, possibly venting frustration over white society's disregard for their socioeconomic achievements and disdainful rejection of them as mere "niggers." . . .

The numbers and characteristics of those apprehended between June 21 and June 30 affected how the riot was interpreted by many people. Of nearly 2,000 arrestees, young, black males comprised the overwhelming majority, followed by far fewer white males and black and white females. These participants recorded a median age of twenty-five years; surprisingly few of the scores of juveniles seen at the riot were arrested. Regardless of age or gender, blacks filled the ranks of arrestees in greater proportions than their population in metropolitan Detroit. Their spokespersons attributed this gross imbalance to police bias, while bluecoat officials explained it in terms of black aggression. . . .

Those who witnessed or read about the rampage also blamed Southern newcomers. When [Mayor Edward] Jeffries stated that an influx of migrant workers contributed to the riot, he sparked the ire of editors like Ralph McGill of the *Atlanta Constitution,* who protested "the cheap and easy habit of blaming any and all racial troubles on the South." Such conflict grew out of civil injustices and economic inequities found in both Detroit and Dixie, lectured McGill, noting also that teenagers, not Southern laborers, had ignited the outburst. Despite McGill's logic, most Detroiters thought like their mayor. Popular *News* columnist W. K. Kelsey ascribed the disorder to scores of Southerners who encountered liberal conditions in the city, where blacks experiencing newfound freedom clashed with whites clinging to "Jim Crow notions." . . .

. . . Of course, more than black hooligans and Southern newcomers participated in the Detroit riot of 1943. Despite contemporary studies and public opinion, hoodlums and migrants shared the streets with lawful, longtime Detroiters. Rioters, in fact, included multitudes of ordinary men and women of both races. Their experiences, as well as those of teenagers, identify more completely those arrested for having been in the crowd. . . .

. . . The largest percentage of black men, slightly more than a quarter, fell between the ages of twenty-eight and thirty-seven, and the median age for all black male participants stood at twenty-seven years. Nearly 63 percent were married, and nearly 75 percent lived in Paradise Valley. Most were literate and employed, and over 85 percent had benefited from the war boom and worked as laborers; 9 percent of the black rioters worked as skilled and semiskilled operatives, suggesting even higher and more stable social standing. Significant also for understanding the spontaneous actions of normally upright residents, most black transgressors were arrested alone and for the first time in their lives. They rioted in their home precincts and within a half mile of their east side addresses.

Information from probation records indicated further social stability for black males. Overwhelmingly born and bred in Alabama, Georgia, and Mississippi, fully half of them had resided in Detroit for nine years or more—the median stay, just short of a decade. Most were married, nearly 40 percent were raising children, and over 50 percent had secured meaningful jobs within the past year; they represented working-class people hopeful of bright futures. Indeed, having endured the Great Depression and blatant racism, they must have sensed the potential for personal and racial advancement: Weekly wages of fifty dollars, median educations of eight years, and several successful protests over housing and employment had surely raised their expectations. . . .

In sum, usually law-abiding and hard-working men stood side-by-side with lawbreakers. No doubt many of both kinds were politically astute and racially proud. Black laborers and skilled workers, particularly those married, with children and education levels approaching that of whites, knew of—might even have participated in—recent DSR* incidents, housing controversies, or hate strikes that sharpened racial animus. Very likely their riot activity arose from the accumulation of blocked socioeconomic opportunities, which they attributed to white racists. They deemed the Belle Isle rampage and accompanying rumors as final provocation in a series of real and occasionally perceived wrongs. Fearful for their newfound prosperity and status, they struck as much to protect their stake in society as to destroy their enemy, as much out of pride as anger. Black repeat offenders probably clashed with lawmen on familiar ground over perennial grudges. Slightly over 25 percent of all black male participants, however, exhibited calculated or mindless theft as they looted east-side stores, expressly those on Hastings Street. And a minute number of arrestees attacked white citizens or patrolmen, perhaps displaying a bloodlust that predated wartime frustrations. In essence, no single profile or motivation moved black males to action. Protestors and lawbreakers alike took part in several different kinds of riot for equally diverse reasons. . . .

Unsurprisingly, white male rioters were as diverse as their black counterparts. Nearly 65 percent of all white men were younger than twenty-three years old. Their ages extended from seventeen to fifty-four, the median age at twenty years—less extreme than the black range of fourteen to sixty-four and significantly younger than the black midpoint of twenty-seven. Consequently, over 70 percent of the white arrestees were single and over 55 percent worked as laborers, with 4 percent as clericals, 5 percent as semiskilled, 23 percent as skilled operatives, and the rest service employees or domestics. And, regardless of marital status or occupation, slightly more than 50 percent of all white participants lived relatively close to Belle Isle or on the fringes of Paradise Valley, and 40 percent more traveled over two miles to riot along its boundaries. Fully three quarters of all white offenders left their home precincts, determined to secure the perimeters of Detroit's color line against integrated housing and black upward mobility. Young adults, ordinarily law-abiding, mobilized to avenge past affronts aboard public conveyances, in municipal parks, and at downtown theaters, stores, and eateries.

Probation data reveals that almost all white arrestees were individuals with roots, on the make, and yet insecure. Most—53 percent—identified their home state as Michigan, and only one named the South as his origin; obviously far fewer white Southerners participated in the upheaval than was believed by officials, black leaders, and residents. Surprisingly, white in-migrants, Southern born or otherwise, stayed pretty clear of the disturbance. Neither Bedford B. nor Leonard O., placed on probation for carrying concealed weapons, qualified as "hillbillies"—those allegedly clannish, dirty, ignorant newcomers

---

*Detroit Street Railway.

from Dixie. One came from a border state, the other from Michigan. Neither possessed police records, and both worked as machinists. They lived with their families, respectively, east of Cass in a neighborhood of white transients and north of Grand Boulevard in a mixed area rapidly becoming an extension of the black ghetto. Separated by nearly twenty years of life (forty-two versus twenty-three) and eight years of education (third grade versus eleventh), they shared little save their whiteness, offenses, and convictions. Both carried weapons, one a butcher knife, the other a nickel-plated revolver, and received sentences of short probation. Occasional drinking problems aside, both met the terms of probation. Having reported regularly, worked steadily, and provided a "suitable home," they were discharged with improvement. Their experiences belied the dominance of Southern or other groups of newcomers among white participants.

Despite . . . Southern cultural deprivation theories, over 80 percent of the white felons had resided in the city more than six years. In fact, 50 percent had lived as Detroiters for over seventeen years. Except for being significantly more single than black felons, they registered similar education levels, time of employment, and wages. They competed with blacks for jobs and status, which personalized and sharpened the racial rivalry. Most probably, they recalled the hardships of depression and, facing black competition on every front, feared slipping backward. . . .

Personal characteristics and riot activity also distinguished black female rioters from males of both races. (No data exist for white women, whose participation in the disturbances was completely ignored for the first two days out of the prejudice or chivalry of out-numbered, overtaxed lawmen.) Ranging from seventeen to forty-five years of age, black women tallied a median age of twenty-four and one-half years. Over 65 percent were single, yet almost half of those had been separated, divorced, or widowed. Regardless of marital status, 69 percent of all black females worked outside the home: 43 percent as domestics, cooks, or similar service workers, and 19 percent as common laborers. Their ages, marital statuses, employment rates, occupational categories, and police records identified most of them as predominantly older, mature, working class, and law-abiding. . . .

Prior to the 1960s, European scholars of collective violence in England and France followed the lead of Gustave Le Bon. They characterized early rioters as criminal, maladjusted, and riffraff, unstable persons fulfilling emotional needs and selfish, apolitical aims. Lacking quantifiable evidence and drawing on psychological interpretations, they posited breakdown and contagion theories: Urbanization and industrialization promoted antisocial behavior in some individuals, and these misfits exploded, drawing others into a "mental unity" of excitement, destruction, and anonymity.

Le Bon's theory is still quite popular with some officials and private citizens, but it began losing its credibility among scholars in the early 1960s. Some, like

E.J. Hobsbawm and E. P. Thompson, resurrected and revised Karl Marx's solidarity theory, and interpreted collective violence as the struggle of working-class people for political power. Non-Marxist historians also explained riot as protest and participants as ordinary people seeking redress. Perhaps most influential is George Rudé's synthesis of preindustrial crowds, which posits violence as collective behavior evolving through a precise set of determinants. Rudé presented history from the bottom up and suggested similarities between food rioters and political rebels. He also encouraged further investigation of the mob in other eras and locales as a "living and many-sided historical phenomenon." Slightly more than a decade later, a comparative history of upheavals in England, France, and Germany between 1830 and 1930 by Charles Tilly, Louise Tilly, and Richard Tilly extended the revised history of collective violence into modern times and suggested parallels for the recent civil disorders in the United States. . . .

In fact, the Detroit rioters of 1943 provided the necessary example for understanding successive generations of white and black participants in riots dating back to the turn of the century and, particularly for blacks, forward to the 1960s. Taken together and allowing for distinctions of time, place, and riot patterns, . . . Detroit profiles have dashed officials' self-serving descriptions of earlier white rioters as riffraff and raised anew the possibility that rioters in other cities . . . represented several classes and ethnic groups. While additional research is needed of all those who erupted before World War II, Detroiters . . . came from the general populace and shared certain traits with them.

Indeed, participants in the 1943 Detroit outburst desired greater participation in society. White rioters felt threatened and their black counterparts resentful, for members of both races had made enough gains to want much more. Unlike more successful residents, they were too impatient to mark time amid democratic rhetoric and wartime change. Younger, more energized, and less influential than those who avoided violence, they sought redress in the streets; they rioted to improve rather than destroy the system. They came forth as neither mainstream nor misfit, but as desperate people seeking respectability through protest that shed blood and ironically reinforced their disrepute in the eyes of the public.

PRIMARY SOURCES

Most of the sources in this section reflect the social and economic conditions of Detroit's African-American population and their view about those conditions. What, if anything, does this evidence reveal about the causes of the Detroit riot and the motives of the rioters?

SOURCE 2   In 1942, African-Americans were accepted as tenants in the Sojourner Truth Homes, a public housing project located in a black-Polish neighborhood. When they arrived to move in, they were greeted by white mobs who beat them and stoned their cars.

A Handbill for White Resistance (1942)

Source: From Archives of Labor and Urban Affairs, Wayne State University.

The Job Situation

What do the following sources reveal about job discrimination in Detroit during World War II?

———◆———

SOURCE 3

Black Employment in Selected Detroit Companies, 1941

Aeronautical Products, Inc.	0.02 percent
Briggs Manufacturing Company	7.0 percent
Chrysler	2.5 percent*
Hudson Motor Company	1.8 percent
Murray Corporation of America	5.0 percent
Packard Corporation	11.0 percent*
Vicker, Inc.	3.0 percent*

*Most were foundry workers or janitors.

Source: Data from Richard W. Thomas, *Life for Us Is What We Make It* (Bloomington: Indiana University Press, 1992), p. 157.

———◆———

SOURCE 4   In early 1943, blacks walked off their jobs at Chrysler and Ford plants to protest the working conditions they encountered. The *Michigan Chronicle,* a black newspaper, offered an explanation for the strikes at Ford.

An Explanation for Strikes (1943)

. . . It is extremely significant that all of the so-called "Negro wild-cat strikes" in the local war plants have arisen in departments in which the Negro workers are jim-crowed and isolated because of their color. Rather than integrate the workers, the companies insist in most cases in creating separate racial gangs

Source: Reprinted from *Michigan Chronicle,* May 8, 1943 by permission of the publisher.

in the factory. They claim that this procedure eliminates trouble, yet the facts reveal that wherever workers are so segregated, the separate groups invariably pit themselves against each other and violence follows the slightest provocation. To the normal problem of general worker relations the companies add the second problem of racial relations.

◆

SOURCE 5   In March 1943, 600 black male workers at the Chrysler Highland Park plant walked out to protest the working conditions of black women at the factory. Here two female workers offer their explanations for the protest.

Black Workers Protest Against Chrysler (1943)

We are not given the same opportunities for promotions that white women are given. In the first place, . . . the superintendent has stated that we have got to do the hard work, such as pulling steel, running jitneys and heavy mopping. Many of us were hired as elevator operators but have never run an elevator at the plant because the men on the elevators refuse to transfer to work we are doing. They say the work is too hard for them. We have taken our complaints to the union—to the proper sources—but there has been no action. . . .

Many of us have trained for skilled jobs, hired as matrons but our jobs soon developed into common labor in the shop-labor for which the company is unable to hire men. White girls turn these jobs down and are given other work, but Negro women are told . . . they must do these jobs or ring their cards and go home. I was fired from my job because I wanted to change my clothes before going out to sweep around the building at 6 a.m. on a cold morning. I had been working in a hot place all night and would have been exposed to catching a severe cold. . . .

We are constantly being intimidated because we insist on eating in the regular places. When we first went to the plant they gave us separate toilets—far from our work—and we were told that we would have to eat our lunch in these restrooms. There is nothing but two benches and a low table in them. We don't know what they were used for before we were hired. Once when a colored girl changed her clothes in a white girl's restroom, she went back and found out that the buttons had been cut off her coat and her galoshes cut into shreds. We complained to the plant committeeman about this but have not heard anything from him.

Source: Reprinted from *Michigan Chronicle,* April 10, 1943 by permission of the publisher.

SOURCE 6   This editorial ran in the Detroit *Tribune,* a black newspaper, in 1939. Note black Detroiters' complaints about the police department.

A Complaint About the Police (1939)

The Detroit Police Department is apparently trying to establish a national record for brutality to Negro citizens. In spite of the many protests made to those in authority, the brutality continues. . . . Since January 1, this year, the number of Negroes slain in cold blood and savagely beaten and clubbed by local police officers has steadily mounted. . . . In addition to these and other murders by Detroit policemen in recent months, many other members of our race have been brutally clubbed and beaten by officers of the law, without just cause. . . . Policemen are paid by the taxpayers to preserve law and order and to protect human lives and public and private property, but they have no right to take the law into their own hands, as so many of them do. It is not their duty to act as judges, juries and executioners, in their dealings with Negroes. Policemen have no legal or moral right to let their racial or religious prejudices lead them to persecute members of our race or any other racial group, and when policemen . . . forget their duty as to indulge in such lawless acts of violence, they should be curbed, reprimanded, and in flagrant cases they should be dismissed from the Police Department and punished by the courts of justice.

Colored citizens of Detroit have been protesting for some time to those in local authority, and appealing to them to put a stop to this police brutality, but our protests thus far seem to have fallen on deaf ears.

Source: Detroit *Tribune,* July 15, 1939.

SOURCE 7   Declining death rates are usually an indication of improving living conditions. Do these tables provide evidence about the expectations of blacks in Northern cities like Detroit? Do they reveal a difference between Detroit and the rest of the nation in that regard?

Changes in White and Black Death Rates, 1910–1940

Changes in White and Black Death Rates in Detroit,
1915–1940 (per 1,000)

Year	White Death Rate	Black Death Rate
1915	12.8	14.7
1920	12.8	24.0
1925	10.4	19.4
1930	8.7	15.6
1940	8.0	12.2

Changes in National Black and White Death Rates
1910–1940 (per 1,000)

Year	White Death Rate	Black Death Rate
1910	14.5	21.7
1920	12.6	17.7
1930	10.8	15.6
1940	10.4	13.9

Source: Richard W. Thomas, *Life for Us Is What We Make It* (Bloomington: Indiana University Press, 1992), pp. 104, 105.

◆

SOURCE 8   As you examine the table on the following pages, determine whether the data support or contradict the main essay's argument about the characteristics of the rioters. Do these statistics indicate significant differences between white and black rioters? More than 1,500 blacks and 250 whites were arrested; can historians draw valid generalizations about the Detroit rioters from such a sample?

A Profile of the Detroit Rioters

Characteristics	Black Males (N = 205)		White Males (N = 30)		Black Females (N = 11)		Total Sample (N = 246)	
	#	%	#	%	#	%	#	%
Black	205		—		11		216	87.7
Male	205		30		—		235	95.5
Median age	27 years		19 years		28 years		26 years	
Range of ages	16 to 64		17 to 41		17 to 38		16 to 64	
Married	129	62.9	11	36.7	4	36.4	144	58.5
Laborer	176	85.9	16	53.3	1	9.1	193	78.5
Employed	197	96.1	28	93.3	6	54.5	231	93.9
Resident precinct 3, 9, 13	150	73.2	10	33.3	10	90.0	170	69.1
Detroit resident	199	97.1	27	90.0	11	100.0	237	96.3
No previous arrest	124	60.5	21	70.0	11	100.0	156	63.4
Riot Behavior								
Felony	115	56.1	12	40.0	6	54.5	133	54.1
Misdemeanor	90	43.9	18	60.0	5	45.5	113	45.9
Weapon	59	28.8	13	43.3	1	9.1	73	29.7
Looting	55	26.8	1	0.03	7	63.6	63	25.6
Conduct	88	42.9	16	53.3	3	27.3	107	43.5
Arrested in home precinct	126	61.5	7	23.3	5	45.5	138	56.1
Arrested within ½ mile of home	106	51.7	7	23.3	9	81.8	122	49.6
Arrested in precinct 1, 3, 9, 13	158	77.1	16	53.3	8	72.7	182	74.0

Source: Excerpted from Dominic J. Capeci, Jr., and Martha Wilkerson, *Layered Violence: The Detroit Rioters of 1943*, p. 210. Copyright © 1991 by the University of Mississippi Press. Reprinted by permission of the University of Mississippi Press.

A Profile of the Detroit Rioters (con't)

Additional Characteristics[1]	Black Males (N = 68)		White Males (N = 5)		Probation Records (N = 73)	
	#	%	#	%	#	%
Home state in South[2]	59	86.8	2	40.0	61	83.6
Acted alone	49	72.1	2	40.0	51	69.9
No children	41	60.3	2	40.0	43	58.9
Protestant	66	97.1	2	60.0	69	94.5
Median education	8 years		9 years		8 years	
Median length of residence	9.5 years		14 years		12 years	
Median length of present employment	1 year		1 year		1 year	
Median weekly salary	$50.00		$50.00		$50.00	

[1]These additional data are drawn from the probation records that could be located for male felons.
[2]South includes the lower South (South Carolina, Mississippi, Louisiana, Alabama, Georgia, Texas, and Florida), upper South (Tennessee, Virginia, Arkansas, and North Carolina), and border states (Kentucky and Missouri).

CONCLUSION

"There's a monotony about the injustices suffered by the poor . . ." the critic Dwight Macdonald once wrote. "Everything seems to go wrong with them. They never win. It's just boring."[8] Although there was nothing boring about the Detroit riot, Macdonald had a point. Unless an eruption had occurred there in 1943, Detroit's wartime slums would draw relatively little notice today. Macdonald's observation points to a problem facing historians looking at history "from the bottom up." The poor are not at the center of power. They normally do not make decisions affecting the lives of millions, and often their lives appear to change little until violence breaks the monotony. Historians would seem to find little worthy of study in them.

Yet wartime Detroit shows that historians must see beyond the "monotony" of everyday life. The city's slums reflected important changes in the lives of many Americans. Historians who wish to understand how World War II changed American society need to understand those who lived in the slums of cities like Detroit or New York. Because historians make generalizations about historical influences, they cannot lose sight of the people at society's bottom. Otherwise, they may explain less than they claim to. That is a good point to remember as we turn next to one historian's explanation regarding the influence of a single factor—anticommunism—on America's postwar culture.

FURTHER READING

Earl Brown, "The Detroit Race Riot of 1943," in *A Documentary History of the Negro People in the United States, 1933–1945,* ed. Herbert Aptheker (Seacus, N.J.: Citadel Press, 1974).

A. Russell Buchanan, *Black Americans in World War II* (Santa Barbara, Calif.: Clio Books, 1977).

Alfred McClung Lee and Norman D. Humphrey, *Race Riot, Detroit 1943* (New York: Octagon Books, 1968).

Elaine Latzman Moon, *Untold Tales, Unsung Heros: An Oral History of Detroit's African-American Community, 1918–1967* (Detroit: Wayne State University Press, 1994).

George Rudé, *The Crowd in History: A Study of Popular Disturbances in France and England, 1730–1848* (New York: John Wiley and Sons, 1964).

Richard W. Thomas, *Life for Us Is What We Make It* [A history of black Detroit] (Bloomington: Indiana University Press, 1992).

NOTES

1. Quoted in Alfred McClung Lee and Norman D. Humphrey, *Race Riot (Detroit, 1943)* (New York: Octagon Books, 1968), p. 38.

2. Ibid.

3. Eric J. Hobsbawm, "History from Below—Some Reflections," in *History from Below: Studies in Popular Protest and Popular Ideology in Honour of George Rudé,* ed. Frederick Krantz (Montreal: Concordia University, 1985), p. 65.

4. Quoted in Robert Conot, *American Odyssey: A Unique History of America Told Through the Life of a Great City* (New York: William Morrow, 1974), p. 379.

5. Quoted in Earl Brown, "The Detroit Race Riot of 1943," in *A Documentary History of the Negro in the United States, 1933–1945,* ed. Herbert Aptheker (New York: Citadel Press, 1969), p. 453.

6. Quoted in Conot, *American Odyssey,* p. 386.

7. Quoted in ibid.

8. Quoted in Michael Sragow, "The Individualist," *The New Yorker,* September 12, 1994, p. 90.

Chapter 10

History as Synthesis:
The Cold War and Popular Culture
in the 1950s

The documents in this chapter deal with the anticommunist climate of the Cold War era.

Secondary Source

1. The Culture of the Cold War (1991), STEPHEN J. WHITFIELD

Primary Sources

2. Advertisement for *Runaway Daughter* (1953)
3. Promotional Material for *Walk East on Beacon* (1952)
4. A Game Show Producer Remembers the Red Scare (1995)
5. A Playwright Recalls the Red Scare (1995)
6. The Hammer Song (1949), LEE HAYES and PETE SEEGER
7. A Folk Singer Remembers the Early 'Fifties (1995)
8. Sixty Minute Man (1951), WILLIAM WARD and ROSE MARKS
9. Sweet Little Sixteen (1958), CHUCK BERRY
10. Pogo (1952), WALT KELLY

*I*n March 1947 the House Un-American Activities Committee (HUAC) came to Hollywood to expose communist influence in the film industry. Ronald Reagan, Gary Cooper, Robert Taylor, Adolph Menjou, and other stars testified as "friendly" witnesses at HUAC's hearings. Menjou declared, "I am a witch hunter if the witches are Communists. . . . I would like to see them all back in Russia."[1] Other witnesses also shared evidence of subversion in Hollywood's studios. Animator Walt Disney told the committee of a communist plot to turn Mickey Mouse into a Marxist. Fervid anticommunist author Ayn Rand pointed to evidence of subversive influence in *Song of Russia* (1943), one of several pro-Soviet wartime films produced when the United States and the Soviet Union were allies in World War II. Rand declared that the movie made her "sick." It showed Russian schoolchildren smiling, and in Russia, Rand pointed out, children never smiled.

The committee, chaired by Representative Parnell Thomas, also heard from ten "unfriendly" witnesses. All of them refused to cooperate with HUAC, and Thomas had armed guards drag them from the hearing room. Later that year all were cited for contempt by the Congress and indicted by a grand jury. By 1950 the "Hollywood ten" were in prison. Two of the ten, screenwriters Ring Lardner, Jr., and Lester Cole, served time in the federal prison at Danbury, Connecticut. By the time they arrived, former HUAC chairman Thomas was already there, convicted in 1949 of padding his office payroll. One day Cole passed Thomas, who was in charge of the prison farm's chicken yard. "I see," Cole observed, "that you're still shoveling chicken shit."[2]

Cole and the other "Hollywood ten" did not get the last laugh with the communist hunters, however. By the time they were released from prison in 1951, anticommunist hysteria had only grown. That year HUAC returned to Hollywood to ferret out more communists and communist sympathizers. The committee obtained more than 300 names. By then, the major studios had begun blacklisting actors, screenwriters, and technicians, making it virtually impossible for them to find work. And the hunt for subversives had also spread well beyond Hollywood. The unexpected Soviet test of an atomic bomb, the conviction of the accused spy Alger Hiss in 1950, and the outbreak of the Korean War the same year had fed a growing fear of communism. So had Senator Joseph McCarthy's shocking accusations of a communist underground in the government. By 1950, the effort to root out alleged communist subversion had spread from Hollywood and the government to television, radio, and schools. When McCarthy was censured by the U.S. Senate four years later, McCarthyism had become a household word and thousands of lives and careers had been ruined.

The postwar anticommunist witch-hunt tarnished reputations, sent people to prison for their political convictions, and even led some to commit suicide.

Because many of the accused were writers and performing artists, it also dramatically affected the postwar era's films, television programs, novels, and other expressions of popular culture. Producers of entertainment—and messages—for mass consumption were visible targets of the communist hunters' investigations. Many were liberal, some were communists, and most had been enthusiastic supporters of America's alliance with the Soviet Union during World War II. It was not an accident that Hollywood was one of the first places to be searched for subversives, or that the search would quickly turn to television and radio networks and to other producers of popular entertainment.

Because of the vulnerability of writers, artists, and entertainers to anticommunist hysteria, popular culture is one of the best places to see the impact of the Cold War on American society. To understand the Cold War's impact on the popular messages in that era, historians must synthesize or combine evidence from such diverse sources as films, plays, songs, television programs, novels, and even comics. In this chapter, we piece together some of this evidence to create a picture of American popular culture in a period of anticommunist hysteria.

SETTING

As is true today, popular culture in the 1950s meant primarily movies, television programs, and recorded music as well as fiction, drama, and even fashion and comics. In the postwar years, however, spreading affluence, new technology, and growing numbers of children and teenagers made this culture more pervasive than ever. Its growing influence was evident in the new medium of television and in new forms of popular entertainment, from TV's situation comedies to rock 'n' roll. And many postwar commentators were appalled by what they saw and heard. Surveying postwar radio, television, movies, and novels, one critic declared popular culture to be "non-art."[3] Other observers lamented the homogenization of culture pitched to a mass audience.

Since the 1950s, scholars have continued to debate the limits and limitations of popular culture. Yet most of them would probably agree about its important characteristics. If "high" culture conforms to rigorous artistic standards, demands some effort to enjoy, and appeals to a limited audience, popular culture adheres to no fixed rules, requires no effort to enjoy and little training to understand, and thus appeals to a broad audience. At the same time, popular culture differs from folk culture: stories, songs, dances, and other forms of artistic expression usually created by a society's illiterate, lower classes. Folk culture is preserved in memory and is passed down orally, often over centuries. By contrast, popular culture is created and marketed by an entertainment industry and transmitted through channels of mass communication, both of which are dominated by large corporations. In other words, it is a commodity to be bought and sold for profit in the marketplace. Like other marketable commodities, it has a short "shelf life." Popular culture, then, travels instantly and disappears quickly, but often not before it has touched all levels of society.

Today, historians who study postwar popular culture are less interested in judging people's tastes than in understanding what its messages reveal about the period. They also see much more variety in the popular culture of the 1950s than did contemporary critics, who often focused on the burgeoning white, middle-class suburbs. Historians also recognize numerous influences on postwar popular culture: growing middle-class affluence, the spread of suburbia, the increasing importance of the automobile, the "baby boom," and the Cold War. Thus their task is to understand popular culture's messages and determine the role of varied influences in shaping them.

The glorification of mothers and homemakers, a dominant theme of postwar popular culture, illustrates the challenge. Undoubtedly, the baby boom and the growth of suburbs played a large role in fashioning this domestic ideal, which was broadcast widely in the movies, television, and magazines of the 1950s. Yet so may have other factors, including the Cold War. The domestic ideal was a comforting image and a useful tool in the battle against communism. The image of the suburban home with its contented homemaker seemed to be compelling evidence of American superiority in the Cold War. Thus when Richard Nixon engaged Soviet leader Nikita Khrushchev in their famous "kitchen debate" at an exhibition of American goods in Moscow in 1959, the vice president praised the American way of life because it had eased the domestic burden of women. Standing in front of a washing machine, Nixon told Khrushchev, "What we want is to make easier the life of our housewives."[4]

The postwar domestic ideal illustrates that popular culture's influence can run in many, often unexpected, directions. It also demonstrates that popular culture can be shaped by numerous influences. To understand its many messages, historians must draw from myriad, often unrelated, sources. And, as with any historical analysis, they must be careful not to attribute too much influence to a single cause.

INVESTIGATION

In the movie *Blackboard Jungle* (1955), an idealistic teacher played by Glenn Ford tells a high school class filled with rebellious students, "All your lives you're gonna hear stories—what some guy tells you, what you see in books and magazines—but you gotta examine these stories, look for the real meaning, and most of all . . . you gotta think for yourselves."[5] It was easy for postwar Americans to enjoy their favorite television programs, movies, music, or popular fiction without thinking much about them. Few perceived in them a common frame of reference. Now, with the advantage of hindsight, historians can synthesize a variety of sources into a coherent picture. In this chapter, we examine a wide array of cultural artifacts to determine the messages, assumptions, and values they reveal. The main problem is to determine what impact the fear of communism had on postwar American popular culture. Your analysis of the culture of the Cold War should address the following questions:

1. **Did the Cold War narrow postwar popular culture?** How did it "distort and enfeeble" cultural expression, according to the main essay? How did it undermine challenges to the status quo?

2. **Did the Cold War affect various forms of popular culture the same way?** Do the sources reveal that some types of popular expression were blander than others? Were some more susceptible to outside pressures? What clues do the sources offer about why?

3. **Is the main essay's argument about the impact of anticommunism on postwar popular culture supported or contradicted by the primary sources?** Do the sources reflect a cultural consensus, or do they demonstrate a clash of discordant messages and resistance to dominant standards? Is popular culture an influential force in American society, or is it merely a commodity that is influenced by other developments?

Before you begin, read the section in your textbook about the Cold War, especially its impact on American society in the 1950s. It will provide background that will help you analyze this chapter's sources. What is its view about the Cold War's impact on cultural expression?

SECONDARY SOURCE

SOURCE 1   In this selection, historian Stephen Whitfield explores the impact of anticommunism on various forms of popular culture. Pay particular attention to his argument about the main messages conveyed by postwar popular culture. What is the most important evidence that anticommunist hysteria influenced popular culture? Are Whitfield's examples representative?

The Culture of the Cold War (1991)

STEPHEN J. WHITFIELD

In 1951, one of the prisoners in a New York jail awaiting sentencing under the Smith Act for conspiring to advocate the violent overthrow of the American government was George Charney. The chairman of the state's Communist party and a member of the national committee, he became acquainted with an Italian-American hoodlum named Bob Raymondi, who since his teens in Brooklyn had associated with Murder, Inc., and was a veteran of seventeen years as an inmate of Dannemora. While dominating the prison population, Raymondi also sought to compensate for his poor formal education by chatting with the Marxist-Leninists who had been inserted among the other prisoners. One Saturday, Raymondi's sister visited him and was startled to learn how close he had gotten with Charney and others convicted under the Smith Act. "My God, Bob," she warned. "You'll get into trouble."

In this era, a specter was haunting America—the specter of Communism. Trying to exorcise it were legislators and judges, union officials and movie studio bosses, policemen and generals, university presidents and corporation executives, clergymen and journalists, Republicans and Democrats, conservatives and liberals. The specter that, a century earlier, Marx and Engels had described as stalking the continent of Europe was extending itself to the United States, . . . By introducing ideological politics, Communism became more loathed than organized crime, exacerbating fears that were to distort and enfeeble American culture throughout the late 1940s and the 1950s. . . .

. . . Censors endorsed the boycott of films that they had not seen; vigilantes favored the removal from library shelves of books that they had not read.

The confusion of the public and private realms was also characteristic of the era. Thus, the Federal Bureau of Investigation compiled dossiers on novelists who seemed unduly critical of their native land, and the bureau got into the movie business by secretly filming the patrons of a left-wing bookstore, Four Continents, in New York. At the same time, some representatives of Hollywood presented themselves to Congress as authorities on the theory and tactics of Marxism-Leninism. An awed member of the House Committee on Un-American Activities (HUAC) hailed even the mother of musical star Ginger Rogers as "one of the outstanding experts on communism in the United

Source: Excerpted from Stephen J. Whitfield, *The Culture of the Cold War,* pp. 1, 2, 10–12, 34, 35, 37, 53, 56, 71, 127, 131–133, 144, 200–203. Copyright © 1991 by Johns Hopkins University Press. Reprinted by permission of Johns Hopkins University Press.

States," for example. While legislators were interrogating musicians and actors about their beliefs, university administrators were using political instead of academic criteria to evaluate the fitness of teachers. Even as some clergymen were advocating ferocious military measures to defeat an enemy that was constantly described as "atheistic," government officials were themselves asserting that the fundamental problem presented by Communism was not political but spiritual. . . .

. . . [T]he effect was . . . the suffocation of liberty and the debasement of culture itself. Even by the narrowest chauvinistic criteria of the Cold War, the United States thus diminished its ability in the global struggle to be seen as an attractive and just society. The politicization of culture might win the allegiance of those who cherished authority, but not of those who valued autonomy. The politicization of culture might appeal to reactionaries abroad, but not to foreigners who appreciated creativity or critical thought.

And though the state was intimately involved in restricting liberty, it acted with popular approval and acquiescence; the will of the majority was not thwarted. In effect, Americans imposed a starchy repression upon themselves. . . .

. . . One response can be explored at the murkier edges of popular sensibility, the locale of novelist Mickey Spillane. . . .

On the top ten fictional bestsellers of the decade of the 1950s, Spillane wrote an astounding six of them: number three, *The Big Kill* (1951); number five, *My Gun Is Quick* (1950); number six, *One Lonely Night* (1951); number seven, *The Long Wait* (1951); number eight, *Vengeance Is Mine* (1950); and number nine, *Kiss Me, Deadly* (1952). This catalogue does not count his most popular novel, *I, the Jury,* which had been published prior to the decade. By 1953, the New American Library had sold seventeen million paperbacks of his first six novels, which meant that having Spillane on the firm's list of authors was like a license to print money.

I, the Jury (1947) introduced a private investigator named Mike Hammer, a World War II veteran of such magnanimity that he harbors no hostility toward Nazis. Though he chose not to become a cop because a "pansy" bureaucracy was emasculating policemen with its rules and regulations, his real contempt is reserved for the professional and intellectual classes, for homosexuals, and above all for swarthy criminals like "the Mafia. The stinking slimy Mafia. An oversized mob of ignorant, lunk-headed jerks who ruled with fear and got away with it because they had the money to back themselves up."

The detective's hairy-chested heroics would have made such novels enormously popular even if they had been devoid of any explicit politics, but the overt anti-Communism of Spillane's fiction engraved it with the signature of the period. Two decades earlier, Hammer might have combated only organized criminals spawned in the lower depths; two decades later, the adversaries would have been a cabal of Third World terrorists. In the early 1950s, however, the Red Scare required his special skills. For the comrades and conspirators in *One Lonely Night,* Hammer has reserved kicks that can shatter bone on impact, bursts of lead from his .45, and the sadistic pleasures of strangulation.

In that novel, which sold more than 3 million copies, the detective seduces a millionaire's estranged granddaughter, whom boredom has driven to Communism. At first Hammer cannot fathom why Ethel Brighton, despite her early exposure to the attractions of capitalism, can embrace the twisted creed of Bolshevism. He suspects that she needs only the substitute of *his* embrace. Confident that his virility can transform her politics, he has her spend one night in his apartment, and concludes, "Now that she had a taste of life[,] maybe she'd go out and seek some different company for a change." He is wrong—or at least seems to be, and realizes that Ethel Brighton has continued to associate with the scum and perverts who comprise the Communist movement. So he strips and whips her. Eventually Hammer poses as a member of the Soviet intelligence apparatus; since no one in this supposedly very clandestine organization thinks of challenging his credentials, he considers these conspirators as "dumb as horse manure." These malignant dreamers of world conquest "had a jackal look of discontent and cowardice." When they are not merely credulous cretins, they are either vicious hypocrites or else clinically insane. The supreme villain in *One Lonely Night* is Oscar Deamer, who is both a Communist and a psychopath. Hammer tells this master criminal, just before choking him to death: "You were a Commie, Oscar, because you were batty. It was the only philosophy that would appeal to your crazy mind. It justified everything you did and you saw a chance of getting back at the world." The explanation for the appeal of Communism is, apparently, insanity.

In destroying such motiveless, psychopathic malevolence, Hammer personifies the rejection of liberalism. The cure for the plague of Communism cannot be the diffusion of New Deal programs to relieve economic misery, or the extension of the Four Freedoms to amplify the meaning of an open society, or more resonant calls to lighten the burden of social injustice. The solution, the creator of Hammer seems to fantasize, is violent prophylaxis. After the detective has saved his naked fiancée from hysterical Bolshevik flagellants, he murders them all, . . . "I killed more people tonight than I have fingers on my hands," he later boasts. "I shot them in cold blood and enjoyed every minute of it. . . . They were Commies. . . . They were red sons-of-bitches who should have died long ago. . . . They never thought that there were people like us in this country. They figured us all to be soft as horse manure and just as stupid." . . .

To appraise the literary significance of such fiction would be utterly irrele-vant, to sermonize against such appalling crudeness equally pointless. What needs underscoring is that, at least in the night battles of the Cold War for which Spillane recruited more Americans than any other author, the proce-dural rules and legal guarantees that helped make a civil society worth defending were treated with savage contempt. Justice was imagined as coming from the barrel of a pistol, and cruelty was not confined to Party headquarters but was exalted in the exploits of Mike Hammer. Because of the official limitations under which formal authority chafed, vigilante ruthlessness was the only effective antidote to unmitigated evil. . . .

The search to define and affirm a way of life, the need to express and celebrate the meaning of "Americanism," was the flip side of stigmatizing Communism; to decipher the culture of the 1950s requires tracing the formu-lation of this national ideology. It was not invented but inherited, and some of its components were intensified under the political pressures of the era. The belief system that most middle-class Americans considered their birthright—the traditional commitment to competitive individualism in social life, to the liberal stress on rights in political life, and to private enterprise in economic life—was adapted to the crisis of the Cold War. . . .

. . . [By the 1950s] the bounties pouring forth from American factories and laboratories, made available in such profusion in stores and markets, had become perhaps the chief ideological prop—the most palpable vindication—of "the American way of life." Success and virtue were so easily equated that, after *Life* magazine published *The Old Man and the Sea* (1952), the industrialist who became Eisenhower's secretary of the treasury was puzzled by the popular fascination with Hemingway's story. "Why would anybody be inter-ested in some old man who was a failure," George M. Humphrey wondered, "and never amounted to anything anyway?"

Such assumptions help account for Barbie (b. 1958), the most popular doll in history. With her own national fan club, she received five hundred letters a week. Eleven and one-half inches tall, this late adolescent was endowed with a three-and-one-quarter-inch bust that smashed an anatomical taboo in the toy market. But what made her something of an icon of the Cold War were the fantasies of consumption that she evoked. Barbie came cheap: three dollars. But her full wardrobe cost more than one hundred dollars, and her appetite for more was insatiable: party dresses and casual attire, prom gowns and eventually a wedding ensemble (her boyfriend's name was Ken), outdoor outfits, professional uniforms. Barbie lived in a split-level house, patronized a beauty parlor, drove a Corvette. She "seemed to be only a product," one scholar concluded, "but she turned out to be a way of life," an affirmation of national supremacy. The capitalist "fetishism of commodities" that Marx found so repellent had advanced to the first line of defense. . . .

. . . The movie industry was conscripted into the Cold War in 1947 when HUAC was invited to Los Angeles. The committee's host was the Motion Picture Alliance for the Preservation of American Ideals, an organization that struck a typical postwar stance in asserting that "co-existence is a myth and neutrality is impossible . . . anyone who is not FIGHTING Communism is HELPING Communism." About fifteen hundred members of the film community had founded the alliance three years earlier; they included John Wayne, Gary Cooper, Walt Disney, Adolphe Menjou, and Cecil B. De Mille. Its first president was director Sam Wood, who felt so strongly about the subject that his will imposed as a condition of inheritance that his relatives (other than his wife) file affidavits in court that they "are not now, nor have they ever been, Communists." . . .

. . . [By the 1950s] it was safer to produce films without any political or economic themes or implications at all. Although *Broken Arrow* (1950) had presented Cochise sympathetically as a peace-loving Apache, Monogram Studios abandoned its plans for a movie on Hiawatha, whose efforts to achieve peace among the Iroquois nations might be interpreted as a boost to Communist peace propaganda. Because novelist Theodore Dreiser had formally converted to Communism shortly before his death in 1945, Paramount got the jitters in adapting his classic of a generation earlier, *An American Tragedy.* So director George Stevens toned down the social analysis and highlighted the romance in *A Place in the Sun* (1951). Stevens's protagonist (Montgomery Clift) is no longer a victim of certain class relationships that Dreiser had shown motivating Clyde Griffiths toward homicide. Then even the inflated love story posed a problem when supporting actress Anne Revere took the Fifth Amendment, so Paramount cut out most of her major scenes. . . .

. . . [I]t was prudent to avoid overtly political films. Consider, for instance, the fate of Universal's *The Senator Was Indiscreet* (1947), a satire about a bumbling Senator (William Powell) who does not realize that a new income tax bill applies to him as well. He runs for the presidency on a platform that includes adding his relatives to the payroll and giving every citizen the right to attend Harvard. The movie also dares to suggest that White House aspirants can be packaged with images that can maximize their appeal to the electorate. *The Senator Was Indiscreet* was written by Charles MacArthur, was rewritten and produced by Nunnally Johnson, and was the only movie that George S. Kaufman ever directed. None of the three was a political activist. All were renowned for their wit, which was lost on Congresswoman Clare Boothe Luce (R-Conn.) when it was screened for her. "Was this picture made by an American?" she demanded to know. *Life,* which her husband published, retracted its own favorable review of the film in a column called "On Second Thought." Editorials in other forums, plus the American Legion, also attacked the un-American propaganda of *The Senator Was Indiscreet.* Having approved the script, the Motion Picture Association of America had somehow missed its incendiary implications, leaving the trade organization with only the option of prohibiting the showing of *The Senator Was Indiscreet* overseas, which it did.

Partly as a result, the few dozen political films that were released in the postwar era bristled with titles like *The Iron Curtain* (1948), *The Red Menace* (1949), *The Red Danube* (1949), *Red Snow* (1952), and *The Steel Fist* (1952). The election year of 1952 was the peak, when twelve explicitly anti-Communist films were produced. Though Elizabeth Taylor and Robert Taylor were featured in *Conspirator* (1950) and John Wayne glamorized HUAC in *Big Jim McLain,* very few of these movies had large budgets or major stars. They were shot on the cheap and usually ended up as the second features on double bills. Because strongly ideological films were considered unlikely to attract the masses anyway, the studios apparently reasoned that anti-Communist pictures might mollify the American Legion and right-wingers in Congress without losing too much money. And although Menjou had predicted to HUAC that such movies "would be an incredible success," the studios' apprehensions proved correct: most of them bombed at the box office.

How was domestic Communism depicted in the films of the Cold War? Its adherents show no respect for national sanctums and symbols, which Party members traduce. They treat the Stars and Stripes with contempt. They conspire to meet one another by carrying an edition of *Reader's Digest* or a TWA flight bag and by picking such agreeable settings as the Boston Public Garden amid the swan boats. Communists are rude, humorless, and "cruel to animals," Nora Sayre noticed. "But we don't know how they treat children, since they never have any." Women in the Party are either disturbingly unfeminine, downright unattractive, or nearly nymphomaniacs. Bereft of the experience of "normal" love, they use sex for political seduction. A Party target in Republic Pictures' *The Red Menace* tells a blonde *femme fatale:* "I always thought the Commies peddled bunk. I didn't know they came as cute as you." After the comely comrade lets the dupe kiss her, she teasingly withdraws, then gives him a copy of *Das Kapital.* . . .

. . . When one independent, left-wing film was produced in 1954, it was unclear what was more impressive—the fact that in so politically parched an atmosphere *Salt of the Earth* could be made at all, or the fact that it faced so many barriers imposed by those who believed that liberty was an ornament of American life.

The movie was based on a 1951–52 strike by Mexican-American zinc miners, who demanded better safety regulations as well as equal treatment with Anglo employees. The strike was conducted by the International Union of Mine, Mill, and Smelter Workers, which the CIO had expelled in 1950 because it was Communist-controlled. Since no Hollywood studio would have touched such a subject in the 1950s, *Salt of the Earth* was a venture of the blacklisted. Director Herbert Biberman was a member of the Hollywood Ten, scenarist Michael Wilson took the Fifth Amendment before HUAC in 1951, and producer Paul Jarrico had co-written *Song of Russia*. . . .

. . . The fragility of the left-wing popular culture that faced extinction during the Cold War was symbolized by an encounter in 1956 in a New Jersey hospital. Harold Leventhal, a Communist who once plugged songs for Irving Berlin, went to Greystone Park to visit one of the inmates. A psychiatrist rummaged through the files on his desk, then exclaimed: "Guthrie, Guthrie, ah, Guthrie! A very sick man. Very sick. Delusional! He says he has written more than a thousand songs! And a novel too. And he says he has made records for the Library of Congress." Leventhal's reply was terse: "He has." . . .

. . . Born in 1912, Woody Guthrie had proudly cultivated an ardent pro-Communism by the late 1930s and did not waver thereafter. . . . A drifter and a loner, Guthrie was even jailed and given a six-month sentence in 1948 for writing obscene letters to a Los Angeles woman. His drinking and self-destructive rages were awful preludes to the congenital disease called Huntington's chorea that would eventually deprive him of control of mind and body. The atrophy would gradually worsen until he would quiver into horrifying disintegration, his brain utterly depleted.

Guthrie was functioning well enough to attend a major concert held in New York in 1956 to honor his work. Over a thousand people filled Pythian Hall, and at the end of the program the entire cast sang "This Land Is Your Land." Guthrie sat in the balcony, and the audience cheered him when it too joined in "This Land Is Your Land." Within a few months of that consolidation of the political culture to which Guthrie had contributed for two decades, he was committed to Greystone Park, and five years later to Brooklyn State Hospital. One pilgrim who came east to visit the hospitalized Guthrie early in 1961 would quickly become his most dazzling successor, taking audiences far beyond the "progressive" confines within which Guthrie had operated. Bob Dylan idolized Guthrie, sang and dressed like him, concocted a similar past, and recorded a "Song to Woody" on his first album in 1962. Born in 1941, the University of Minnesota dropout was immune to Guthrie's pro-Soviet politics. But Dylan transmitted an outrage against social injustice and war in such early songs as "Blowin' in the Wind" and "A Hard Rain's Gonna Fall" that outstripped the appeal of Guthrie's music a generation earlier, though the successor himself soon abandoned the leftist orientation to which Guthrie himself had been so faithful. . . .

In the 1950s, when dissent was too easily equated with disloyalty, the influence of such figures sharply diminished. As a result, talents were thwarted, creative possibilities were stifled, and the development of a more vital and various national culture was unrealized.

PRIMARY SOURCES

This section contains a variety of sources, from movie advertisements to popular songs, reflecting postwar popular culture. Together, the primary sources offer important clues about the impact of anticommunism on the popular culture of the period. All of them may not support the same conclusion.

Movie Advertising and the Anticommunist Hysteria

After Germany invaded the Soviet Union in 1941, Hollywood movie studios produced numerous pro-Soviet films. Warner Brothers' *Mission to Moscow* (1943), based on former United States Ambassador Joseph Davies' memoir, was a good example. In the movie, Davies (Walter Huston) tells Stalin, "I believe, sir, that history will record you as a great benefactor of mankind."[6] By 1947, the Soviet Union was no longer an ally in the battle against Nazism and the HUAC was investigating alleged communist subversion in Hollywood. Studios were under intense pressure to demonstrate their anticommunist credentials. One result was the blacklisting of actors and other studio personnel. Another was a stream of B-grade movies exposing the dangerous menace of communist subversion. Although never big hits at the box office, these films showed that Hollywood took seriously the growing fear of domestic subversion. As you examine material produced to market several of these movies, determine what messages they give. Think about their impact on the public. Are these movies evidence of Hollywood's influence, or of its vulnerability to outside influences?

◆

SOURCE 2   In 1935, United Artists released the movie *Red Salute,* starring Barbara Stanwyck and Robert Young. When a rich college girl becomes too friendly with a campus radical, her father sends her off to Mexico. There she meets a handsome border patrolman. The all-American patrolman quickly wins the girl's heart and the young student radical is sent packing by the patrolman and the student body. In 1953, *Red Salute* was re-released under the title *Runaway Daughter.*

Advertisement for *Runaway Daughter* (1953)

Source: Michael Barson, *"Better Red Than Dead!"* (New York: Hyperion, 1992), no page; originally from RKO Radio Pictures.

SOURCE 3   In this movie from Columbia Pictures, the FBI battles a vast communist spy network in Boston, where spies hope to steal the results of "an extraordinary scientific experiment" involving a new computer. The movie opens with the narrator praising the FBI for "protecting" Americans and then shows FBI agents opening other people's mail.

Promotional Material for *Walk East on Beacon* (1952)

Source: *Walk East on Beacon*. Copyright © 1952, renewed 1980 RD.DR Corporation. All rights reserved. Courtesy of Columbia Pictures.

SOURCE 4   Mark Goodson was a producer of television game shows, including *What's My Line, I've Got a Secret, Password,* and *Family Feud.* Before he died in 1992, Goodson was the subject of an oral history, a tape recorded interview designed to preserve an individual's experiences and to share them with a broader audience. What does this portion of Goodson's oral history reveal about the forces that made television particularly vulnerable to the communist hysteria?

A Game Show Producer Remembers the Red Scare (1995)

I'm not sure when it began, but I believe it was early 1950. At that point, I had no connection with the blacklisting that was going on, although I had heard about it in the motion picture business and heard rumors about things that had happened on other shows, like *The Aldrich Family*. My first experience really was when we settled into a fairly regular panel on *What's My Line?* in mid-1950. The panel consisted of the poet Louis Untermeyer, Dorothy Kilgallen, Arlene Francis, and Hal Block, a comedy writer. Our sponsor was Stopette, a deodorant.

A few months into the show, I began getting mail on [left-wing poet] Louis Untermeyer. He had been listed in *Red Channels*.* He was one of those folks who had supported the left-wing forces against Franco in Spain. I know that he also had allowed his name to be affiliated with the Joint Anti-Fascist Refugee Committee and had been a sponsor of the 1948 May Day parade. Back in the early 1920s, he had written articles for *The Masses*. But he was certainly not an active political person, at least as far as I knew.

CBS and Stopette also began receiving letters of protest. First, it was just a few postcards. Then it grew. Members of the Catholic War Veterans put stickers on drugstore windows, red, white, and blue stickers, warning "Stop Stopette Until Stopette stops Untermeyer."

We didn't pay too much attention until we got the call from CBS. Untermeyer and I were summoned to Ralph Colin's office, who was the general counsel for CBS at the time. Louis and Colin knew each other. Ralph asked him why he lent his name to the group. "I thought it was a good cause," Untermeyer said. "Louis, you're being very naive. These are very difficult times and you've put us in a bad spot. We're going to have to drop you." Untermeyer was very apologetic, but the decision had been made. He was let go.

I remember leaving that office feeling embarrassed. Untermeyer was in his sixties, a man of considerable dignity. He was a good American poet and I liked him; he was funny and articulate on the show. What's more, I had no political ax to grind.

That was the last of that kind of meeting. Soon afterwards, CBS installed a clearance division. There wasn't any discussion. We would just get the word—"Drop that person"—and that was supposed to be it. Whenever we booked a guest or a panelist on *What's My Line?* or *I've Got a Secret*, one of our assistants would phone up and say, "We're going to use so-and-so." We'd either get the

---

Red Channels: The Report of Communist Influence in Radio and Television was a private publication that listed names of people affiliated with communist "causes." After it appeared in June 1950, it quickly became known as "the Bible of Madison Avenue." Advertising agencies, the television networks, and sponsors used it to remove "subversives" from the airwaves.

Source: From *Red Scare: Memories of the American Inquisition: An Oral History* by Griffin Fariello. Copyright © 1995 by Griffin Fariello. Reprinted by permission of W. W. Norton & Company.

okay, or they'd call back and say, "Not clear," or "Sorry, can't use them." Even advertising agencies—big ones, like Young & Ribicam and BBD&O—had their own clearance departments. They would never come out and say it. They would just write off somebody by saying, "He's a bad actor." You were never supposed to tell the person what it was about; you'd just unbook them. They never admitted there was a blacklist. It just wasn't done.

Some fairly substantial names were off-limits—big stars like Leonard Bernstein, Harry Belafonte, Abe Burrows, Gypsy Rose Lee, Judy Holliday, Jack Gilford, Uta Hagen, and Hazel Scott. Everyone, from the stars to the bit-part actors, was checked. We once did a show in California called *The Rebel,* and we used wranglers to take care of the horses—we had to clear all of their names. CBS, in particular, asked for loyalty oaths to be signed by everybody, making sure that you were not un-American. So far as I know, no one ever refused.

In 1952, *I've Got a Secret* got a new sponsor, R. J. Reynolds Tobacco Company, with its advertising agency, William Este. When they came aboard, someone from the agency called me and said, "Please get rid of Henry Morgan," one of the regular panelists on the show. Morgan had been named in *Red Channels.* I had known Henry for a long time; he was one of those young curmudgeons who was acidic at times, but he was by no means a Communist. His wife was involved with radical politics, but they were getting a divorce, and to some extent his name was just smeared.

I went to the agency and told them that they were crazy to try and get rid of Henry Morgan. They agreed that the charge in *Red Channels* was absurd, but they said they couldn't take the risk. That was the main thing—mail accusing them of being pro-Communist was not going to sell cigarettes. They gave me an ultimatum: dump Morgan or face the show's cancellation.

So I went to Garry Moore, the MC of the show and an established comedian. He was a conservative, a Republican from Maryland. I know that he liked Morgan. I said that if he'd be willing to back me up, I'd tell the agency I'd do the show without a sponsor. He agreed without hesitation. I phoned up William Este and said, "We're not going to do the show without Henry." The people at the agency were flabbergasted. It was virtually unheard-of to have this kind of confrontation. They told me they'd think about it, and in the end, they actually backed down. The show was not canceled, and some weeks later Morgan's name simply vanished from *Red Channels.*

Morgan never even knew. When I wrote the article about my experience, Henry called me. "I did not know that I was about to be dropped," he said. "I knew I was in *Red Channels* and I was outraged about that, but I didn't know I was about to be dropped." It was a revelation for him.

The Morgan episode was my first act of resistance. It was not something my lawyers ever encouraged. The watchword in the business is "Don't make waves."

The studios and the advertising agencies didn't have to subscribe to *Red Channels.* It was one of about a dozen publications. There were several private lists, and the major agencies and networks exchanged lists, most of which had several names each. I'd help you out by giving you my list and you'd help me out by giving me your list. There was a big interchange of listings. A fellow called Danny O'Shea was in charge of the listings at CBS, an ex-FBI man. *Red Channels* would maybe have a couple of hundred names, but there might be on the other list at CBS several hundred more. Anybody could show up on a list, stars, technicians, cowboys.

◆

SOURCE 5   Arthur Miller, author of *Death of a Salesman* (1949), *The Crucible* (1953), and other plays, discusses anticommunist pressures on Broadway in this oral history. In 1956, Miller appeared before HUAC. Refusing to testify, he was convicted for contempt of Congress, a decision later overturned by a higher court. Note Miller's explanation for Broadway's relative immunity from the anticommunist hysteria. Do the previous sources reflect his point about the difference between Broadway, on the one hand, and Hollywood and the broadcasting industry, on the other?

A Playwright Recalls the Red Scare (1995)

I drew some attention when I became involved with the Conference for Peace at the Waldorf in 1949. That was a kind of crossroads, I guess, at the time: when the Russians were—in fact, up to that moment almost—our allies and then suddenly they were turned into our enemy, and that conference was very important from that point of view.

At the time I was not working in films or for any broadcasting companies, or advertisers, so the effect on me was more obscure. It was simply that I would be attacked in the press from time to time. But I had no job to lose, so it was quite a bit different than it was for a lot of other writers who had either actual jobs that they would be thrown out of, or contracts with publishers that would have been affected. I didn't have anything like that, and obviously the Broadway situation was quite different, because we didn't have any big corporations investing in Broadway, there were just a lot of small investors who threw in their money to put a play on. So they were not so easily tampered with as the big companies were in Hollywood or the broadcasting industry. They could maintain more independence.

They had blacklists of writers, and as it later turned out, practically every American writer was on it. But not all of them were out front the way I found myself, because they weren't putting plays on, especially not in the Middle

West. So the impact was greater on me than it would have been on, let's say, Steinbeck or somebody else.

We had a road company of *Death of a Salesman* in the Middle West that we finally had to close down. The American Legion especially, and I think the Catholic War Veterans, picketed it so heavily everywhere that people were intimidated and they didn't come. So there wasn't much business. They were attacking the play and me as being an anti-American.

Death of a Salesman questioned the ethos of the business civilization, which the play intimates has no real respect for individual human beings, whereas the going mythology was quite the opposite: in that nobody of any competence ever fails and that everything was pretty sound and terrific for everybody. So to put a play on where somebody who believes in the system, as Willy Loman does to his dying minute, ends up a suicide, it was rather a shock.

In fact, when they made the film they made Willy appear crazy. That was the whole drift of the film; that's why it was such a bad film in my opinion. They made him into a lunatic, and consequently you could observe him with the same distance you observe any crazy person, you don't really identify with him. In my opinion that was to make the play politically more palatable, but there were other artistic problems with that production which I disagreed with, but certainly this was the major one.

Columbia Studios actually made a short, cost them a couple of hundred thousand dollars, which they wanted to run before each showing of the film in the movie theaters. The short was shot at City College in New York City and was basically a very boring set of lectures by business administration professors who made it clear that Willy Loman represented nobody and that the play was really quite absurd and that the system was altogether different than as it was portrayed in the play and that the salesman's job was one of the best imaginable careers that a person could have and indeed that the system was based on salesmanship. When they got finished with this kind of analysis you wondered why they had produced the play at all as a film. I managed to make an empty threat that I would sue them if they did this, but in fact I think they themselves saw that the absurdity of the whole thing was even too much for them. They may have shown it, somebody told me that he had seen it once in some theater, but I don't think it was very widespread.

◆

SOURCE 6   Lee Hayes and Pete Seeger were leaders in People's Artists, a left-wing music organization founded in 1949. People's Artists emphasized peace, civil rights, and the protection of civil liberties. From the beginning, its messages were not well received. Vigilantes in Peekskill, New York, broke up the organization's first concert. When it was rescheduled, mobs stoned the cars of concert-goers and more than 150 people were hospitalized. In 1950, People's

Artists began publishing *Sing Out!,* a song magazine that helped to promote the folk music revival early in the decade. Its title was taken from *The Hammer Song,* which was featured on the cover of the first issue. After the magazine's release, one subscriber cancelled his subscription, protesting that "all you left out of that song was the sickle."[7] In the early 1960s, however, folk trio Peter, Paul, and Mary would turn *If I Had a Hammer* into a huge hit record. What does this song and its history say about the relationship between the Cold War and cultural expression?

The Hammer Song (1949)

LEE HAYES AND PETE SEEGER

Source: © Sing Out Corporation, reprinted with permission.

SOURCE 7   Ronnie Gilbert was the only female member of The Weavers, a popular folk music quartet whose hit *Goodnight Irene* sold two million records in the early 1950s. As you read this excerpt from Gilbert's oral history, note what effect the anticommunist crusade had on the group. Was popular music more or less susceptible to blacklisting than Hollywood, television, or Broadway?

A Folk Singer Remembers the Early 'Fifties (1995)

My interest in the Weavers was political as well as musical. We sang for unions. We sang for the Henry Wallace campaign.* I was all of eighteen or nineteen at the time. My background was political. My mother was a rank-and-file union-ist, belonged to the International Ladies Garment Workers Union, and she was a singer. She taught me all the songs. So I come from a very proud, political union background. That was part of my nature and my life, you know. I still sing political songs. There's a different style and shape, I'm not so much a "folksinger" as I was then. I sing a wide variety of musical styles. But the lyrics that attract me are lyrics about something.

We incubated most of our material at the Village Vanguard. We were there for six months. It was a small club in New York that did all kinds of stuff, radical stuff, nonradical stuff, jazz. . . .

We sang everything that we sang later on. But we were very aware that we were entertainers. We would never even think of singing a song that wasn't good fun to do. Sure, we sang Spanish Civil War songs, one or two of them, 'cause they were musically exciting. And we would refer to them and say that this was a song that was written during the Spanish Civil War, and that perhaps if Hitler had been turned back during that war, we would never have had World War Two. We said really "subversive" things like that. And every now and then we'd sing something that related to a union. Very subversive, you know. You bet, that's the kind of thing we did. But when we appeared on television, we knew that we were singing for a very broad audience that wouldn't sit still for the explanation of a song. The song had to be directly of interest to them, and we sang what we thought was best in American folk music, and that was what we represented.

The Weavers were headline-makers. We were the hottest thing to come along in a long time in the music industry. . . . Had we not made "Goodnight Irene,"

---

*FDR's vice president and Progressive Party candidate for president in 1948.
Source: From *Red Scare: Memories of the American Inquisition: An Oral History* by Griffin Fariello. Copyright © 1995 by Griffin Fariello. Reprinted by permission of W. W. Norton & Company, Inc.

had we not become hot performing artists, it's very possible that we would never have been caught up in the blacklist, because we wouldn't have been worth anything to anybody.

I mean, why are entertainers picked up in a blacklist like that? 'Cause they made headlines for the committee. The headlines you see in these old movies from the thirties—the Criminal or the Hunted Person comes into a hotel lobby, and everybody's reading the papers: "So-and-So Wanted," you know? Well, that actually happened to us. We were playing a nightclub engagement in Springfield, Illinois. And we came into the hotel lobby, and there were people reading the newspaper, and it said "Weavers Named Reds!" [Laughs.] And there we were! . . .

We were being followed all the time. I remember walking down the street in some place in Ohio, it might have been Akron, with these two guys following us behind. I was terrified. By that time it was very scary, because it involved groups like the American Legion, the Catholic War Veterans, and a very patriotic kind of macho. I was present at Peekskill, at the Paul Robeson concert, where people were badly injured by rock-throwing goons, with the police standing by doing absolutely nothing. So I knew that kind of thing could happen very easily. These guys followed us a long ways. I stopped and turned around and confronted them. One of them seemed very surprised, and he said, "Well, do you want your subpoena here, or in the club, while you're perform-ing?" I said, "I'll take it now!" [Laughs.] . . .

I never did get subpoenaed again. Very quickly our work came down to nothing, there was no work to be had. We stuck together as long as we possibly could, and then it was pointless. Decca was not going to do any more recording. Decca was in the red when we recorded for them and we pulled them right out. It didn't help. It didn't make them loyal to us. [Laughs.] The music industry is the music industry. The Weavers were merchandise. Our songs were merchandise, just the way people are now.

From Rhythm and Blues to Rock 'n' Roll

By the early 1950s, black rhythm and blues (R & B) was beginning to move out of the ghetto and up the white pop charts. Within a few years, R & B had helped to inspire a new, highly charged form of popular culture known as rock 'n' roll. Although devoid of political content, early rock flaunted mainstream cultural standards. It appealed to a growing sense of teenage rebellion against authority and conformity. Do the following lyrics, from two popular hits of the 1950s, support the main essay's argument that popular culture in the 1950s reveals how "Americans imposed a starchy repression on themselves"?

◆

SOURCE 8   Recorded by the R & B group The Dominoes in 1951, *Sixty Minute Man* became a number-one rhythm and blues hit. Within several months, however, it also appeared on the pop record charts. In spite of its "suggestive" lyrics, the song was one of the pioneer crossovers from the black R & B to the white pop charts.

Sixty Minute Man (1951)

WILLIAM WARD AND ROSE MARKS

Sixty Minute Man

Sixty Minute Man
Sixty Minute Man
Look here girls I'm telling you now
They call me loving Dan
I rock 'em roll 'em all night long
I'm a sixty minute man
If you don't believe I'm all I say
Come up here and take my hand
When I let you go you'll cry
Oh yes, he's a sixty minute man

There'll be fifteen minutes of kissing
Then you'll holler, please don't stop
There'll be fifteen minutes of teasin'
There'll be fifteen minutes of squeezin'
And fifteen minutes of blowin' my top
Mop! Mop! Mop!

If your old man ain't treatin' you right
Come up and see old Dan
I rock 'em roll 'em all night long
I'm a sixty minute man
Sixty Minute Man
They call me loving Dan
I rock 'em roll 'em all night long
I'm a sixty minute man

SOURCE 9   Chuck Berry, a black former hairdresser from St. Louis, recorded his first big pop hit, *Maybelline,* in 1955. It was followed by a string of hits, including *School Days, Roll Over Beethoven,* and *Sweet Little Sixteen.* In his songs, Berry wrote about teenagers' lives. "Everything I wrote about wasn't about me," he later said, "but about the people listening to my songs."[8] In *Sweet Little Sixteen,* a million seller, Berry sang of a girl's excitement over collecting autographed pictures and seeing the singing stars perform. With this ordinary subject, Berry coyly conveyed an image of sexuality and captured adolescent joys and frustrations.

Sweet Little Sixteen (1958)

CHUCK BERRY

They're really rocking in Boston, in Pittsburgh, Pa.,
Deep in the heart of Texas and 'round the Frisco Bay,
All over St. Louis, way down in New Orleans,
All the cats want to dance with Sweet Little Sixteen.

Sweet little sixteen, she's just got to have
About a half a million famed autographs.
Her wallet's filled with pictures, she gets 'em one by one.
Become so excited, watch her, look at her run.

Oh, Mommy, Mommy, please may I go,
Such a sight to see, somebody steal the show.
Oh Daddy, Daddy, I beg of you,
Whisper to Mommy, it's all right with you.

Sweet Little Sixteen, she's got the grown-up blues
Tight dresses and lipstick, she's sportin' high-heeled shoes.
Oh but tomorrow morning she'll have to change her trend
And be sweet sixteen and back in class again.

Source: Chuck Berry, *Sweet Little Sixteen,* © Jewell Music Publishing Co., Ltd., London.

SOURCE 10   In his popular animal comic strip, Walt Kelly often targeted political figures. In the strip below, Kelly introduces a lynx named Simple J. Malarkey, who bears a striking resemblance to Joseph McCarthy. Malarkey takes over the Okefenokke Swamp's Bird Watching Club. Note Kelly's message about Malarkey's methods. Why was Kelly able to get away with such criticism while other popular artists and entertainers were not?

Pogo (1952)

WALT KELLY

Source: Estate of Walt Kelly, reprinted with permission from *The Pogo Papers,* 1952.

CONCLUSION

Before historians can judge the importance of historical developments, they need to determine their influence. To understand the impact of anticommunist hysteria after World War II, for instance, historians make connections between seemingly unrelated developments, from detective fiction to popular music. To do this, they synthesize, or combine various parts into a whole. Historical synthesis, in turn, depends on skills emphasized in earlier chapters: the ability to evaluate evidence carefully, to detect causal influences, to understand the role of ideology in history, and to examine the past from many perspectives. In the case of the postwar period, this ability to synthesize allows us to reconstruct what one historian called the "mentality of the fifties" and to understand its impact on American society. It also gives historians the power to analyze later changes in American society. Involvement in Vietnam, the topic of the next chapter, was one powerful cause for the decline of a fifties mindset. And, as we shall see later, the women's movement of the 1960s and 1970s was also a cause—and consequence—of its demise.

FURTHER READING

David Caute, *The Great Fear: The Anti-Communist Purge Under Truman and Eisenhower* (New York: Simon and Schuster, 1978).

Griffin Fariello, *Red Scare: Memories of the American Inquisition: An Oral History* (New York: W. W. Norton and Company, 1995).

Richard Pells, *The Liberal Mind in a Conservative Age: American Intellectuals in the 1940s and 1950s* (New York: Harper and Row, 1985).

Edward Pessen, *Losing Our Souls: The American Experience in the Cold War* (Chicago: Ivan R. Dee, 1993).

Nora Sayre, *Running Time: Films of the Cold War* (New York: Dial Press, 1982).

NOTES

1. Quoted in David Caute, *The Great Fear: The Anti-Communist Purge Under Truman and Eisenhower* (New York: Simon and Schuster, 1978), p. 493.
2. Quoted in Griffin Fariello, *Red Scare: Memories of the American Inquisition: An Oral History* (New York: W. W. Norton, 1995), p. 263.
3. Dwight Macdonald, *Against the American Grain: Essays on the Effects of Mass Culture* (New York: Vintage Books, 1952), p. 4.
4. Quoted in Elaine Tyler May, *Homeward Bound: American Families in the Cold War Era* (New York: Basic Books, 1988), p. 16.

5. Quoted in Peter Biskind, *Seeing Is Believing: How Hollywood Taught Us to Stop Worrying and Love the Fifties* (New York: Pantheon Books, 1983), p. 6.

6. Quoted in Nora Sayre, *Running Time: Films of the Cold War* (New York: Dial Press, 1982), p. 61.

7. Peter Seeger Oral History in Griffin Fariello, *Red Scare: Memories of the American Inquisition: An Oral History* (New York: W. W. Norton, 1995), p. 364.

8. Quoted in Arnold Shaw, *The Rockin' '50s* (New York: Hawthorn Books, 1974), p. 146.

Chapter 11

Causation and the Lessons of History: Explaining America's Longest War

This chapter presents two secondary sources and several primary sources dealing with America's involvement in the Vietnam War.

Secondary Sources

1. Fighting in "Cold Blood": LBJ's Conduct of Limited War in Vietnam (1994), GEORGE HERRING
2. God's Country and American Know-How (1986), LOREN BARITZ

Primary Sources

3. Lyndon Johnson Defends the American Commitment to Vietnam (April 1965)
4. LBJ Expresses Doubts about Vietnam (June 1965)
5. LBJ Recalls His Decision to Escalate (1971)
6. The Central Intelligence Agency Reports on the War (1967)
7. McNamara Recalls the Decision to Escalate (1995)
8. A Medical Corpsman Recalls the Vietnamese People (1981)
9. Fighting a Technological War of Attrition (1977)

The end of the Vietnam War came suddenly in 1975. For eighteen hours on April 29, marine and air force helicopters hovered over landing pads on the roofs of a few of Saigon's tallest buildings. As the Viet Cong and North Vietnamese troops advanced on the capital, the helicopters lifted more than 1,000 Americans and 5,000 South Vietnamese to waiting ships in the South China Sea. Meanwhile, the U.S. embassy was a scene of confusion. Thousands of South Vietnamese desperately looking for a way out of their country had come to the compound. When they tried to scale the walls, marine guards used their boots and rifle butts to force them back. One North Vietnamese commander said they were "fighting their way in, smashing doors, climbing walls, climbing each other's backs, tussling, brawling, and trampling each other as they sought to flee."[1]

At 5:00 the next morning the American ambassador, under orders from President Ford to get out "without a moment's delay," boarded a CH-46 helicopter. Then nine more CH-46s landed and took off with the remaining marines, who had to spray Mace to fend off the Vietnamese still trying to break into the compound. When the last helicopter lifted off, three years after the last American combat troops had gone home, American involvement in Vietnam was finally over. Within hours, so was the war that the United States had officially abandoned two years before. By the afternoon, communist troops rolled into the heart of Saigon, smashed their way into the presidential palace, and raised their single-starred flag in triumph.

The United States expended an estimated $600 billion to defend South Vietnam. American planes dropped more than 10 million tons of bombs on the Southeast Asian country. About 2.7 million American soldiers fought there. Approximately 300,000 of them were wounded, and nearly 58,000 lost their lives. All of it had been done to prevent what happened in Saigon on April 30. Confronting failure, many Americans could only wonder what the effort had been for. "Now it's all gone down the drain and it hurts," said one Pennsylvanian who had lost a son in Vietnam. "What did he die for?"[2] In the two decades since the fall of South Vietnam, the sense of failure and personal loss has gradually lessened. Now many historians study the Vietnam War to discover why the United States fought this war as it did. They also want to know why it turned out as it did and what it would have taken for it to end differently. In this chapter we turn to those questions about America's longest war and its biggest military loss.

SETTING

Four years before the fall of South Vietnam, Lyndon Johnson predicted that the debate about Vietnam would continue for a long time as historians made "judgments on the decisions made and the actions taken."[3] In fact, the historical debate about Vietnam started even before LBJ left the presidency. With the war still raging, many historians wanted to know how the United States had come to be involved in Vietnam in the first place. Contemporary answers to that question varied. Such radical historians as Patrick J. Hearden and Gabriel Kolko saw the war as the result of a rational assessment by American policymakers concerned about a capitalist economy's need for markets and resources. Other students of the war, including Arthur Schlesinger and David Halberstam, argued that successive administrations made a series of mistakes that gradually and unthinkingly led the United States into a quagmire. Still others disputed the notion that the United States ended up in Vietnam by accident. Daniel Ellsberg, the Defense Department analyst who leaked *The Pentagon Papers*—a secret history of the war—to the *New York Times,* argued that presidents from Truman to LBJ were concerned about losing Vietnam to communism. These presidents, Ellsberg argued, made clear-sighted decisions and had no illusions about the chances of long-run success. Other scholars have also argued against the unthinking nature of America's commitment to Vietnam. In a study of the foreign policy elite, for instance, John Donovan argued that American policymakers were guided by a belief in containing communist expansion and simply misapplied the policy to Vietnam.

After the fall of South Vietnam, the debates shifted focus. They now reflected the failure of America's commitment and an increasingly conservative national mood. By the late 1970s, such revisionists as Harry G. Summers, Jr., and Norman Podhoretz began to treat the American effort in Vietnam more sympathetically. Instead of asking why the United States fought there, they inquired how the war was fought and how it could have turned out differently. Their guiding assumption was that the United States could have won. Rejecting earlier assessments that saw Vietnam as a mistake, they also drew a different lesson from America's military experience there. Rather than accept the conclusion that the United States should "never again" become involved militarily in distant lands, revisionists pointed to the dangers of isolationism and "appeasement."

More recently, Loren Baritz, Gary Hess, Larry Berman, and other scholars have taken on the revisionists. These postrevisionists are critical of American intervention in Vietnam and argue that the United States could not have won the war for many reasons, including the American ignorance about Vietnamese culture and society. Some of them are also more sympathetic to Lyndon Johnson, who was responsible for the rapid American military escalation in the late 1960s. Far from the blundering and thoughtless hawk of many earlier accounts, they view LBJ as a cautious leader who understood the difficulty of military success in Vietnam and actually expressed doubts about escalation. Many postrevisionists argue that the way America fought the war was determined by domestic political considerations. LBJ chose to escalate the war in a limited way to save his Great Society domestic program. A masterful politician, Johnson simply miscalculated when it came to the war. Ironically, while pointing to LBJ's flawed judgment, these postrevisionists also demonstrate that he got one thing right about Vietnam: It will be a long time before this war loses its power to elicit deeply felt debate.

INVESTIGATION

In this chapter you have the opportunity to compare two historians' assessments of the war in Vietnam. Their discussions focus on the policies and conduct of the war by the Johnson administration. Your primary job is to compare and evaluate these two historians' conclusions about the reason for the American failure in Vietnam and about the lessons that they draw from it. Your analysis should address the following main questions:

1. **What assumptions guided the escalation of the war in Vietnam, according to the main essays?** Why do the authors think these assumptions were flawed? How do the authors respond to the argument that the war could have turned out differently?

2. **What role do the essays assign to Lyndon Johnson in explaining the American failure in Vietnam?** Do the authors agree about the role of Johnson's personality and beliefs in determining American war policy?

3. **Are the essays' arguments supported by the evidence in the primary sources?** Do the primary sources suggest that the main reason for the American failure in Vietnam was the inherent difficulty of fighting a limited war, false assumptions rooted in American culture, or some other factor?

Before you begin, read the sections about Vietnam in your textbook, especially those dealing with the escalation of the war during the Johnson administration.

SECONDARY SOURCES

◆

SOURCE 1   In this selection, historian George Herring offers an explanation for the way the United States fought in Vietnam. It focuses on the Johnson administration's decision to fight a limited war: one that would not arouse the passions of Americans, but rather could be fought in "cold blood." Note Herring's explanation for the American leaders' lack of an overall strategy for fighting the war and the extent to which Johnson's personality shaped American war policy. Does Herring explain why the Johnson administration failed to wage limited war successfully?

Fighting in "Cold Blood": LBJ's Conduct of Limited War in Vietnam (1994)

GEORGE HERRING

Of the two great questions concerning involvement in Vietnam—why did the United States intervene and why did it fail—the latter has provoked the most emotional controversy. Historically, as a nation, America has been uniquely successful, so much so that its people have come to take success for granted. When failure occurs, scapegoats are sought and myths concocted to explain what is otherwise inexplicable. In the case of Vietnam, many critics of America's conduct of the war have thus insisted that a different approach would have produced the "proper" results. Such arguments can never be proven, of course, and they are suspect in method. As Wayne Cole observed many years ago of a strikingly similar debate in the aftermath of World War II, the "most heated controversies . . . do not center on those matters for which the facts and truth can be determined with greatest certainty. The interpretive controversies, on the contrary, rage over questions about which the historian is least able to determine the truth." . . .

The most glaring deficiency is that in an extraordinarily complex war there was no real strategy. President Johnson and Secretary of Defense Robert S. McNamara provided no firm strategic guidance to those military and civilian advisers who were running programs in the field. They set no clearcut limits on what could be done, what resources might be employed, and what funds expended. Without direction from the top, each service or agency did its own thing. Strategy emerged from the field on an improvised basis without careful calculation of the ends to be sought and the means used to attain them.

Perhaps equally important and less generally recognized, despite widespread and steadily growing dissatisfaction among the president's top advisers with the way the war was being fought and the results that were being obtained, there was no change of strategy or even systematic discussion of such a change. Not until the shock of the 1968 Tet offensive compelled it were the basic issues of how the war was being fought even raised. Even then, they were quickly dropped and left largely unresolved. Despite talk among the president's top advisers of borrowing a page from the communists' book and fighting while negotiating, the administration after Tet replaced one makeshift strategy with another, perpetuating and in some ways exacerbating the problems that had afflicted its management of the war from the beginning.

Closely related to and to some extent deriving from the absence of strategy was the lack of coordination of the numerous elements of what had become by 1966 a sprawling, multifarious war effort. Johnson steadfastly refused to assume overall direction of the war, and he would not create special machinery or designate someone else to run it. In Vietnam, therefore, each service or agency tended to go about its own business without much awareness of the impact of its actions in other areas or on other programs. The air war against North Vietnam operated separately from the ground war in South Vietnam (and the air war in Laos was run separately from both). . . .

It is more difficult to determine why these problems existed. In part, no doubt, institutional imperatives were at fault. The rule in bureaucracy . . . is that when an organization does not know what to do—or is not told what to do—it does what it knows how to do. Thus, in the absence of strong leadership from the top, the various services and agencies acted on the basis of their own standard operating procedures whether or not they were appropriate or compatible. CIA operative William Colby recalls warning McGeorge Bundy during the U.S. buildup in 1965 that the growing militarization of the war was diverting attention from the more urgent problems in the villages of South Vietnam. He pleaded with the presidential adviser to refocus the administration's attention toward the proper area. "You may be right, Bill," Colby remembered Bundy answering, "but the structure of the American government won't permit it." "What he meant," Colby concluded, "was that the Pentagon had to fight the only war it knew how to fight, and there was no American organization that could fight any other." This was most true of the army, air force, and navy, but it was also true of the civilian agencies.

Limited war theory also significantly influenced the way the war was fought. Korea and especially the Truman-MacArthur controversy stimulated a veritable cult of limited war in the 1950s and 1960s, the major conclusion of which was that in a nuclear age where total war was unthinkable limited war was essential. McNamara, William and McGeorge Bundy, Rusk,* and indeed Lyndon Johnson were deeply imbued with limited war theory, and it determined in many crucial ways their handling of Vietnam. Coming of age in World War II, they were convinced of the essentiality of deterring aggression to avoid a major war. Veterans of the Cuban missile crisis, they lived with the awesome responsibility of preventing nuclear conflagration and they were thus committed to fighting in "cold blood" and maintaining tight operational control over the military. They also operated under the mistaken assumption that limited war was more an exercise in crisis management than the application of strategy, and they were thus persuaded that gradual escalation would achieve their limited goals without provoking the larger war they so feared. Many of their notions, of course, turned out to be badly flawed.

To an even greater extent, Lyndon Johnson's own highly personalized style indelibly marked the conduct of the war and contributed to its peculiar frustrations. LBJ was a "kind of whirlwind," David Lilienthal has observed, a

---

*William Brady was assistant secretary of state for eastern affairs; McGeorge Bundy was a national security advisor; Dean Rusk was secretary of state.

man of seemingly boundless energy who attempted to put his personal brand on everything he dealt with. He dominated the presidency as few others have. He sought to run the war as he ran his household and ranch, his office and *his* government, with scrupulous attention to the most minute detail. As with every other personal and political crisis he faced he worked tirelessly at the job of commander in chief of a nation at war. His approach was best typified by his oft-quoted and characteristically hyperbolic boast that U.S. airmen could not bomb an outhouse in North Vietnam without his approval. In the case of Vietnam, however, the result was the worst of both worlds, a strategic vacuum and massive intrusion at the tactical level, micromanagement without real control. Whether he would admit it or not, moreover, LBJ quickly found in Vietnam a situation that eluded his grasp and dissipated even *his* seemingly inexhaustible storehouse of energy.

In so many ways, the conduct of the war reflected Johnson's modus operandi. The reluctance to provide precise direction and define a mission and explicit limits, the highly politicized, for Johnson characteristically middle-of-the-road approach that gave everybody something and nobody what they wanted, that emphasized consensus and internal harmony over results on the battlefield or at the negotiating table, all these were products of a thoroughly political and profoundly insecure man, a man especially ill at ease among military issues and military people.

Johnson's intolerance for any form of intragovernmental dissent and his unwillingness to permit, much less order, a much-needed debate on strategic issues deserve special note. It was not, as his most severe critics have argued, the result of his determination to impose a hermetically sealed system or his preference for working with sycophants, the so-called Caligula syndrome. LBJ was a domineering individual, to be sure, and he did have a strong distaste for conflict in his official family. As David Barrett and others have pointed out, however, he eagerly sought out and indeed opened himself to a wide diversity of viewpoints. Whatever their faults, the people that worked with him were anything but sycophants.

The problem went much deeper than that. In part, it reflected the peculiar mix of personalities involved, the rigorous standards of loyalty of a Rusk or McNamara, Harriman's determination to retain influence at the cost of principle and candor. From Johnson's standpoint, it was largely a matter of control. "He wanted to control everything," Joe Califano* recalled. "His greatest outbursts of anger were triggered by people or situations that escaped his control." He therefore discouraged the sort of open exchange of ideas, freewheeling discussion of alternatives, or ranging policy reviews that might in any way threaten his control. His admonition to McGeorge Bundy that his

*W. Averell Harriman was an ambassador-at-large; Joseph Califano was a presidential aide.

advisers must not "gang up" on him reflected his reluctance to permit them to engage in discussions except under his watchful eye. . . .

It would be a serious mistake to attribute America's failure in Vietnam solely or even largely to bureaucratic imperatives, the false dogmas of limited war theory, or the eccentricities of Johnson leadership style. Had the United States looked all over the world in 1965 it might not have been able to find a more difficult place to fight. The climate and terrain were singularly inhospitable. More important, perhaps, was the formless, yet lethal, nature of warfare in Vietnam, a conflict without distinct battlelines or fixed objectives where traditional concepts of victory and defeat were blurred. And from the outset, the balance of forces was stacked against the United States in the form of a weak, divided, and far too dependent client lacking in political legitimacy and a fanatically determined and resilient enemy that early on seized and refused to relinquish the banner of Vietnamese nationalism.

American military leaders have left ample testimony of the complex and often baffling challenge they faced in Vietnam and on the home front. Speaking of the "fog of war" in December 1967, [General Earle] Wheeler observed that Vietnam was the "foggiest war" in his memory and the first where the fog was "thicker away from the scene of the conflict than on the battlefield." Marine Gen. Lewis Walt concurred. "Soon after I arrived in Vietnam," he later admitted, "it became obvious to me that I had neither a real understanding of the nature of the war nor any clear idea how to win it." Abysmal ignorance of Vietnam and the Vietnamese on the part of Lyndon Johnson, his advisers, and the nation as a whole thickened the fog of war, contributing to a mistaken decision to intervene, mismanagement of the conflict, and ultimate failure.

A considerable part of the problem also lay in the inherent difficulty of waging limited war. Limited wars, as Stephen Peter Rosen has noted, are by their very nature "*strange* wars." They combine political, military, and diplomatic dimensions in the most complicated way. Conducting them effectively requires rare intellectual ability, political acumen, and moral courage.

Johnson and his advisers went into the conflict confident—probably overconfident—that they knew how to wage limited war, and only when the strategy of escalation proved bankrupt and the American people unwilling or unable to fight in cold blood did they confront their tragic and costly failure. . . .

Nor is there any obvious solution to the dilemma of domestic opinion. Vietnam exposed the enormous difficulties of fighting in cold blood. Without arousing popular emotions and especially without measurable success on the battlefield it was impossible over a long period of time to sustain popular support. Frederick the Great's dictum that war could only be successful when people did not know about it could not possibly work in the age of instant communications and mass media, especially when, as in the case of Vietnam, the size of the U.S. commitment quickly outgrew the presumed parameters of limited war. On the other hand, trying to play down the war also caused major problems. The Johnson and Nixon administrations both went to considerable lengths to maintain the semblance of normality at home. Thus, as D. Michael Shafer has observed, "those fighting [in Vietnam] faced the bitter irony that back in 'The World' life went on as normal while they risked their lives in a war their government did not acknowledge and many fellow citizens considered unnecessary or even immoral."

Johnson's inability to wage war in cold blood produced what appears on the surface a great anomaly—one of the shrewdest politicians of the twentieth century committing a form of political suicide by taking the nation into a war he would have preferred not to fight. To some extent, of course, LBJ was the victim of his considerable political acumen. He took the nation to war so quietly, with such consummate skill (and without getting a popular mandate) that when things turned sour the anger was inevitably directed at him. His inability to manage effectively the war he got [in] so skillfully is typical of his leadership record. He was also much more effective in getting domestic programs through Congress than in managing them once enacted. In the final analysis, however, Johnson's failure reflects more than anything else the enormity of the problem and the inadequacy of the means chosen to address it.

Partial mobilization or a declaration of war provides at best debatable alternatives. George Bush's apparent success in mobilizing support for the Persian Gulf War in 1991 confirmed in the eyes of some critics the deficiencies of Johnson's leadership in Vietnam. In fact, the remarkable popular support for the Gulf War and especially for the troops was in a very real sense an expiation of lingering guilt for nonsupport in Vietnam. It also owed a great deal to perceptions of military success and the rapidity with which the war ended. In any event, Johnson's and Rusk's reservations about the dangers of a declaration of war in the Cold War international system were well taken, and congressional sanction in the War of 1812 and the Mexican War did nothing to stop rampant and at times crippling domestic opposition.

However much we might deplore the limitations of Johnson's leadership and the folly of limited war theory, they alone are not responsible for America's failure in Vietnam. That conflict posed uniquely complex challenges for U.S. war managers both in terms of the conditions within Vietnam itself and the international context in which it was fought. American policymakers thus took on in Vietnam a problem that was in all likelihood beyond their control.

In the new world order of the post–Cold War era, the conditions that appeared to make limited war essential and that made the Vietnam War especially difficult to fight will probably not be replicated, and the "lessons" of Vietnam will have at best limited relevance. There are many different kinds of limited war, however. Korea, Vietnam, the Persian Gulf War (which was, after all, limited in both ends and means) were as different from each other as

each was from World War II. What they shared was the complexity in establishing ends and formulating means that is inherent in the institution of limited
war itself. Even in this new era, therefore, it would be well for us to remember
Vietnam and to recall Lady Bird Johnson's 1967 lament: "It is unbearably hard
to fight a limited war."

SOURCE 2   In his study of the Vietnam War, historian Loren Baritz argues that
American culture not only led the United States into Vietnam but also determined
the way Americans fought the war. Note how Baritz explains the American failure
in Vietnam and how the cause of failure manifested itself in the actions of the
Johnson administration and American military personnel. How does Baritz
account for the American determination to fight in "cold blood" and for the
failure of the Johnson administration to formulate a war strategy? How does his
explanation for failure in Vietnam differ from Herring's?

God's Country and American Know-How (1986)

LOREN BARITZ

America was involved in Vietnam for thirty years, but never understood
the Vietnamese. We were frustrated by the incomprehensible behavior of our
Vietnamese enemies and bewildered by the inexplicable behavior of our Vietnamese friends. For us, this corner of Asia was inscrutable. These Asians
successfully masked their intentions in smiles, formal courtesies, and exotic
rituals. The organic nature of Vietnamese society, the significance of village
life, the meaning of ancestors, the relationship of the family to the state, the
subordinate role of the individual, and the eternal quest for universal agreement, not consensus or majorities, were easily lost on the Americans.

Most of the Vietnamese were so poor, American GIs said that they lived like
animals. Some said they were animals. They did not bathe, had no toilets, and
ate food whose smell made some young Americans vomit. There was something about the very great age of Vietnamese culture that seemed to resist our
best efforts to understand. . . . They were not part of our century and not part
of our world.

When we did try to impose changes, for the better of course, the resistance
of the people could seem like ingratitude or stupidity, as it did to a young GI,

Source: From Loren Baritz, *Backfire: A History of How American Culture Led Us into Vietnam and
Made Us Fight the Way We Did.* Copyright © 1985 by Loren Baritz. Originally published by William
Morrow & Company, New York. Reprinted with permission of Gerald McCauley Agency, Inc.

Steve Harper. The Vietnamese enraged him. "We were there to help but Vietnamese are so stupid they can't understand that a great people want to help a weak people." He said that "somebody had to show poor people better ways of livin', like sewer disposal and sanitation and things like that." He once watched an American team enter a village to teach the peasants sanitation while members of South Vietnam's army stood around laughing because they thought it was a pointless waste of energy. His worst experience was his R&R tour in Tokyo, "the greatest sin city":

> I would walk down the Ginza, their main street, and look at all the slant eyes and I swear I'd start to get sick. I was even tempted by some of the prostitutes but one look at their faces and I'd walk away in disgust. . . . I began to get angry at Asians and at my own country. Why couldn't they take care of their own problems?

Americans who were most responsible for our Vietnam policies often complained about how little they knew about the Vietnamese. They mistakenly thought they were especially uninformed about the northerners. For example, General Maxwell Taylor, America's ambassador to Saigon, admitted that "we knew very little about the Hanoi leaders . . . and virtually nothing about their individual or collective intentions." . . .

Our difficulties were not with the strangeness of the land or the inscrutability of its people. Modern, secular, well-educated people, such as we are, such as General Taylor and Dr. Kissinger* were, can learn about exotic people in distant places. Our difficulty was not with the peculiarities of the Vietnamese. The problem was us, not them. Our difficulty was that the foot soldier slogging through a rice paddy, the general in his Saigon office planning great troop movements, the official in the Pentagon, and the Presidents who made the war were all Americans. Peer de Silva, a CIA chief of station in Saigon, said, "The American official posted in Asia very often finds himself, whether he realizes it or not, standing solemnly before the Asians, his finger pointed skyward and the word 'repent' on his lips." We wanted the Vietnamese to repent for being Vietnamese. There was something about the condition of being an American that prevented us from understanding the "little people in black pajamas" who beat the strongest military force in the world.

In common with most Asians, the Vietnamese had one custom that American soldiers could not tolerate. The people of Vietnam hold hands with their friends. Two Vietnamese soldiers would walk down the street holding hands. An American marine from south Boston noticed this custom: "They all hold hands, see. I fucking hated that." The intensity of this marine's reaction was characteristic of America's fighting men. The custom proved to the GIs that

---

*Henry Kissinger was a national security advisor and, later, secretary of state.

South Vietnamese men were homosexuals, and this diagnosis explained why the Vietnamese were incompetent warriors, raising the question about why Americans had to die in defense of perverts. . . .

This could all be dismissed as just another example of American cultural ignorance except that it occasionally had hideous consequences. A marine's truck was stopped by South Vietnamese soldiers who wanted the Americans to take a wounded South Vietnamese soldier to a hospital. His leg had been shot off. One of the marines said, "Fuck him. Let him hop." But the commander of the truck told the wounded man to climb in. "The fucking little slope grabbed my leg." The truck commander said that he had been in Vietnam long enough "to know that most of them are queer. They hold hands and stuff." One of the Americans "whacked" the wounded soldier and told the driver to get going. They threw the wounded man out of the moving truck: "The poor fucking bastard was screaming and crying and begging us. 'Fuck you, you slope. Out you go.' "

The Americans did not see guerrillas or North Vietnamese strolling hand in hand down the street, or if they did they did not realize they were North Vietnamese. It was usual for grunts to respect the enemy more than the ally. As GIs watched our gunships pulverize an area, one said, "You couldn't believe that anyone would have the courage to deal with that night after night . . . and you cultivated a respect for the Viet Cong and NVA [North Vietnamese army] . . . ." He also told of a lone sniper firing at a marine base from his hold in the ground. The marines fired everything they had at him, but he always reappeared to fire another round. Finally, napalm was dropped on his position and the entire area was burned to the ground. "When all of it cleared, the sniper popped up and fired off a single round, and the Marines in the trenches cheered. They called him Luke the Gook, and after that no one wanted anything to happen to him."

Thomas Bailey, an interrogation officer stationed in Saigon in the early seventies, believed that Americans did not understand themselves well enough to understand the Vietnamese. He became frustrated because "their civilization was so much older than ours, although we would characterize them as being uncivilized. I would have a difficult time defining the way in which they were more civilized than we were, but they were. It's my gut feeling." It was difficult for the young Americans who were sent to save the South Vietnamese both from themselves and from North Vietnam to encounter people who did not want to be saved in the way we intended. "Government is not important," a villager said, "rice is important." America corrupted the urban elites of South Vietnam by dangling riches in front of them. But it was the city dwellers, especially the Buddhists, who struggled hardest against the other corruption, the cultural pride and myopia of the Americans. They were as proud of their traditions and culture as we were of ours. . . .

Americans were ignorant about the Vietnamese not because we were stupid, but because we believe certain things about ourselves. Those things necessarily distorted our vision and confused our minds in ways that made learning extraordinarily difficult. To understand our failure we must think about what it means to be an American.

The necessary text for understanding the condition of being an American is a single sentence written by Herman Melville in his novel *White Jacket*: "And we Americans are the peculiar, chosen people—the Israel of our time; we bear the ark of the liberties of the world." This was not the last time this idea was expressed by Americans. It was at the center of thought of the men who brought us the Vietnam War. It was at the center of the most characteristic American myth. . . .

In countless ways Americans know in their gut—the only place myths can live—that we have been Chosen to lead the world in public morality and to instruct it in political virtue. We believe that our own domestic goodness results in strength adequate to destroy our opponents who, by definition, are enemies of virtue, freedom, and God. Over and over, the founding Puritans described their new settlement as a beacon in the darkness, a light whose radiance could keep Christian voyagers from crashing on the rocks, a light that could brighten the world. In his inaugural address John Kennedy said, "The energy, the faith, the devotion which we bring to this endeavor [defending freedom] will light our country and all who serve it—and the glow from that fire can truly light the world." . . .

In other words, we assumed that we had a superior moral claim to be in Vietnam, and because, despite their quite queer ways of doing things, the Vietnamese shared our values, they would applaud our intentions and embrace our physical presence. Thus, Vice-President Humphrey later acknowledged that all along we had been ignorant of Vietnam. He said that "to LBJ, the Mekong and the Pedernales were not that far apart." Our claim to virtue was based on the often announced purity of our intentions. It was said, perhaps thousands of times, that all we wanted was freedom for other people, not land, not resources, and not domination. . . .

Joining the American sense of its moral superiority with its technological superiority was a marriage made in heaven, at least for American nationalists. We told ourselves that each advantage explained the other, that the success of our standard of living was a result of our virtue, and our virtue was a result of our wealth. Our riches, our technology, provided the strength that had earlier been missing, that once had forced us to rely only on our virtue. Now, as Hiroshima demonstrated conclusively, we could think of ourselves not only as morally superior, but as the most powerful nation in history. The inevitable offspring of this marriage of an idea with a weapon was the conviction that the United States could not be beaten in war—not by any nation, and not by any combination of nations. For that moment we thought that we could fight where, when, and how we wished, without risking failure. For that moment we thought that we could impose our will on the recalcitrant of the earth. . . .

In Vietnam we had to find a technology to win without broadening the war. The nuclear stalemate reemphasized our need to find a more limited ground, to find, so to speak, a way to fight a domesticated war. We had to find a technology that would prevail locally, but not explode internationally. No assignment is too tough for the technological mentality. In fact, it was made to order for the technicians who were coming into their own throughout all of American life. This war gave them the opportunity to show what they could do. This was to be history's most technologically sophisticated war, most carefully analyzed and managed, using all of the latest wonders of managerial procedures and systems. It was made to order for bureaucracy. . . .

In summary, our national myth showed us that we were good, our technology made us strong, and our bureaucracy gave us standard operating procedures. It was not a winning combination. . . .

To make matters worse, President Johnson had a warm and giving nature. He genuinely believed that all the peoples of the earth were the same in their need for food, health, and education, as of course they are. He had no comprehension that different cultures search for the satisfaction of these essential needs in quite different ways. His understanding of the Vietnamese, North and South, was minimal. His textbook was his own experience in west Texas; his textbook was his own life. That is what Vice-President Humphrey meant when he said that for LBJ the Pedernales and the Mekong were not so far apart. That is why the President could even think of offering a massive flood-control project to the North Vietnamese if they would only please stop fighting. He could imagine trading an enormous TVA project in exchange for the ideology of the North. With typical enthusiasm, he said "We're going to turn the Mekong into a Tennessee Valley." North Vietnam responded that this was a "bribe." . . .

He believed that his was the voice of "the common people" because he thought he was one of them, and believed that he therefore understood their needs and dreams whether in America or Vietnam. While he was destroying the country with bombing, defoliation, and napalm, he could without cynicism speak of peace and progress. He believed that the destruction was unfortunately necessary before the construction could occur. That was Ho Chi Minh's fault. . . .

War is a product of culture. It is an expression of the way a culture thinks of itself and the world. Different cultures go to war for different reasons and fight in different ways. There is an American way of war. Our Vietnam War was started and fought in ways our culture required. . . .

American political culture—the self-righteousness of our nationalism— merged with the impulses of our technological culture—tell us what to do and we'll do it, no questions asked. President Kennedy's enthusiasm for counter-insurgency led the nation to assume that we could successfully intervene in Vietnamese politics in ways that were foreign to America's genius. Our managerial sophistication and technological superiority resulted in our trained incompetence in guerrilla warfare.

The conclusion is obvious: If this nation cannot use its managerial and technological strengths in international conflict, it would be wise to avoid engagement. If our expensive weapon systems will not contribute to victory, it would be wise not to pretend that we have other resources. . . .

The technician's mind is organized around the question *how.* He is motivated by a desire, sometimes a need, to solve problems. He is rational, practical, hardheaded, and believes that if an idea can be transformed into a solution that actually works, the idea was true. Most of the war's planners exhibited these traits. Three other attributes of the technological mentality had an even more direct impact on the war. The technician's language is amoral, dispassionate, and optimistic. For example, Secretary McNamara's perception of Vietnam as a limited war reveals all these habits of mind: "The greatest contribution Vietnam is making—right or wrong is beside the point—is that it is developing an ability in the United States to fight a limited war, to go to war without the necessity of arousing the public ire." . . .

North Vietnam finally won its war because it was willing to accept more death than we considered rational. That is why the bombing campaigns failed. It is not that our technology failed. Our cultural perceptions failed when so many intelligent men in high positions simply assumed that our enemy's culture was sufficiently like ours that he would quit at a point where we believed we would quit.

We lost the war because we were never clear about the guerrillas, their popular support, the North Vietnamese, or ourselves. Our marvelously clever technology did not help us to understand the war and, in fact, confused us even more because it created our unquestioning faith in our own power. Finally, the North's decision to continue fighting, and our decision to stop, were each consistent with the cultural imperatives of each nation. Because the army of South Vietnam was trained by us to fight in the American style, it was forever dependent on a supply of hardware and fuel. That army was incongruent with the culture it was trying to defend.

This is why the military's continuing claim that we could have won the war if it had been allowed to fight differently is pointless. We could not have fought it differently. The constraints on the tactics of the war, and the absence of a political goal to shape those tactics, were products of American culture at the time. It is meaningless to argue that "next time we'll do it differently and win." The only reasonable prediction about the cultural pressures surrounding a "next time" is that they will at least resemble those that existed in the 1960s and exist now.

PRIMARY SOURCES

The Vietnam War left historians with a wealth of primary sources. Many of them reveal the thinking of policymakers, including LBJ and his top advisers. Others reflect the experience of military personnel in Vietnam. Some of the primary sources in this chapter document the concerns of policymakers in the Johnson administration as they considered military options. Others demonstrate the nature of the Vietnam War, the consequences of the administration's war policies, and the attitudes of Americans about Vietnam. Together such sources can help historians understand, perhaps better than many of the participants themselves, why the United States fought the war the way it did and why the war ended as it did.

◆

SOURCE 3   The decisions to wage a bombing campaign in Vietnam, to commit American combat troops to the war, and to increase their numbers were ultimately Lyndon Johnson's. Thus LBJ is a central figure in historians' debates about the limited war in Vietnam. What does this speech, delivered at Johns Hopkins University, reveal about his perception of the problem in Vietnam and his objectives there? Were his objectives realistic?

Lyndon Johnson Defends the American Commitment to Vietnam (April 1965)

Why must this nation hazard its ease, its interest, and its power for the sake of a people so far away?

We fight because we must fight if we are to live in a world where every country can shape its own destiny, and only in such a world will our own freedom be finally secure. . . .

The confused nature of this conflict cannot mask the fact that it is the new face of an old enemy.

Over this war—and all Asia—is another reality: the deepening shadow of Communist China. The rulers in Hanoi are urged on by Peking. This is a regime which has destroyed freedom in Tibet, which has attacked India and has been condemned by the United Nations for aggression in Korea. It is a nation which is helping the forces of violence in almost every continent. The contest in Viet-Nam is part of a wider pattern of aggressive purposes.

Source: Robert J. McMahon, *Major Problems in the History of the Vietnam War,* 2nd ed. (Lexington, Mass.: D. C. Health and Company, 1995), pp. 210–211, 212–213.

Why are these realities our concern? Why are we in South Viet-Nam?

We are there because we have a promise to keep. Since 1954 every American President has offered support to the people of South Viet-Nam. We have helped to build, and we have helped to defend. Thus, over many years, we have made a national pledge to help South Viet-Nam defend its independence.

And I intend to keep that promise. . . .

We are also there because there are great stakes in the balance. Let no one think for a moment that retreat from Viet-Nam would bring an end to conflict. The battle would be renewed in one country and then another. The central lesson of our time is that the appetite of aggression is never satisfied. To withdraw from one battlefield means only to prepare for the next. We must say in Southeast Asia—as we did in Europe—in the words of the Bible: "Hitherto shalt thou come, but no further." . . .

And we do this to convince the leaders of North Viet-Nam—and all who seek to share their conquest—of a simple fact:

We will not be defeated.

We will not grow tired.

We will not withdraw, either openly or under the cloak of a meaningless agreement.

We know that air attacks alone will not accomplish all of these purposes. But it is our best and prayerful judgment that they are a necessary part of the surest road to peace. . . .

The task is nothing less than to enrich the hopes and existence of more than a hundred million people. And there is much to be done.

The vast Mekong River can provide food and water and power on a scale to dwarf even our own T.V.A.

The wonders of modern medicine can be spread through villages where thousands die every year from lack of care.

Schools can be established to train people in the skills needed to manage the process of development.

And these objectives, and more, are within the reach of a cooperative and determined effort.

I also intend to expand and speed up a program to make available our farm surpluses to assist in feeding and clothing the needy in Asia. We should not allow people to go hungry and wear rags while our own warehouses overflow with an abundance of wheat and corn and rice and cotton. . . .

We must also expect that nations will on occasion be in dispute with us. It may be because we are rich, or powerful, or because we have made some mistakes, or because they honestly fear our intentions. However, no nation need ever fear that we desire their land, or to impose our will, or to dictate their institutions.

But we will always oppose the effort of one nation to conquer another nation.

◆────────────

SOURCE 4   One month before Johnson decided to send an additional 125,000 American combat troops to Vietnam, he told Secretary of Defense Robert McNamara what he foresaw there. Do the doubts LBJ expresses here help to explain the Johnson administration's later conduct of the war?

LBJ Expresses Doubts about Vietnam (June 1965)

I think that in time . . . it's going to be difficult for us to very long prosecute effectively a war that far away from home with the divisions that we have here and particularly the potential divisions. And it's really had me concerned for a month and I'm very depressed about it because I see no program from either Defense or State that gives me much hope of doing anything except just praying and grasping to hold on during [the] monsoon [season] and hope they'll quit. And I don't believe they're ever goin' to quit. And I don't see . . . that we have any . . . plan for victory militarily or diplomatically. . . . Russell* thinks we ought to take one of these [regime] changes to get out of there. I do not think we can get out of there with our treaty like it is and with what all we've said and I think it would just lose us face in the world and I just shudder to think what all of 'em would say.

*Richard B. Russell (D-Ga.), Johnson's old Senate mentor and powerful chairman of the Senate Armed Services Committee.
Source: Robert S. McNamara, *In Retrospect: The Tragedy and Lessons of Vietnam* (New York: Random House, Inc., 1995), pp. 190–191; originally from June 21, 1965, 12:15 p.m., Tape 6506.04, Program Number 18, Presidential Recordings, Lyndon Baines Johnson Library.

◆────────────

SOURCE 5   Because they are often written to justify past actions and policies, memoirs must be evaluated very carefully, particularly when such sources deal with such a controversial subject as Vietnam. In his memoir, Johnson defended his decision to seek a middle course in Vietnam. Note how he justifies his decision in this excerpt. Were his assumptions well founded? How does this statement compare to that in Source 4?

LBJ Recalls His Decision to Escalate (1971)

We continued our review of the military situation and the requirement for additional forces. Our military commanders had refined their estimates and indicated they could meet the immediate demand with 50,000 men. I called a meeting of the National Security Council two days later, on July 27. I asked McNamara at that time to summarize again the current need as he saw it.

McNamara noted that the Viet Cong had increased in size through local recruitment and replacements from the North. Regular North Vietnamese army units had increased in number and strength. Communist control of the countryside was growing. A dozen provincial capitals were virtually isolated from surrounding rural areas. The South Vietnamese army was growing, but not nearly fast enough to keep pace with the expanding enemy forces. Without additional armed strength, South Vietnam would inevitably fall to Hanoi. I told the NSC there were five possible choices available to us.

"We can bring the enemy to his knees by using our Strategic Air Command," I said, describing our first option. "Another group thinks we ought to pack up and go home."

"Third, we could stay there as we are—and suffer the consequences, continue to lose territory and take casualties. You wouldn't want your own boy to be out there crying for help and not get it."

"Then, we could go to Congress and ask for great sums of money; we could call up the reserves and increase the draft; go on a war footing; declare a state of emergency. There is a good deal of feeling that ought to be done. We have considered this. But if we go into that kind of land war, then North Vietnam would go to its friends, China and Russia, and ask them to give help. They would be forced into increasing aid. For that reason I don't want to be overly dramatic and cause tensions. I think we can get our people to support us without having to be too provocative and warlike.

"Finally, we can give our commanders in the field the men and supplies they say they need."

I had concluded that the last course was the right one. I had listened to and weighed all the arguments and counterarguments for each of the possible lines of action. I believed that we should do what was necessary to resist aggression but that we should not be provoked into a major war. We would get the required appropriation in the new budget, and we would not boast about what we were doing. We would not make threatening noises to the Chinese or the Russians by calling up reserves in large numbers. At the same time, we would

Source: Lyndon Johnson, *The Vantage Point: Perspectives of the Presidency, 1963–1969* (New York: Holt, Rinehart and Winston, 1971), pp. 148–149.

press hard on the diplomatic front to try to find some path to a peaceful settlement.

I asked if anyone objected to the course of action I had spelled out. I questioned each man in turn. Did he agree? Each nodded his approval or said "yes."

◆

SOURCE 6   In 1965, the Johnson administration initiated Rolling Thunder, a bombing campaign against North Vietnam. As you read this assessment, note the CIA's conclusion about the effects of that campaign and what this report reveals about the problems the United States confronted in waging a war in Vietnam using sophisticated technology.

The Central Intelligence Agency Reports on the War (1967)

Through the end of April 1967 the US air campaign against North Vietnam—Rolling Thunder—had significantly eroded the capacities of North Vietnam's limited industrial and military base. These losses, however, have not meaningfully degraded North Vietnam's material ability to continue the war in South Vietnam.

Total damage through April 1967 was over $233 million, of which 70 percent was accounted for by damage to economic targets. The greatest amount of damage was inflicted on the so-called logistics target system—transport equipment and lines of communication.

By the end of April 1967 the US air campaign had attacked 173 fixed targets, over 70 percent of the targets on the JCS [Joint Chiefs of Staff] list. This campaign included extensive attacks on almost every major target system in the country. The physical results have varied widely. . . .

North Vietnam's ability to recuperate from the air attacks has been of a high order. The major exception has been the electric power industry. . . .

The recuperability problem is not significant for the other target systems. The destroyed petroleum storage system has been replaced by an effective system of dispersed storage and distribution. The damaged military target systems—particularly barracks and storage depots—have simply been abandoned, and supplies and troops dispersed throughout the country. The inventories of transport and military equipment have been replaced by large infusions of military and economic aid from the USSR and Communist China.

Source: Robert J. McMahon, *Major Problems in the History of the Vietnam War,* 2nd ed. (Lexington, Mass.: D. C. Heath and Company, 1995), pp. 248, 249.

Damage to bridges and lines of communications is frequently repaired within a matter of days, if not hours, or the effects are countered by an elaborate system of multiple bypasses or pre-positioned spans.

◆

SOURCE 7   Twenty years after the fall of South Vietnam, Robert McNamara published his memoir. In this excerpt, he discusses LBJ's decision to commit combat troops to Vietnam. Note McNamara's explanation for LBJ's determination to downplay the escalation of the war and how his recollection of this decision differs from Johnson's. What accounts for the difference?

McNamara Recalls the Decision to Escalate (1995)

On January 27, 1965—just one week after the inauguration—Mac* and I gave President Johnson a short but explosive memorandum. Mac and I believed events were at a critical juncture. We told LBJ:

> The worst course of action is to continue in this essentially passive role which can only lead to eventual defeat and an invitation to get out in humiliating circumstances. We see two alternatives. The first is to use our military power in the Far East and to force a change in Communist policy. The second is to deploy all our resources along a track of negotiation, aimed at salvaging what little can be preserved with no major addition to our present military risks. [We] tend to favor the first course, but we believe that both should be carefully studied.

After months of uncertainty and indecision, we had reached the fork in the road.

The first six months of 1965 that followed our memo marked the most crucial phase of America's thirty-year involvement in Indochina. Between January 28 and July 28, 1965, President Johnson made the fateful choices that locked the United States onto a path of massive military intervention in Vietnam, an intervention that ultimately destroyed his presidency and polarized America like nothing since the Civil War.

During this fateful period, Johnson initiated bombing of North Vietnam and committed U.S. ground forces, raising the total U.S. troop strength from 23,000 to 175,000—with the likelihood of another 100,000 in 1966 and perhaps even more later. All of this occurred without adequate public disclosure or debate, planting the seeds of an eventually debilitating credibility gap. . . .

Why did President Johnson refuse to take the American people into his confidence? Some point to his innate secretiveness, but the answer is far more

*National Security Adviser McGeorge Bundy.
Source: From *In Retrospect: The Tragedy and Lessons of Vietnam* by Robert S. McNamara. Copyright © 1995 by Robert S. McNamara. Reprinted by permission of Time Books, a division of Random House, Inc.

complex. One factor was his obsession with securing Congress's approval and financing of his Great Society agenda; he wanted nothing to divert attention and resources from his cherished domestic reforms. The other was his equally strong fear of hard-line pressure (from conservatives in both parties) for greater—and far riskier—military action that might trigger responses, especially nuclear, by China and/or the Soviet Union. The president coped with his dilemma by obscuring it—an unwise and ultimately self-defeating course. . . .

From the beginning of our involvement in Vietnam, the South Vietnamese forces had been giving us poor intelligence and inaccurate reports. Sometimes these inaccuracies were conscious attempts to mislead; at other times they were the product of too much optimism. And sometimes the inaccuracies merely reflected the difficulty of gauging progress accurately.

But I insisted we try to measure progress. Since my years at Harvard, I had gone by the rule that it is not enough to conceive of an objective and a plan to carry it out; you must monitor the plan to determine whether you are achieving the objective. If you discover you are not, you either revise the plan or change the objective. I was convinced that, while we might not be able to track a front line, we could find variables that would indicate our success or failure. So we measured the targets destroyed in the North, the traffic down the Ho Chi Minh Trail, the number of captives, the weapons seized, the enemy body count, and so on.

The body count was a measurement of the adversary's manpower losses; we undertook it because one of Westy's* objectives was to reach a so-called crossover point, at which the Vietcong and North Vietnamese casualties would be greater than they could sustain. Critics point to use of the body count as an example of my obsession with numbers. "This guy McNamara," they said, "he tries to quantify everything." Obviously, there are things you cannot quantify; honor and beauty, for example. But things you can count, you ought to count. Loss of life is one, when you are fighting a war of attrition. We tried to use body counts as a measurement to help us figure out what we should be doing in Vietnam to win the war while putting our troops at the least risk.

American Soldiers in Vietnam

Americans fought against the Vietnamese and alongside them in an unconventional war waged by an often unseen enemy. In oral histories, memoirs, and interviews, many of the soldiers expressed their thoughts about the war, the South Vietnamese, and the enemy. What do these sources reveal about American attitudes toward the Vietnamese and about the problems Americans encountered

---

*General William Westmoreland.

as they fought an unconventional war? What do they reveal about policymakers' assumptions regarding the war?

◆───────────────

SOURCE 8   Medic David Ross, who served in Vietnam from 1965 until 1967, provided an oral history of his experience.

A Medical Corpsman Recalls the Vietnamese People (1981)

When Americans are talking about Vietnamese or people in India or somewhere similar, it's not like we're looking at them like they're our next-door neighbors. If someone came to our neighborhood and burned all of our houses and most of our possessions and put us in flying saucers which we'd never seen before and zipped us across the universe, setting us down somewhere in tent city in the middle of a sandbox with wire all around us, I guess we might not be too excited about it. Most of us were never able to see the Vietnamese as real people. I remember President Johnson in one of the psy-op [psychological warfare] flicks we saw saying that the communists weren't like us—they didn't have feelings. But I always remembered that old woman or remembered after a B-52 strike going into this area where there was a little girl with her leg . . . traumatic amputation . . . and . . . still alive. Her mother dead. The whole place turned upside down, a few people still screaming, some people wandering around with the look of the dead, a totally shocked daze. I wondered how people would feel in Pittsburgh if the Vietnamese came over in B-52s and bombed them. And while I feel some real sympathy for the POWs who were airmen, I pick Pittsburgh simply because it's a steel city and it has the image of the real hard-working honest American man. I'm trying to imagine a bunch of steelworkers after their wives, children, fiancées, parents, grandparents, have been blown up or are running around screaming in agony and some Vietnamese pilot comes swooping down in a parachute. I don't imagine they'd give him a very friendly reception. . . .

There was another thing I remember, too. We were going through a rice-paddy area in armored personnel carriers, and of course track vehicles going through a rice paddy isn't . . . The amount of labor they put into maintaining the rice and the paddy berms and the irrigation system and everything—it's all by hand. They don't have the equipment. It's all built a basket of dirt at a time and things have built up over generations. We're just ripping through

Source: Al Santoli, *Everything We Had: An Oral History of the Vietnam War by Thirty-three American Soldiers Who Fought It* (New York: Ballantine Books, 1981), pp. 47–49.

there on the tracks, tearing the whole damn thing apart. This farmer out there is stomping on his hat and and beating his hand against his head. I guess, really, the bottom line is that all his stocks and bonds and his future and his Mercedes and his dreams he hoped for his kids, we just drove through there and in three or four minutes made a helluva mess of it.

———————◆———————————

SOURCE 9   Philip Caputo was a marine lieutenant in Vietnam in 1965. His memoir, *A Rumor of War,* describes his experiences there.

Fighting a Technological War of Attrition (1977)

Everything rotted and corroded quickly over there: bodies, boot leather, canvas, metal, morals. Scorched by the sun, wracked by the wind and rain of the monsoon, fighting in alien swamps and jungles, our humanity rubbed off of us as the protective bluing rubbed off the barrels of our rifles. We were fighting in the cruelest kind of conflict, a people's war. It was no orderly campaign, as in Europe, but a war for survival waged in a wilderness without rules or laws; a war in which each soldier fought for his own life and the lives of the men beside him, not caring who he killed in that personal cause or how many or in what manner and feeling only contempt for those who sought to impose on his savage struggle the mincing distinctions of civilized warfare— that code of battlefield ethics that attempted to humanize an essentially inhuman war. According to those "rules of engagement," it was morally right to shoot an unarmed Vietnamese who was running, but wrong to shoot one who was standing or walking; it was wrong to shoot an enemy prisoner at close range, but right for a sniper at long range to kill an enemy soldier who was no more able than a prisoner to defend himself; it was wrong for infan- trymen to destroy a village with white-phosphorus grenades, but right for a fighter pilot to drop napalm on it. Ethics seemed to be a matter of distance and technology. You could never go wrong if you killed people at long range with sophisticated weapons. And then there was that inspiring order issued by General Greene: kill VC. In the patriotic fever of the Kennedy years, we had asked, "What can we do for our country?" and our country answered, "Kill VC." That was the strategy, the best our best military minds could come up with: organized butchery. But organized or not, butchery was butchery, so who was to speak of rules and ethics in a war that had none?

CONCLUSION

History is the collective memory that we use to guide us in the present. However, sometimes its lessons are not clear. Few wars have been more carefully scrutinized as the Vietnam War, but historians disagree about the lessons it yields. They have different explanations for the way Americans fought it and thus for the way it turned out.

Some historians locate the cause of America's defeat in its leaders' decisions about how to fight the war. These decisions, in turn, reflected such forces as personality or bureaucratic mentality. For these historians, the lesson of Vietnam is to avoid similar decisions in the future. Other historians see a deeper cause for defeat in certain American assumptions that made military disaster a virtual certainty. For these historians America's failure in Vietnam can be traced to a single powerful force: American culture.

Yet Vietnam may hold a lesson that has nothing to do with avoiding future military disasters. It involves the unintended consequences that wars have on societies fighting them. As we saw by examining nativism in Chapter 6 and the Cold War in the previous chapter, cultural assumptions can have powerful consequences. Yet culture is not static, as Vietnam's impact on Americans makes clear. The disillusionment fostered by this war helped crack a powerful Cold War culture. Ideas about gender made up one prominent strand woven into that culture. As we will see next, changing ideas about gender contributed to its unraveling in the 1960s and 1970s.

FURTHER READING

Larry Berman, *Lyndon Johnson's War: The Road to Stalemate in Vietnam* (New York: W. W. Norton and Company, 1989).

Frances FitzGerald, *Fire in the Lake: The Vietnamese and the Americans in Vietnam* (Boston: Little, Brown, 1972).

George Herring, *America's Longest War: The United States in Vietnam, 1950–1975*, rev. ed. (New York: McGraw-Hill, Inc., 1986).

David Levy, *The Debate over Vietnam* (Baltimore: Johns Hopkins University Press, 1991).

Norman Podhoretz, *Why We Were in Vietnam* (New York: Simon and Schuster, 1982).

Al Santoli, *Everything We Had: An Oral History of the Vietnam War by Thirty-three American Soldiers Who Fought It* (New York: Ballantine Books, 1981).

NOTES

1. Quoted in "A North Vietnamese Commander Celebrates the 'Great Spring Victory,' " in *Major Problems in the History of the Vietnam War*, ed. Robert J. McMahon, 2nd ed. (Lexington, Mass.: D. C. Heath, 1995), p. 578.

2. Quoted in George C. Herring, *America's Longest War: The United States in Vietnam, 1950–1975* (New York: John Wiley, 1979), p. 264.

3. Lyndon B. Johnson, *The Vantage Point: Perspectives of the Presidency, 1963–1969* (New York: Holt Rinehart and Winston, 1971), p. x.

Chapter 12

Gender, Ideology, and Historical Change: Explaining the Women's Movement

The sources in this chapter relate to the rise of the women's movement in the 1960s and 1970s.

Secondary Sources

1. Feminism and Family Change: 1960–1980 (1983), MARY P. RYAN
2. Cold War Ideology and the Rise of Feminism (1988), ELAINE TYLER MAY

Primary Sources

3. The Problem That Has No Name (1963), BETTY FRIEDAN
4. Civil Rights and the Rise of Feminism (1987), MARY KING
5. NOW's Statement of Purpose (1966)
6. Redstockings Manifesto (1969)
7. On Women and Sex (1972), JOYCE MAYNARD
8. Our Bodies, Ourselves (1973)
9. The Politics of Housework (ca. 1970), PAT MAINARDI
10. Sex Ratios of High School and College Graduates in the United States, 1940–1980
11. Women's Labor Force Participation, by Marital Status, 1940–1987
12. Median Earnings of Year-round, Full-time Workers, by Sex, 1955–1985

*C*vidence of coming turmoil was everywhere in 1965. In the first week of June, *Newsweek* detailed several scenarios for the growing war in Vietnam. One of them read that the United States "steadily enlarges its ground combat commitment but its hopes are frustrated; there is no conclusion to the war in sight."[1] The same week, *U.S. News & World Report* covered an "uproar" in Chicago over segregated public schools, yet another sign that the civil rights movement had moved north by the mid-1960s. In the same issue, *U.S. News* reported on the growing campus demonstrations against U.S. foreign policy: "Speakers draw cheers with demands for American withdrawal from the war against the Communists in Vietnam."[2]

Far less obvious was the hint of looming trouble in *Time*'s cover story the following week on the best-selling poet Phyllis McGinley, a suburban Connecticut housewife. McGinley proclaimed that women exercise their greatest influence in the home. She "finds herself the sturdiest exponent of the glory of housewifery," *Time* observed, "standing almost alone against a rising chorus of voices summoning women away from the hearth." The loudest voice in the chorus, the story also noted, belonged to Betty Friedan, whose best-selling "broadside," *The Feminine Mystique* (1963), proclaimed "that the college-educated woman who seeks fulfillment in domesticity will never find it. . . ." Given McGinley's nine books of poetry, two volumes of essays, fifteen children's books, and one Pulitzer Prize, *Time* could only conclude that Friedan's attitude was "tinged with envy."[3]

Values are often defended only when they are no longer taken for granted. *Time*'s profile of McGinley exposed growing doubts by 1965 that women could find happiness only at home. Indeed, in the coming years the rejection of domesticity fed a powerful women's movement that transformed the way homes, workplaces, churches, and the halls of government looked and functioned. Three decades after a suburban housewife like Phyllis McGinley could become a controversial figure, historians ask what gave rise to a women's movement that caught most Americans off guard in the 1960s. In this chapter, we consider some of their answers.

SETTING

By 1970, the growing women's protest had a name: the "women's liberation movement." Journalists, commentators, and women activists themselves had other labels for it as well. Some called it the "women's rights movement." Others labeled it "feminist protest," and later many settled on "the women's movement."

The failure to pin one name on the women's revolt of the 1960s and 1970s reveals something about it. First, it was a movement only in the loosest sense. As *Newsweek* put it in 1970, "the women's liberation movement [is] a very loose designation for a multiplicity of small groups led by a multiplicity of women."[4] All of the participants might agree that women were subject to sexism and sexual discrimination and thus did not enjoy full equality in American society. Yet not all women activists shared the same analysis of their problems. Nor did they agree on what to do about them. Liberation, they discovered, could mean many things.

Women's diverse backgrounds influenced their analysis of the gender problem. Social class, education, occupation, marital status, and even sexual orientation influenced women's views of equality. Thus the women's movement had little appeal for many black, Hispanic, and working-class women, who often saw their inequality in economic or racial terms. On the other hand, it attracted many educated, middle-class women, for whom *The Feminine Mystique* struck a responsive chord. Friedan had asserted that education and employment outside the home was the solution for women's unhappiness and lack of self-esteem. When the National Organization for Women (NOW) was formed in 1966 with Friedan as its first president, its ranks were filled with professional women who faced discrimination in the job market and felt bridled by traditional attitudes about women's domestic duties. NOW denied hostility toward men, however. Rather, it called for "a fully equal partnership of the sexes," and pressed for an end to sexual discrimination through such measures as the Equal Rights Amendment.

By the late 1960s, younger women began to challenge NOW with different analyses of women's oppression and alternative responses to it. Often veterans of the civil rights and antiwar movements or New Left political organizations, these radical feminists dismissed NOW's efforts to end sexual discrimination through political action as "bourgeois" and insufficient. They also pointed out that gaining equality in the workplace, the political arena, the media, and elsewhere in the "public" sphere was not enough. With no equality in the "private" sphere of domestic relations, women would be expected to "do it all."

For radical feminists, NOW's legislative solutions were too narrow, and women could not be truly liberated without a radical restructuring of society. Some insisted that women's liberation could only be achieved with the rejection of capitalism. Yet most radical feminists advanced cultural rather than economic radicalism. They divided with moderates not on questions about the economic order but on the matters of marriage and family. Radicals like Kate Millett and Susan Brownmiller, for instance, argued that women could liberate themselves through communal living arrangements and even by ending women's function as childbearers. Others, such as the Radicalesbians, insisted that the problem lay in heterosexual relations. Rather than point to the barriers to access, radical feminists emphasized the oppressive nature of a male-dominated society and the need to view all relations between men and women in political terms.

The difference, said some feminists, was between the moderates' "egalitarian ethic" and the radicals' "liberation ethic." Yet it was not quite that simple. Friedan and other moderates had advocated the liberation of women from an ideology of domesticity, and radicals were guided by the ideal of gender equality. In addition, both moderates and radicals proclaimed opposition to sexism. Moreover, by the mid-1970s there were thousands of feminist groups raising numerous issues supported by both sides, including legal abortion, domestic violence, women's health, and child care. Maybe the most accurate assessment of the growth of women's groups was offered by one feminist writer, who proclaimed, "It's not a movement, it's a State of Mind."[5]

By 1975, that "state of mind" had influenced public consciousness. The protests and lobbying of women's groups and a flood of books and articles by such feminists as Kate Millett, Gloria Steinem, and Robin Morgan had raised awareness of women's issues. Feminism had gained legitimacy, although not in the radical sense of eliminating gender differences. By the end of the 1970s, laws and court decisions embodied many demands of the women's movement. Although factionalized and under a conservative counterattack, women had succeeded in altering their status as a group and changing the lives of countless women and men.

INVESTIGATION

Like the antebellum women's rights movement, the feminist revolt of the 1960s and 1970s was led mostly by middle-class women. Also like the earlier movement, it rebelled against an ideology at the same time that it was divided by ideology. And like the pre–Civil War women's protest, it arose at a time of widespread unrest. To understand the rise of feminist protest in the 1960s and 1970s, historians must therefore study a number of influences on women. They must also consider the power of ideology to stimulate and define the limits of reform.

This chapter examines what led many women to become women's rights advocates seeking legal equality and equal treatment in the workplace, or even to become feminists seeking to completely redefine the meaning of gender. It presents two historians' contrasting views about the changes responsible for the rise of the women's movement. Your main assignment is to evaluate these arguments and develop an explanation for the rise of the women's movement in the 1960s and 1970s. Your analysis should explain the impact of economic, social, political, and cultural changes on women's views about their status. It should also address the following main questions:

1. **How do the essays' explanations for the rise of the women's movement differ?** Which one better explains its rise? Why? Are their explanations mutually exclusive?

2. **What do the primary sources reveal about the experiences that led many women to change their views about their status?** What did major economic, cultural, political, and economic trends, including the civil rights and antiwar movements and the sexual revolution, have to do with the rise of the women's movement?

3. **What do the sources reveal about the major goals of the women's movement and the most important factors limiting their attainment?** How do the essays' explanations for the limits of the women's movement differ?

Before you begin, read the sections in your textbook on the status of women in postwar society and on the women's movement of the 1960s and 1970s. Note how your text accounts for the rise of this movement.

SECONDARY SOURCES

◆

SOURCE 1   In this selection, historian Mary Ryan discusses some of the generational experiences of women. Look for Ryan's explanation for the changes in the women's movement between the 1960s and 1970s. How did women's involvement in antiwar protest and the civil rights movement contribute to the rise of the women's movement? Finally, pay particular attention to Ryan's argument about the "structures of womanhood," experiences that gave two generations of women a "reprieve from domesticity." Note her argument about the way "factors intrinsic to the gender system itself" helped to stimulate a women's movement and also to limit the attainment of equality by the 1980s.

Feminism and Family Change, 1960–1980 (1983)

MARY P. RYAN

Even during the high tide of the feminine mystique the discerning observer could identify undercurrents of gender change. Social scientists noted that

Source: Mary P. Ryan, "Feminism and Family Change, 1960–1980," from *Womanhood in America from Colonial Times to the Present,* 3rd ed., Franklin Watts, 1983, pp. 307–311, 312, 317, 321. Excerpted by permission of Franklin Watts.

many women were uncomfortable with their assigned places; sociologists talked about role conflict and psychologists worried about identity crises. The editors of the *Ladies' Home Journal* were surprised by the voluminous correspondence generated by articles on "Mothers Who Run Away," and "Why Women Feel Trapped." These quiet tremors of discontent were hardly all that lurked beneath the peaceful domestic surface of the 1950s.

Countless wives and mothers had taken their personal dilemmas into their own hands, often half-consciously and without any societal endorsement, to remodel gender roles more to their own liking. . . . The millions of women who went back to school or back to work in the 1950s may not have been self-conscious feminists, but their individual acts of confidence and courage were the makings of a major transformation in the gender system.

Not until well into the 1960s, however, were these personal decisions articulated as a conscious break with convention or organized into a political or social movement. The word "feminism" was scarcely uttered during the 1940s and 1950s, except to refer to musty relics of the past. Women's politics was confined to voluntary service in the community, feminism to a few veterans of the Woman's party who doggedly introduced the Equal Rights Amendment before Congress year after year. Explicitly women's issues were not placed on the political agenda in any visible way until 1961, when John F. Kennedy appointed a Presidential Commission on the Status of Women. . . .

The first report of the Commission, issued in 1963, put this old-fashioned social feminism on full display. It focused on the wages and conditions of women's work, skirted the issue of the Equal Rights Amendment, and disavowed any intention of undermining women's domestic roles. Nonetheless, the Kennedy Commission marked a new beginning as well. It gave women's issues a prominent place on the political agenda for the first time in decades and, perhaps more importantly, put a group of women and men together and set them to thinking concertedly about questions of gender. By sponsoring auxiliary state organizations and providing for extended deliberations, the Commission put into operation a small but viable and visible network of women's politics. It provided an institutional base for the revival of feminism. Whether the Commission on the Status of Women was dealing with industrial workers or educated professional women, its members could not escape the contradictions of the kaleidoscope of roles.

At about the same time that the Commission sat down to work on this problem, Betty Friedan was facing a critical moment in the female life cycle—returning to the labor force after years of childrearing. From her position on the editorial staff of a women's magazine, Friedan began to overhear and then publicize murmurings of discontent among the home-bound women of suburbia. In the *Feminine Mystique*, published in 1963, Friedan became a best-selling author on the strength of her attack upon domestic womanhood. The quagmire of woman's dual role was given scholarly attention in 1964 in the spring issue of the prestigious journal, *Daedalus*. In a path-breaking article entitled "Equality of the Sexes: An Immodest Proposal," the sociologist Alice Rossi translated these inchoate grumblings into an explicitly feminist manifesto. Slowly the smoldering complaints of workingwomen and restless housewives began to cohere as a platform for reform.

All these concerns came together in Washington, D.C., in 1966 when women assembled for a meeting of the National Conference of Commissions on the Status of Women. In Betty Friedan's hotel room the National Organization of Women (NOW) was founded, the first explicit feminist organization since the suffrage era. In the early years of its existence, NOW propounded a legalistic brand of feminism, demanding equality of opportunity and speaking to the concerns of the educated, relatively affluent professional women who comprised its initial constituency. This first impulse of organization in behalf of women seemed to take clues from moderate civil rights organizations such as the National Association for the Advancement of Colored People. The aim of NOW, as reputedly scribbled on a napkin in a Washington hotel, was "To take actions needed to bring women into the mainstream of American society now with full equality for women in fully equal partnership with men."

Even at the outset, however, this women's movement of the 1960s distinguished itself from the older feminism in critical ways. It had, first of all, stepped clearly outside women's sphere and set its mind on the integrationist goal of "full partnership with men." Second, NOW proclaimed its intention to critically assess and reform the private and domestic realm. "We believe," said the founding members of NOW, "that true partnership between the sexes demands a different concept of marriage, and equitable sharing of the responsibilities of home and children and the economic and social value of homemaking and child care." Clearly, an eventful span of history had intervened between the culmination of the suffrage movement and the formation of NOW in 1966. . . . Still, the largely professional and middle-aged women who founded NOW could conceive of only traditional political means of working toward their novel goals. Their policy statement on domestic issues concluded rather lamely, "To these ends, we will seek to open a reexamination of laws and mores governing marriage and divorce."

By the mid-1970s NOW claimed 800 chapters and 55,000 members and a much broader program of reforms. Its original focus on legal equality and labor-force discrimination had been extended to encompass such issues as legalized abortion, day care, political power, and family reform. It began to champion the rights of the poor, minorities, and lesbians. The expansion of NOW's program was inspired by the protests of an independent flank of the nascent women's movement, one associated with younger women allied with the New Left and calling itself Women's Liberation.

Feminist consciousness seemed to erupt just as suddenly on college campuses as it had among the career women who founded NOW. Yet Women's

Liberation was rooted in basic structural changes in womanhood that were evolving within the life cycles of these younger women. The generation of women that unfurled the banners of Women's Liberation was composed in large part of the daughters of those middle-aged women who were returning to work in ever larger numbers. The younger women, however, should they follow in their mothers' footsteps, would advance into the labor force with greater planning, skills, and forethought. While their mothers had often dropped out of high school during the depression and rarely completed college, the women of the 1960s left secondary school with their diplomas in hand and fully one-third of them went on to college where, by 1968, they constituted 40 percent of the student body.

As education was prolonged, so was marriage delayed; the median age of brides, which had fallen to its all-time low in 1950, began slowly to rise. At college, these women drew away from the parental home and entered into a sphere of independent activity, casual association with male peers, and co-equal involvement in preparing and planning for the deployment of their knowledge and talents. By the 1970s, 37 percent of the women between the ages of twenty and twenty-four were single. More women than ever before were at a point in their life cycles and a place in the social system where they could seriously contemplate a choice between marriage and a career. The community of their peers, the experience of their working mothers, the example of NOW, all inspired a conscious assessment of the choices open to them as women.

The turbulent campus politics of the 1960s combined with this shifting structure of womanhood to catalyze a special breed of feminism. Women students had entered freely and fully into the enlivened political arena of the '60s. They went south to claim civil rights for black men and women; they denounced the war in Vietnam; and they participated in the ideological stirrings that defined a New Left in America. The women who lent their wholehearted support to these movements, however, confronted some particularly grating exhibitions of misogyny. In the New Left they were routinely delegated the most menial tasks, like leafleting, mimeographing, and generally serving as secretaries to the revolution. They were often expected to be sexually accommodating as well, best suited to a "prone" position, according to one leader of the Student Nonviolent Coordinating Committee (SNCC) and "saying yes to men who say no" in the antidraft movement.

It was a group of black women working in the South with SNCC who first began to protest against this kind of treatment. In 1966 a women named Ruby Dory Smith Robinson issued a formal attack on the sexual politics of the civil-rights movement, particularly the relations between black men and white women. Two white women, Casey Hayden and Mary King, responded to these stirrings of discontent with a position paper entitled "Sex and Caste: A Kind of Memo." It received national circulation in the April issue of the New-Left periodical *Liberation*. The first volley in what was to be the women's liberation movement had been fired. . . .

It would be mistaken to place too much emphasis on strictly political history, be it the Kennedy administration, the civil rights movement, or the New Left, as the point of origin for the new feminism. In some ways the collision with conventional politics was incidental to more basic causal factors intrinsic to the gender system itself. The Women's Liberation movement grew directly out of at least three structures of womanhood which had evolved in the twentieth century.

First of all, feminism grew up within the crevices between women's multiple roles as they unfolded over the course of the female life cycle. For the cohort of middle-class women who formed NOW, the empty-nest stage was the seedtime of feminism. When maternal responsibilities subsided and women began to contemplate returning to school or to the labor force, they became acutely conscious of the restrictions of gender. Domestic roles were suspended in a more radical way for the generation which created the Women's Liberation movement. In the late 1960s more women than ever before in American history were in college, living away from their parental homes, and freed by the affluence of the era from the exigencies of earning their own living as well. Suspended between the families of their birth and the family of marriage, these women were in an ideal position to reconsider woman's place. Those women who went south to participate in the civil rights movement, and ended up in the vanguard of a new feminism, illustrate this principle in the extreme. Almost entirely college educated, three-quarters of them planned to go on to graduate or professional school. One of their number captured the possibilities of this moment in the female life cycle in just a few words: "I have no husband to consult . . . no degree to finish."

Thus, two generations of women, each in their own ways enjoying a reprieve from domesticity, worked unconsciously in tandem to resurrect feminism. This generational cross-fertilization is a second structural base of the feminist revival. In some cases, for example, when founders of Women's Liberation recalled being introduced to *The Feminine Mystique* by their mothers, the matrilineage of the women's movement was direct and explicit. More often the influence of the mother's generation was more diffuse, but equally powerful. As the daughters left for college, their own mothers presented models of something more than domesticity: they engaged in voluntary work, resumed their education, or reentered the labor force. The life cycles of the two generations, in other words, intersected in such a way as to reinforce the impression that womanhood was no longer a simple and single matter of homemaking.

The feminism which emerged at this juncture was deeply marked by a third circumstance of its founding. Unlike the nineteenth-century women's movement, the new feminism emerged from conditions of contact and similarity between the sexes, not out of a separate woman's sphere. For the older group associated with NOW, women's revolt was stimulated by contact with the labor force, a previously male sphere. On the job, in a breadwinning role parallel to that of their husbands, the women of the 1960s saw sexual discrimination with a new clarity, in the stark reality of unequal paychecks.

The special anger of the younger cohort of feminists was kindled by abrasive contact with their male peers—in the classroom, the political meeting, and the bedroom and kitchen as well. Intimate contacts between the sexes proved especially explosive. The college students of the 1960s were the first generation in American history to engage in premarital promiscuity and cohabitation in any appreciable numbers. When sexual contacts and shared housekeeping occurred outside the bonds of engagement or matrimony, the conventional sexual division of power and of work became suspect. Women began to complain about male roommates who enjoyed the privileges of the bed but wouldn't make it. It was contact with males or the male world, that is, participation in the heterosocial atmosphere of twentieth-century women, that sparked the anger so essential to the resuscitation of American feminism.

The conditions which enkindled feminist consciousness in the late 1960s all turned into major historical trends in the decade that followed. Women's participation in the labor force grew at an unprecedented rate in the 1970s until it accounted for the majority of women, regardless of marital status. Female college enrollment mounted at a similar pace while the marriage rate declined, and the proportion of young women living on their own more than doubled. The generational continuity was also maintained as the daughters of working mothers demonstrated greater career ambitions, and the new generation of women built securely on the work rate of their mothers to rise to even higher levels of employment. Whether in the labor force or in the playgrounds of the swinging '70s, finally, the mingling of the sexes continued to mark women's experience and generate both sexual combat and gender consciousness. . . .

Women awakened in the 1970s to discover, along with their new-found strength and confidence, that they were still in many ways the second sex. The massing of women in the labor force had made at least one species of sexual inequity patently obvious, for now a woman's secondary status could be measured by the clear and definitive standard of her paycheck, which usually amounted to several thousand dollars less than a male's annual income. The demand for equal pay for equal work became almost as all-American as apple pie and was edging out motherhood as the preoccupation of contemporary women. In fact, the majority of Americans endorsed Women's Liberation as a package. In 1971, 42 percent of the population expressed general agreement with the goals of the women's movement, and by 1975 feminism was endorsed by a solid majority, 59 percent of the American people. . . .

The past history of their sex would suggest, however, that during the '70s and '80s the young women who grew up with the feminist movement were fast approaching a critical period in their life cycles. It remained to be seen whether marriage and motherhood would diminish their appetite for a hefty masculine portion of power and wealth. When less ambitious and privileged women returned to work after the interruptions of infant care, they might be bound all the more tightly to low-level jobs. Women of the last quarter of the twentieth century still face these formidable domestic hurdles.

◆

SOURCE 2   In the previous selection, Mary Ryan deemphasizes the role of political history in explaining the rise of modern feminism. In this selection, Elaine Tyler May examines the impact of political changes on American families, specifically the relationship between the demise of a Cold War ideology and the ideal of domesticity in the 1960s. Pay attention to May's argument about the way a Cold War ideology "contained" women. Does she make a convincing case that a domestic ideology and Cold War militance rose and fell together? Do you think the postwar marriage and baby booms were the result of Cold War ideology or of other factors, such as the return of peace and prosperity? Also think about whether the idea of containment can be applied to family relations and if May shows that containment cut off pre–Cold War changes within families. How does she explain the limited success of the women's movement, and how does her explanation differ from Ryan's?

Cold War Ideology and the Rise of Feminism (1988)

ELAINE TYLER MAY

The politics of the cold war and the ideology and public policies that it spawned were crucial in shaping postwar family life and gender roles. . . .

With security as the common thread, the cold war ideology and the domestic revival reinforced each other. The powerful political consensus that supported cold war policies abroad and anticommunism at home fueled conformity to the suburban family ideal. In turn, the domestic ideology encouraged private solutions to social problems and further weakened the potential for challenges to the cold war consensus. Personal adaptation, rather than political resistance, characterized the era. But postwar domesticity never fully delivered on its promises. The baby-boom children who grew up in suburban homes abandoned the containment ethos when they came of age.

As young adults in the 1960s, they challenged both the imperatives of the cold war and the domestic ideology that came with it. At the same time, they forged new paths to pursue the unfulfilled dreams of their parents. . . .

. . . Among the first to criticize the status quo were postwar parents themselves. In 1963, Betty Friedan published her exposé of domesticity, *The Feminine Mystique.* Friedan gave a name to the "problem that has no name" for career homemakers. A postwar wife and mother herself, Friedan spoke directly to women . . . who had lived according to the domestic containment ideology. She urged them to break away from their domestic confines, go back to school, pursue careers, and revive the vision of female independence that had been alive before World War II. *The Feminine Mystique* became an immediate best-seller and created a national sensation. The book enabled discontented women across the country to find their voices. It was as if someone was finally willing to say that the emperor had no clothes; soon a chorus joined in support. Hundreds of readers wrote to Friedan, telling their stories. These personal testimonies reveal the stated and unstated messages that this generation of parents gave their children.

The letters to Friedan reveal widespread disenchantment among women who had struggled to conform to the prevailing familial norm. Some of the writers were children of activist parents who had fought for equal rights in the early part of the century. Nearly all expressed the hope that their children would avoid the domestic trap in which they found themselves. . . .

A Mount Holyoke graduate who joined the "stampede back to the nest" described her path into domesticity: "I entered graduate school at Yale, met a man, left school, and married in 1951. I have since then moved thirteen times, lived in eight states, had four miscarriages and produced two children." But she also struggled at home and alone to become a painter. So "finally, when I fill out the income tax now, it is occupation: Painter, not housewife. . . .

Friedan's book sparked readers to comment not only on the connection between women's and men's fate, but between domesticity and cold war politics. One woman believed that political activism was the only way to bring women out of "their cozy cocoons in America," but she also perceived that challenges to women's roles would be seen as un-American. Women would need to "make determined efforts to free themselves," she noted, "and they may expect hostility from conservative elements politically as well as from their fellow timid sisters and timid men. I am not advocating that women become Communist sympathizers, but I am expecting that progressive women will be so labelled." . . .

Many of the women who wrote to Friedan were those who could respond to her call for self-realization through education and careers. They were affluent. If married, they had husbands who provided an income that was adequate enough to allow them to develop outside interests for self-fulfillment. But there were others who found Friedan's message troubling. It was fine to have ambitions, but it was another matter to work out of necessity, face a sex-segregated job market, and do double duty at home as well.

One woman expressed her irritation at "the false emphasis that is placed on the entire matter of women fulfilling themselves through a career. The vast majority of working women don't have careers. We have jobs, just like men. We work for money to buy things that our families need. If we're lucky, we like our jobs, and find some satisfaction in doing them well, but it is hard to hold a commercial job, raise a family and keep a house." . . .

As these letters indicate, domestic containment was not going to die a quick or natural death. Yet it was clearly doomed from its own internal contradictions. Betty Friedan spoke for a generation whose children would later be credited with initiating a decade of political and social upheaval, but many of their parents had paved the way. Even those who thought that it was too late to change their own ways and routines knew it was not too late for their children. They encouraged their children—implicitly if not explicitly—to follow new paths. Frustrated women and exhausted men provided ambiguous role models for children hoping to avoid the discontent of their mothers and the pressure and ill health the stresses of the work place had inflicted on their fathers.

Still, change came slowly. In the early 1960s, it was not immediately obvious that a unique historical era was coming to an end. Signs that the postwar consensus was beginning to crack were hardly more visible than they had been in the fifties: a few voices of dissent from the intelligentsia, the growing popularity of counterculture heroes such as Elvis Presley and James Dean, and the spread of the civil rights movement from black activists in the South to northern whites. Oral contraceptives first became available in 1960, but they did not immediately bring about a change in behavior, even though years later, many would credit (or blame) "The Pill" for the "sexual revolution." Most cultural signs still pointed toward the cold war consensus at home and abroad, and the ideology of domesticity was still alive and well. . . .

On November 1, 1961, 50,000 American housewives walked out of their homes and jobs in a massive protest, "Women Strike for Peace." These activists were among the first postwar middle-class whites to organize against the social and political status quo. Several of the leaders of the strike were part of a small group of feminists who had worked on behalf of women's rights throughout the forties and the fifties. According to *Newsweek*, the strikers "were perfectly ordinary looking women. . . . They looked like the women you would see driving ranch wagons, or shopping at the village market, or attending PTA meetings . . . many [were] wheeling baby buggies or strollers." Within a year their numbers grew to several hundred thousand.

Anticommunists worried that Women Strike for Peace signaled that "the pro-Reds have moved in on our mothers and are using them for their own purposes," and the Federal Bureau of Investigation kept the group under surveillance from its inception in 1961. The following year, the leaders of Women Strike for Peace were called before the House Un-American Activities Committee. Under questioning, these women spoke as mothers, claiming that saving American children from nuclear extinction was the essence of "Americanism," thereby turning the ideology of domesticity against the assumptions of the cold war. These women carried the banner of motherhood into politics, much like their reformist Victorian sisters in the last century. But their ability to attack the cold war with domesticity as their tool and make a mockery of the congressional hearings indicates that the familial–cold war consensus was beginning to lose its grip.

Increasing political pressure resulted in several important new public policies that challenged the status quo. In 1961, President Kennedy established the President's Commission on the Status of Women, chaired appropriately by an activist from the 1930s, Eleanor Roosevelt. Within the next three years, Congress passed the Equal Pay Act and Title VII of the Civil Rights Act (which prohibited discrimination on the basis of sex, as well as race, color, religion, and national origin), and the United States and the Soviet Union signed the first treaty banning the atmospheric testing of nuclear weapons.

While these policies were taking shape, Students for a Democratic Society (SDS), inspired largely by the civil rights movement, gained thousands of members in chapters across the country. Out of the student movement came the antiwar movement and the new feminism. By the late sixties, hundreds of thousands of young activists mobilized against the gender assumptions as well as the cold war policies that had prevailed since World War II.

The simultaneous attack on domestic containment and the cold war ideology also found expression in the popular culture. Within a few months of the publication of *The Feminine Mystique* came Stanley Kubrick's film, *Dr. Strangelove: Or, How I Learned to Stop Worrying and Love the Bomb*, a biting satire that equated the madness of the cold war with Americans' unresolved sexual neuroses. Such attacks against the sanctity of the postwar domestic ideology and the politics of the cold war would have been risky endeavors ten years earlier. The film probably would have been suppressed and its creators called before the House Un-American Activities Committee. By the early sixties, however, although the cold war was still in full force, and some viewers found the film offensive and un-American, critics as well as audiences were, for the most part, wildly enthusiastic.

By the end of the decade, the new feminist movement had pushed beyond Betty Friedan's call for self-realization into a full-fledged assault on sexism in all its forms, organized by younger women who emerged from their activism in the civil rights movement and the New Left with newly discovered skills and strengths. The new feminists demanded access to professional occupations and skilled jobs, protested low wages, and worked for pay equity. They formed consciousness-raising groups all over the country, challenged the gender division of labor in the home, and railed against the sexual double standard. In a 1970 survey of women entering an open-admission, tuition-free public university, most saw their future role as "married career woman with children"—a vast change from the 1950s when most women of all classes saw their future career as homemaker. . . .

Married or divorced, professional as well as nonprofessional wage-earning women continued to face inequalities at work and at home. Nevertheless, political activism opened up new opportunities for women to achieve autonomy that had been unavailable to their mothers. Women of the fifties, constrained by tremendous cultural and economic pressures to conform to domestic containment, gave up their independence and personal ambitions. Once they made the choice to embrace domesticity, they did their best to thrive within it and claimed that their sacrifices were ultimately worthwhile. Many of their daughters abandoned security and material comfort to follow a more autonomous path that brought them face to face with economic hardship and pervasive discrimination. Yet, like their mothers, many would say that the struggles were worth it. Their mothers paid a price for security and dependence; the daughters paid a price for autonomy and independence. In both cases, the lack of equal opportunity for women limited their options. Yet there is no question that the daughters had more opportunities than their mothers as a result of the hard-won political achievements of the sixties and seventies: they were no longer bound to the home.

Political goals were only partially achieved, however. Even before the end of the 1960s, the "silent majority" rose up against the noisy, youthful minority. In 1968, the quintessential fifties politician, Richard Nixon, was back in the White House, this time as president. The ideology of the cold war, although dealt a serious blow by the disastrous war in Vietnam, remained a powerful force in national politics—and it continued to be tied to the ideology of domesticity. Those who claimed that South Vietnam fell as a result of softness against communism also blamed feminism for what they perceived as the destruction of the family.

It is no accident that in the wake of feminism, the sexual revolution, and the peace movement of the 1960s, the New Right emerged in the 1970s and 1980s as a powerful political force with the dual aims of reviving the cold war and reasserting the ideology of domesticity. It should not be surprising that the most vigorous opponent of the Equal Rights Amendment, Phyllis Schlafly, began her career as an avid Cold Warrior. Proponents of the New Right gained strength by calling for militance in foreign policy, opposing the Equal Rights Amendment, and condemning student radicalism, the counterculture, feminism, and the sexual revolution. They went on to triumph in 1980, with the election of Ronald Reagan to the presidency.

Reagan, like Nixon, received his political groundings in the late 1940s and 1950s as an anticommunist crusader in California. Appropriately, his media image was that of the family man par excellence, as he promoted home-centered consumerism as host of the General Electric Theater. The all-electric home that Reagan advertised (and also inhabited) was virtually identical to the "model home" Nixon praised in Moscow in 1959. In the 1960s, Reagan carried his image into California politics, where he promised to crack down on student protestors. With Reagan in the White House in the 1980s, the rhetoric of containment returned, with its support for cold-war militance and calls for a strengthened "traditional" family. . . .

It is clear that in recent decades, the domestic ideology and cold war militance have risen and fallen together. Immediately after World War II, stable family life seemed necessary for national security, civil defense, and the struggle for supremacy over the Soviet Union. For a generation of young adults who grew up amid depression and war, domestic containment was a logical response to specific historical circumstances. It allowed them to pursue, in the midst of a tense and precarious world situation, the quest for a sexually fulfilling, consumer-oriented personal life that was free from hardship. But the circumstances were different for their children, who broke the consensus surrounding the cold war and domestic containment. Whether the baby-boom children will ultimately be more successful than their parents in achieving fulfilling lives and a more just and tolerant world remains to be seen. But one thing is certain: gender, family, and national politics are still intertwined in the ongoing saga of postwar cultural change.

PRIMARY SOURCES

The sources in this section will help you further analyze the two essays and thus formulate answers to the main questions in the Investigation section. These sources reflect a number of economic, cultural, political, and demographic influences on the women's movement. They also illustrate the varied ways women attempted to achieve equality and some of the obstacles they confronted.

SOURCE 3   Friedan attacked the postwar domestic ideal in her best-selling book, *The Feminine Mystique.* As you read this excerpt, note what problem accompanied the widespread acceptance of the domestic ideal, according to Friedan. Why was the feminine mystique so powerful in the 1950s? Did its hold have more to do with demographic or with political factors?

The Problem That Has No Name (1963)

BETTY FRIEDAN

The problem lay buried, unspoken, for many years in the minds of American women. It was a strange stirring, a sense of dissatisfaction, a yearning that women suffered in the middle of the twentieth century in the United States. Each suburban wife struggled with it alone. As she made the beds, shopped for groceries, matched slipcover material, ate peanut butter sandwiches with her children, chauffeured Cub Scouts and Brownies, lay beside her husband at night—she was afraid to ask even of herself the silent question—"Is this all?"

For over fifteen years there was no word of this yearning in the millions of words written about women, for women, in all the columns, books and articles by experts telling women their role was to seek fulfillment as wives and mothers. Over and over women heard in voices of tradition and of Fruedian sophistication that they could desire no greater destiny than to glory in their own femininity. Experts told them how to catch a man and keep him, how to breastfeed children and handle their toilet training, how to cope with sibling rivalry and adolescent rebellion; how to buy a dishwasher, bake bread, cook gourmet meals, and building a swimming pool with their own hands; how to dress, look, and act more feminine and make marriage more exciting; how to keep their husbands from dying young and their sons from growing into delinquents. They were taught to pity the neurotic, unfeminine, unhappy women who wanted to be poets or physicists or presidents. They learned that truly feminine women do not want careers, higher education, political rights—the independence and the opportunities that the old-fashioned feminists fought for. Some women, in their forties and fifties, still remembered painfully giving up those dreams, but most of the younger women no longer even thought about them. A thousand expert voices applauded their femininity, their adjustment, their new maturity. All they had to do was devote their lives from earliest girlhood to finding a husband and bearing children. . . .

The suburban housewife—she was the dream image of the young American women and the envy, it was said, of women all over the world. The American housewife—freed by science and labor-saving appliances from the drudgery, the dangers of childbirth and the illnesses of her grandmother. She was healthy, beautiful, educated, concerned only about her husband, her children, her home. She had found true feminine fulfillment. As a housewife and mother, she was respected as a full and equal partner to man in his world. She was free to choose automobiles, clothes, appliances, supermarkets; she had everything that women ever dreamed of.

In the fifteen years after World War II, this mystique of feminine fulfillment became the cherished and self-perpetuating core of contemporary American culture. Millions of women lived their lives in the image of those pretty pictures of the American suburban housewife, kissing their husbands goodbye in front of the picture window, depositing their station-wagonsful of children at school, and smiling as they ran the new electric waxer over the spotless kitchen floor. They baked their own bread, sewed their own and their children's clothes, kept their new washing machines and dryers running all day. They changed the sheets on the beds twice a week instead of once, took the rug-hooking class in adult education, and pitied their poor frustrated mothers, who had dreamed of having a career. Their only dream was to be perfect wives and mothers; their highest ambition to have five children and a beautiful house, their only fight to get and keep their husbands. They had no thought for the unfeminine problems of the world outside the home; they wanted the men to make the major decisions. They gloried in their role as women, and wrote proudly on the census blank "Occupation: housewife." . . .

If a woman had a problem in the 1950's and 1960's, she knew that something must be wrong with her marriage, or with herself. Other women were satisfied with their lives, she thought. What kind of a woman was she if she did not feel this mysterious fulfillment waxing the kitchen floor? She was so ashamed to admit her dissatisfaction that she never knew how many other women shared it. If she tried to tell her husband, he didn't understand what she was talking about. She did not really understand it herself. For over fifteen years women in America found it harder to talk about this problem than about sex.

———◆———————

SOURCE 4   Like pre–Civil War women's rights activists, many modern feminists were first involved in other reforms or protests before becoming committed to feminism. Mary King, the author of this selection, was a white civil rights worker involved in the Student Non-violent Coordinating Committee, a civil rights organization founded in 1960 to coordinate efforts to desegregate the South. Many black and white college students were members of SNCC. What effect did involvement in the civil rights movement have on King as a woman?

Civil Rights and the Rise of Feminism (1987)

MARY KING

1. Staff was involved in crucial constitutional revisions at the Atlanta staff meeting in October. A large committee was appointed to present revisions to the staff. The committee was all men.
2. Two organizers were working together to form a farmers league. Without asking any questions, the male organizer immediately assigned the clerical work to the female organizer although both had had equal experience in organizing campaigns.
3. Although there are women in Mississippi project who have been working as long as some of the men, the leadership group in COFO is all men.
4. A woman in a field office wondered why she was held responsible for day to day decisions, only to find out later that she had been appointed project director but not told.
5. A fall 1964 personnel and resources report on Mississippi projects lists the number of people in each project. The section on Laurel however, lists not the number of persons, but "three girls."
6. One of SNCC's main administrative officers apologizes for appointment of a woman as interim project director in a key Mississippi project area.
7. A veteran of two years work for SNCC in two states spends her day typing and doing clerical work for other people in her project. . . .

Undoubtedly this list will seem strange to some, petty to others, laughable to most. The list could continue as far as there are women in the movement. Except that most women don't talk about these kinds of incidents, because the whole subject is not discussable—strange to some, petty to others, laughable to most. The average white person finds it difficult to understand why the Negro resents being called "boy," or being thought of as "musical" and "athletic," because the average white person doesn't realize that *he assumes he is superior.* And naturally he doesn't understand the problem of paternalism. So too the average SNCC worker finds it difficult to discuss the woman problem because of the assumption of male superiority. Assumptions of male superiority are as widespread and deep rooted and every much as crippling to the woman as the assumptions of white supremacy are to the Negro. Consider why it is in SNCC that women who are competent, qualified and experienced, are automatically assigned to the "female" kinds of jobs such as typing, desk work, telephone work, filing, library work, cooking and the assistant kind of administrative work but rarely the "executive" kind.

The woman in SNCC is often in the same position as that token Negro hired in a corporation. The management thinks that it has done its bit. Yet every day the Negro bears an atmosphere, attitudes and actions which are tinged with condescension and paternalism, the most telling of which are when he is not promoted as the equally or less skilled whites are. . . .

◆

SOURCE 5   The National Organization for Women proclaimed its premises and goals at its first meeting in 1966. Note what NOW saw as the principal problems confronting women. Did its proposals to achieve equality pertain to the "public" or the "private" sphere? How does this statement reflect the influence of other developments in American society by the 1960s?

NOW's Statement of Purpose (1966)

We, men and women who hereby constitute ourselves as the National Organization for Women, believe that the time has come for a new movement toward true equality for all women in America, and toward a fully equal partnership of the sexes, as part of the world-wide revolution of human rights now taking place within and beyond our national borders.

The purpose of NOW is to take action to bring women into full participation in the mainstream of American society now, exercising all the privileges and responsibilities thereof in truly equal partnership with men.

We believe the time has come to move beyond the abstract argument, discussion and symposia over the status and special nature of women which has raged in America in recent years: the time has come to confront, with concrete action, the conditions that now prevent women from enjoying the equality of opportunity and freedom of choice which is their right as individual Americans, and as human beings.

NOW is dedicated to the proposition that women first and foremost are human beings, who, like all other people in our society, must have the chance to develop their fullest human potential. We believe that women can achieve such equality only by accepting to the full the challenges and responsibilities they share with all other people in our society, as part of the decision-making mainstream of American political, economic and social life.

We organize to initiate or support action, nationally or in any part of this nation, by individuals or organizations, to break through the silken curtain of

Source: National Organization for Women, 1966, pp. 397–398, 399.

prejudice and discrimination against women in government, industry, the professions, the churches, the political parties, the judiciary, the labor unions, in education, science, medicine, law, religion and every other field of importance in American society. . . .

There is no civil rights movement to speak for women, as there has been for Negroes and other victims of discrimination. The National Organization for Women must therefore begin to speak.

WE BELIEVE that the power of American law, and the protection guaranteed by the U.S. Constitution to the civil rights of all individuals, must be effectively applied and enforced to isolate and remove patterns of sex discrimination, to ensure equality of opportunity in employment and education, and equality of civil and political rights and responsibilities on behalf of women, as well as for Negroes and other deprived groups. . . .

WE DO NOT ACCEPT the token appointment of a few women to high-level positions in government and industry as a substitute for a serious continuing effort to recruit and advance women according to their individual abilities. To this end, we urge American government and industry to mobilize the same resources of ingenuity and command with which they have solved problems of far greater difficulty than those now impeding the progress of women.

WE BELIEVE that this nation has a capacity at least as great as other nations, to innovate new social institutions which will enable women to enjoy true equality of opportunity and responsibility in society, without conflict with their responsibilities as mothers and homemakers. In such innovations, America does not lead the Western world, but lags by decades behind many European countries. We do not accept the traditional assumption that a woman has to choose between marriage and motherhood, on the one hand, and serious participation in industry or the professions on the other. We question the present expectation that all normal women will retire from job or profession for ten or fifteen years, to devote their full time to raising children, only to reenter the job market at a relatively minor level. . . .

WE REJECT the current assumptions that a man must carry the sole burden of supporting himself, his wife, and family, and that a woman is automatically entitled to lifelong support by a man upon her marriage, or that marriage, home and family are primarily woman's world and responsibility—hers, to dominate, his to support. We believe that a true partnership between the sexes demands a different concept of marriage, an equitable sharing of the responsibilities of home and children and of the economic burdens of their support. We believe that proper recognition should be given to the economic and social value of homemaking and child care. To these ends, we will seek to open a reexamination of laws and mores governing marriage and divorce, for we believe that the current state of "half-equality" between the sexes discriminates against both men and women, and is the cause of much unnecessary hostility between the sexes.

———————◆———————

SOURCE 6   Redstockings was one of many radical feminist organizations that had sprung up by the late 1960s. How does this analysis of women's inequality differ from NOW's? Do Redstockings's analysis and rhetoric reveal the influence of other protest movements in the 1960s?

Redstockings Manifesto (1969)

I.   After centuries of individual and preliminary political struggle, women are uniting to achieve their final liberation from male supremacy. Redstockings is dedicated to building this unity and winning our freedom.

II.   Women are an oppressed class. Our oppression is total, affecting every facet of our lives. We are exploited as sex objects, breeders, domestic servants, and cheap labor. We are considered inferior beings, whose only purpose is to enhance men's lives. Our humanity is denied. Our prescribed behavior is enforced by the threat of physical violence.

Because we have lived so intimately with our oppressors, in isolation from each other, we have been kept from seeing our personal suffering as a political condition. This creates the illusion that a woman's relationship with her man is a matter of interplay between two unique personalities, and can be worked out individually. In reality, every such relationship is a *class* relationship, and the conflicts between individual men and women are *political* conflicts that can only be solved collectively.

III.   We identify the agents of our oppression as men. Male supremacy is the oldest, most basic form of domination. All other forms of exploitation and oppression (racism, capitalism, imperialism, etc.) are extensions of male supremacy: men dominate women, a few men dominate the rest. All power structures throughout history have been male-dominated and male-oriented. Men have controlled all political, economic and cultural institutions and backed up this control with physical force. They have used their power to keep women in an inferior position. *All men* receive economic, sexual,

Source: Mary Beth Norton, *Major Problems in American Women's History* (Lexington, Mass.: D. C. Heath and Company, 1989), p. 400.

and psychological benefits from male supremacy. *All men* have oppressed women.

The Sexual Revolution and the Women's Movement

The civil rights and antiwar movements brought important changes to American society in the 1960s. So, too, did a sexual revolution. As you read these selections, think about the relationship between a sexual revolution in the 1960s and the rise of the women's movement. How did a more liberated social climate bring both liberation and tyranny for women?

◆

SOURCE 7   In this selection a writer looks at the effects of the sexual revolution.

On Women and Sex (1972)

JOYCE MAYNARD

For about three weeks of my freshman year at college I had two roommates instead of one—the girl in the bottom bunk and her friend, who made our quarters especially cramped because, in addition to being six feet tall with lots of luggage, he was male. We slept in shifts—they together, until I came back to the room at night, then he outside in the living room on the couch, until she got up, then he in her bed and I in mine, or I in hers and he in mine, because it was easier for me to get out from the bottom without waking him, and he needed his sleep. . . . We never made it a threesome, but the awkwardness was always there (those squeaking bedsprings . . .), as it was for many girls I knew, and many boys. Coming back to the room and announcing my presence loudly with a well-directed, well-projected cough or a casual murmur, "Hmmmm—I think I'll go to my room now," it occurred to me that it wasn't my roommate but I—the one who slept alone, the one whose only pills were vitamins and aspirin—I was the embarrassed one. How has it happened, what have we come to, that the scarlet letter these days isn't A, but V? . . .

   The sexual revolution. It's a cliché, but it exists all right, and its pressures are everywhere. All the old excuses ("I might get pregnant," "I'm not that kind

Source: Reprinted by permission of the author from *Looking Back* by Joyce Maynard (New York: Doubleday, 1973).

of girl") are gone. Safe and increasingly available contraceptives (for anyone brave and premeditative enough to get them) make premarital sex possible; changing moral standards, an increased naturalness, make it commonplace; elegant models of sexual freedom—Julie Christie, Catherine Deneuve—have made it fashionable. Consider a virgin in the movies. Is there a single pretty young heroine who doesn't hop unself-consciously into bed? (Who is there left for her to identify with—Doris Day?) Then there are magazines, filled with discussions of intricate sexual problems (the timing of orgasms . . . do I get one? do I give one?) while the virgin remains on a whole other level—her fears compounded. (Our old, junior high notion of sex was that it got done to you; the girl with the purple eyeshadow just let it happen. Today all kinds of problems in technique make the issue much more complicated for an inexperienced, media-blitzed girl: not just *will I* but *can I.*) The people who've been making nice, simple love for years now, while the virgin became more and more unique, have, quite understandably, gone on to other things. There is foreplay and afterplay and the 999 positions of the *Kamasutra* . . . The train has left the station before the virgin's bought her ticket or even, maybe, packed her bags. . . .

◆

SOURCE 8   This source is an excerpt from the preface to the first edition of a book that has had a long history and a wide influence.

Our Bodies, Ourselves (1973)

The history of this book, *Our Bodies, Ourselves,* is lengthy and satisfying.

It began in a small discussion group on "women and their bodies" which was part of a women's conference held in Boston in the spring of 1969, one of the first gatherings of women meeting specifically to talk with other women. For many of us it was the very first time we had joined together with other women to talk and think about our lives and what we could to about them. Before the conference was over, some of us decided to keep on meeting as a group to continue the discussion, and so we did.

In the beginning we called ourselves "the doctors group." We had all experienced similar feelings of frustration and anger toward specific doctors and the medical maze in general, and initially we wanted to do something about those doctors who were condescending, paternalistic, judgmental and non-informative. As we talked and shared our experiences with one another, we realized just how much we had to learn about our bodies. So we decided on a summer project—to research those topics which we felt were particularly pertinent to learning about our bodies, to discuss in the group what we had learned, then to write papers individually or in groups of two or three, and finally to present the results in the fall as a course for women on women and their bodies.

As we developed the course we realized more and more that we really *were* capable of collecting, understanding, and evaluating medical information. Together we evaluated our reading of books and journals, our talks with doctors and friends who were medical students. We found we could discuss, question and argue with each other in a new spirit of cooperation rather than competition. We were equally struck by how important it was for us to be able to open up with one another and share our feelings about our bodies. The process of talking was as crucial as the facts themselves. Over time the facts and feelings melted together in ways that touched us very deeply, and that is reflected in the changing titles of the course and then the book—from *Women and Their Bodies* to *Women and Our Bodies* to, finally, *Our Bodies, Ourselves*. . . .

Many, many other women have worked with us on the book. A group of gay women got together specifically to do the chapter on lesbianism. Other chapters were done still differently. For instance, the mother of one woman in the group volunteered to work on menopause with some of us who have not gone through that experience ourselves. . . .

From the very beginning of working together, first on the course that led to this book and then on the book itself, we have felt exhilarated and energized by our new knowledge. Finding out about our bodies and our bodies' needs, starting to take control over that area of our lives, has released for us an energy that has overflowed into our work, our friendships, our relationships with men and women, and for some of us, our marriages and our parenthood. . . .

A second important result of this kind of learning is that we are better prepared to evaluate the institutions that are supposed to meet our health needs—the hospitals, clinics, doctors, medical schools, nursing schools, public health departments, Medicaid bureaucracies and so on. For some of us it was the first time we had looked critically, and with strength, at the existing institutions serving us. The experience of learning just how little control we had over our lives and bodies, the coming together out of isolation to learn from each other in order to define what we needed, and the experience of supporting one another in demanding the changes that grew out of our developing critique—all were crucial and formative political experiences for us. We have felt our potential power as a force for political and social change.

The learning we have done while working on *Our Bodies, Ourselves* has been a good basis for growth in other areas of life for still another reason. For women throughout the centuries, ignorance about our bodies has had one major consequence—pregnancy. Until very recently pregnancies were all but inevitable, biology *was* our destiny—that is, because our bodies are designed to get pregnant and give birth and lactate that is what all or most of us did. . . . It was not until we researched carefully and learned more about birth-control methods and abortion, about laws governing birth control and abortion, and not until we put all this information together with what it meant to us to be female, that we began to feel we could truly set out to control whether and when we would have babies.

This knowledge has freed us to a certain extent from the constant, energy-draining anxiety about becoming pregnant. It has made our pregnancies better because they no longer happen to us, but we actively choose them and enthusiastically participate in them. It has made our parenthood better because it is our choice rather than our destiny. . . . This is why people in the women's movement have been so active in fighting against the inhumane legal restrictions, the imperfections of available contraceptives, the poor sex education, the highly priced and poorly administered health care that keep too many women from having this crucial control over their bodies.

There is a fourth reason why knowledge about our bodies has generated so much new energy. For us, body education is core education. Our bodies are the physical bases from which we move out into the world; ignorance, uncertainty—even, at worst, shame—about our physical selves create in us an alienation from ourselves that keeps us from being the whole people that we could be. Picture a woman trying to do work and to enter into equal and satisfying relationships with other people—when she feels physically weak because she has never tried to be strong; when she drains her energy trying to change her face, her figure, her hair, her smells, to match some ideal norm set by magazines, movies and TV; when she feels confused and ashamed of the menstrual blood that every month appears from some dark place in her body; when her internal body processes are a mystery to her and surface only to cause her trouble (an unplanned pregnancy, or cervical cancer); when she does not understand or enjoy sex and concentrates her sexual drives into aimless romantic fantasies, perverting and misusing a potential energy because she had been brought up to deny it. Learning to understand, accept, and be responsible for our physical selves, we are freed of some of these preoccupations and can start to use our untapped energies. Our image of ourselves is on a firmer base, we can be better friends and better lovers, better *people,* more self-confident, more autonomous, stronger and more whole.

◆

SOURCE 9   *The Feminine Mystique* proclaimed that women would find fulfillment through work outside the home. Note how this essay illustrates some of the problems women faced as they began to reject domesticity. Does it help to explain why feminists began to put increasing emphasis on reform within the "private" sphere?

The Politics of Housework (ca. 1970)

PAT MAINARDI

Liberated women—very different from Women's Liberation! The first signals all kinds of goodies, to warm the hearts (not to mention other parts) of the most radical men. The other signals—HOUSEWORK. The first brings sex without marriage, sex before marriage, cozy housekeeping arrangements ("I'm living with this chick") and the self-content of knowing that you're not the kind of man who wants a doormat instead of a woman. That will come later. After all, who wants that old commodity anymore, the Standard American Housewife, all husband, home and kids. The New Commodity, the Liberated Woman, has sex a lot and has a Career, preferably something that can be fitted in with the household chores—like dancing, pottery, or painting.

On the other hand is Women's Liberation—and housework. What? You say this is all trivial? Wonderful! That's what I thought. It seemed perfectly reasonable. We both had careers, both had to work a couple of days a week to earn enough to live on, so why shouldn't we share the housework? So I suggested it to my mate and he agreed—most men are too hip to turn you down flat. You're right, he said. It's only fair.

Then an interesting thing happened. I can only explain it by stating that we women have been brainwashed more than even we can imagine. Probably too many years of seeing television women in ecstasy over their shiny waxed floors or breaking down over their dirty shirt collars. Men have no such conditioning. They recognize the essential fact of housework right from the very beginning. Which is that it stinks.

Here's my list of dirty chores: buying groceries, carting them home and putting them away; cooking meals and washing dishes and pots; doing the laundry; digging out the place when things get out of control; washing floors. The list could go on but the sheer necessities are bad enough. All of us have to

Source: Pat Mainardi, "The Politics of Housework," as reprinted in *Women's Liberation in the 20th Century,* edited by Mary C. Lynn. Copyright © 1975 by Pat Mainardi. Reprinted by permission of John Wiley & Sons, Inc.

do these things, or get someone else to do them for us. The longer my husband contemplated these chores, the more repulsed he became, and so proceeded the change from the normally sweet considerate Dr. Jekyll into the crafty Mr. Hyde who would stop at nothing to avoid the horrors of—housework. As he felt himself backed into a corner laden with dirty dishes, brooms, mops and reeking garbage, his front teeth grew longer and pointier, his fingernails haggled and his eyes grew wild. Housework trivial? Not on your life! Just try to share the burden. . . .

Participatory democracy begins at home. If you are planning to implement your politics, there are certain things to remember:

1. He *is* feeling it more than you. He's losing some leisure and you're gaining it. The measure of your oppression is his resistance.
2. A great many American men are not accustomed to doing monotonous repetitive work which never issues in any lasting, let alone important, achievement. This is why they would rather repair a cabinet than wash dishes. If human endeavors are like a pyramid with man's highest achievements at the top, then keeping oneself alive is at the bottom. Men have always had servants (us) to take care of this bottom strata of life while they have confined their efforts to the rarefied upper regions. It is thus ironic when they ask of women—where are your great painters, statesmen, etc. Mme Matisse ran a millinery shop so he could paint. Mrs. Martin Luther King kept his house and raised his babies.
3. It is a traumatizing experience for someone who has always thought of himself as being against any oppression or exploitation of one human being by another to realize that in his daily life he has been accepting and implementing (and benefiting from) this exploitation; that his rationalization is little different from that of the racist who says "Black people don't feel pain" (women don't mind doing the shitwork); and that the oldest form of oppression in history has been the oppression of 50% of the population by the other 50%. . . .

I was just finishing this when my husband came in and asked what I was doing. Writing a paper on housework. Housework? he said, *Housework?* Oh my god how trivial can you get. A paper on housework.

Women's Changing Education and Employment Experience

As it can for other population groups, statistical information can reveal important changes in women's lives. As you examine these charts, consider whether they reveal reasons why many women in the 1960s rejected domesticity and joined the women's movement. Do they also provide evidence for the impact of that movement?

SOURCE 10

Sex Ratios of High School and College Graduates in the United States, 1940–1980

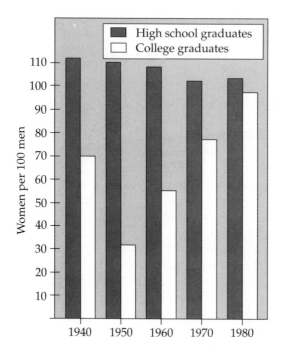

Source: U.S. Bureau of the Census, *Historical Statistics of the United States, Colonial Times to 1970* (Washington: GPO, 1975), 379, 385–86; U.S. Bureau of the Census, *Statistical Abstract of the United States: 1988* (Washington: GPO, 1987, 108th ed.), 140.

SOURCE 11

Women's Labor Force Participation, by Marital Status, 1940–1987

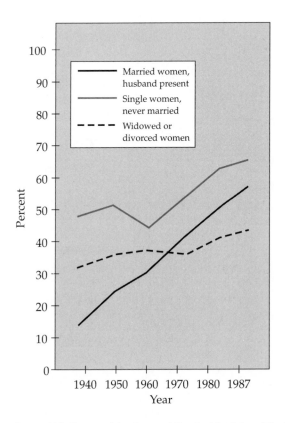

Source: U.S. Bureau of the Census, *Historical Statistics of the United States, Colonial Times to 1970* (Washington: GPO, 1975), 133; U.S. Bureau of the Census, *Statistical Abstract of the United States: 1988* (Washington: GPO, 1987, 108th ed.), 373.

SOURCE 12

Median Earnings of Year-round, Full-time Workers, by Sex, 1955–1985

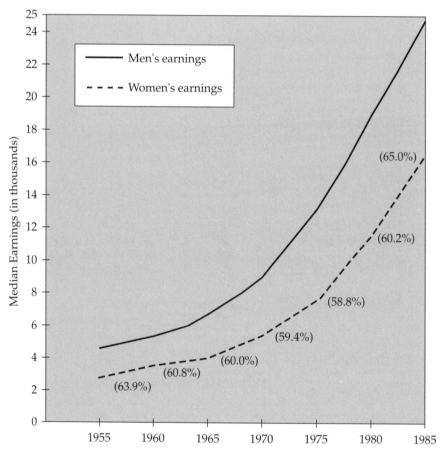

* Numbers in parentheses are women's earnings as a percentage of men's.

Source: U.S. Department of Labor, Women's Bureau, Bulletin 298, *Time of Change: 1983 Handbook on Women Workers* (Washington: GPO, 1983), 82; U.S. Bureau of the Census, *Money Income of Households, Families and Persons in the United States: 1986.* Current Population Reports, Series P-60, no. 159, 100–101.

CONCLUSION

One month before *Time* magazine proclaimed 1975 "The Year of the Women" and a decade after it put Phyllis McGinley on its cover, *Newsweek* magazine ran a story on the exploding field of women's history. The timing of the stories was no coincidence. One of the most important consequences of the women's movement was the interest it stimulated in uncovering women's past. As we have already seen in this volume, our view of the past is shaped by the way people think about the present—and vice versa. As women began to think in new ways about their status in contemporary society, they also began to think differently about their place in the past. They found women mostly excluded from the pages of history, a reflection of their subordinate position in American society. Like African-Americans, women began to recapture their past when they began to fight for equality.

The women's movement, which greatly stimulated the study of women's history, is now history itself. As this chapter's secondary sources demonstrate, women's historians do not write about it only to "raise consciousness," to prove past oppression, or to recount women's past contributions. More important, they are interested in placing women in the mainstream of the American past. They seek to understand the way women's experience influenced and in turn was influenced by American society and culture. Thus they illustrate important points about historical inquiry that we have seen repeatedly in this volume. For instance, to understand the rise of the women's movement, historians must consider the effects of many causal influences. To understand the motivations of feminists, moreover, those influences can rarely be considered apart from ideology. The study of the contemporary women's movement also reminds us that history happens to elites and nonelites alike. In fact, it is a double reminder of that message, because the voices of women in general and nonelite women in particular have usually not been heard in the past. By making connections between the "private" sphere of family life and the "public" sphere, the women's movement demonstrates why historians must be interested in more than the activities of statesmen and generals.

Finally, the modern women's movement illustrates the importance of historians' motivations. As we have seen in this chapter, historians are guided by contemporary concerns even as they seek to understand the past on its own terms. Although they may write history that serves to defend or attack contemporary policies, historians do not turn to the past merely to do that. That is a good lesson to keep in mind as we turn in the next chapter to the "Reagan revolution."

FURTHER READING

Lois Banner, *Women in Modern America: A Brief History* (San Diego: Harcourt Brace Jovanovich, 1984).

Nancy Cott, *The Grounding of Modern Feminism* (New Haven: Yale University Press, 1987).

Sara Evans, *Personal Politics: The Roots of Women's Liberation in the Civil Rights Movement and the New Left* (New York: Vintage Books, 1979).

Betty Friedan, *The Feminine Mystique* (New York: W. W. Norton and Company, 1963).

Mary Thom, ed., *Letters to Ms., 1972–1987* (New York: Henry Holt and Company, 1987).

Winifred Wandersee, *On the Move: American Women in the 1970s* (Boston: Twayne Publishers, 1988).

NOTES

1. *Newsweek,* June 7, 1965, p. 55.
2. *U.S. News & World Report,* June 7, 1965, pp. 12, 53.
3. *Time,* June 18, 1965, pp. 75, 78.
4. *Newsweek,* March 23, 1970, pp. 71–72.
5. Quoted in Nancy Woloch, *Women and the American Experience* (New York: McGraw-Hill, 1984), p. 518.

Chapter 13

Why Historical Interpretation Matters: Assessing the "Reagan Revolution"

The documents in this chapter give various perspectives on the performance of the Reagan administration in the 1980s.

Secondary Sources

1. Roosevelt Revolution, Reagan Counterrevolution (1988), RICHARD POLENBERG
2. Summing Up the Reagan Era (1990), KARL ZINSMEISTER

Primary Sources

3. Five-Year Economic Program for the U.S. (1980), RONALD REAGAN
4. The Budget: Guns Up, People Down (1982), SIDNEY WEINTRAUB
5. The Triumph of Politics (1986), DAVID STOCKMAN
6. The Unfinished Agenda (1987), MICHAEL BOSKIN
7. The Contract with America (1994)
8. Real Average Weekly Earnings, 1947–1986 (in 1986 dollars)
9. Pay of Workers and Corporate Chief Executives, 1965–1988
10. Federal Budget Priorities, 1980–1987
11. Total Government Expenditures, 1929–1990
12. Federal Budget Deficits, 1980–1990

*N*ot since Andrew Jackson's raucous supporters celebrated the triumph of the "common man" in 1829 had a presidential inauguration made such a declaration. Private jets carrying corporate executives and celebrities crowded Washington's National Airport. All over the capital, limousines carried men in formal attire and women in furs and designer dresses. One caterer noted that there were ten times as many parties as at the last inaugural. Four years earlier, when Jimmy Carter had walked down Pennsylvania Avenue after taking the oath of office, all of the inaugural events had been open to the public. Now they were by invitation only, and getting in could cost as much as $10,000. As one observer noted, it was "the costliest, most opulent inauguration in American history."[1]

As president, Ronald Reagan often communicated through symbols. In the opening hours of his presidency in 1981, he sent the country a clear signal of changes ahead. The departing Carter had called upon Americans to accept limits, to lower their thermostats and their expectations. Reagan's inauguration represented a glittery reaffirmation of acquisitive values and individual success. One reveler said, "This is what America's all about. It looks like a bunch of people who want to get back to what America really means."[2] In retrospect, many observers also saw the inaugural celebration as a fitting symbol to mark the beginning of the "Reagan revolution," a domestic program of lower taxes, reduced spending on social programs, less government regulation, and increased military expenditures. For the next eight years, the president would use his formidable communications skills to promote this program, which came to be known simply as Reaganomics.

By the time Reagan had stepped down in 1989, few observers could deny that he was popular. In another sweeping victory in 1984 he had won a second term, which ended with overwhelming approval ratings in public opinion polls. Nor was there much dispute that Reagan made many Americans feel good about themselves and their country. Less clear was what Reaganomics had actually wrought and how revolutionary it really was. Both supporters and opponents disagreed about whether the "Reagan revolution" brought significant changes or, like Reagan's first inaugural, was merely symbolic.

Two presidents later, historians in increasing numbers have joined this debate. Like the journalists and former Reagan administration officials who initially dominated the discussion, historians ask whether there was a "Reagan revolution," how much America was changed by the Reagan administration's policies, and what Reagan had to do with the changes that *did* occur in the 1980s. In this chapter we seek answers to these questions.

SETTING

Historians, economists, journalists, and even former Reagan administration officials disagree about the effects of the "Reagan revolution." They do agree, however, that it was based on economic ideas radically different from those that had guided the government's economic policies for decades. Labeled "supply-side" economics in the late 1970s, these ideas represented a rejection of Keynesian economic principles, pioneered by British economist John Maynard Keynes during the Great Depression. Keynesian economics emphasizes the importance of demand for goods and services as the key to prosperity. Keynesians see government spending as a stabilizing economic influence because it helps to create demand. They also argue that taxation and social policies should encourage consumer demand. Graduated income taxes, which increase tax rates as incomes rise, help to ensure prosperity by encouraging a broader distribution of income. So do social welfare programs, which provide money and other benefits to the poor.

Supply-siders, on the other hand, were inspired by the "classical economics" of the eighteenth-century economist Adam Smith, who insisted that producing a supply of goods automatically created a demand for them. In the late 1970s, such supply-siders as George Gilder, Arthur Laffer, and Charles Murray argued that economic policy should therefore be concerned with the factors affecting production, not demand. "Nonproductive" government expenditures should be cut. As a spur to initiative and more production, taxes should also be cut, especially on the rich. Production, incomes, and tax revenues would then rise. Coupled with cuts in government expenditures, rising tax revenue would lower the budget deficit. Moreover, growing prosperity would "trickle down" to the middle and lower classes in the form of more jobs and higher incomes. Finally, this "trickle-down" effect would justify the reduction in government expenditures primarily through a cutback in social welfare programs.

At the heart of the battle over the Reagan revolution are questions about the impact of supply-side economics and the extent to which Reaganomics actually carried it out. That battle began even before Reagan left office. In a farewell address to the nation in early 1989, for instance, Reagan himself gave an upbeat assessment of the revolution that bore his name. Pointing to a decade's expanding economy, an "explosion" of research and new technology, and the "recovery of our morale," he judged it a resounding success. "We meant to change the nation," he proudly declared, "and instead, we changed a world."[3]

Other observers, including some of the president's former aides, were not so sure. Before Reagan's second term was over, three cabinet secretaries, a deputy chief of staff, the chief White House press spokesman, a senior economic adviser, and a director of the Office of Management and Budget had offered their views from inside the Reagan White House. Although often born of self-serving motives, several of these memoirs provided early negative judgments about the "Reagan revolution." Former budget director David Stockman, for instance, found little evidence of a revolution after eight years. A supply-sider, Stockman evaluated the Reagan administration on its promise to reduce the deficit and cut the size of the government. In *The Triumph of Politics* (1986), he showed a president stubbornly committed to increasing military spending even after a massive tax cut in 1981. Moreover, because of the political costs, Reagan had no intention to cut domestic programs, said Stockman. Pointing to the $1.5 trillion added to the federal deficit in the Reagan years, he concluded that the result was not revolution but "fiscal disaster."[4]

Economists in and outside the Reagan administration were sharply divided about the impact of Reaganomics. Most economists rejected Reagan's contention that tax cuts would increase government revenue by increasing incentives to produce. Nonetheless, many of them credited Reaganomics with an end to "stagflation," the sluggish economic growth and high inflation of the 1970s. Martin Feldstein, Harvard economist and chairman of Reagan's Council of Economic Advisers, also defended Reaganomics' recognition "that a higher saving rate would be a good thing for the American economy."[5] Toward the end of the Reagan years, Stanford economist Michael Boskin praised Reaganomics for achieving growth with low inflation and for halting the trend "toward a European-style welfare state."[6] Liberal economists, however, decried Reaganomics' other effects. John Kenneth Galbraith, for instance, pointed to the rising wealth of the rich, the increasing numbers of the poor, and the stagnating incomes of the middle class as consequences of Reagan's economic policies. Rejecting supply-side assumptions, Galbraith compared the trickle-down of wealth to feeding a horse. "If one feeds the horse enough oats," he noted, "some will pass to the road for the sparrows."[7]

Meanwhile, many journalists have also assessed the "Reagan revolution," although mostly without supply-side assumptions. In *Sleepwalking Through History* (1991), for instance, Haynes Johnson concluded that Reagan had accomplished much that he had set out to do and that he had "truly altered the condition of the country." Johnson pointed to tax cuts, cuts in domestic programs, and a redistribution of wealth. "The poor had been left poorer, the rich, richer; the social compact, if not broken, had been severely weakened," Johnson asserted. And, he suggested, Reagan brought an even more important change. By "the personal example and tone he set," the President had changed people's attitudes toward politics, especially their assumptions about government's role in solving problems.[8] Other journalists agreed. The Washington *Post*'s Thomas Edsall concluded that the Reagan administration's domestic policies blunted arguments for more government programs by focusing attention on tax burdens. That assessment was shared by Robert Kuttner, economics correspondent for *Business Week,* the Boston *Globe,* and *The New Republic.* The Reagan revolution was "remarkably successful at paralyzing the liberal impulse," Kuttner concluded.[9]

Historians who have inherited the debate about the Reagan revolution often echo the conclusions of journalists that there was in fact a revolution and that its effects were not good. In *Reagan's America* (1988), for instance, Garry Wills argued that Reagan's self-deception allowed him to promote Reaganomics "with a straight face" and thus to change the nation's "moral energies."[10] Like journalist Haynes Johnson, University of Arizona historian Michael Schaller found a dreamlike quality to the Reagan years. In *Reckoning with Reagan* (1992), Schaller maintained that the Reagan administration's impact was less than Reagan claimed but more than many of his critics conceded. Moreover, much of this "more" was negative. Although Reagan increased Americans' pride, he asserted that Reagan administration policies encouraged the growth of a "culture of greed" while neglecting such social problems as rising drug use, teen pregnancy, and the spread of AIDS. "As in a daydream," Schaller concluded, "anything seemed possible. Deficits did not exist, were someone else's fault, or did not matter [and] the poor caused their own plight or were impoverished because they received too much money from the government. . . ."[11] More recently, University of Wisconsin historian Paul Boyer noted that "Reagan did not single-handedly cause the materialism, selfishness, and preening vulgarity of the 1980s." In *Promises to Keep* (1995), however, Boyer also concluded that the president's constant touting of individualism encouraged the neglect of "festering problems," from inner-city joblessness to environmental degradation.[12]

As historians evaluate Reaganomics, most of them are clearly more interested in its long-run social effects than in its short-run economic consequences. Moreover, in assessing the effects of Reaganomics, historians have an advantage over economists, journalists, and former Reagan administration officials because they can base their evaluations on knowledge of social conditions and government policies earlier in American history. And as time goes on, they will have another advantage. Reaganomics is part of a debate about the role of the government in American society that goes back two centuries to Thomas Jefferson's vision of minimal government and Alexander Hamilton's promotion of an activist state. As Americans continue this debate in the future, the long-run impact of Reagan's policies will become clearer. Thus historians will be in a better position to see whether Reaganomics was a dramatic turn or only a transitory stage in American history.

INVESTIGATION

In this chapter, you have the opportunity to compare two views of Reaganomics. Your main job is to determine whether there was a "Reagan revolution." To do that, you will need to determine the economic and social impact of the Reagan administration's policies. You will need to compare the conclusions of the two essays and, with the aid of primary sources, determine which one's assessment of the Reagan years is more accurate. Your analysis should also address the following main questions:

1. **What does the evidence suggest to you about the success or failure of Reaganomics?** What were the most important effects of the Reagan administration's economic policies?

2. **What is the evidence that Reagan administration policies reversed long-term economic or social trends?** Were the important economic and social changes in the 1980s brought about by Reaganomics or were they continuations of long-term trends?

3. **Which of the essays is better supported by the evidence?** Which author's views about Reaganomics is better supported by the statistical evidence presented in the primary sources?

4. **What is the most important lesson to be drawn from the "Reagan revolution"?** What evidence supports that lesson?

Before you begin, read the sections in your textbook on the Reagan administration and on American society in the 1980s. You will also find it helpful to read about the political, economic, social, and cultural developments since the late 1980s. This will help you determine whether Reaganomics' effects endured or ended quickly.

SECONDARY SOURCES

◆

SOURCE 1 In this selection, historian Richard Polenberg compares the "Reagan revolution" to Franklin Roosevelt's New Deal. He concludes that Reagan's policies actually represented a "counterrevolution." Note how Polenberg compares FDR's and Reagan's goals. What is his main evidence that the Reagan administration achieved a significant reversal of policy? What were the main results of Reagan's polices, and does Polenberg approve of them?

Roosevelt Revolution, Reagan Counterrevolution (1988)

RICHARD POLENBERG

Franklin Delano Roosevelt established a set of national priorities that lasted for thirty-five years after his death. His Democratic successors—Harry S Truman, John F. Kennedy, and Lyndon B. Johnson—adhered to those priorities, and so did Republicans Dwight Eisenhower, Richard Nixon, and Gerald Ford—however reluctant they were to admit it. But since 1981, there has been a drastic reordering of Roosevelt's priorities. Ronald Reagan has brought about a fundamental redirection of American politics. . . .

. . . Let us see how, by examining Roosevelt's and Reagan's use of presidential power, their economic policies, and their attempts to institutionalize their programs.

Franklin Roosevelt is, by common consent, a president who exploited the full potential of his office. Theodore Roosevelt and Woodrow Wilson had employed executive power but not to the same degree. Franklin Roosevelt exerted a near-magnetic influence over Congress and the bureaucracy. More systematically than his predecessors, he used patronage to get congressmen to do what he wanted. Under FDR, it became standard practice for the executive branch to draft legislation and for Congress to react to the administration's initiative. . . .

Roosevelt further enhanced presidential power by appealing directly to the voters. He used the radio, especially the fireside chat, to explain—rather, to advocate—his policies and build popular support for them. . . .

Roosevelt also used press conferences to get his point of view across to the people. Recognizing that most newspaper publishers opposed his programs—some publishers, he observed, deserved "neither hate not praise, only pity for their unbalanced mentalities"—Roosevelt understood the importance of establishing a good working relationship with reporters. . . .

One of the reasons Roosevelt was so comfortable and effective in these meetings was that he had an extraordinarily detailed knowledge of governmental policy. Observers were always impressed with his grasp of what was happening in Washington, in the nation, and in the world. He had an uncanny command of the facts. Nothing seemed to escape his attention. When he wanted to explain a complicated proposal to reporters, he would tell them it was time for a "seminar," and for an hour or more he would hold their attention with a line-by-line analysis of that proposal. If he did not know

Source: "Roosevelt Revolution, Reagan Counterrevolution" from *The Reagan Revolution?* by B. B. Kymlicka and Jean Mathews. Copyright © 1988 by Harcourt Brace & Company. Reprinted by permission of the publisher.

everything there was to know about government, and, of course, no one could, he gave the impression he did.

For thirty years after Franklin Roosevelt's death in 1945, under Democrats and Republicans alike, there was a further expansion of presidential power. By the time Richard Nixon was reelected in 1972, people were talking about "King Richard" and the dangers of an "imperial presidency." What appeared to be a dramatic reversal then occurred as a reaction to Vietnam and Watergate. In 1974, Congress passed the War Powers Resolution restricting the president's ability to conduct certain kinds of military operations without obtaining legislative approval, and the Supreme Court decided that a claim of "executive privilege" did not mean that all presidential communications could be withheld from the courts. The Ford and Carter years witnessed an erosion of presidential authority. By 1980, Gerald Ford claimed that the presidency was no longer "imperial," but "imperiled," and Water Mondale said, still more pungently, that the presidency had become "the fire hydrant of the nation."

By the mid-1980s, however, no one was making such statements, for Ronald Reagan had, by all accounts, refurbished executive authority. But his use of presidential power differs from Franklin Roosevelt's in important respects. Reagan does not have the same mastery of issues that Roosevelt did. Even disregarding the harsher comments of his critics—for example, that he is the "president with the seven-minute attention span"—it would be impossible to contend that Reagan knows about or cares about intricate details of economic policy. Nor can one envision the president leading an hour-long seminar for reporters as Roosevelt sometimes did. Reagan has been notoriously reluctant to hold press conferences, not so much because he is worried about making an offhand statement that will have harmful repercussions, but because he does not wish to expose his limited knowledge of controversial issues. Even one of his friendlier biographers, Lou Cannon, admits that the president's knowledge gap makes every press conference an "adventure into the unexplored regions of his mind." In his first four years in office, Reagan held 26 press conferences compared to Roosevelt's 337.

Nevertheless, Reagan has been a strong president. He has exerted an influence over Congress that, only a decade ago, seemed impossible for any president to exert. His administration has been highly effective in establishing legislative priorities and in showing a willingness to compromise when necessary (but only when necessary) to achieve its goals. The president has also put his own brand on the federal bureaucracy. Where Franklin Roosevelt dealt with conservative bureaucrats by creating emergency agencies and staffing them with dedicated New Dealers, Ronald Reagan has dealt with liberal bureaucrats by centralizing the budgetary process in the Office of Management and Budget and staffing it with diehard supply siders. Finally, Reagan has used television to appeal directly to the people in much the same way, and with much the same effect, as Roosevelt used radio. So it is not surprising that when voters are asked whether President Reagan has "strong qualities of leadership" that nearly three out of four answer "yes."

Just as the two presidents employed different techniques to enhance their power, they also used that authority for sharply contrasting purposes. During Franklin Roosevelt's twelve years in the White House, the government assumed increasing responsibility for the welfare of large numbers of jobless or impoverished people; the government also introduced a system of taxation that produced a modest redistribution of income from the rich to the poor. By Ronald Reagan's seventh year as president, the government had jettisoned many welfare programs, and it had implemented what can only be termed a Robin Hood-in-reverse tax program.

The fundamental assumption on which the New Deal was based should not be lost in the welter of alphabet agencies: that the great majority of those who were unemployed or impoverished were not personally to blame. They were not lazy; they were just unfortunate. They were not individual failures; they were social casualties. Whatever the potential risks involved in providing federal relief, the actual risks involved in not providing it were more severe. Roosevelt knew that a person who received federal assistance could become dependent on such handouts; but he also knew that a person who did not obtain aid would experience intense suffering. An astute politician, and a cautious one, Roosevelt did not go as far in this direction as many wanted, or even as far as he might have gone. But in providing federal relief—as in creating a social security system, in guaranteeing unemployment insurance, and in establishing a minimum wage—he recognized that the important thing was not how far a particular measure went, but the general direction in which it took the nation. The direction during the Roosevelt years was toward an assumption of new responsibilities by the federal government.

The redistribution of income that Roosevelt presided over occurred during World War II. The redistribution resulted partly from new tax laws, and it reflected the impact of full employment and wartime prosperity on the working class. From 1941–45, the incomes of the poorest fifth of American families increased by 10 percent, while the incomes of the wealthiest fifth increased by 20 percent. During those same years, the share of national income held by the wealthiest 5 percent of the people declined from 23.7 to 16.8 percent. Of course, wealthy individuals were considerably better off at the end of the war since 16.8 percent of the 1945 national income amounted to more than 23.7 percent of the 1941 national income. Relatively speaking, however, the final years of the Roosevelt administration had seen a modest redistribution of wealth in a downward direction.

Franklin Roosevelt created an agenda for American politics, and for thirty-five years, until 1980, politicians committed themselves to fulfilling it—Democrats eagerly, Republicans more grudgingly. The programs Roosevelt instituted were beneficial to many groups, and those groups provided built-in constituencies for maintaining the programs and for extending them. They were immediately institutionalized. The relevant political questions were not whether to increase social security benefits, provide more comprehensive unemployment insurance, or raise the minimum wage; the relevant questions were: By how much?

In 1935, Roosevelt was discussing the Social Security Act with his advisers. They warned him that payroll deductions amounted to a regressive system of taxation since all workers, no matter what their income, paid at the same rate. It would make more sense, they claimed, to have government fund the program. Roosevelt admitted that the bill was bad economics, but he insisted it was good politics. So long as social security rested on individuals' taxes, he said, "no damn politician can ever scrap my social security system." How could Roosevelt have known that somewhere in the Midwest, at that very moment, was a twenty-four-year-old radio announcer, Ronald Reagan, who would one day sit in the White House?

The Reagan administration has endeavored to turn the welfare state clock back, not to 1929 or even 1939, but to 1959. The administration had proposed, and obtained, much more stringent cuts in the Great Society programs of the 1960s than in the New Deal programs of the 1930s. The administration's budget proposal for the fiscal year 1985 would have cut spending for such New Deal programs as social security and unemployment insurance by 11 percent (compared with prior policy levels), but it would have cut medicaid, food stamps, rent supplements, and other Great Society low-income assistance programs by more than 25 percent (compared with the same pre-1980 baseline figures). Congress agreed to cut social welfare spending by about half as much as Reagan proposed. As in Roosevelt's case, however, the point was not how far a measure went, but its general direction.

The income tax reduction that the Reagan administration won from Congress in 1981 also represented a reversal of trends established during the Roosevelt years. The measure provided for reductions of 5 percent the first year and an additional 10 percent in each of the succeeding two years. But special interest groups won benefits in the form of accelerated depreciation, lucrative write-offs, and near elimination of the estate tax. As David Stockman, Reagan's budget chief at the time, admitted: "The hogs were really feeding. The greed level, the level of opportunism, just got out of control." The Treasury Department estimated that, over three years, 9 percent of the total tax relief would go to people earning under $15,000, and 36 percent would go to people earning more than $50,000. The 162,000 families with incomes of $200,000 or more saw their taxes cut by $3.6 billion; the 31,700,000 families who earned $15,000 or less realized a savings of $2.9 billion. From 1980 to 1984, the real disposable income of the poorest fifth of American families declined by nearly 8 percent, while the real disposable income of the wealthiest fifth jumped by almost 9 percent. The Reagan administration has presided over a major redistribution of income away from the poor and toward the rich.

Reagan seems to have been as successful as Roosevelt in institutionalizing his policies. But where Roosevelt introduced programs that offered tangible benefits to large numbers of voters who then had a vested interest in preserving them, Reagan has simply run up a massive federal deficit. By cutting taxes, and by increasing defense spending, Reagan has created enormous pressure on Congress to slash spending for social purposes. When Reagan took office, the national debt was $800 billion; four years later, it had nearly doubled to $1.5 trillion. Nearly as much debt accumulated during Reagan's first term in office as had accumulated in the nation's history prior to his election. About one dollar in every seven spent by the federal government went to pay interest on that debt. As some observers pointed out, such deficits were "a means of advancing the Reagan revolution."

The success of that revolution—or, more properly, counterrevolution—can be gauged not so much by the results of the 1984 election, which saw Reagan capture 59 percent of the popular vote and carry 49 of the 50 states, but rather by the kind of campaign waged by his Democratic opponent. Walter Mondale was properly regarded as a spokesman for a traditional brand of liberalism, but one would not know it from hearing his speech accepting the nomination. Mondale called for a well-managed, not merely well-meaning, government; a president who could say "no" to special interest groups; a strong military posture with no major cuts in defense spending; policies to ensure private rather than public-sector economic growth; and the maintenance of family values. "I will cut the deficit by two-thirds," the liberal Democrat pledged; "we must cut spending and pay as we go." Mondale attacked Reagan for pandering to the rich, but he said little about social welfare or racial justice.

Ronald Reagan established the terms of political debate for the 1980s as surely as Franklin Roosevelt had for the 1930s and 1940s. Whether Reagan's agenda will last for thirty-five years, as Roosevelt's did, remains to be seen.

———————◆———————

SOURCE 2   In this selection, Karl Zinsmeister, an analyst at the American Enterprise Institute, argues that although the Reagan administration achieved some important changes, the "Reagan revolution" was an "underachiever." How do the evidence and conclusions in this essay compare to those in the previous selection? Why does Zinsmeister conclude that the Reagan administration failed to achieve its goals? Keep in mind what he sees as the most important economic and social changes in the 1980s. Does he attribute them to Reagan policies? Then compare his statistics with those in Sources 8–12. Finally, why does Zinsmeister believe that Reagan's was "the most important presidency since World War II"?

Summing Up the Reagan Era (1990)

KARL ZINSMEISTER

For all the academic ink devoted to the subject of revolution, history is rarely discontinuous, rarely an affair of dramatic leaps or breaks. While rhetoric and the emotional environment can shift quickly, the actual workings of a society usually change at about the same rate as the proverbial freight train. Just the same, there are occasional turning points in any nation's life, when the engine crests a hill or enters a deep curve. The train remains a train—momentum intact—but thanks to a thousand small changes in pressure and direction among its moving parts a different hum rises from the tracks.

Since we now find ourselves at the end of a decade, the question naturally presents itself: Were the 1980s such a time for America?

Viewed presidentially, the '80s were one part Jimmy Carter, eight parts Ronald Reagan, and one part George Bush. The decade seems destined to be known, however, as the era of the "Reagan Revolution." Just how revolution-ary a time it was depends upon where you set your gaze, but the range of sub-possibilities extends from "More than you might think," to "A lot less than you've been told."

At its self-proclaimed core, the revolution was a clear underachiever. For an epoch supposedly characterized by its backlash against government spend-ing, government intrusion, and government presence in national life, there was far less action than fanfare. Not a single public housing project was privatized. The sagebrush rebellion didn't pry any western lands out of Uncle Sam's grasp. Zooming farm subsidies and protections cost a total of $200 billion during the 1980s, by far the highest figure in our history. Enterprise zones, school prayers, and "the anti-communist resistance" in Nicaragua were so real to White House staffers as to have earned their own function keys on the speechwriting computers. But to average Americans they remained just slogans. Not a single tuition or social-service voucher was ever handed to a poor person over the head of a bureaucrat. And not only is there still a Department of Education, it spent one-and-a-half times as much in 1989 as it did ten years earlier.

In fiscal year 1980 the federal budget totaled 22.1 percent of U.S. GNP. By 1989, the figure had dropped all the way to 22.2 percent. No axe job! Not even any whittling! No decrease at all! (For ancient history buffs, the figure was 16.0 percent in 1950.) That's the revenge of the Neanderthal conservatives?

Even on the narrower front of federal taxes, where it is constantly claimed that the Reagan administration made cuts of "irresponsible" proportions, the changes were distinctly mouse-like: Over the decade, the proportion of national output channeled into the federal till went from 19.4 to 19.3 percent (compared with 14.8 percent in 1950). And if state and local taxes are taken into consideration, one can only conclude that during the 1980s the American people took a little more government onto their backs.

Mathematicians in the audience will detect a mismatch between the taxes-in and spending-out figures cited above. That discrepancy is called "the deficit," a definite growth sector and the favorite subject of the policy class during most of the last decade. The federal deficit stood at $74 billion in 1980, peaked at $221 billion in 1986, and weighed in at $115 billion by decade's end. So much for fiscal prudence and other pinched Republican concepts.

Accumulated and metamorphosed over the years like so much sea-bottom silt, federal deficits eventually become federal debt, an increasingly plentiful quantity in America during the 1980s. On New Year's Eve 1979 the national debt stood at $834 billion. Ten Auld Lang Syne's later it hit $2.3 trillion. These figures inspired rare harmonic caterwauls from both the right and the left. . . .

If we sharpen our focus on U.S. budget figures even further and look toward the supposed heart of the Reagan hit list—social welfare spending—we still see little evidence of any adherence to an anti-bloat diet. Federal spending on Social Security, Aid to Families with Dependent Children, health, housing, education, and anti-poverty measures totaled 4.9 percent of GNP in 1960, 7.8 percent in 1970, 11.3 percent in 1980, and 11.3 percent in 1987. Much ballyhooed overhauls of the Social Security and welfare systems, replete with "blue-ribbon" commissions, presidential task forces, and "shadow committee" proposals resulted in the end in two distinct "Poofs!" that could be heard hundreds of miles from the nation's capital. Both reform efforts ultimately carried far more fingerprints of steady-as-she-goes Democratic Senator Daniel Patrick Moynihan than of the would-be earthquake inducers in the Reagan administration.

The Reagan presidency was not without its effect on the budget, however. Raising spending is a lot easier than reducing it, naturally, and in the area of national defense a notable expansion was accomplished. From its 1980 level of just under $200 billion, defense spending was increased to slightly more than $300 billion in the late 1980s (both figures in 1989 dollars). Here too, though, ephemerality was the byword. Defense outlays, which had represented 9.5 percent of GNP in 1960, 8.3 percent in 1970, and 5.0 percent in 1980, bobbed up to a peak of 6.5 percent of GNP in 1986 before dribbling back under 6 percent again by the decade's end. . . .

The two lasting political effects of Reaganism are disparate: Party identification has taken a so-far enduring swing toward the GOP, with self-described

Republicans even becoming a majority among some young voting cohorts. Among 18- to 29-year-olds, for instance, 52 percent inclined to Republicanism in the first quarter of 1989, versus 33 percent in 1980. (While young voters tend to be comparatively liberal on issues like race and gender, they toe a more conservative line on economics, crime, and foreign policy.) And the Supreme Court, with five reasonably solid right-leaning justices, has been transformed from a clearly liberal institution of more than 20 years standing to what most observers describe as a "moderately conservative" one. (The same is true for the federal judiciary generally.) Again, however, the transmogrifying jump was distinctly un-quantum like.

But the federal fisc and Washington are not the nation. In the myriad private universes of America, movement during the last 10 years was much more rapid. Indeed, change ranging between gradual and dizzying was virtually the rule.

For one thing, the pace of technical innovation—which accelerates largely without regard to ditherings beyond the laboratory—continues to defy most people's expectations. Scientific advances initiated in the 1980s include the first higher-temperature superconductivity, the first anomalous indications that nuclear fusion may be possible at sub-stellar temperatures, creation of the first genetically altered animals, and the first field tests of genetically engineered plants.

It must be remembered that personal computers and workstations—of which there are nearly 60 million now in operation—were only invented in the 1980s. Likewise cellular phones (a couple million in motion), laser printers (more than 3 million), any number of new drugs, and a host of other daily-life-changing products. Undoubtedly, though their significance is often hard to grasp at the moment of breakthrough, the advances now sweeping electronics, biotechnology, chemistry and other hard sciences will eventually cause our era to be thought of as an epochal one in human civilization.

The results of these quiet marches can be seen in fundamental indicators like life expectancy. Average life expectation for a child born in the United States was 70.8 years in 1970, 73.7 in 1980, and 75.0 in 1987. With each passing year during the 1980s, average life spans increased 67 days. (To lay a prominent Reagan-attack to rest, infant mortality rates also continued to improve steadily during this period, falling from 12.6 deaths per 1,000 births to 9.9 in the first eight years of the decade.) . . .

To return for a moment to the subject of life and limb, there is one very troubling 1980s retrogression that must be noted. Life expectancy for black Americans has actually *fallen* since 1984, an unprecedented occurrence. Given the health-care spending surge and all the countervailing technological factors regularly pushing life spans up, only a serious breakdown in the social arena could drag the figure lower. Unfortunately, such a breakdown exists today, in the form of the drug abuse and homicide epidemics which are tragically sweeping black communities across the nation. Jesse Jackson has taken to saying that dope is doing more damage to African-Americans than KKK ropes ever did, and on this critical statistical axis he is literally correct. . . .

. . . The 1980s were the decade when the family arrived as a political issue. The public saw infant strollers clogging neighborhoods full of baby-boomers and concluded that the return to traditional family values the president was calling for had actually taken place. Not so. The divorce rate did finally level off in the early 1980s, but that is mostly because the marriage rate had fallen so low. And divorce has stabilized at a level more than double the pre-1970s norm. (Current rates, extrapolated into the future, suggest that half of today's marriages will eventually break up.) . . .

And traditionalism is hardly on a roll. During the first seven years of the 1980s, right in the midst of a supposedly calm and conservatizing era, the number of births out of wedlock soared 40 percent. The astonishing result is that by the end of the decade one-quarter of all children born in America arrived without benefit of married parents. Literally a majority of them will depend upon welfare payments instead of a contributing father.

The combined result of 1980s divorce and illegitimacy patterns is that 27 percent of all children in this country now live apart from one or both of their parents. (In Japan, 96 percent of all children live in two-parent families. Could broken homes, with known negative effects on "human capital," be part of our competitiveness problem?) An even more frightening fact is this: At *some* point in their childhood, at least 60 percent of all American youngsters born in the 1980s will spend time in a single-parent home.

If family salvation and shrunken government were Reaganisms that just didn't happen, a few other battle cries translated more successfully into reality. While critics worried that greed and self-interest would overwhelm the voluntarism and individual accountability called for by the president, Americans remained very generous during the 1980s. Private giving for philanthropic purposes increased from $49 billion to $104 billion in the first eight years of the decade. More than four-fifths of that was comprised of individual donations. Corporate giving also jumped, by 66 percent in seven years. Mutual aid and fraternal cooperation are alive and well in the United States, as further indicated by the jump in national non-profit associations, from 14,726 in 1980 to 21,911 in 1989.

The Reaganites always insisted that the best aid program in the world was economic growth, and of that there was a surprisingly large measure during the 1980s. As this is being written in the weaning weeks of 1989 the United States is entering its 85th straight month of economic growth, the second longest expansion since record-keeping began in 1854, and one that economist Herbert Stein characterizes as "the longest and strongest *noninflationary* expansion in our history."

In addition to confounding economists of varying hues, this long expansion did nice things to the pocketbooks of American citizens. Median family income, in constant 1988 dollars, stood at $29,919 in 1980. The decade-opening recession pushed it down to $28,708 by 1982. Then over the next six years it zipped up to $32,191. Income per capita, in many ways a purer indicator because it is not distorted by changes in family configuration over time, grew even more strongly: up a total of 17 percent from 1980 to 1988, or an annual rate of 2 percent since the expansion began.

Two percent annual growth sounds unexceptional, until you realize that it would *double* your standard of living in 35 years. For most of human history, an increase in life quality of that magnitude would have taken many generations. Today it is the legacy of a single presidential term.

Growth like that also has a way of eating up surplus labor. Early in the decade the air was full of talk of long-term "structural" unemployment. By late 1989 unemployment was just a bit over 5 percent, and a record 63 percent of all Americans 16 and over were in harness. The raw aggregates too are quite impressive: As of 1979, 100 million Americans were earning a paycheck. In 1989 it was up to 119 million. There has been a whole lot of shaking going on in the world of job creation. . . .

A factual survey like this necessarily concentrates on subjects that can be measured and expressed statistically. But many of the most important shifts of the 1980s fell in softer categories, loosely organizable under the topic "cultural attitudes." In the long run, the new cultural thinking that coincided with the Reagan era (I do not wish to make a case here concerning cause and effect) may be more significant to the life of the nation than anything that happened in, say, the governmental or financial realms.

There was, for instance, a pronounced religious revival, with most of the action taking place within evangelical and theologically conservative churches. Even though the total percentage of Americans who attend church weekly is about the same today as it was in 1939—40 percent—the number of persons reporting they watch religious television rose from 42 percent in 1980 to 49 percent in 1989. A network of thousands of religious bookstores has spread across the country. Twenty-five hundred retail stores were members of the Christian Booksellers Association in 1980, versus 3,000 in 1989. If sales figures from such shops were included by the tabulators, religious books by authors like James Dobson, Charles Swindoll, Frank Peretti, Jeanette Oke, Robert Schuller, and Rabbi Harold Kushner would have appeared prominently on U.S. best-seller lists during the 1980s (with around 30 million books sold among them). . . .

On television and in film, too, new values—or at least a new wistfulness for old values—became apparent. Among the movies that American audiences consumed most hungrily during the 1980s were ones like "Chariots of Fire,"

"Top Gun," "Hoosiers," and "Trading Places"—films that treated religion sympathetically, that frankly admired military values, that celebrated small-town virtue, that were anti-communist, that were pro-entrepreneurial and anti-bureaucratic. Among the most popular television fare was "The Bill Crosby Show," with its full embrace of traditional bourgeois family values (top rated for four of its five full seasons to date), and the attacks on liberalism in criminal justice on "Hill Street Blues" (winner of 25 Emmy awards).

The currents and crosscurrents of the 1980s had their cumulative effect in subtle but significant ways. Toward the end of the decade an extremely average American woman named Anita Folmar, one of many conservative Democrats whom Ronald Reagan had induced to become a Republican, was quoted in an unimportant little newspaper piece praising the president for being a "return to morality . . . wearing jeans where jeans should be worn, not all the time." That is about as good a summary of the most important presi-dency since World War II as we are likely to get. Ronald Reagan—himself more a cultural icon, an embodied idea, than an actual motive force—was important mostly because he presented an *altered picture* to America in the 1980s.

In his own daffy way, Reagan characterized the decade perfectly. He wasn't quite the man he claimed to be, and he, like us, didn't carry through on a lot of his boldest resolutions. Few molds got broken during the 1980s. But Reagan projected an idealized image that was rather different from what we had become used to, and he quite sincerely aspired to fill it. He, and we, deeply wanted us to be the old shining city on the hill.

His was a wishful era. And wishes, we know, are very important.

PRIMARY SOURCES

This section contains sources related to the Reagan administration's economic policies and to economic changes in the 1980s. They reflect a variety of viewpoints and thus do not support a single conclusion. Look for evidence of economic and social changes and for proof that Reagan administration policies were responsible for them.

SOURCE 3   Reagan outlined his economic goals in a speech to the Interna-tional Business Council several weeks before the election. As you read this selection, note his main goals. Did his administration achieve them?

Five-Year Economic Program for the U.S. (1980)

RONALD REAGAN

I'd like to speak to you today about a new concept of leadership . . . based on faith in the American people, confidence in the American economy, and a firm commitment to see to it that the Federal Government is once more responsive to the people.

That concept is rooted in a strategy for growth, a program that sees the American economic system as it is—a huge, complex, dynamic system which demands not piecemeal Federal packages, or pious hopes wrapped in soothing words, but the hard work and concerted programs necessary for real growth.

We must first recognize that the problem with the U.S. economy is swollen, inefficient government, needless regulation, too much taxation, too much printing-press money. . . .

Our country is in a downward cycle of progressive economic deterioration that must be broken if the economy is to recover and move into a vigorous growth cycle in the 1980's.

We must move boldly, decisively and quickly to control the runaway growth of Federal spending, to remove the tax disincentives that are throttling the economy, and to reform the regulatory web that is smothering it.

We must have and I am proposing a new strategy for the 1980's.

Only a series of well-planned economic actions, taken so that they complement and reinforce one another, can move our economy forward again.

We must keep the rate of growth of government spending at reasonable and prudent levels.

We must reduce personal income tax rates and accelerate and simplify depreciation schedules in an orderly, systematic way to remove disincentives to work, savings, investment and productivity.

We must review regulations that affect the economy and change them to encourage economic growth.

We must establish a stable, sound and predictable monetary policy.

And we must restore confidence by following a consistent national economic policy that does not change from month to month. . . . We must balance the budget, reduce tax rates and restore our defenses. . . .

Let us look at how we can meet this challenge.

One of the most critical elements of my economic program is the control of government spending. Waste, extravagance, abuse and outright fraud in

Source: Ronald Reagan, Speech Delivered Before the International Business Council, Chicago, September 9, 1980, in *Vital Speeches of the Day* 46, No. 24 (October 1, 1980), 738–741 (excerpts).

Federal agencies and programs must be stopped. Billions of the taxpayers' dollars are wasted every year throughout hundreds of Federal programs, and it will take a major, sustained effort over time to effectively counter this.

Federal spending is now projected to increase to over $900 billion a year by fiscal year 1985. But, through a comprehensive assault on waste and inefficiency, I am confident that we can squeeze and trim 2 percent out of the budget in fiscal year 1981, and that we will be able to increase this gradually to 7 percent of what otherwise would have been spent in fiscal year 1985.

Now this is based on projections that have been made by groups in the government. Actually I believe we can do even better. My goal will be to bring about spending reductions of 10 percent by fiscal year 1984. . . .

The second major element of my economic program is a tax rate reduction plan. This plan calls for an across-the-board, three-year reduction in personal income tax rates—10 percent in 1981, 10 percent in 1982 and 10 percent in 1983. My goal is to implement three reductions in a systematic and planned manner.

More than any single thing, high rates of taxation destroy incentive to earn, to save, to invest. And they cripple productivity, lead to deficit financing and inflation, and create unemployment.

We can go a long way toward restoring the economic health of this country by establishing reasonable, fair levels of taxation.

But even the extended tax rate cuts which I am recommending still leave too high a tax burden on the American people. In the second half of the decade ahead we are going to need, and we must have, additional tax rate reductions. . . .

A fundamental part of my strategy for economic growth is the restoration of confidence. If our business community is going to invest and build and create new, well-paying jobs, they must have a future free from arbitrary government action. They must have confidence that the economic "rules-of-the-game" won't be changed suddenly or capriciously. . . .

The time has come for the American people to reclaim their dream. Things don't have to be this way. We can change them. We must change them. Mr. Carter's American tragedy must and can be transcended by the spirit of the American people, working together.

Let's get America working again.

The time is now.

———◆———

SOURCE 4   Weintraub, a University of Pennsylvania economist, blasted Reagan's 1983 budget proposals in this article from the *New Leader*. What does he consider to be the main results of Reaganomics?

The Budget: Guns Up, People Down (1982)

SIDNEY WEINTRAUB

Thumbing his nose at his own long and uninformed babbling about the economy, Ronald Reagan is destined as President to become king of the deficit-makers and undisputed master of the national debt mountain. John Wayne and Bela Lugosi, in their respectively macho and fiendish movie incarnations, would have undoubtedly applauded the "Guns Up, People Down" Reagan budget for fiscal 1983. . . .

The discrepancy between the expenditure and revenue figures translates into the $91.5 billion deficit that has traumatized the conservative Reagan Regulars. Of course, the President extols his deficits as an act of statecraft, strutting out on the hustings to challenge others "to put up or shut up." Obvious alternatives that occur instantly are to defer some tax cuts for his cronies, alter some of the queer corporate investment-credit tax rules, and install an Incomes Policy to ease the monetary stand-off that is taking us down disaster road and, among other things, ensuring a massive future housing shortage. Only Hollywood speech writers could inject so sterile a platform ploy into presumably substantive Presidential remarks.

Our never wasteful, never extravagant military—tell that to anyone who has served in our Armed Forces—is slated to grab $216 billion, an increase of 18 percent. Between military and interest outlays, given the incredible Reagan interest rate mismanagement, 42 per cent of the budget sums is absorbed, with the military taking 29 and interest charges 13 per cent. The interest statistic is understated, based as it is on the "assumption" that short-term Treasury bills, will yield about 10.5 per cent despite the present 14.5 per cent range. Don't wager more than a penny on this calculation, for this Administration's predictions have been as shrewd as those of the man who continually bets that temperatures in Buffalo will be lower in July than in January.

Other budget allotments follow the Reagan non-compassion pattern: Education, down nearly 15 per cent (on top of the inflation erosion); mass transportation lopped by 38 per cent, highway funds out 21 per cent. Amtrack 30 per cent. Reagan never rides trains and his limos avoid potholes. This is a magnificent example of a "think-small" aldermanic approach to a great country's potential. Reagan's New Old Federalism involves a vision of a public sector about the size of a Mom and Pop store. Up with bigger Duponts, Mobils, IBMs, United States Steels, and other sprawling corporate giants to safeguard the public interest. One has to wonder how conservatives can call this theology a realistic political philosophy.

Source: "The Budget: Guns Up, People Down." Reprinted with permission from *The New Leader,* February 22, 1982. Copyright © the American Labor Conference on International Affairs, Inc.

Housing and Urban Development and the Labor Department would be chopped by 10 and 17 per cent, respectively; apparently our cities are already flourishing. Food stamps, which always make Reagan choleric, would drop by 10 per cent; perhaps the President has found a new cheater in Chicago—or is it in Orange County this time, among his rich friends? Welfare payments down, to $5.4 billion from $7.8. Drawing on the experience of his arduous work life as a sports announcer, movie actor and TV hawker, states would be required to exact work from welfare recipients. Shades of the WPA under FDR! Will we see news clips of leaf raking? . . .

FDR was a piker by Deficit-Ronnie standards. Between 1933–40 the New Deal spender added about $20 billion to the national debt. Including World War II, the ascent was about $235 billion. Reagan will dash ahead by $350 billion on the Reagan-Stockman estimates, and by about $650 billion according to the CBO figures. Either way, Reagan will stand out luminously in our debt annals. . . .

◆

SOURCE 5   David Stockman was Ronald Reagan's budget director from 1981 until he quit in 1985. As you read this excerpt from his memoir, pay attention to Stockman's view of what went wrong with Reaganomics and his view of the consequences.

The Triumph of Politics (1986)

DAVID STOCKMAN

"You ain't seen nothing yet." The White House made that its official campaign slogan for 1984. When it did, I knew that my own days were numbered, and that even the reluctant loyalty I had maintained during the long battle to reverse the President's tax policy was no longer defensible. Now I had to resort to out-and-out subversion—scheming with the congressional leaders during the first half of 1985 to force a tax hike. But that failed too, leaving me with no choice but to resign in the knowledge that my original ideological excesses had given rise to a fiscal and political disorder that was probably beyond correction. . . .

"You ain't seen nothing yet" was to have unintended, ironic meaning. It pointed to a frightful day of reckoning, a day that will reveal just how arrogant, superficial, and willfully ignorant the White House phrase-makers really were.

By the end of 1985 the economic expansion was three years old and the numbers demonstrated no miracle. Real GNP growth had averaged 4.1 percent—an utterly unexceptional, prosaic business cycle recovery by historical standards, and especially so in light of the extraordinary depth of the 1981–82 recession. The glowing pre-election GNP and employment numbers, therefore, had manifested only the truism that when the business cycle turns down, it will inevitably bounce back for a while.

Still, the White House breastbeating had to do with the future, and that depends upon the fundamental health of the economy and the soundness of policy. Yet how can economic growth remain high and inflation low for the long run when the administration's de facto policy is to consume two thirds of the nation's net private savings to fund the federal deficit?

The fundamental reality of 1984 was not the advent of a new day, but a lapse into fiscal indiscipline on a scale never before experienced in peacetime. There is no basis in economic history or theory for believing that from this wobbly foundation a lasting era of prosperity can actually emerge.

Indeed, just beneath the surface the American economy was already being twisted and weakened by Washington's free lunch joy ride. Thanks to the half-revolution adopted in July 1981, more than a trillion dollars has already been needlessly added to our national debt—a burden that will plague us indefinitely. Our national savings has been squandered to pay for a tax cut we could not afford. . . .

One reason I plotted to raise taxes in 1985, then, was to help correct an economic policy course that was leading to long-run disaster.

But there was also another, more compelling reason. As the original architect of the fiscal policy error now threatening so much grief, I was appalled by the false promises of the 1984 campaign. Ronald Reagan had been induced by his advisers and his own illusions to embrace one of the more irresponsible platforms of modern times. He had promised, as it were, to alter the laws of arithmetic. No program that had a name or line in the budget would be cut; no taxes would be raised. Yet the deficit was pronounced intolerable and it was pledged to be eliminated.

This was the essence of the unreality. The President and his retainers promised to eliminate the monster deficit with spending cuts when for all practical purposes they had already embraced or endorsed 95 percent of all the spending there was to cut.

The White House itself had surrendered to the political necessities of the welfare state early on. By 1985, only the White House speechwriters carried on a lonely war of words, hurling a stream of presidential rhetoric at a ghostly abstraction called Big Government.

◆

SOURCE 6   Michael Boskin, a Stanford University economist, gives Reaganomics mixed marks in his book *Reagan and the Economy*. What does Boskin see as Reaganomics' biggest success and failure? Does his analysis support the view that there was a "Reagan revolution?"

The Unfinished Agenda (1987)

MICHAEL BOSKIN

In judging the successes and failures of the Reagan economic program, one must focus on the present, looking at what has been accomplished, what has failed, and how what has been done affects the policy agenda in the immediate future. Then, of course, there is the longer-term future, especially the question of whether the Reagan program will be viewed twenty years from now as a turning point, with many enduring accomplishments influencing economic policy and performance over the long haul, or whether it will be viewed only as an aberration—a temporary suspension of the long-run trend from Franklin Roosevelt's New Deal toward a European-style welfare state. . . .

. . . [T]he prospect of sustaining the Reagan program beyond the President's personal popularity remains in doubt. Nevertheless, much has been accomplished. The Reagan economic program, while far from perfect, has created an *opportunity* for a much-improved economy for the balance of the century, by eliminating rising and fluctuating double-digit inflation, explosive growth of nondefense government spending, high and rising marginal tax rates, ever-growing government regulation, and outright government control through incomes policies or wage and price controls. It is worth recalling that these were serious problems as recently as 1980.

In my view, however, the most important accomplishment of Reaganomics is intangible: Reaganomics changed the general understanding of what constitutes a reasonable economic policy. Only a few years ago, fine-tuning demand management, wage and price controls, incomes policies, retaliatory protectionism, expanding government regulation, public sector employment, industrial policy, public works programs, and national development banks were considered sensible economic policies. Some of them had been tried and found wanting, but were recycled once again. Today, one hears much less talk

Source: Michael J. Boskin, *Reagan and the Economy: The Successes, Failures, and Unfinished Agenda,* ICS Press, 1987. Copyright © 1987 by Michael J. Boskin. Reprinted by permission of the author.

of such policies than even a few years ago. Perhaps this is because inflation has been substantially reduced. Bad ideas tend not to die out; they wait to be recycled. But the once-popular notion that the government, especially the federal government, is the proper answer to *all* of society's economic problems has been dealt a serious blow. Following the terrible economic performance of the 1970s, the Reagan economic program seems to have accomplished the important but intangible objective of discrediting this idea, making it more difficult for ill-advised policies to appear at the expense of the taxpayer and the economy. New spending programs will have to pass tougher tests for years to come, and that means less automatic budget growth in the future. Even if nothing else is done, the repudiation of bad policies will stand as a major accomplishment.

SOURCE 7   In 1994, Republicans in the House of Representatives drafted a Contract with America as a campaign platform for the congressional elections. That year, Republicans took control of the Congress. Does this document represent an important legacy of a "Reagan revolution?"

The Contract with America (1994)

On the first day of the 104th Congress, the new Republican majority will immediately pass the following major reforms, aimed at restoring the faith and trust of the American people in their government:

First, require all laws that apply to the rest of the country also apply equally to the Congress;

Second, select a major independent auditing firm to conduct a comprehensive audit of Congress for waste, fraud, or abuse;

Third, cut the number of House committees, and cut committee staff by one-third;

Fourth, limit the terms of all committee chairs;

Fifth, ban the casting of proxy votes in committee;

Sixth, require committee meetings to be open to the public;

Source: Ed Gillespie and Bob Schellas, eds., *Contract with America: The Bold Plan by Rep. Newt Gingrich, Rep. Dick Armey and the House Republicans to Change the Nation* (New York: Random House, Inc., 1994), pp. 8–9, 10.

Seventh, require a three-fifths majority vote to pass a tax increase;

Eighth, guarantee an honest accounting of our federal budget by implementing zero baseline budgeting.

Thereafter, within the first hundred days of the 104th Congress, we shall bring to the House Floor the following bills, each to be given full and open debate, each to be given a clear and fair vote, and each to be immediately available this day for public inspection and scrutiny.

The Fiscal Responsibility Act

A balanced budget/tax limitation amendment and a legislative line-item veto to restore fiscal responsibility to an out-of-control Congress, requiring them to live under the same budget constraints as families and businesses. . . .

The Personal Responsibility Act

Discourage illegitimacy and teen pregnancy by prohibiting welfare to minor mothers and denying increased AFDC for additional children while on welfare, cut spending for welfare programs, and enact a tough two-years-and-out provision with work requirements to promote individual responsibility. . . .

The American Dream Restoration Act

A $500-per-child tax credit, begin repeal of the marriage tax penalty, and creation of American Dream Savings Accounts to provide middle-class tax relief.

Economic Trends in the Reagan Era

One way to determine the impact of Reaganomics is to look at evidence of long-term economic changes contained in charts and tables. As you examine the following sources, note the most important changes they reflect. To what extent can these changes be attributed to Reagan administration policies? Does this evidence support the argument that Reaganomics was revolutionary?

SOURCE 8

Real Average Weekly Earnings, 1947–1986 (in 1986 dollars)

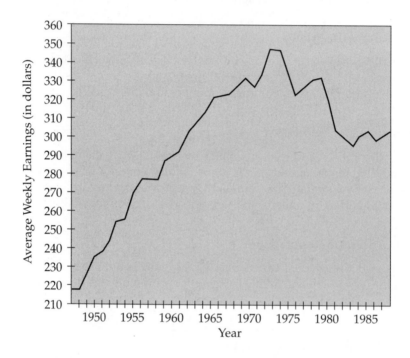

Source: Council of Economic Advisers, *Economic Report of the President, 1987* (Washington, D.C.: U.S. Government Printing Office, 1987).

SOURCE 9

Pay of Workers and Corporate Chief Executives, 1965–1988

Average annual pay	Hourly-paid production workers	Chief executives' total compensation
1968	$ 6,370	$157,000
1978	$12,962	$373,000
1988	$21,735	$773,000

American pay, 1965 = 100

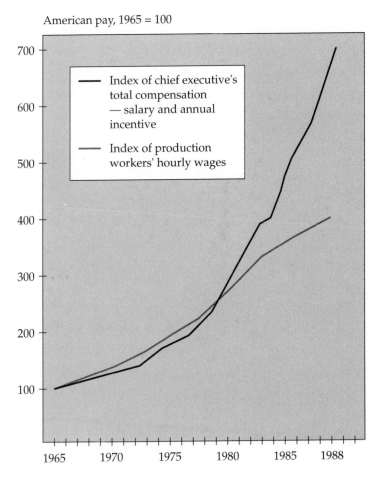

Source: The Economist, June 17, 1989.

SOURCE 10

Federal Budget Priorities, 1980–1987

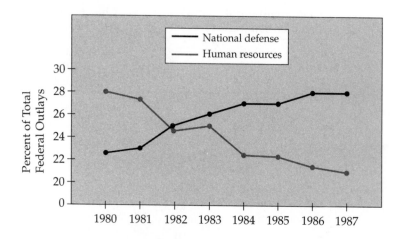

Source: Center on Budget and Policy Priorities.

SOURCE 11

Total Government Expenditures, 1929–1990

Index: 1929=100

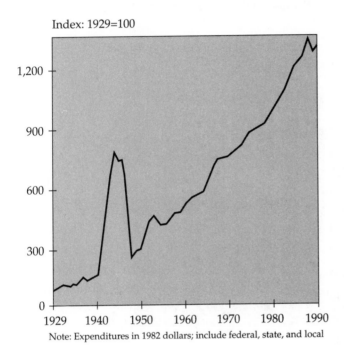

Note: Expenditures in 1982 dollars; include federal, state, and local

Source: Data from Herbert Stein and Murray Foss, *An Illustrated Guide to the American Economy* (Washington, D.C.: AEI Press, 1992), p. 221.

SOURCE 12

Federal Budget Deficits, 1980–1990 (National Income and Product Accounts Basis, Billions of Dollars)

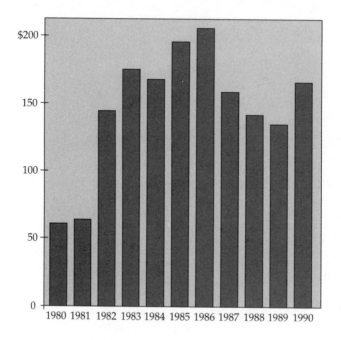

Source: Data from Herbert Stein and Murray Foss, *An Illustrated Guide to the American Economy* (Washington, D.C.: AEI Press, 1992), p. 195.

CONCLUSION

"It will take historians years to balance the successes and failures of Reagan's administration," predicted the Denver *Post* shortly after Reagan's farewell. By now, you probably agree. The Reagan era is not easy to assess because it is so close in time. As time passes, however, it will become easier to evaluate the "Reagan revolution." Economic and social trends in the intervening years will give historians additional perspective on economic and social changes in the 1980s. With their own society as a reference point, they will be able to trace the long-term influence of developments in the Reagan years. Decisions that once appeared to have lasting impact may well appear as insignificant.

However, although it will take time for historians to see the enduring legacies of the "Reagan revolution," the *Post*'s prediction was only half right. Unfortunately, judgments about Reagan's contribution will never achieve some "objective" balance. Although historians may well arrive at some consensus about various aspects or effects of "Reaganomics," the final impartial word on the Reagan administration or anything else of historical importance is like a desert mirage: The closer we seem to get, the further it recedes from us. First, as we have seen repeatedly in this volume, historians' views of the past are shaped by the times. As circumstances change, so too do their historical interpretations. Moreover, much like your own conclusion about Reaganomics, historical analysis inevitably reflects the values of the historian. And history, as we have also seen, is shaped by the historian's assumptions about historical inquiry itself. Whether expressed or not, all historians' work reflects views about the role of ideology in history, the importance of individual actions as opposed to economic, technological, demographic, or other "grand" forces, and whether history is better written from the "top down" or the "bottom up." Thus no matter how many years have passed, there will never be a last word on the Reagan administration or on any other part of the past.

This does not mean that our historical interpretations do not matter, however. The national debate that began with Jefferson and Hamilton about the proper role of the government in American society still continues. Today it takes the form of disagreements about welfare, government regulation, the proper role of the government in ensuring equal treatment of people, and even the budget deficit and taxes. These issues affect all of us, and consequently we all have a vested interest in how they are resolved. Because experience is a powerful teacher, debates about these issues often turn on the lessons of the past. It follows that we also have a vested interest in what historians say about the Reagan administration's recent experience in dealing with these issues. Historical assessments of the Reagan administration thus illustrate how those who interpret the past have the power to influence decisions that affect the future. To the list of the "Reagan revolution's" legacies we can therefore add one more: It is a powerful reminder of the importance of historical interpretation.

FURTHER READING

Michael J. Boskin, *Reagan and the Economy: The Successes, Failures, and Unfinished Agenda* (San Francisco: Institute for Contemporary Studies, 1987).

Haynes Johnson, *Sleepwalking Through History: America in the Reagan Years* (New York: W. W. Norton and Company, 1991).

Bruce W. Kinzey, *Reaganomics* (St. Paul, Minn.: West Publishing Co., 1983).

Kevin Phillips, *The Politics of Rich and Poor: Wealth and the American Electorate in the Reagan Aftermath* (New York: Random House, 1990).

Michael Schaller, *Reckoning with Reagan: America and Its President in the 1980's* (New York: Oxford University Press, 1992).

NOTES

1. Haynes Johnson, *Sleepwalking Through History: America in the Reagan Years* (New York: W. W. Norton, 1991), p. 20.
2. Quoted in ibid., p. 23.
3. Ronald Reagan, "Farewell Address to the American People," in Paul Boyer, *Reagan as President: Contemporary Views of the Man, His Politics, and His Policies* (Chicago: Ivan R. Dee, 1990), p. 264.
4. David Stockman, *The Triumph of Politics: How the Reagan Revolution Failed* (New York: Harper and Row, 1986), p. 13.
5. Martin Feldstein, "The Conceptual Foundation of Supply-Side Economics," in Federal Reserve Bank of Atlanta, *Supply-Side Economics in the 1980s* (Westport, Conn.: Quorum Books, 1982), p. 151.
6. Michael Boskin, *Reagan and the Economy: The Successes, Failures, and Unfinished Agenda* (San Francisco: ICS Press, 1987), p. 255.
7. John Kenneth Galbraith, *The Culture of Contentment* (Boston: Houghton Mifflin, 1992), p. 108.
8. Johnson, *Sleepwalking Through History,* p. 455.
9. Quoted in Sidney Blumenthal and Thomas B. Edsall, *The Reagan Legacy* (New York: Pantheon Books, 1988), p. xiii.
10. Garry Wills, *Reagan's America* (New York: Penguin, 1987), p. 466.
11. Michael Schaller, *Reckoning with Reagan* (New York: Oxford University Press, 1992), p. 181.
12. Paul Boyer, *Promises to Keep: The United States Since World War II* (Lexington, Mass.: D. C. Heath, 1995), p. 477.